TO MY READERS.

Nay, blame me not; I might have spared
  Your patience many a trivial verse,
Yet these my earlier welcome shared,
  So, let the better shield the worse.

And some might say, "Those ruder songs
  Had freshness which the new have lost;
To spring the opening leaf belongs,
  The chestnut-burs await the frost."

When those I wrote, my locks were brown,
  When these I write—ah, well-a-day!
The autumn thistle's silvery down
  Is not the purple bloom of May!

Go, little book, whose pages hold
  Those garnered years in loving trust;
How long before your blue and gold
  Shall fade and whiten in the dust?

O sexton of the alcoved tomb,
  Where souls in leathern cerements lie,
Tell me each living poet's doom!
  How long before his book shall die?

It matters little, soon or late,
  A day, a month, a year, an age,—
I read oblivion in its date,
  And Finis on its title-page.

Before we sighed, our griefs were told;
  Before we smiled, our joys were sung;
And all our passions shaped of old
  In accents lost to mortal tongue.

In vain a fresher mould we seek,—
  Can all the varied phrases tell
That Babel's wandering children speak
  How thrushes sing or lilacs smell?

Caged in the poet's lonely heart,
  Love wastes unheard its tenderest tone;
The soul that sings must dwell apart,
  Its inward melodies unknown.

Deal gently with us, ye who read!
  Our largest hope is unfulfilled,—
The promise still outruns the deed,—
  The tower, but not the spire, we build.

Our whitest pearl we never find;
  Our ripest fruit we never reach;
The flowering moments of the mind
  Drop half their petals in our speech.

These are my blossoms; if they wear
  One streak of morn or evening's glow
Accept them; but to me more fair
  The buds of song that never blow.

April 8, 1862.

FROM the first gleam of morning to the gray
    Of peaceful evening, lo, a life unrolled!
    In woven pictures all its changes told,
Its lights, its shadows, every flitting ray,
Till the long curtain, falling, dims the day,
    Steals from the dial's disk the sunlight's gold,
    And all the graven hours grow dark and cold
Where late the glowing blaze of noontide lay.
Ah! the warm blood runs wild in youthful veins, —
    Let me no longer play with painted fire;
    New songs for new-born days! I would not tire
The listening ears that wait for fresher strains
In phrase new-moulded, new-forged rhythmic chains,
    With plaintive measures from a worn-out lyre.

August 2, 1881.

LIST OF ILLUSTRATIONS.

———◆———

CONTENTS.

The Riverside Press, Cambridge, Mass., U. S. A.
Printed by H. O. Houghton & Company.

THE

POETICAL WORKS

OF

OLIVER WENDELL HOLMES

Household Edition

WITH ILLUSTRATIONS

BOSTON AND NEW YORK
HOUGHTON, MIFFLIN AND COMPANY
The Riverside Press, Cambridge

Oliver Wendell Holmes.

Carrie C. Strong,
January, 1892.
P. H. S.

EARLIER POEMS.

1830-1836.

OLD IRONSIDES.

AY, tear her tattered ensign down!
 Long has it waved on high,
And many an eye has danced to see
 That banner in the sky;
Beneath it rung the battle shout,
 And burst the cannon's roar; —
The meteor of the ocean air
 Shall sweep the clouds no more!

Her deck, once red with heroes' blood,
 Where knelt the vanquished foe,
When winds were hurrying o'er the flood,
 And waves were white below,
No more shall feel the victor's tread,
 Or know the conquered knee; —
The harpies of the shore shall pluck
 The eagle of the sea!

O better that her shattered hulk
 Should sink beneath the wave;
Her thunders shook the mighty deep,
 And there should be her grave;
Nail to the mast her holy flag,
 Set every threadbare sail,
And give her to the god of storms,
 The lightning and the gale!

THE LAST LEAF.

I SAW him once before,
As he passed by the door,
 And again

The pavement stones resound,
As he totters o'er the ground
 With his cane.

They say that in his prime,
Ere the pruning-knife of Time
 Cut him down,
Not a better man was found
By the Crier on his round
 Through the town.

But now he walks the streets,
And he looks at all he meets
 Sad and wan,
And he shakes his feeble head,
That it seems as if he said,
 "They are gone."

The mossy marbles rest
On the lips that he has prest
 In their bloom,
And the names he loved to hear
Have been carved for many a year
 On the tomb.

My grandmamma has said —
Poor old lady, she is dead
 Long ago —
That he had a Roman nose,
And his cheek was like a rose
 In the snow.

But now his nose is thin,
And it rests upon his chin
 Like a staff,

And a crook is in his back,
And a melancholy crack
    In his laugh.

I know it is a sin
For me to sit and grin
    At him here ;
But the old three-cornered hat,
And the breeches, and all that,
    Are so queer !

And if I should live to be
The last leaf upon the tree
    In the spring,
Let them smile, as I do now,
At the old forsaken bough
    Where I cling.

THE CAMBRIDGE CHURCHYARD.

OUR ancient church ! its lowly tower,
    Beneath the loftier spire,
Is shadowed when the sunset hour
    Clothes the tall shaft in fire ;
It sinks beyond the distant eye,
    Long ere the glittering vane,
High wheeling in the western sky,
    Has faded o'er the plain.

Like Sentinel and Nun, they keep
    Their vigil on the green ;
One seems to guard, and one to weep,
    The dead that lie between ;
And both roll out, so full and near,
    Their music's mingling waves,
They shake the grass, whose pennoned spear
    Leans on the narrow graves.

The stranger parts the flaunting weeds,
    Whose seeds the winds have strown
So thick beneath the line he reads,
    They shade the sculptured stone ;
The child unveils his clustered brow,
    And ponders for a while

The graven willow's pendent bough,
    Or rudest cherub's smile.

But what to them the dirge, the knell ?
    These were the mourner's share ;
The sullen clang, whose heavy swell
    Throbbed through the beating air ;
The rattling cord, — the rolling stone, —
    The shelving sand that slid,
And, far beneath, with hollow tone,
    Rung on the coffin's lid.

The slumberer's mound grows fresh and
        green,
    Then slowly disappears ;
The mosses creep, the gray stones lean,
    Earth hides his date and years ;
But, long before the once-loved name
    Is sunk or worn away,
No lip the silent dust may claim,
    That pressed the breathing clay.

Go where the ancient pathway guides,
    See where our sires laid down
Their smiling babes, their cherished
        brides,
    The patriarchs of the town ;
Hast thou a tear for buried love ?
    A sigh for transient power ?
All that a century left above,
    Go, read it in an hour !

The Indian's shaft, the Briton's ball,
    The sabre's thirsting edge,
The hot shell, shattering in its fall,
    The bayonet's rending wedge, —
Here scattered death ; yet, seek the spot,
    No trace thine eye can see,
No altar, — and they need it not
    Who leave their children free !

Look where the turbid rain-drops stand
    In many a chiselled square ;
The knightly crest, the shield, the brand
    Of honored names were there ; —

Alas ! for every tear is dried
    Those blazoned tablets knew,
Save when the icy marble's side
    Drips with the evening dew.

Or gaze upon yon pillared stone,
    The empty urn of pride ;
There stand the Goblet and the Sun, —
    What need of more beside ?
Where lives the memory of the dead,
    Who made their tomb a toy ?
Whose ashes press that nameless bed ?
    Go, ask the village boy !

Lean o'er the slender western wall,
    Ye ever-roaming girls ;
The breath that bids the blossom fall
    May lift your floating curls,
To sweep the simple lines that tell
    An exile's date and doom ;
And sigh, for where his daughters dwell,
    They wreathe the stranger's tomb.

And one amid these shades was born,
    Beneath this turf who lies,
Once beaming as the summer's morn,
    That closed her gentle eyes ;
If sinless angels love as we,
    Who stood thy grave beside,
Three seraph welcomes waited thee,
    The daughter, sister, bride !

I wandered to thy buried mound
    When earth was hid below
The level of the glaring ground,
    Choked to its gates with snow,
And when with summer's flowery waves
    The lake of verdure rolled,
As if a Sultan's white-robed slaves
    Had scattered pearls and gold.

Nay, the soft pinions of the air,
    That lift this trembling tone,
Its breath of love may almost bear,
    To kiss thy funeral stone ;

And, now thy smiles have passed away,
    For all the joy they gave,
May sweetest dews and warmest ray
    Lie on thine early grave !

When damps beneath, and storms above,
    Have bowed these fragile towers,
Still o'er the graves yon locust-grove
    Shall swing its Orient flowers ;
And I would ask no mouldering bust,
    If e'er this humble line,
Which breathed a sigh o'er other's dust,
    Might call a tear on mine.

TO AN INSECT.

I LOVE to hear thine earnest voice,
    Wherever thou art hid,
Thou testy little dogmatist,
    Thou pretty Katydid !
Thou mindest me of gentlefolks, —
    Old gentlefolks are they, —
Thou say'st an undisputed thing
    In such a solemn way.

Thou art a female, Katydid !
    I know it by the trill
That quivers through thy piercing notes,
    So petulant and shrill ;
I think there is a knot of you
    Beneath the hollow tree, —
A knot of spinster Katydids, —
    Do Katydids drink tea ?

O tell me where did Katy live,
    And what did Katy do ?
And was she very fair and young,
    And yet so wicked, too ?
Did Katy love a naughty man,
    Or kiss more cheeks than one ?
I warrant Katy did no more
    Than many a Kate has done.

Dear me ! I 'll tell you all about
    My fuss with little Jane,

And Ann, with whom I used to walk
  So often down the lane,
And all that tore their locks of black,
  Or wet their eyes of blue, —
Pray tell me, sweetest Katydid,
  What did poor Katy do?

Ah no! the living oak shall crash,
  That stood for ages still,
The rock shall rend its mossy base
  And thunder down the hill,
Before the little Katydid
  Shall add one word, to tell
The mystic story of the maid
  Whose name she knows so well.

Peace to the ever-murmuring race!
  And when the latest one
Shall fold in death her feeble wings
  Beneath the autumn sun,
Then shall she raise her fainting voice,
  And lift her drooping lid,
And then the child of future years
  Shall hear what Katy did.

THE DILEMMA.

Now, by the blessed Paphian queen,
Who heaves the breast of sweet sixteen;
By every name I cut on bark
Before my morning star grew dark
By Hymen's torch, by Cupid's dart,
By all that thrills the beating heart;
The bright black eye, the melting blue, —
I cannot choose between the two.

I had a vision in my dreams; —
I saw a row of twenty beams;
From every beam a rope was hung,
In every rope a lover swung;
I asked the hue of every eye,
That bade each luckless lover die;
Ten shadowy lips said, heavenly blue,
And ten accused the darker hue.

I asked a matron which she deemed
With fairest light of beauty beamed;
She answered, some thought both were
    fair, —
Give her blue eyes and golden hair.
I might have liked her judgment well,
But, as she spoke, she rung the bell,
And all her girls, nor small nor few,
Came marching in, — their eyes were blue.

I asked a maiden; back she flung
The locks that round her forehead hung,
And turned her eye, a glorious one,
Bright as a diamond in the sun,
On me, until beneath its rays
I felt as if my hair would blaze;
She liked all eyes but eyes of green;
She looked at me; what could she mean?

Ah! many lids Love lurks between,
Nor heeds the coloring of his screen;
And when his random arrows fly,
The victim falls, but knows not why.
Gaze not upon his shield of jet,
The shaft upon the string is set;
Look not beneath his azure veil,
Though every limb were cased in mail.

Well, both might make a martyr break
The chain that bound him to the stake;
And both, with but a single ray,
Can melt our very hearts away;
And both, when balanced, hardly seem
To stir the scales, or rock the beam;
But that is dearest, all the while,
That wears for us the sweetest smile.

MY AUNT.

My aunt! my dear unmarried aunt!
  Long years have o'er her flown;
Yet still she strains the aching clasp
  That binds her virgin zone;
I know it hurts her, — though she looks
  As cheerful as she can;

Her waist is ampler than her life,
    For life is but a span.

My aunt ! my poor deluded aunt !
    Her hair is almost gray ;
Why will she train that winter curl
    In such a spring-like way ?
How can she lay her glasses down,
    And say she reads as well,
When, through a double convex lens,
    She just makes out to spell ?

Her father — grandpapa ! forgive
    This erring lip its smiles —
Vowed she should make the finest girl
    Within a hundred miles ;
He sent her to a stylish school ;
    'T was in her thirteenth June ;
And with her, as the rules required,
    "Two towels and a spoon."

They braced my aunt against a board,
    To make her straight and tall ;
They laced her up, they starved her down,
    To make her light and small ;
They pinched her feet, they singed her hair,
    They screwed it up with pins ;—
O never mortal suffered more
    In penance for her sins.

So, when my precious aunt was done,
    My grandsire brought her back ;
(By daylight, lest some rabid youth
    Might follow on the track ;)
"Ah !" said my grandsire, as he shook
    Some powder in his pan,
"What could this lovely creature do
    Against a desperate man !"

Alas ! nor chariot, nor barouche,
    Nor bandit cavalcade,
Tore from the trembling father's arms
    His all-accomplished maid.

For her how happy had it been !
    And Heaven had spared to me
To see one sad, ungathered rose
    On my ancestral tree.

REFLECTIONS OF A PROUD PEDES-TRIAN.

I SAW the curl of his waving lash,
    And the glance of his knowing eye,
And I knew that he thought he was cutting a dash,
    As his steed went thundering by.

And he may ride in the rattling gig,
    Or flourish the Stanhope gay,
And dream that he looks exceeding big
    To the people that walk in the way ;

But he shall think, when the night is still,
    On the stable-boy's gathering numbers,
And the ghost of many a veteran bill
    Shall hover around his slumbers ;

The ghastly dun shall worry his sleep,
    And constables cluster around him,
And he shall creep from the wood-hole deep
    Where their spectre eyes have found him !

Ay ! gather your reins, and crack your thong,
    And bid your steed go faster ;
He does not know, as he scrambles along,
    That he has a fool for his master ;

And hurry away on your lonely ride,
    Nor deign from the mire to save me ;
I will paddle it stoutly at your side
    With the tandem that nature gave me !

DAILY TRIALS.

BY A SENSITIVE MAN.

O, THERE are times
When all this fret and tumult that we
  hear
Do seem more stale than to the sexton's
  ear
  His own dull chimes.

Ding dong ! ding dong !
The world is in a simmer like a sea
Over a pent volcano, — woe is me
  All the day long !

From crib to shroud !
Nurse o'er our cradles screameth lullaby,
And friends in boots tramp round us as
  we die,
  Snuffling aloud.

At morning's call
The small-voiced pug-dog welcomes in
  the sun,
And flea-bit mongrels, wakening one by
  one,
  Give answer all.

When evening dim
Draws round us, then the lonely cater-
  waul,
Tart solo, sour duet, and general squall,—
  These are our hymn.

Women, with tongues
Like polar needles, ever on the jar ;
Men, plugless word-spouts, whose deep
  fountains are
  Within their lungs.

Children, with drums
Strapped round them by the fond pater-
  nal ass ;
Peripatetics with a blade of grass
  Between their thumbs.

Vagrants, whose arts
Have caged some devil in their mad ma-
  chine,
Which grinding, squeaks, with husky
  groans between,
  Come out by starts.

Cockneys that kill
Thin horses of a Sunday, — men, with
  clams,
Hoarse as young bisons roaring for their
  dams
  From hill to hill.

Soldiers, with guns,
Making a nuisance of the blessed air,
Child-crying bellmen, children in de-
  spair,
  Screeching for buns.

Storms, thunders, waves !
Howl, crash, and bellow till ye get your
  fill ;
Ye sometimes rest ; men never can be still
  But in their graves.

EVENING.

BY A TAILOR.

DAY hath put on his jacket, and around
His burning bosom buttoned it with stars.
Here will I lay me on the velvet grass,
That is like padding to earth's meagre
  ribs,
And hold communion with the things
  about me.
Ah me ! how lovely is the golden braid
That binds the skirt of night's descend-
  ing robe !
The thin leaves, quivering on their silken
  threads,
Do make a music like to rustling satin,
As the light breezes smooth their downy
  nap.

Ha! what is this that rises to my touch,
So like a cushion? Can it be a cabbage?
It is, it is that deeply injured flower,
Which boys do flout us with; — but yet
    I love thee,
Thou giant rose, wrapped in a green sur-
    tout.
Doubtless in Eden thou didst blush as
    bright
As these, thy puny brethren; and thy
    breath
Sweetened the fragrance of her spicy air;
But now thou seemest like a bankrupt
    beau,
Stripped of his gaudy hues and essences,
And growing portly in his sober garments.

Is that a swan that rides upon the
    water?
O no, it is that other gentle bird,
Which is the patron of our noble calling.
I well remember, in my early years,
When these young hands first closed
    upon a goose;
I have a scar upon my thimble finger,
Which chronicles the hour of young am-
    bition.
My father was a tailor, and his father,
And my sire's grandsire, all of them
    were tailors;
They had an ancient goose, — it was an
    heirloom
From some remoter tailor of our race.
It happened I did see it on a time
When none was near, and I did deal
    with it,
And it did burn me, — O, most fearfully!

It is a joy to straighten out one's limbs,
And leap elastic from the level counter,
Leaving the petty grievances of earth,
The breaking thread, the din of clashing
    shears,
And all the needles that do wound the
    spirit,

For such a pensive hour of soothing si-
    lence.
Kind Nature, shuffling in her loose un-
    dress,
Lays bare her shady bosom; — I can feel
With all around me; — I can hail the
    flowers
That sprig earth's mantle, — and yon
    quiet bird,
That rides the stream, is to me as a
    brother.
The vulgar know not all the hidden
    pockets,
Where Nature stows away her loveliness.
But this unnatural posture of the legs
Cramps my extended calves, and I must go
Where I can coil them in their wonted
    fashion.

THE DORCHESTER GIANT.

THERE was a giant in time of old,
  A mighty one was he;
He had a wife, but she was a scold,
So he kept her shut in his mammoth fold;
  And he had children three.

It happened to be an election day,
  And the giants were choosing a king;
The people were not democrats then,
They did not talk of the rights of men,
  And all that sort of thing.

Then the giant took his children three,
  And fastened them in the pen;
The children roared; quoth the giant,
    "Be still!"
And Dorchester Heights and Milton Hill
  Rolled back the sound again.

Then he brought them a pudding stuffed
    with plums,
  As big as the State-House dome;
Quoth he, "There's something for you
    to eat;

So stop your mouths with your 'lection
    treat,
    And wait till your dad comes home."

So the giant pulled him a chestnut stout,
    And whittled the boughs away ;
The boys and their mother set up a shout,
Said he, " You 're in, and you can't get
    out,
    Bellow as loud as you may."

Off he went, and he growled a tune
    As he strode the fields along ;
'T is said a buffalo fainted away,
And fell as cold as a lump of clay,
    When he heard the giant's song.

But whether the story 's true or not,
    It is n't for me to show ;
There 's many a thing that 's twice as
    queer
In somebody's lectures that we hear,
    And those are true, you know.

      *   *   *

What are those lone ones doing now,
    The wife and the children sad ?
O, they are in a terrible rout,
Screaming, and throwing their pudding
    about,
    Acting as they were mad.

They flung it over to Roxbury hills,
    They flung it over the plain,
And all over Milton and Dorchester too
Great lumps of pudding the giants threw;
    They tumbled as thick as rain.

      *   *   *

Giant and mammoth have passed away,
    For ages have floated by ;
The suet is hard as a marrow-bone,
And every plum is turned to a stone,
    But there the puddings lie.

And if, some pleasant afternoon,
    You 'll ask me out to ride,

The whole of the story I will tell,
And you shall see where the puddings fell,
    And pay for the punch beside.

TO THE PORTRAIT OF "A LADY."

IN THE ATHENÆUM GALLERY.

WELL, Miss, I wonder where you live,
    I wonder what 's your name,
I wonder how you came to be
    In such a stylish frame ;
Perhaps you were a favorite child,
    Perhaps an only one ;
Perhaps your friends were not aware
    You had your portrait done !

Yet you must be a harmless soul ;
    I cannot think that Sin
Would care to throw his loaded dice,
    With such a stake to win ;
I cannot think you would provoke
    The poet's wicked pen,
Or make young women bite their lips,
    Or ruin fine young men.

Pray, did you ever hear, my love,
    Of boys that go about,
Who, for a very trifling sum,
    Will snip one's picture out?
I 'm not averse to red and white,
    But all things have their place,
I think a profile cut in black
    Would suit your style of face !

I love sweet features ; I will own
    That I should like myself
To see my portrait on a wall,
    Or bust upon a shelf ;
But nature sometimes makes one up
    Of such sad odds and ends,
It really might be quite as well
    Hushed up among one's friends !

THE COMET.

THE Comet ! He is on his way,
  And singing as he flies ;
The whizzing planets shrink before
  The spectre of the skies ;
Ah ! well may regal orbs burn blue,
  And satellites turn pale,
Ten million cubic miles of head,
  Ten billion leagues of tail !

On, on by whistling spheres of light
  He flashes and he flames ;
He turns not to the left nor right,
  He asks them not their names ;
One spurn from his demoniac heel, —
  Away, away they fly,
Where darkness might be bottled up
  And sold for "Tyrian dye."

And what would happen to the land,
  And how would look the sea,
If in the bearded devil's path
  Our earth should chance to be ?
Full hot and high the sea would boil,
  Full red the forests gleam ;
Methought I saw and heard it all
  In a dyspeptic dream !

I saw a tutor take his tube
  The Comet's course to spy ;
I heard a scream, — the gathered rays
  Had stewed the tutor's eye ;
I saw a fort, — the soldiers all
  Were armed with goggles green ;
Pop cracked the guns ! whiz flew the balls !
  Bang went the magazine !

I saw a poet dip a scroll
  Each moment in a tub,
I read upon the warping back,
  " The Dream of Beelzebub " ;
He could not see his verses burn,
  Although his brain was fried,
And ever and anon he bent
  To wet them as they dried.

I saw the scalding pitch roll down
  The crackling, sweating pines,
And streams of smoke, like water-spouts,
  Burst through the rumbling mines ;
I asked the firemen why they made
  Such noise about the town ;
They answered not, — but all the while
  The brakes went up and down.

I saw a roasting pullet sit
  Upon a baking egg ;
I saw a cripple scorch his hand
  Extinguishing his leg ;
I saw nine geese upon the wing
  Towards the frozen pole,
And every mother's gosling fell
  Crisped to a crackling coal.

I saw the ox that browsed the grass
  Writhe in the blistering rays,
The herbage in his shrinking jaws
  Was all a fiery blaze ;
I saw huge fishes, boiled to rags,
  Bob through the bubbling brine ;
And thoughts of supper crossed my soul;
  I had been rash at mine.

Strange sights ! strange sounds ! O fear-
    ful dream !
  Its memory haunts me still,
The steaming sea, the crimson glare,
  That wreathed each wooded hill ;
Stranger ! if through thy reeling brain
  Such midnight visions sweep,
Spare, spare, O, spare thine evening meal,
  And sweet shall be thy sleep !

THE MUSIC-GRINDERS.

THERE are three ways in which men take
  One's money from his purse,
And very hard it is to tell
  Which of the three is worse ;
But all of them are bad enough
  To make a body curse.

You 're riding out some pleasant day,
    And counting up your gains ;
A fellow jumps from out a bush,
    And takes your horse's reins,
Another hints some words about
    A bullet in your brains.

It 's hard to meet such pressing friends
    In such a lonely spot ;
It 's very hard to lose your cash,
    But harder to be shot ;
And so you take your wallet out,
    Though you would rather not.

Perhaps you 're going out to dine, —
    Some odious creature begs
You 'll hear about the cannon-ball
    That carried off his pegs,
And says it is a dreadful thing
    For men to lose their legs.

He tells you of his starving wife,
    His children to be fed,
Poor little, lovely innocents,
    All clamorous for bread, —
And so you kindly help to put
    A bachelor to bed.

You 're sitting on your window-seat,
    Beneath a cloudless moon ;
You hear a sound, that seems to wear
    The semblance of a tune,
As if a broken fife should strive
    To drown a cracked bassoon.

And nearer, nearer still, the tide
    Of music seems to come,
There 's something like a human voice,
    And something like a drum ;
You sit in speechless agony,
    Until your ear is numb.

Poor "home, sweet home " should seem to be
    A very dismal place ;

Your " auld acquaintance " all at once
    Is altered in the face ;
Their discords sting through Burns and Moore,
    Like hedgehogs dressed in lace.

You think they are crusaders, sent
    From some infernal clime,
To pluck the eyes of Sentiment,
    And dock the tail of Rhyme,
To crack the voice of Melody,
    And break the legs of Time.

But hark ! the air again is still,
    The music all is ground,
And silence, like a poultice, comes
    To heal the blows of sound ;
It cannot be, — it is, — it is, —
    A hat is going round !

No !   Pay the dentist when he leaves
    A fracture in your jaw,
And pay the owner of the bear
    That stunned you with his paw,
And buy the lobster that has had
    Your knuckles in his claw ;

But if you are a portly man,
    Put on your fiercest frown,
And talk about a constable
    To turn them out of town ;
Then close your sentence with an oath,
    And shut the window down !

And if you are a slender man,
    Not big enough for that,
Or, if you cannot make a speech,
    Because you are a flat,
Go very quietly and drop
    A button in the hat !

THE TREADMILL SONG.

THE stars are rolling in the sky,
    The earth rolls on below,
And we can feel the rattling wheel
    Revolving as we go.

Then tread away, my gallant boys,
　And make the axle fly ;
Why should not wheels go round about,
　Like planets in the sky ?

Wake up, wake up, my duck-legged man,
　And stir your solid pegs !
Arouse, arouse, my gawky friend,
　And shake your spider legs ;
What though you 're awkward at the
　　trade,
　There 's time enough to learn, —
So lean upon the rail, my lad,
　And take another turn.

They 've built us up a noble wall,
　To keep the vulgar out ;
We 've nothing in the world to do
　But just to walk about ;
So faster, now, you middle men,
　And try to beat the ends, —
It 's pleasant work to ramble round
　Among one's honest friends.

Here, tread upon the long man's toes,
　He sha' n't be lazy here, —
And punch the little fellow's ribs,
　And tweak that lubber's ear, —
He 's lost them both, — don't pull his
　　hair,
　Because he wears a scratch,
But poke him in the further eye,
　That is n't in the patch.

Hark ! fellows, there 's the supper-bell,
　And so our work is done ;
It 's pretty sport, — suppose we take
　A round or two for fun !
If ever they should turn me out,
　When I have better grown,
Now hang me, but I mean to have
　A treadmill of my own !

THE SEPTEMBER GALE.

I 'M not a chicken ; I have seen
　Full many a chill September,
And though I was a youngster then,
　That gale I well remember ;
The day before, my kite-string snapped,
　And I, my kite pursuing,
The wind whisked off my palm-leaf
　　hat ; —
　For me two storms were brewing !

It came as quarrels sometimes do,
　When married folks get clashing ;
There was a heavy sigh or two,
　Before the fire was flashing, —
A little stir among the clouds,
　Before they rent asunder, —
A little rocking of the trees,
　And then came on the thunder.

Lord ! how the ponds and rivers boiled !
　They seemed like bursting craters !
And oaks lay scattered on the ground
　As if they were p'taters ;
And all above was in a howl,
　And all below a clatter, —
The earth was like a frying-pan,
　Or some such hissing matter.

It chanced to be our washing-day,
　And all our things were drying ;
The storm came roaring through the
　　lines,
　And set them all a flying ;
I saw the shirts and petticoats
　Go riding off like witches ;
I lost, ah ! bitterly I wept, —
　I lost my Sunday breeches !

I saw them straddling through the
　　air,
　Alas ! too late to win them ;
I saw them chase the clouds, as if
　The devil had been in them ;
They were my darlings and my pride,
　My boyhood's only riches, —
" Farewell, farewell," I faintly cried, —
　" My breeches ! O my breeches ! "

That night I saw them in my dreams,
  How changed from what I knew them !
The dews had steeped their faded threads,
  The winds had whistled through them !
I saw the wide and ghastly rents
  Where demon claws had torn them ;
A hole was in their amplest part,
  As if an imp had worn them.

I have had many happy years,
  And tailors kind and clever,
But those young pantaloons have gone
  Forever and forever !
And not till fate has cut the last
  Of all my earthly stitches,
This aching heart shall cease to mourn
  My loved, my long-lost breeches !

THE HEIGHT OF THE RIDICULOUS.

I WROTE some lines once on a time
  In wondrous merry mood,
And thought, as usual, men would say
  They were exceeding good.

They were so queer, so very queer,
  I laughed as I would die ;
Albeit, in the general way,
  A sober man am I.

I called my servant, and he came ;
  How kind it was of him
To mind a slender man like me,
  He of the mighty limb !

"These to the printer," I exclaimed,
  And, in my humorous way,
I added, (as a trifling jest,)
  "There 'll be the devil to pay."

He took the paper, and I watched,
  And saw him peep within ;
At the first line he read, his face
  Was all upon the grin.

He read the next ; the grin grew broad,
  And shot from ear to ear ;
He read the third ; a chuckling noise
  I now began to hear.

The fourth ; he broke into a roar ;
  The fifth ; his waistband split ;
The sixth ; he burst five buttons off,
  And tumbled in a fit.

Ten days and nights, with sleepless eye,
  I watched that wretched man,
And since, I never dare to write
  As funny as I can.

THE LAST READER.

I SOMETIMES sit beneath a tree,
  And read my own sweet songs ;
Though naught they may to others be,
  Each humble line prolongs
A tone that might have passed away,
But for that scarce remembered lay.

I keep them like a lock or leaf
  That some dear girl has given ;
Frail record of an hour, as brief
  As sunset clouds in heaven,
But spreading purple twilight still
High over memory's shadowed hill.

They lie upon my pathway bleak,
  Those flowers that once ran wild,
As on a father's careworn cheek
  The ringlets of his child ;
The golden mingling with the gray,
And stealing half its snows away.

What care I though the dust is spread
  Around these yellow leaves,
Or o'er them his sarcastic thread
  Oblivion's insect weaves,
Though weeds are tangled on the stream,
It still reflects my morning's beam.

And therefore love I such as smile
  On these neglected songs

No, deem that flattery's needless wile
   My opening bosom wrongs ;
For who would trample, at my side,
A few pale buds, my garden's pride ?

It may be that my scanty ore
   Long years have washed away,
And where were golden sands before,
   Is naught but common clay ;
Still something sparkles in the sun
For memory to look back upon.

And when my name no more is heard,
   My lyre no more is known,
Still let me, like a winter's bird,
   In silence and alone,
Fold over them the weary wing
Once flashing through the dews of spring.

Yes, let my fancy fondly wrap
   My youth in its decline,
And riot in the rosy lap
   Of thoughts that once were mine,
And give the worm my little store
When the last reader reads no more !

POETRY :

A METRICAL ESSAY, READ BEFORE THE
Φ B K SOCIETY, HARVARD UNIVER-
SITY, AUGUST, 1836.

TO CHARLES WENTWORTH UPHAM, THE FOLLOW-
ING METRICAL ESSAY IS AFFECTION-
ATELY INSCRIBED.

SCENES of my youth ! awake its slum-
   bering fire !
Ye winds of Memory, sweep the silent
   lyre !
Ray of the past, if yet thou canst appear,
Break through the clouds of Fancy's
   waning year ;
Chase from her breast the thin autumnal
   snow,
If leaf or blossom still is fresh below !

Long have I wandered ; the returning
   tide

Brought back an exile to his cradle's side ;
And as my bark her time-worn flag un-
   rolled,
To greet the land-breeze with its faded
   fold,
So, in remembrance of my boyhood's
   time,
I lift these ensigns of neglected rhyme ;
O more than blest, that, all my wander-
   ings through,
My anchor falls where first my pennons
   flew !

   The morning light, which rains its
     quivering beams
Wide o'er the plains, the summits, and
   the streams,
In one broad blaze expands its golden
   glow
On all that answers to its glance below ;
Yet, changed on earth, each far re-
   flected ray
Braids with fresh hues the shining brow
   of day ;
Now, clothed in blushes by the painted
   flowers,
Tracks on their cheeks the rosy-fingered
   hours ;
Now, lost in shades, whose dark en-
   tangled leaves
Drip at the noontide from their pendent
   eaves,
Fades into gloom, or gleams in light again
From every dew-drop on the jewelled
   plain.

   We, like the leaf, the summit, or the
     wave,
Reflect the light our common nature gave,
But every sunbeam, falling from her
   throne,
Wears on our hearts some coloring of our
   own ;
Chilled in the slave, and burning in the
   free,

Like the sealed cavern by the sparkling
    sea ;
Lost, like the lightning in the sullen
    clod,
Or shedding radiance, like the smiles of
    God,
Pure, pale in Virtue, as the star above,
Or quivering roseate on the leaves of
    Love ;
Glaring like noontide, where it glows
    upon
Ambition's sands, — the desert in the
    sun ;
Or soft suffusing o'er the varied scene
Life's common coloring, — intellectual
    green.

  Thus Heaven, repeating its material
    plan,
Arched over all the rainbow mind of man;
But he who, blind to universal laws,
Sees but effects, unconscious of their
    cause, —
Believes each image in itself is bright,
Not robed in drapery of reflected light,—
Is like the rustic who, amidst his toil,
Has found some crystal in his meagre
    soil,
And, lost in rapture, thinks for him alone
Earth worked her wonders on the spark-
    ling stone,
Nor dreams that Nature, with as nice a
    line,
Carved countless angles through the
    boundless mine.

  Thus err the many, who, entranced
    to find
Unwonted lustre in some clearer mind,
Believe that Genius sets the laws at
    naught
Which chain the pinions of our wildest
    thought ;
Untaught to measure, with the eye of
    art,

The wandering fancy or the wayward
    heart ;
Who match the little only with the less,
And gaze in rapture at its slight excess,
Proud of a pebble, as the brightest gem
Whose light might crown an emperor's
    diadem.

  And, most of all, the pure ethereal
    fire,
Which seems to radiate from the poet's
    lyre,
Is to the world a mystery and a charm,
An Ægis wielded on a mortal's arm,
While Reason turns her dazzled eye
    away,
And bows her sceptre to her subject's
    sway ;
And thus the poet, clothed with godlike
    state,
Usurped his Maker's title — to create ;
He, whose thoughts differing not in
    shape, but dress,
What others feel, more fitly can express,
Sits like the maniac on his fancied
    throne,
Peeps through the bars, and calls the
    world his own.

  There breathes no being but has some
    pretence
To that fine instinct called poetic sense :
The rudest savage roaming through the
    wild ;
The simplest rustic bending o'er his
    child ;
The infant listening to the warbling bird ;
The mother smiling at its half-formed
    word ;
The boy uncaged, who tracks the fields
    at large ;
The girl, turned matron to her babe-like
    charge ;
The freeman, casting with unpurchased
    hand

The vote that shakes the turrets of the
 land ;
The slave, who, slumbering on his rusted
 chain,
Dreams of the palm-trees on his burning
 plain ;
The hot-cheeked reveller, tossing down
 the wine,
To join the chorus pealing "Auld lang
 syne " ;
The gentle maid, whose azure eye grows
 dim,
While Heaven is listening to her evening
 hymn ;
The jewelled beauty, when her steps
 draw near
The circling dance and dazzling chandelier ;
E'en trembling age, when Spring's renewing air
Waves the thin ringlets of his silvered
 hair ; —
All, all are glowing with the inward
 flame,
Whose wider halo wreathes the poet's
 name,
While, unembalmed, the silent dreamer
 dies,
His memory passing with his smiles and
 sighs !

If glorious visions, born for all man-
 kind,
The bright auroras of our twilight mind ;
If fancies, varying as the shapes that
 lie
Stained on the windows of the sunset
 sky ;
If hopes, that beckon with delusive
 gleams,
Till the eye dances in the void of dreams ;
If passions, following with the winds
 that urge
Earth's wildest wanderer to her farthest
 verge ; —

If these on all some transient hours
 bestow
Of rapture tingling with its hectic glow,
Then all are poets ; and, if earth had
 rolled
Her myriad centuries, and her doom
 were told,
Each moaning billow of her shoreless
 wave
Would wail its requiem o'er a poet's
 grave !

If to embody in a breathing word
Tones that the spirit trembled when it
 heard ;
To fix the image all unveiled and warm,
And carve in language its ethereal form,
So pure, so perfect, that the lines express
No meagre shrinking, no unlaced excess ;
To feel that art, in living truth, has
 taught
Ourselves, reflected in the sculptured
 thought ; —
If this alone bestow the right to claim
The deathless garland and the sacred
 name ;
Then none are poets, save the saints on
 high,
Whose harps can murmur all that words
 deny !

But though to none is granted to
 reveal,
In perfect semblance, all that each may
 feel,
As withered flowers recall forgotten love,
So, warmed to life, our faded passions
 move
In every line, where kindling fancy
 throws
The gleam of pleasures, or the shade of
 woes.

When, schooled by time, the stately
 queen of art

Had smoothed the pathways leading to
the heart,
Assumed her measured tread, her solemn
tone,
And round her courts the clouds of fable
thrown,
The wreaths of heaven descended on
her shrine,
And wondering earth proclaimed the
Muse divine.
Yet, if her votaries had but dared pro-
fane
The mystic symbols of her sacred reign,
How had they smiled beneath the veil
to find
What slender threads can chain the
mighty mind!

Poets, like painters, their machinery
claim,
And verse bestows the varnish and the
frame;
Our grating English, whose Teutonic jar
Shakes the racked axle of Art's rattling
car,
Fits like mosaic in the lines that gird
Fast in its place each many-angled word;
From Saxon lips Anacreon's numbers
glide,
As once they melted on the Teian tide,
And, fresh transfused, the Iliad thrills
again
From Albion's cliffs as o'er Achaia's
plain!
The proud heroic, with its pulse-like
beat,
Rings like the cymbals clashing as they
meet;
The sweet Spenserian, gathering as it
flows,
Sweeps gently onward to its dying close,
Where waves on waves in long succes-
sion pour,
Till the ninth billow melts along the
shore;

The lonely spirit of the mournful lay,
Which lives immortal as the verse of
Gray,
In sable plumage slowly drifts along,
On eagle pinion, through the air of
song;
The glittering lyric bounds elastic by,
With flashing ringlets and exulting eye,
While every image, in her airy whirl,
Gleams like a diamond on a dancing
girl!

Born with mankind, with man's ex-
panded range
And varying fates the poet's numbers
change;
Thus in his history may we hope to find
Some clearer epochs of the poet's mind,
As from the cradle of its birth we trace,
Slow wandering forth, the patriarchal
race.

I.

WHEN the green earth, beneath the
zephyr's wing,
Wears on her breast the varnished buds
of Spring;
When the loosed current, as its folds
uncoil,
Slides in the channels of the mellowed
soil;
When the young hyacinth returns to
seek
The air and sunshine with her emerald
beak;
When the light snowdrops, starting from
their cells,
Hang each pagoda with its silver bells;
When the frail willow twines her trailing bow
With pallid leaves that sweep the soil
below;
When the broad elm, sole empress of
the plain,

Whose circling shadow speaks a century's reign,
Wreathes in the clouds her regal diadem, —
A forest waving on a single stem ; —
Then mark the poet ; though to him unknown
The quaint-mouthed titles, such as scholars own,
See how his eye in ecstasy pursues
The steps of Nature tracked in radiant hues ;
Nay, in thyself, whate'er may be thy fate,
Pallid with toil, or surfeited with state,
Mark how thy fancies, with the vernal rose,
Awake, all sweetness, from their long repose ;
Then turn to ponder o'er the classic page,
Traced with the idyls of a greener age,
And learn the instinct which arose to warm
Art's earliest essay, and her simplest form.

To themes like these her narrow path confined
The first-born impulse moving in the mind ;
In vales unshaken by the trumpet's sound,
Where peaceful Labor tills his fertile ground,
The silent changes of the rolling years,
Marked on the soil, or dialled on the spheres,
The crested forests and the colored flowers,
The dewy grottos and the blushing bowers,
These, and their guardians, who, with liquid names,
Strephons and Chloes, melt in mutual flames,
Woo the young Muses from their mountain shade,
To make Arcadias in the lonely glade.

Nor think they visit only with their smiles
The fabled valleys and Elysian isles ;
He who is wearied of his village plain
May roam the Edens of the world in vain.
'T is not the star-crowned cliff, the cataract's flow,
The softer foliage, or the greener glow,
The lake of sapphire, or the spar-hung cave,
The brighter sunset, or the broader wave,
Can warm his heart whom every wind has blown
To every shore, forgetful of his own.

Home of our childhood ! how affection clings
And hovers round thee with her seraph wings !
Dearer thy hills, though clad in autumn brown,
Than fairest summits which the cedars crown !
Sweeter the fragrance of thy summer breeze
Than all Arabia breathes along the seas !
The stranger's gale wafts home the exile's sigh,
For the heart's temple is its own blue sky !

O happiest they, whose early love unchanged,
Hopes undissolved, and friendship unestranged,
Tired of their wanderings, still can deign to see
Love, hopes, and friendship, centring all in thee !

And thou, my village! as again I
tread
Amidst thy living, and above thy dead;
Though some fair playmates guard with
chaster fears
Their cheeks, grown holy with the lapse
of years;
Though with the dust some reverend
locks may blend,
Where life's last mile-stone marks the
journey's end;
On every bud the changing year recalls,
The brightening glance of morning mem-
ory falls,
Still following onward as the months
unclose
The balmy lilac or the bridal rose;
And still shall follow, till they sink once
more
Beneath the snow-drifts of the frozen
shore,
As when my bark, long tossing in the
gale,
Furled in her port her tempest-rended
sail!

What shall I give thee? Can a simple lay,
Flung on thy bosom like a girl's bouquet,
Do more than deck thee for an idle
hour,
Then fall unheeded, fading like the
flower?
Yet, when I trod, with footsteps wild
and free,
The crackling leaves beneath yon linden-
tree,
Panting from play, or dripping from the
stream,
How bright the visions of my boyish
dream!
Or, modest Charles, along thy broken
edge,
Black with soft ooze and fringed with
arrowy sedge,

As once I wandered in the morning sun,
With reeking sandal and superfluous
gun;
How oft, as Fancy whispered in the gale,
Thou wast the Avon of her flattering
tale!
Ye hills, whose foliage, fretted on the
skies,
Prints shadowy arches on their evening
dyes,
How should my song with holiest charm
invest
Each dark ravine and forest-lifting crest!
How clothe in beauty each familiar scene,
Till all was classic on my native green!

As the drained fountain, filled with
autumn leaves,
The field swept naked of its garnered
sheaves;
So wastes at noon the promise of our
dawn,
The springs all choking, and the harvest
gone.

Yet hear the lay of one whose natal star
Still seemed the brightest when it shone
afar;
Whose cheek, grown pallid with ungra-
cious toil,
Glows in the welcome of his parent soil;
And ask no garlands sought beyond the
tide,
But take the leaflets gathered at your
side.[1]

II.

But times were changed; the torch
of terror came,
To light the summits with the beacon's
flame;
The streams ran crimson, the tall mountain pines
Rose a new forest o'er embattled lines;

1 For "The Cambridge Churchyard," see p. 2

The bloodless sickle lent the warrior's
   steel,
The harvest bowed beneath his chariot
   wheel ;
Where late the wood-dove sheltered her
   repose
The raven waited for the conflict's close ;
The cuirassed sentry walked his sleepless round
Where Daphne smiled or Amaryllis
   frowned ;
Where timid minstrels sung their blushing charms,
Some wild Tyrtæus called aloud, "To
   arms ! "

When Glory wakes, when fiery spirits
   leap,
Roused by her accents from their tranquil sleep,
The ray that flashes from the soldier's
   crest
Lights, as it glances, in the poet's
   breast ; —
Not in pale dreamers, whose fantastic
   lay
Toys with smooth trifles like a child at
   play,
But men, who act the passions they in-
   spire,
Who wave the sabre as they sweep the
   lyre !

Ye mild enthusiasts, whose pacific
   frowns
Are lost like dew-drops caught in burning towns,
Pluck as ye will the radiant plumes of
   fame,
Break Cæsar's bust to make yourselves
   a name ;
But, if your country bares the avenger's
   blade
For wrongs unpunished, or for debts
   unpaid,

When the roused nation bids her armies
   form,
And screams her eagle through the gathering storm,
When from your ports the bannered
   frigate rides,
Her black bows scowling to the crested
   tides,
Your hour has past ; in vain your feeble
   cry,
As the babe's wailings to the thundering
   sky !

Scourge of mankind ! with all the
   dread array
That wraps in wrath thy desolating way,
As the wild tempest wakes the slumber-
   ing sea,
Thou only teachest all that man can
   be.
Alike thy tocsin has the power to charm
The toil-knit sinews of the rustic's arm,
Or swell the pulses in the poet's veins,
And bid the nations tremble at his
   strains.

The city slept beneath the moonbeam's
   glance,
Her white walls gleaming through the
   vines of France,
And all was hushed, save where the
   footsteps fell,
On some high tower, of midnight sentinel.
But one still watched ; no self-encircled
   woes
Chased from his lids the angel of repose ;
He watched, he wept, for thoughts of
   bitter years
Bowed his dark lashes, wet with burning
   tears :
His country's sufferings and her children's shame
Streamed o'er his memory like a forest's
   flame,

Each treasured insult, each remembered
  wrong,
Rolled through his heart and kindled
  into song :
His taper faded ; and the morning gales
Swept through the world the war-song
  of Marseilles !

Now, while around the smiles of Peace
  expand,
And Plenty's wreaths festoon the laugh-
  ing land ;
While France ships outward her reluc-
  tant ore,
And half our navy basks upon the shore ;
From ruder themes our meek-eyed Muses
  turn
To crown with roses their enamelled urn.

If e'er again return those awful days
Whose clouds were crimsoned with the
  beacon's blaze,
Whose grass was trampled by the sol-
  dier's heel,
Whose tides were reddened round the
  rushing keel,
God grant some lyre may wake a nobler
  strain
To rend the silence of our tented plain !
When Gallia's flag its triple fold dis-
  plays,
Her marshalled legions peal the Mar-
  seillaise ;
When round the German close the war-
  clouds dim,
Far through their shadows floats his
  battle-hymn ;
When, crowned with joy, the camps of
  England ring,
A thousand voices shout, "God save the
  King !"
When victory follows with our eagle's
  glance,
Our nation's anthem pipes a country
  dance !

Some prouder Muse, when comes the
  hour at last,
May shake our hillsides with her bugle-
  blast ;
Not ours the task ; but since the lyric
  dress
Relieves the statelier with its sprightli-
  ness,
Hear an old song, which some, per-
  chance, have seen
In stale gazette, or cobwebbed magazine.
There was an hour when patriots dared
  profane
The mast that Britain strove to bow in
  vain ;
And one, who listened to the tale of
  shame,
Whose heart still answered to that
  sacred name,
Whose eye still followed o'er his coun-
  try's tides
Thy glorious flag, our brave Old Iron-
  sides !
From yon lone attic, on a summer's morn,
Thus mocked the spoilers with his
  school-boy scorn.[1]

III.

WHEN florid Peace resumed her golden
  reign,
And arts revived, and valleys bloomed
  again ;
While War still panted on his broken
  blade,
Once more the Muse her heavenly wing
  essayed.
Rude was the song ; some ballad, stern
  and wild,
Lulled the light slumbers of the soldier's
  child ;
Or young romancer, with his threatening
  glance

[1] For "Old Ironsides," see p. 1.

And fearful fables of his bloodless lance,
Scared the soft fancy of the clinging girls,
Whose snowy fingers smoothed his raven
curls.
But when long years the stately form
had bent,
And faithless memory her illusions lent,
So vast the outlines of Tradition grew,
That History wondered at the shapes
she drew,
And veiled at length their too ambitious
hues
Beneath the pinions of the Epic Muse.

Far swept her wing; for stormier days
had brought
With darker passions deeper tides of
thought.
The camp's harsh tumult and the con-
flict's glow,
The thrill of triumph and the gasp of woe,
The tender parting and the glad return,
The festal banquet and the funeral urn,—
And all the drama which at once uprears
Its spectral shadows through the clash
of spears,
From camp and field to echoing verse
transferred,
Swelled the proud song that listening
nations heard.

Why floats the amaranth in eternal
bloom
O'er Ilium's turrets and Achilles' tomb?
Why lingers fancy, where the sunbeams
smile
On Circe's gardens and Calypso's isle?
Why follows memory to the gate of
Troy
Her plumed defender and his trembling
boy?
Lo! the blind dreamer, kneeling on the
sand,
To trace these records with his doubtful
hand;

In fabled tones his own emotion flows,
And other lips repeat his silent woes;
In Hector's infant see the babes that
shun
Those deathlike eyes, unconscious of the
sun,
Or in his hero hear himself implore,
"Give me to see, and Ajax asks no
more!"

Thus live undying through the lapse
of time
The solemn legends of the warrior's
clime;
Like Egypt's pyramid, or Pæstum's fane,
They stand the heralds of the voiceless
plain;
Yet not like them, for Time, by slow
degrees,
Saps the gray stone, and wears the em-
broidered frieze,
And Isis sleeps beneath her subject
Nile,
And crumbled Neptune strews his
Dorian pile;
But Art's fair fabric, strengthening as
it rears
Its laurelled columns through the mist
of years,
As the blue arches of the bending skies
Still gird the torrent, following as it
flies,
Spreads, with the surges bearing on
mankind,
Its starred pavilion o'er the tides of
mind!

In vain the patriot asks some lofty lay
To dress in state our wars of yesterday.
The classic days, those mothers of ro-
mance,
That roused a nation for a woman's
glance;
The age of mystery with its hoarded
power,

That girt the tyrant in his storied tower,
Have past and faded like a dream of
    youth,
And riper eras ask for history's truth.

On other shores, above their moulder-
    ing towns,
In sullen pomp the tall cathedral frowns,
Pride in its aisles, and paupers at the
    door,
Which feeds the beggars whom it fleeced
    of yore.
Simple and frail, our lowly temples
    throw
Their slender shadows on the paths
    below ;
Scarce steal the winds, that sweep his
    woodland tracks,
The larch's perfume from the settler's
    axe,
Ere, like a vision of the morning air,
His slight-framed steeple marks the
    house of prayer ;
Its planks all reeking, and its paint
    undried,
Its rafters sprouting on the shady side,
It sheds the raindrops from its shingled
    eaves,
Ere its green brothers once have changed
    their leaves.

Yet Faith's pure hymn, beneath its
    shelter rude,
Breathes out as sweetly to the tangled
    wood,
As where the rays through pictured glo-
    ries pour
On marble shaft and tessellated floor ;—
Heaven asks no surplice round the heart
    that feels,
And all is holy where devotion kneels.

Thus on the soil the patriot's knee
    should bend,
Which holds the dust once living to
    defend ;

Where'er the hireling shrinks before
    the free,
Each pass becomes "a new Thermopy-
    læ" !
Where'er the battles of the brave are
    won,
There every mountain "looks on Mara-
    thon" !

Our fathers live ; they guard in glory
    still
The grass-grown bastions of the for-
    tressed hill ;
Still ring the echoes of the trampled gorge,
With *God and Freedom! England and
    Saint George !*
The royal cipher on the captured gun
Mocks the sharp night-dews and the
    blistering sun ;
The red-cross banner shades its captor's
    bust,
Its folds still loaded with the conflict's
    dust ;
The drum, suspended by its tattered
    marge,
Once rolled and rattled to the Hessian's
    charge ;
The stars have floated from Britannia's
    mast,
The redcoat's trumpets blown the rebel's
    blast.

Point to the summits where the brave
    have bled,
Where every village claims its glorious
    dead ;
Say, when their bosoms met the bay-
    onet's shock,
Their only corselet was the rustic frock ;
Say, when they mustered to the gather-
    ing horn,
The titled chieftain curled his lip in
    scorn,
Yet, when their leader bade his lines
    advance,

No musket wavered in the lion's glance ;
Say, when they fainted in the forced
    retreat,
They tracked the snow-drifts with their
    bleeding feet,
Yet still their banners, tossing in the
    blast,
Bore *Ever Ready*, faithful to the last,
Through storm and battle, till they
    waved again
On Yorktown's hills and Saratoga's
    plain !

Then, if so fierce the insatiate pa-
    triot's flame,
Truth looks too pale, and history seems
    too tame,
Bid him await some new Columbiad's
    page,
To gild the tablets of an iron age,
And save his tears, which yet may fall
    upon
Some fabled field, some fancied Wash-
    ington !

IV.

BUT once again, from their Æolian
    cave,
The winds of Genius wandered on the
    wave.
Tired of the scenes the timid pencil
    drew,
Sick of the notes the sounding clarion
    blew ;
Sated with heroes who had worn so long
The shadowy plumage of historic song ;
The new-born poet left the beaten
    course,
To track the passions to their living
    source.

Then rose the Drama ; — and the
    world admired
Her varied page with deeper thought
    inspired ;

Bound to no clime, for Passion's throb
    is one
In Greenland's twilight or in India's
    sun ;
Born for no age, — for all the thoughts
    that roll
In the dark vortex of the stormy soul,
Unchained in song, no freezing years
    can tame ;
God gave them birth, and man is still
    the same.

So full on life her magic mirror shone,
Her sister Arts paid tribute to her
    throne ;
One reared her temple, one her canvas
    warmed,
And Music thrilled, while Eloquence
    informed.
The weary rustic left his stinted task
For smiles and tears, the dagger and
    the mask ;
The sage, turned scholar, half forgot his
    lore,
To be the woman he despised before ;
O'er sense and thought she threw her
    golden chain,
And Time, the anarch, spares her death-
    less reign.

Thus lives Medea, in our tamer age,
As when her buskin pressed the Grecian
    stage;
Not in the cells where frigid learning
    delves
In Aldine folios mouldering on their
    shelves ;
But breathing, burning in the glitter-
    ing throng,
Whose thousand bravoes roll untired
    along,
Circling and spreading through the
    gilded halls,
From London's galleries to San Carlo's
    walls !

Thus shall he live whose more than
    mortal name
Mocks with its ray the pallid torch of
    Fame ;
So proudly lifted, that it seems afar
No earthly Pharos, but a heavenly star ;
Who, unconfined to Art's diurnal
    bound,
Girds her whole zodiac in his flaming
    round,
And leads the passions, like the orb
    that guides,
From pole to pole, the palpitating tides !

V.

Though round the Muse the robe of
    song is thrown,
Think not the poet lives in verse alone.
Long ere the chisel of the sculptor
    taught
The lifeless stone to mock the living
    thought ;
Long ere the painter bade the canvas glow
With every line the forms of beauty
    know ;
Long ere the iris of the Muses threw
On every leaf its own celestial hue ;
In fable's dress the breath of genius
    poured,
And warmed the shapes that later times
    adored.

Untaught by Science how to forge the
    keys,
That loose the gates of Nature's myste-
    ries ;
Unschooled by Faith, who, with her
    angel tread,
Leads through the labyrinth with a
    single thread,
His fancy, hovering round her guarded
    tower,
Rained through its bars like Danae's
    golden shower.

He spoke ; the sea-nymph answered
    from her cave :
He called ; the naiad left her mountain
    wave :
He dreamed of beauty ; lo, amidst his
    dream,
Narcissus, mirrored in the breathless
    stream ;
And night's chaste empress, in her bri-
    dal play,
Laughed through the foliage where
    Endymion lay ;
And ocean dimpled, as the languid swell
Kissed the red lip of Cytherea's shell :
Of power, — Bellona swept the crimson
    field,
And blue-eyed Pallas shook her Gor-
    gon shield ;
O'er the hushed waves their mightier
    monarch drove,
And Ida trembled to the tread of Jove !

So every grace that plastic language
    knows
To nameless poets its perfection owes.
The rough-hewn words to simplest
    thoughts confined
Were cut and polished in their nicer
    mind ;
Caught on their edge, imagination's ray
Splits into rainbows, shooting far
    away ; —
From sense to soul, from soul to sense,
    it flies,
And through all nature links analogies ;
He who reads right will rarely look
    upon
A better poet than his lexicon !

There is a race, which cold, ungenial
    skies
Breed from decay, as fungous growths
    arise ;
Though dying fast, yet springing fast
    again,

Which still usurps an unsubstantial
   reign,
With frames too languid for the charms
   of sense,
And minds worn down with action too
   intense ;
Tired of a world whose joys they never
   knew,
Themselves deceived, yet thinking all
   untrue ;
Scarce men without, and less than girls
   within,
Sick of their life before its cares begin ; —
The dull disease, which drains their
   feeble hearts,
To life's decay some hectic thrills imparts,
And lends a force, which, like the
   maniac's power,
Pays with blank years the frenzy of an
   hour.

And this is Genius ! Say, does
   Heaven degrade
The manly frame, for health, for action
   made ?
Break down the sinews, rack the brow
   with pains,
Blanch the bright cheek, and drain the
   purple veins,
To clothe the mind with more extended
   sway,
Thus faintly struggling in degenerate
   clay ?

No ! gentle maid, too ready to admire,
Though false its notes, the pale enthusi-
   ast's lyre ;
If this be genius, though its bitter springs
Glowed like the morn beneath Aurora's
   wings,
Seek not the source whose sullen bosom
   feeds

But fruitless flowers, and dark, enven-
   omed weeds.

But, if so bright the dear illusion
   seems,
Thou wouldst be partner of thy poet's
   dreams,
And hang in rapture on his bloodless
   charms,
Or die, like Raphael, in his angel arms ;
Go, and enjoy thy blessed lot, — to
   share
In Cowper's gloom, or Chatterton's despair !

Not such were they, whom, wandering o'er the waves,
I looked to meet, but only found their
   graves ;
If friendship's smile, the better part of
   fame,
Should lend my song the only wreath I
   claim,
Whose voice would greet me with a
   sweeter tone,
Whose living hand more kindly press
   my own,
Than theirs, — could Memory, as her
   silent tread
Prints the pale flowers that blossom o'er
   the dead,
Those breathless lips, now closed in
   peace, restore,
Or wake those pulses hushed to beat no
   more ?

Thou calm, chaste scholar ! I can see
   thee now,
The first young laurels on thy pallid
   brow,
O'er thy slight figure floating lightly
   down
In graceful folds the academic gown,
On thy curled lip the classic lines, that
   taught

How nice the mind that sculptured
 them with thought,
And triumph glistening in the clear
 blue eye,
Too bright to live, — but O, too fair to
 die !

 And thou, dear friend, whom Science
 still deplores,
And love still mourns, on ocean-severed
 shores,
Though the bleak forest twice has bowed
 with snow,
Since thou wast laid its budding leaves
 below,
Thine image mingles with my closing
 strain,
As when we wandered by the turbid Seine,
Both blest with hopes, which revelled,
 bright and free,
On all we longed, or all we dreamed to
 be ;
To thee the amaranth and the cypress
 fell, —
And I was spared to breathe this last
 farewell !

 But lived there one in unremembered
 days,
Or lives there still, who spurns the poet's
 bays,
Whose fingers, dewy from Castalia's
 springs,
Rest on the lyre, yet scorn to touch the
 strings ?
Who shakes the senate with the silver
 tone
The groves of Pindus might have sighed
 to own ?

Have such e'er been ?   Remember Can-
 ning's name !
Do such still live ? Let "Alaric's Dirge"
 proclaim !

 Immortal Art ! where'er the rounded
 sky
Bends o'er the cradle where thy children
 lie,
Their home is earth, their herald every
 tongue
Whose accents echo to the voice that
 sung.
One leap of Ocean scatters on the sand
The quarried bulwarks of the loosening
 land ;
One thrill of earth dissolves a century's
 toil
Strewed like the leaves that vanish in
 the soil ;
One hill o'erflows, and cities sink below,
Their marbles splintering in the lava's
 glow ;
But one sweet tone, scarce whispered to
 the air,
From shore to shore the blasts of ages
 bear ;
One humble name, which oft, perchance,
 has borne
The tyrant's mockery and the courtier's
 scorn,
Towers o'er the dust of earth's forgotten
 graves,
As once, emerging through the waste of
 waves,
The rocky Titan, round whose shattered
 spear
Coiled the last whirlpool of the drowning
 sphere !

ADDITIONAL POEMS.

1837-1848.

THE PILGRIM'S VISION.

In the hour of twilight shadows
 The Pilgrim sire looked out ;
He thought of the "bloudy Salvages"
 That lurked all round about,
Of Wituwamet's pictured knife
 And Pecksuot's whooping shout ;
For the baby's limbs were feeble,
 Though his father's arms were stout.

His home was a freezing cabin,
 Too bare for the hungry rat,
Its roof was thatched with ragged grass,
 · And bald enough of that ;
The hole that served for casement
 Was glazed with an ancient hat ;
And the ice was gently thawing
 From the log whereon he sat.

Along the dreary landscape
 His eyes went to and fro,
The trees all clad in icicles,
 The streams that did not flow ;
A sudden thought flashed o'er him, —
 A dream of long ago, —
He smote his leathern jerkin,
 And murmured, "Even so !"

"Come hither, God-be-Glorified,
 And sit upon my knee,
Behold the dream unfolding,
 Whereof I spake to thee

By the winter's hearth in Leyden
 And on the stormy sea ;
True is the dream's beginning, —
 So may its ending be !

"I saw in the naked forest
 Our scattered remnant cast,
A screen of shivering branches
 Between them and the blast ;
The snow was falling round them,
 The dying fell as fast ;
I looked to see them perish,
 When lo, the vision passed.

"Again mine eyes were opened ; —
 The feeble had waxed strong,
The babes had grown to sturdy men,
 The remnant was a throng ;
By shadowed lake and winding stream,
 And all the shores along,
The howling demons quaked to hear
 The Christian's godly song.

"They slept, — the village fathers, —
 By river, lake, and shore,
When far adown the steep of Time
 The vision rose once more ;
I saw along the winter snow
 A spectral column pour,
And high above their broken ranks
 A tattered flag they bore.

"Their Leader rode before them,
 Of bearing calm and high,

The light of Heaven's own kindling
    Throned in his awful eye ;
These were a Nation's champions
    Her dread appeal to try ;
God for the right ! I faltered,
    And lo, the train passed by.

"Once more ; — the strife is ended,
    The solemn issue tried,
The Lord of Hosts, his mighty arm
    Has helped our Israel's side ;
Gray stone and grassy hillock
    Tell where our martyrs died,
But peaceful smiles the harvest,
    And stainless flows the tide.

"A crash, — as when some swollen cloud
    Cracks o'er the tangled trees !
With side to side, and spar to spar,
    Whose smoking decks are these ?
I know Saint George's blood-red cross,
    Thou Mistress of the Seas, —
But what is she, whose streaming bars
    Roll out before the breeze ?

"Ah, well her iron ribs are knit,
    Whose thunders strive to quell
The bellowing throats, the blazing lips,
    That pealed the Armada's knell !
The mist was cleared, — a wreath of
        stars
    Rose o'er the crimsoned swell,
And, wavering from its haughty peak,
    The cross of England fell !

"O trembling Faith ! though dark the
        morn,
    A heavenly torch is thine ;
While feebler races melt away,
    And paler orbs decline,
Still shall the fiery pillar's ray,
    Along thy pathway shine,
To light the chosen tribe that sought
    This Western Palestine !

" I see the living tide roll on ;
    It crowns with flaming towers
The icy capes of Labrador,
    The Spaniard's 'land of flowers' !
It streams beyond the splintered ridge
    That parts the Northern showers ;
From eastern rock to sunset wave
    The Continent is ours ! "

He ceased, — the grim old soldier-saint, —
    Then softly bent to cheer
The pilgrim-child, whose wasting face
    Was meekly turned to hear ;
And drew his toil-worn sleeve across,
    To brush the manly tear
From cheeks that never changed in woe,
    And never blanched in fear.

The weary pilgrim slumbers,
    His resting-place unknown ;
His hands were crossed, his lids were
        closed,
    The dust was o'er him strown ;
The drifting soil, the mouldering leaf,
    Along the sod were blown ;
His mound has melted into earth,
    His memory lives alone.

So let it live unfading,
    The memory of the dead,
Long as the pale anemone
    Springs where their tears were shed,
Or, raining in the summer's wind
    In flakes of burning red,
The wild rose sprinkles with its leaves
    The turf where once they bled !

Yea, when the frowning bulwarks
    That guard this holy strand
Have sunk beneath the trampling surge
    In beds of sparkling sand,
While in the waste of ocean
    One hoary rock shall stand,
Be this its latest legend, —
    HERE WAS THE PILGRIM'S LAND !

THE STEAMBOAT.

SEE how yon flaming herald treads
  The ridged and rolling waves,
As, crashing o'er their crested heads,
  She bows her surly slaves !
With foam before and fire behind,
  She rends the clinging sea,
That flies before the roaring wind,
  Beneath her hissing lee.

The morning spray, like sea-born flow-
    ers,
  With heaped and glistening bells,
Falls round her fast, in ringing show-
    ers,
  With every wave that swells ;
And, burning o'er the midnight deep,
  In lurid fringes thrown,
The living gems of ocean sweep
  Along her flashing zone.

With clashing wheel, and lifting keel,
  And smoking torch on high,
When winds are loud, and billows reel,
  She thunders foaming by ;
When seas are silent and serene,
  With even beam she glides,
The sunshine glimmering through the
    green
  That skirts her gleaming sides.

Now, like a wild nymph, far apart
  She veils her shadowy form,
The beating of her restless heart
  Still sounding through the storm ;
Now answers, like a courtly dame,
  The reddening surges o'er,
With flying scarf of spangled flame,
  The Pharos of the shore.

To-night yon pilot shall not sleep,
  Who trims his narrowed sail ;
To-night yon frigate scarce shall keep
  Her broad breast to the gale ;

And many a foresail, scooped and
    strained,
  Shall break from yard and stay,
Before this smoky wreath has stained
  The rising mist of day.

Hark ! hark ! I hear yon whistling
    shroud,
  I see yon quivering mast ;
The black throat of the hunted cloud
  Is panting forth the blast !
An hour, and, whirled like winnowing
    chaff,
  The giant surge shall fling
His tresses o'er yon pennon staff,
  White as the sea-bird's wing!

Yet rest, ye wanderers of the deep ;
  Nor wind nor wave shall tire
Those fleshless arms, whose pulses leap
  With floods of living fire ;
Sleep on, — and, when the morning
    light
  Streams o'er the shining bay,
O think of those for whom the night
  Shall never wake in day !

LEXINGTON.

SLOWLY the mist o'er the meadow was
    creeping,
  Bright on the dewy buds glistened
    the sun,
When from his couch, while his chil-
    dren were sleeping,
  Rose the bold rebel and shouldered
    his gun.
      Waving her golden veil
      Over the silent dale,
Blithe looked the morning on cottage
    and spire ;
      Hushed was his parting sigh,
      While from his noble eye
Flashed the last sparkle of liberty's fire.

On the smooth green where the fresh
  leaf is springing
  Calmly the first-born of glory have
    met ;
Hark ! the death-volley around them is
  ringing !
  Look ! with their life-blood the
    young grass is wet !
    Faint is the feeble breath,
    Murmuring low in death,
"Tell to our sons how their fathers
  have died " ;
    Nerveless the iron hand,
    Raised for its native land,
Lies by the weapon that gleams at its
  side.

Over the hillsides the wild knell is
  tolling,
  From their far hamlets the yeomanry
    come ;
As through the storm-clouds the thun-
  der-burst rolling,
  Circles the beat of the mustering
    drum.
    Fast on the soldier's path
    Darken the waves of wrath,
Long have they gathered and loud shall
  they fall ;
    Red glares the musket's flash,
    Sharp rings the rifle's crash,
Blazing and clanging from thicket and
  wall.

Gayly the plume of the horseman was
  dancing,
  Never to shadow his cold brow again ;
Proudly at morning the war-steed was
  prancing,
  Reeking and panting he droops on the
    rein ;
    Pale is the lip of scorn,
    Voiceless the trumpet horn,
Torn is the silken-fringed red cross on
  high ;

Many a belted breast
Low on the turf shall rest,
Ere the dark hunters the herd have
  passed by.

Snow-girdled crags where the hoarse
  wind is raving,
  Rocks where the weary floods murmur
    and wail,
Wilds where the fern by the furrow is
  waving,
  Reeled with the echoes that rode on
    the gale ;
    Far as the tempest thrills
    Over the darkened hills,
Far as the sunshine streams over the
  plain,
    Roused by the tyrant band,
    Woke all the mighty land,
Girded for battle, from mountain to
  main.

Green be the graves where her martyrs
  are lying !
  Shroudless and tombless they sunk to
    their rest, —
While o'er their ashes the starry fold
  flying
  Wraps the proud eagle they roused
    from his nest.
    Borne on her Northern pine,
    Long o'er the foaming brine
Spread her broad banner to storm and
  to sun ;
    Heaven keep her ever free,
    Wide as o'er land and sea
Floats the fair emblem her heroes have
  won !

ON LENDING A PUNCH-BOWL.

THIS ancient silver bowl of mine, it
  tells of good old times,
Of joyous days, and jolly nights, and
  merry Christmas chimes ;

They were a free and jovial race, but
honest, brave, and true,
That dipped their ladle in the punch
when this old bowl was new.

A Spanish galleon brought the bar ; so
runs the ancient tale ;
'T was hammered by an Antwerp smith,
whose arm was like a flail ;
And now and then between the strokes,
for fear his strength should fail,
He wiped his brow, and quaffed a cup
of good old Flemish ale.

'T was purchased by an English squire
to please his loving dame,
Who saw the cherubs, and conceived a
longing for the same ;
And oft as on the ancient stock another
twig was found,
'T was filled with caudle spiced and hot,
and handed smoking round.

But, changing hands, it reached at
length a Puritan divine,
Who used to follow Timothy, and take
a little wine,
But hated punch and prelacy ; and so it
was, perhaps,
He went to Leyden, where he found
conventicles and schnaps.

And then, of course, you know what 's
next, — it left the Dutchman's shore
With those that in the Mayflower came,
— a hundred souls and more, —
Along with all the furniture, to fill their
new abodes, —
To judge by what is still on hand, at
least a hundred loads.

'T was on a dreary winter's eve, the
night was closing dim,
When brave Miles Standish took the
bowl, and filled it to the brim ;

The little Captain stood and stirred the
posset with his sword,
And all his sturdy men-at-arms were
ranged about the board.

He poured the fiery Hollands in, — the
man that never feared, —
He took a long and solemn draught, and
wiped his yellow beard ;
And one by one the musketeers — the
men that fought and prayed —
All drank as 't were their mother's
milk, and not a man afraid.

That night, affrighted from his nest, the
screaming eagle flew,
He heard the Pequot's ringing whoop,
the soldier's wild halloo ;
And there the sachem learned the rule
he taught to kith and kin,
"Run from the white man when you
find he smells of Hollands gin !"

A hundred years, and fifty more, had
spread their leaves and snows,
A thousand rubs had flattened down
each little cherub's nose,
When once again the bowl was filled,
but not in mirth or joy,
'T was mingled by a mother's hand to
cheer her parting boy.

Drink, John, she said, 't will do you
good, — poor child, you 'll never
bear
This working in the dismal trench, out
in the midnight air ;
And if — God bless me ! — you were
hurt, 't would keep away the chill ;
So John *did* drink, — and well he
wrought that night at Bunker's Hill !

I tell you, there was generous warmth
in good old English cheer ;
I tell you, 't was a pleasant thought to
bring its symbol here ;

'T is but the fool that loves excess;
  hast thou a drunken soul?
Thy bane is in thy shallow skull, not in
  my silver bowl !

I love the memory of the past, — its
  pressed yet fragrant flowers, —
The moss that clothes its broken walls,
  — the ivy on its towers ; —
Nay, this poor bawble it bequeathed, —
  my eyes grow moist and dim,
To think of all the vanished joys that
  danced around its brim.

Then fill a fair and honest cup, and bear
  it straight to me ;
The goblet hallows all it holds, whate'er
  the liquid be ;
And may the cherubs on its face protect
  me from the sin,
That dooms one to those dreadful words,
  — "My dear, where *have* you been?"

A SONG

FOR THE CENTENNIAL CELEBRATION OF
HARVARD COLLEGE, 1836.

WHEN the Puritans came over,
  Our hills and swamps to clear,
The woods were full of catamounts,
  And Indians red as deer,
With tomahawks and scalping-knives,
  That make folks' heads look queer;—
O the ship from England used to bring
  A hundred wigs a year !

The crows came cawing through the air
  To pluck the pilgrims' corn,
The bears came snuffing round the door
  Whene'er a babe was born,
The rattlesnakes were bigger round
  Than the but of the old ram's horn
The deacon blew at meeting time
  On every "Sabbath" morn.

But soon they knocked the wigwams
  down,
  And pine-tree trunk and limb
Began to sprout among the leaves
  In shape of steeples slim ;
And out the little wharves were stretched
  Along the ocean's rim,
And up the little school-house shot
  To keep the boys in trim.

And, when at length the College rose,
  The sachem cocked his eye
At every tutor's meagre ribs
  Whose coat-tails whistled by :
But when the Greek and Hebrew words
  Came tumbling from their jaws,
The copper-colored children all
  Ran screaming to the squaws.

And who was on the Catalogue
  When college was begun ?
Two nephews of the President,
  And *the* Professor's son ;
(They turned a little Indian by,
  As brown as any bun ;)
Lord ! how the seniors knocked about
  The freshman class of one !

They had not then the dainty things
  That commons now afford,
But *succotash* and *homony*
  Were smoking on the board ;
They did not rattle round in gigs,
  Or dash in long-tail blues,
But always on Commencement days
  The tutors blacked their shoes.

God bless the ancient Puritans !
  Their lot was hard enough ;
But honest hearts make iron arms,
  And tender maids are tough ;
So love and faith have formed and fed
  Our true-born Yankee stuff,
And keep the kernel in the shell
  The British found so rough !

THE ISLAND HUNTING-SONG.

No more the summer floweret charms,
  The leaves will soon be sere,
And Autumn folds his jewelled arms
  Around the dying year ;
So, ere the waning seasons claim
  Our leafless groves awhile,
With golden wine and glowing flame
  We 'll crown our lonely isle.

Once more the merry voices sound
  Within the antlered hall,
And long and loud the baying hounds
  Return the hunter's call ;
And through the woods, and o'er the hill,
  And far along the bay,
The driver's horn is sounding shrill, —
  Up, sportsmen, and away !

No bars of steel, or walls of stone,
  Our little empire bound,
But, circling with his azure zone,
  The sea runs foaming round ;
The whitening wave, the purpled skies,
  The blue and lifted shore,
Braid with their dim and blending dyes
  Our wide horizon o'er.

And who will leave the grave debate
  That shakes the smoky town,
To rule amid our island-state,
  And wear our oak-leaf crown ?
And who will be awhile content
  To hunt our woodland game,
And leave the vulgar pack that scent
  The reeking track of fame ?

Ah, who that shares in toils like these
  Will sigh not to prolong
Our days beneath the broad-leaved trees,
  Our nights of mirth and song ?
Then leave the dust of noisy streets,
  Ye outlaws of the wood,
And follow through his green retreats
  Your noble Robin Hood.

DEPARTED DAYS.

YES, dear departed, cherished days,
  Could Memory's hand restore
Your morning light, your evening rays
  From Time's gray urn once more, —
Then might this restless heart be still,
  This straining eye might close,
And Hope her fainting pinions fold,
  While the fair phantoms rose.

But, like a child in ocean's arms,
  We strive against the stream,
Each moment farther from the shore
  Where life's young fountains gleam ; —
Each moment fainter wave the fields,
  And wider rolls the sea ;
The mist grows dark, — the sun goes
    down, —
  Day breaks, — and where are we ?

THE ONLY DAUGHTER.

ILLUSTRATION OF A PICTURE.

THEY bid me strike the idle strings,
  As if my summer days
Had shaken sunbeams from their wings
  To warm my autumn lays ;
They bring to me their painted urn,
  As if it were not time
To lift my gauntlet and to spurn
  The lists of boyish rhyme ;
And, were it not that I have still
  Some weakness in my heart
That clings around my stronger will
  And pleads for gentler art,
Perchance I had not turned away
  The thoughts grown tame with toil,
To cheat this lone and pallid ray,
  That wastes the midnight oil.

Alas ! with every year I feel
  Some roses leave my brow ;
Too young for wisdom's tardy seal,
  Too old for garlands now ;

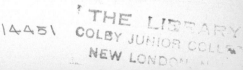

Yet, while the dewy breath of spring
  Steals o'er the tingling air,
And spreads and fans each emerald wing
  The forest soon shall wear,
How bright the opening year would seem,
  Had I one look like thine,
To meet me when the morning beam
  Unseals these lids of mine !
Too long I bear this lonely lot,
  That bids my heart run wild
To press the lips that love me not,
  To clasp the stranger's child.

How oft beyond the dashing seas,
  Amidst those royal bowers,
Where danced the lilacs in the breeze,
  And swung the chestnut-flowers,
I wandered like a wearied slave
  Whose morning task is done,
To watch the little hands that gave
  Their whiteness to the sun ;
To revel in the bright young eyes,
  Whose lustre sparkled through
The sable fringe of Southern skies
  Or gleamed in Saxon blue !
How oft I heard another's name
  Called in some truant's tone ;
Sweet accents ! which I longed to claim,
  To learn and lisp my own !

Too soon the gentle hands, that pressed
  The ringlets of the child,
Are folded on the faithful breast
  Where first he breathed and smiled ;
Too oft the clinging arms untwine,
  The melting lips forget,
And darkness veils the bridal shrine
  Where wreaths and torches met ;
If Heaven but leaves a single thread
  Of Hope's dissolving chain,
Even when her parting plumes are spread,
  It bids them fold again ;
The cradle rocks beside the tomb ;
  The cheek now changed and chill

Smiles on us in the morning bloom
  Of one that loves us still.

Sweet image ! I have done thee wrong
  To claim this destined lay ;
The leaf that asked an idle song
  Must bear my tears away.
Yet, in thy memory shouldst thou keep
  This else forgotten strain,
Till years have taught thine eyes to weep,
  And flattery's voice is vain ;
O then, thou fledgling of the nest,
  Like the long-wandering dove,
Thy weary heart may faint for rest,
  As mine, on changeless love ;
And while these sculptured lines retrace
  The hours now dancing by,
This vision of thy girlish grace
  May cost thee, too, a sigh.

SONG

WRITTEN FOR THE DINNER GIVEN TO
CHARLES DICKENS, BY THE YOUNG
MEN OF BOSTON, FEB. 1, 1842.

THE stars their early vigils keep,
  The silent hours are near,
When drooping eyes forget to weep, —
  Yet still we linger here ;
And what — the passing churl may ask —
  Can claim such wondrous power,
That Toil forgets his wonted task,
  And Love his promised hour ?

The Irish harp no longer thrills,
  Or breathes a fainter tone ;
The clarion blast from Scotland's hills,
  Alas ! no more is blown ;
And Passion's burning lip bewails
  Her Harold's wasted fire,
Still lingering o'er the dust that veils
  The Lord of England's lyre.

But grieve not o'er its broken strings,
  Nor think its soul hath died.

While yet the lark at heaven's gate sings,
  As once o'er Avon's side ; —
While gentle summer sheds her bloom,
  And dewy blossoms wave,
Alike o'er Juliet's storied tomb
  And Nelly's nameless grave.

Thou glorious island of the sea !
  Though wide the wasting flood
That parts our distant land from thee,
  We claim thy generous blood ;
Nor o'er thy far horizon springs
  One hallowed star of fame,
But kindles, like an angel's wings,
  Our western skies in flame !

LINES

RECITED AT THE BERKSHIRE FESTIVAL.

COME back to your mother, ye children,
    for shame,
Who have wandered like truants, for
    riches or fame !
With a smile on her face, and a sprig in
    her cap,
She calls you to feast from her bountiful
    lap.

Come out from your alleys, your courts,
    and your lanes,
And breathe, like young eagles, the air
    of our plains ;
Take a whiff from our fields, and your
    excellent wives
Will declare it 's all nonsense insuring
    your lives.

Come you of the law, who can talk, if
    you please,
Till the man in the moon will allow it 's
    a cheese,
And leave "the old lady, that never tells
    lies,"
To sleep with her handkerchief over her
    eyes.

Ye healers of men, for a moment decline
Your feats in the rhubarb and ipecac
    line ;
While you shut up your turnpike, your
    neighbors can go,
The old roundabout road, to the regions
    below.

You clerk, on whose ears are a couple of
    pens,
And whose head is an ant-hill of units
    and tens ;
Though Plato denies you, we welcome
    you still
As a featherless biped, in spite of your
    quill.

Poor drudge of the city ! how happy he
    feels,
With the burs on his legs, and the grass
    at his heels !
No *dodger* behind, his bandannas to
    share,
No constable grumbling, "You must n't
    walk there !"

In yonder green meadow, to memory
    dear,
He slaps a mosquito and brushes a tear;
The dew-drops hang round him on blos-
    soms and shoots,
He breathes but one sigh for his youth
    and his boots.

There stands the old school-house, hard
    by the old church ;
That tree at its side had the flavor of
    birch ;
O sweet were the days of his juvenile
    tricks,
Though the prairie of youth had so many
    "big licks."

By the side of yon river he weeps and
    he slumps,
The boots fill with water, as if they were
    pumps,

Till, sated with rapture, he steals to his bed,
With a glow in his heart and a cold in his head.

'T is past, — he is dreaming, — I see him again ;
The ledger returns as by legerdemain ;
His neckcloth is damp with an easterly flaw,
And he holds in his fingers an omnibus straw.

He dreams the chill gust is a blossomy gale,
That the straw is a rose from his dear native vale ;
And murmurs, unconscious of space and of time,
"A 1.   Extra super.   Ah, is n't it PRIME !"

O what are the prizes we perish to win
To the first little "shiner" we caught with a pin !
No soil upon earth is so dear to our eyes
As the soil we first stirred in terrestrial pies !

Then come from all parties, and parts, to our feast ;
Though not at the "Astor," we 'll give you at least
A bite at an apple, a seat on the grass,
And the best of old — water — at nothing a glass.

NUX POSTCŒNATICA.

I WAS sitting with my microscope, upon my parlor rug,
With a very heavy quarto and a very lively bug ;
The true bug had been organized with only two antennæ,
But the humbug in the copperplate would have them twice as many.

And I thought, like Dr. Faustus, of the emptiness of art,
How we take a fragment for the whole, and call the whole a part,
When I heard a heavy footstep that was loud enough for two,
And a man of forty entered, exclaiming, — "How d'ye do ?"

He was not a ghost, my visitor, but solid flesh and bone ;
He wore a Palo Alto hat, his weight was twenty stone ;
(It 's odd how hats expand their brims as riper years invade,
As if when life had reached its noon, it wanted them for shade !)

I lost my focus, — dropped my book, — the bug, who was a flea,
At once exploded, and commenced experiments on me.
They have a certain heartiness that frequently appalls, —
Those mediæval gentlemen in semilunar smalls !

"My boy," he said, — (colloquial ways, — the vast, broad-hatted man,) —
"Come dine with us on Thursday next, — you must, you know you can ;
We 're going to have a roaring time, with lots of fun and noise,
Distinguished guests, et cetera, the JUDGE, and all the boys."

Not so, — I said, — my temporal bones are showing pretty clear.
It 's time to stop, — just look and see that hair above this ear ;
My golden days are more than spent, — — and, what is very strange,
If these are real silver hairs, I 'm getting lots of change.

Besides — my prospects — don't you know that people won't employ

A man that wrongs his manliness by
laughing like a boy ?
And suspect the azure blossom that unfolds upon a shoot,
As if wisdom's old potato could not
flourish at its root ?

It 's a very fine reflection, when you 're
etching out a smile
On a copperplate of faces that would
stretch at least a mile,
That, what with sneers from enemies,
and cheapening shrugs of friends,
It will cost you all the earnings that a
month of labor lends !

It 's a vastly pleasing prospect, when
you 're screwing out a laugh,
That your very next year's income is
diminished by a half,
And a little boy trips barefoot that
Pegasus may go,
And the baby's milk is watered that
your Helicon may flow !

No ; — the joke has been a good one, —
but I 'm getting fond of quiet,
And I don't like deviations from my
customary diet ;
So I think I will not go with you to
hear the toasts and speeches,
But stick to old Montgomery Place, and
have some pig and peaches.

The fat man answered : — Shut your
mouth, and hear the genuine creed ;
The true essentials of a feast are only
fun and feed ;
The force that wheels the planets round
delights in spinning tops,
And that young earthquake t' other day
was great at shaking props.

I tell you what, philosopher, if all the
longest heads

That ever knocked their sinciputs in
stretching on their beds
Were round one great mahogany, I 'd
beat those fine old folks
With twenty dishes, twenty fools, and
twenty clever jokes !

Why, if Columbus should be there, the
company would beg
He 'd show that little trick of his of
balancing the egg !
Milton to Stilton would give in, and
Solomon to Salmon,
And Roger Bacon be a bore, and Francis
Bacon gammon !

And as for all the "patronage" of all
the clowns and boors
That squint their little narrow eyes at
any freak of yours,
Do leave them to your prosier friends,
— such fellows ought to die
When rhubarb is so very scarce and
ipecac so high !

And so I come, — like Lochinvar, to
tread a single measure,
To purchase with a loaf of bread a sugar-
plum of pleasure,
To enter for the cup of glass that 's run
for after dinner,
Which yields a single sparkling draught,
then breaks and cuts the winner.

Ah, that 's the way delusion comes, —
a glass of old Madeira,
A pair of visual diaphragms revolved by
Jane or Sarah,
And down go vows and promises with-
out the slightest question
If eating words won't compromise the
organs of digestion !

And yet, among my native shades, beside my nursing mother,

Where every stranger seems a friend,
  and every friend a brother,
I feel the old convivial glow (unaided)
  o'er me stealing, —
The warm, champagny, old-particular,
  brandy-punchy feeling.

We're all alike ; — Vesuvius flings the
  scoriæ from his fountain,
But down they come in volleying rain
  back to the burning mountain ;
We leave, like those volcanic stones, our
  precious Alma Mater,
But will keep dropping in again to see
  the dear old crater.

VERSES FOR AFTER-DINNER.

Φ B K SOCIETY, 1844.

I was thinking last night, as I sat in
  the cars,
With the charmingest prospect of cinders and stars,
Next Thursday is — bless me ! — how
  hard it will be,
If that cannibal president calls upon me !

There is nothing on earth that he will
  not devour,
From a tutor in seed to a freshman in
  flower ;
No sage is too gray, and no youth is too
  green,
And you can't be too plump, though you
  're never too lean.

While others enlarge on the boiled and
  the roast,
He serves a raw clergyman up with a
  toast,
Or catches some doctor, quite tender and
  young,
And basely insists on a bit of his tongue.

Poor victim, prepared for his classical
  spit,

With a stuffing of praise, and a basting
  of wit,
You may twitch at your collar, and wrinkle your brow,
But you 're up on your legs, and you 're
  in for it now.

O think of your friends, — they are waiting to hear
Those jokes that are thought so remark-
  ably queer ;
And all the Jack Horners of metrical
  buns
Are prying and fingering to pick out the
  puns.

Those thoughts which, like chickens,
  will always thrive best
When reared by the heat of the natural
  nest,
Will perish if hatched from their embryo
  dream
In the mist and the glow of convivial
  steam.

O pardon me, then, if I meekly retire,
With a very small flash of ethereal fire ;
No rubbing will kindle your Lucifer
  match,
If the *fiz* does not follow the primitive
  scratch.

Dear friends, who are listening so sweetly
  the while,
With your lips double-reefed in a snug
  little smile, —
I leave you two fables, both drawn from
  the deep, —
The shells you can drop, but the pearls
  you may keep.

*   *   *

The fish called the FLOUNDER, perhaps
  you may know,
Has one side for use and another for
  show ;

One side for the public, a delicate brown,
And one that is white, which he always
keeps down.

A very young flounder, the flattest of
flats,
(And they 're none of them thicker than
opera hats,)
Was speaking more freely than charity
taught
Of a friend and relation that just had
been caught.

" My ! what an exposure ! just see what
a sight !
I blush for my race, — he is showing his
white !
Such spinning and wriggling, — why,
what does he wish ?
How painfully small to respectable fish ! ''

Then said an old SCULPIN, — " My freedom excuse,
But you 're playing the cobbler with holes
in your shoes ;
Your brown side is up, — but just wait
till you 're tried
And you 'll find that all flounders are
white on one side.''

    *   *   *

There 's a slice near the PICKEREL's pec-
toral fins,
Where the *thorax* leaves off and the
venter begins ;
Which his brother, survivor of fish-hooks
and lines,
Though fond of his family, never declines.

He loves his relations ; he feels they 'll
be missed ;
But that one little titbit he cannot resist ;
So your bait may be swallowed, no matter how fast,
For you catch your next fish with a piece
of the last.

And thus, O survivor, whose merciless
fate
Is to take the next hook with the president's bait,
You are lost while you snatch from the
end of his line
The morsel he rent from this bosom of
mine !

A MODEST REQUEST

COMPLIED WITH AFTER THE DINNER AT
PRESIDENT EVERETT'S INAUGURATION.

SCENE, — a back parlor in a certain
square,
Or court, or lane, — in short, no matter
where ;
Time, — early morning, dear to simple
souls
Who love its sunshine, and its fresh-
baked rolls ;
Persons, — take pity on this telltale
blush,
That, like the Æthiop, whispers, "Hush,
O hush ! "

Delightful scene ! where smiling comfort
broods,
Nor business frets, nor anxious care in-
trudes ;
O si sic omnia ! were it ever so !
But what is stable in this world below ?
Medio e fonte, — Virtue has her faults,—
The clearest fountains taste of Epsom
salts ;
We snatch the cup and lift to drain it
dry, —
Its central dimple holds a drowning fly!
Strong is the pine by Maine's ambrosial
streams,
But stronger augers pierce its thickest
beams ;
No iron gate, no spiked and panelled
door,

Can keep out death, the postman, or the
bore ; —
O for a world where peace and silence
reign,
And blunted dulness terebrates in vain !
— The door-bell jingles, — enter Richard Fox,
And takes this letter from his leathern
box.

" Dear Sir,
In writing on a former day,
One little matter I forgot to say ;
I now inform you in a single line,
On Thursday next our purpose is to *dine.*
The act of feeding, as you understand,
Is but a fraction of the work in hand ;
Its nobler half is that ethereal meat
The papers call ' the intellectual treat ';
Songs, speeches, toasts, around the fes-
tive board
Drowned in the juice the College pumps
afford ;
For only water flanks our knives and
forks,
So, sink or float, we swim without the
corks.
Yours is the art, by native genius taught,
To clothe in eloquence the naked thought ;
Yours is the skill its music to prolong
Through the sweet effluence of melliflu-
ous song ;
Yours the quaint trick to cram the pithy
line
That cracks so crisply over bubbling wine ;
And since success your various gifts at-
tends,
We — that is, I and all your numerous
friends —
Expect from you — your single self a
host —
A speech, a song, excuse me, *and* a toast ;
Nay, not to haggle on so small a claim,
A few of each, or several of the same.
(Signed), Yours, *most truly,* —— "

No ! my sight must fail, —
If that ain't Judas on the largest scale !

Well, this *is* modest ; — nothing else
than that ?
My coat ? my boots ? my pantaloons ?
my hat ?
My stick ? my gloves ? as well as all
my wits,
Learning and linen, — everything that
fits !

Jack, said my lady, is it grog you 'll try,
Or punch, or toddy, if perhaps you 're
dry ?
Ah, said the sailor, though I can't re-
fuse,
You know, my lady, 't ain't for me to
choose ; —
I 'll take the grog to finish off my lunch,
And drink the toddy while you mix the
punch.

THE SPEECH. (The speaker, rising to
be seen,
Looks very red, because so very green.)
I rise — I rise — with unaffected fear,
(Louder ! — speak louder ! — who the
deuce can hear ?)
I rise — I said — with undisguised dis-
may —
— Such are my feelings as I rise, I say !
Quite unprepared to face this learned
throng,
Already gorged with eloquence and song;
Around my view are ranged on either
hand
The genius, wisdom, virtue, of the land ;
" Hands that the rod of empire might
have swayed "
Close at my elbow stir their lemonade ;
Would you like Homer learn to write
and speak,
That bench is groaning with its weight
of Greek ;

Behold the naturalist who in his teens
Found six new species in a dish of greens;
And lo, the master in a statelier walk,
Whose annual ciphering takes a ton of
chalk ;
And there the linguist, who by common
roots
Thro' all their nurseries tracks old Noah's
shoots, —
How Shem's proud children reared the
Assyrian piles,
While Ham's were scattered through the
Sandwich Isles !

— Fired at the thought of all the pres-
ent shows,
My kindling fancy down the future
flows :
I see the glory of the coming days
O'er Time's horizon shoot its streaming
rays ;
Near and more near the radiant morning
draws.
In living lustre (rapturous applause) ;
From east to west the blazing heralds run,
Loosed from the chariot of the ascend-
ing sun,
Through the long vista of uncounted
years
In cloudless splendor (three tremendous
cheers).
My eye prophetic, as the depths unfold,
Sees a new advent of the age of gold ;
While o'er the scene new generations
press,
New heroes rise the coming time to
bless, —
Not such as Homer's, who, we read in
Pope,
Dined without forks and never neard of
soap, —
Not such as May to Marlborough Chapel
brings,
Lean, hungry, savage, anti-everythings,

Copies of Luther in the pasteboard
style, —
But genuine articles, — the true Carlyle ;
While far on high the blazing orb shall
shed
Its central light on Harvard's holy head,
And Learning's ensigns ever float un-
furled
Here in the focus of the new-born world .

The speaker stops, and, trampling down
the pause,
Roars through the hall the thunder of
applause,
One stormy gust of long-suspended Ahs !
One whirlwind chaos of insane hurrahs !

———

The Song.   But this demands a briefer
line, —
A shorter muse, and not the old long
Nine ; —
Long metre answers for a common song,
Though common metre does not answer
long.

She came beneath the forest dome
     To seek its peaceful shade,
An exile from her ancient home, —
     A poor, forsaken maid ;
No banner, flaunting high above,
     No blazoned cross, she bore ;
One holy book of light and love
     Was all her worldly store.

The dark brown shadows passed away,
     And wider spread the green,
And, where the savage used to stray,
     The rising mart was seen ;
So, when the laden winds had brought
     Their showers of golden rain,
Her lap some precious gleanings caught,
     Like Ruth's amid the grain.

But wrath soon gathered uncontrolled
     Among the baser churls,

To see her ankles red with gold,
  Her forehead white with pearls ;
" Who gave to thee the glittering bands
  That lace thine azure veins ?
Who bade thee lift those snow-white
    hands
  We bound in gilded chains ? "

" These are the gems my children gave,"
  The stately dame replied ;
" The wise, the gentle, and the brave,
  I nurtured at my side ;
If envy still your bosom stings,
  Take back their rims of gold ;
My sons will melt their wedding-rings,
  And give a hundred-fold ! "

———

THE TOAST. O tell me, ye who thought-
    less ask
Exhausted nature for a threefold task,
In wit or pathos if one share remains,
A safe investment for an ounce of brains ?
Hard is the job to launch the desperate
    pun,
A pun-job dangerous as the Indian one.
Turned by the current of some stronger
    wit
Back from the object that you mean to
    hit,
Like the strange missile which the Aus-
    tralian throws,
Your verbal *boomerang* slaps you on the
    nose.
One vague inflection spoils the whole
    with doubt,
One trivial letter ruins all, left out ;
A knot can choke a felon into clay,
A not will save him, spelt without the k ;
The smallest word has some unguarded
    spot,
And danger lurks in i without a dot.

Thus great Achilles, who had shown his
    zeal

In healing wounds, died of a wounded
    heel ;
Unhappy chief, who, when in childhood
    doused,
Had saved his bacon, had his feet been
    soused !
Accursed heel that killed a hero stout !
O, had your mother known that you
    were out,
Death had not entered at the trifling
    part
That still defies the small chirurgeon's
    art
With corns and bunions, — not the glo-
    rious John,
Who wrote the book we all have pon-
    dered on, —
But other bunions, bound in fleecy hose,
To " Pilgrim's Progress " unrelenting
    foes !   ———

A health, unmingled with the reveller's
    wine,
To him whose title is indeed divine ;
Truth's sleepless watchman on her mid-
    night tower,
Whose lamp burns brightest when the
    tempests lower.
O who can tell with what a leaden flight
Drag the long watches of his weary
    night,
While at his feet the hoarse and blind-
    ing gale
Strews the torn wreck and bursts the
    fragile sail,
When stars have faded, when the wave
    is dark,
When rocks and sands embrace the
    foundering bark,
And still he pleads with unavailing cry,
Behold the light, O wanderer, look or
    die !

A health, fair Themis !   Would the
    enchanted vine

Wreathed its green tendrils round this
    cup of thine ;
If Learning's radiance fill thy modern
    court,
Its glorious sunshine streams through
    Blackstone's port !
Lawyers are thirsty, and their clients too,
Witness at least, if memory serve me
    true,
Those old tribunals, famed for dusty
    suits,
Where men sought justice ere they
    brushed their boots ; —
And what can match, to solve a learned
    doubt,
The warmth within that comes from
    " cold without " ?

Health to the art whose glory is to give
The crowning boon that makes it life to
    live.
Ask not her home ; — the rock where
    nature flings
Her arctic lichen, last of living things,
The gardens, fragrant with the orient's
    balm,
From the low jasmine to the star-like
    palm,
Hail her as mistress o'er the distant
    waves,
And yield their tribute to her wandering
    slaves.
Wherever, moistening the ungrateful
    soil,
The tear of suffering tracks the path of
    toil,
There, in the anguish of his fevered
    hours,
Her gracious finger points to healing
    flowers ;
Where the lost felon steals away to die,
Her soft hand waves before his closing
    eye ;
Where hunted misery finds his darkest
    lair,

The midnight taper shows her kneeling
    there !
VIRTUE, — the guide that men and
    nations own ;
And LAW, — the bulwark that protects
    her throne ;
And HEALTH, — to all its happiest
    charm that lends ;
These and their servants, man's untiring
    friends ;
Pour the bright lymph that Heaven itself
    lets fall, —
In one fair bumper let us toast them all !

THE STETHOSCOPE SONG.

A PROFESSIONAL BALLAD.

THERE was a young man in Boston town,
    He bought him a STETHOSCOPE nice
       and new,
All mounted and finished and polished
    down,
    With an ivory cap and a stopper too.

It happened a spider within did crawl,
    And spun him a web of ample size,
Wherein there chancëd one day to fall
    A couple of very imprudent flies.

The first was a bottle-fly, big and blue,
    The second was smaller, and thin and
       long ;
So there was a concert between the two,
    Like an octave flute and a tavern gong.

Now being from Paris but recently,
    This fine young man would show his
       skill ;
And so they gave him, his hand to try,
    A hospital patient extremely ill.

Some said that his *liver* was short of *bile*,
    And some that his *heart* was over size,

While some kept arguing all the while
  He was crammed with *tubercles* up to
    his eyes.

This fine young man then up stepped he,
  And all the doctors made a pause ;
Said he, — The man must die, you see,
  By the fifty-seventh of Louis's laws.

But since the case is a desperate one,
  To explore his chest it may be well ;
For if he should die and it were not done,
  You know the *autopsy* would not tell.

Then out his stethoscope he took,
  And on it placed his curious ear ;
Mon Dieu! said he, with a knowing look,
  Why here is a sound that 's mighty
    queer !

The *bourdonnement* is very clear, —
  Amphoric buzzing, as I 'm alive !
Five doctors took their turn to hear ;
  Amphoric buzzing, said all the five.

There 's *empyema* beyond a doubt ;
  We 'll plunge a *trocar* in his side. —
The diagnosis was made out,
  They tapped the patient ; so he died.

Now such as hate new-fashioned toys
  Began to look extremely glum ;
They said that *rattles* were made for boys,
  And vowed that his *buzzing* was all a
    hum.

There was an old lady had long been
    sick,
  And what was the matter none did
    know :
Her pulse was slow, though her tongue
    was quick ;
  To her this knowing youth must go.

So there the nice old lady sat,
  With phials and boxes all in a row ;

She asked the young doctor what he
    was at,
  To thump her and tumble her ruffles so.

Now, when the stethoscope came out,
  The flies began to buzz and whiz ; —
O ho ! the matter is clear, no doubt ;
  An *aneurism* there plainly is.

The *bruit de râpe* and the *bruit de scie*
  And the *bruit de diable* are all com-
    bined ;
How happy Bouillaud would be,
  If he a case like this could find !

Now, when the neighboring doctors
    found
  A case so rare had been descried,
They every day her ribs did pound
  In squads of twenty ; so she died.

Then six young damsels, slight and frail,
  Received this kind young doctor's
    cares ;
They all were getting slim and pale,
  And short of breath on mounting
    stairs.

They all made rhymes with "sighs" and
    " skies,"
  And loathed their puddings and but-
    tered rolls,
And dieted, much to their friends' sur-
    prise,
  On pickles and pencils and chalk and
    coals.

So fast their little hearts did bound,
  The frightened insects buzzed the
    more ;
So over all their chests he found
    The *râle sifflant*, and *râle sonore*.

He shook his head ; — there 's grave
    disease, —
  I greatly fear you all must die ;

"Still the r d beacon pours its evening rays." Page 45.

A slight *post-mortem*, if you please,
  Surviving friends would gratify.

The six young damsels wept aloud,
  Which so prevailed on six young men,
That each his honest love avowed,
  Whereat they all got well again.

This poor young man was all aghast ;
  The price of stethoscopes came down ;
And so he was reduced at last
  To practise in a country town.

The doctors being very sore,
  A stethoscope they did devise,
That had a rammer to clear the bore,
  With a knob at the end to kill the flies.

Now use your ears, all you that can,
  But don't forget to mind your eyes,
Or you may be cheated, like this young man,
  By a couple of silly, abnormal flies.

EXTRACTS FROM A MEDICAL POEM.

THE STABILITY OF SCIENCE.

THE feeble sea-birds, blinded in the storms,
On some tall lighthouse dash their little forms,
And the rude granite scatters for their pains
Those small deposits that were meant for brains.
Yet the proud fabric in the morning's sun
Stands all unconscious of the mischief done ;
Still the red beacon pours its evening rays
For the lost pilot with as full a blaze,
Nay, shines, all radiance, o'er the scattered fleet
Of gulls and boobies brainless at its feet.
  I tell their fate, though courtesy disclaims

To call our kind by such ungentle names ;
Yet, if your rashness bid you vainly dare,
Think of their doom, ye simple, and beware !
  See where aloft its hoary forehead rears
The towering pride of twice a thousand years !
Far, far below the vast incumbent pile
Sleeps the gray rock from art's Ægean isle ;
Its massive courses, circling as they rise,
Swell from the waves to mingle with the skies ;
There every quarry lends its marble spoil,
And clustering ages blend their common toil ;
The Greek, the Roman, reared its ancient walls,
The silent Arab arched its mystic halls ;
In that fair niche, by countless billows laved,
Trace the deep lines that Sydenham engraved ;
On yon broad front that breasts the changing swell,
Mark where the ponderous sledge of Hunter fell ;
By that square buttress look where Louis stands,
The stone yet warm from his uplifted hands ;
And say, O Science, shall thy life-blood freeze,
When fluttering folly flaps on walls like these ?

A PORTRAIT.

THOUGHTFUL in youth, but not austere in age ;
Calm, but not cold, and cheerful though a sage ;
Too true to flatter, and too kind to sneer,
And only just when seemingly severe ;
So gently blending courtesy and art,

That wisdom's lips seemed borrowing
　　friendship's heart.
Taught by the sorrows that his age had
　　known
In others' trials to forget his own,
As hour by hour his lengthened day de-
　　clined,
A sweeter radiance lingered o'er his
　　mind.
Cold were the lips that spoke his early
　　praise,
And hushed the voices of his morning
　　days,
Yet the same accents dwelt on every
　　tongue,
And love renewing kept him ever young.

A SENTIMENT.

'Ο βίος βραχύς, — life is but a song ;
'Η τέχνη μακρή, — art is wondrous long ;
Yet to the wise her paths are ever fair,
And Patience smiles, though Genius may
　　despair.
Give us but knowledge, though by slow
　　degrees,
And blend our toil with moments bright
　　as these ;
Let Friendship's accents cheer our doubt-
　　ful way,
And Love's pure planet lend its guiding
　　ray, —
Our tardy Art shall wear an angel's wings,
And life shall lengthen with the joy it
　　brings !

THE PARTING WORD.

I MUST leave thee, lady sweet !
Months shall waste before we meet ;
Winds are fair, and sails are spread,
Anchors leave their ocean bed ;
Ere this shining day grow dark,
Skies shall gird my shoreless bark ;

Through thy tears, O lady mine,
Read thy lover's parting line.

When the first sad sun shall set,
Thou shalt tear thy locks of jet ;
When the morning star shall rise,
Thou shalt wake with weeping eyes ;
When the second sun goes down,
Thou more tranquil shalt be grown,
Taught too well that wild despair
Dims thine eyes, and spoils thy hair.

All the first unquiet week
Thou shalt wear a smileless cheek ;
In the first month's second half
Thou shalt once attempt to laugh ;
Then in Pickwick thou shalt dip,
Slightly puckering round the lip,
Till at last, in sorrow's spite,
Samuel makes thee laugh outright.

While the first seven mornings last,
Round thy chamber bolted fast,
Many a youth shall fume and pout,
"Hang the girl, she's always out !"
While the second week goes round,
Vainly shall they ring and pound ;
When the third week shall begin,
"Martha, let the creature in."

Now once more the flattering throng
Round thee flock with smile and song,
But thy lips, unweaned as yet,
Lisp, "O, how can I forget !"
Men and devils both contrive
Traps for catching girls alive ;
Eve was duped, and Helen kissed, —
How, O how can you resist ?

First be careful of your fan,
Trust it not to youth or man ;
Love has filled a pirate's sail
Often with its perfumed gale.
Mind your kerchief most of all,
Fingers touch when kerchiefs fall ;

Shorter ell than mercers clip
Is the space from hand to lip.

Trust not such as talk in tropes,
Full of pistols, daggers, ropes ;
All the hemp that Russia bears
Scarce would answer lovers' prayers ;
Never thread was spun so fine,
Never spider stretched the line,
Would not hold the lovers true
That would really swing for you.

Fiercely some shall storm and swear,
Beating breasts in black despair ;
Others murmur with a sigh,
You must melt, or they will die ;
Painted words on empty lies,
Grubs with wings like butterflies ;
Let them die, and welcome, too ;
Pray what better could they do ?

Fare thee well, if years efface
From thy heart love's burning trace,
Keep, O keep that hallowed seat
From the tread of vulgar feet ;
If the blue lips of the sea
Wait with icy kiss for me,
Let not thine forget the vow,
Sealed how often, Love, as now.

A SONG OF OTHER DAYS.

As o'er the glacier's frozen sheet
  Breathes soft the Alpine rose,
So, through life's desert springing sweet,
  The flower of friendship grows ;
And as, where'er the roses grow,
  Some rain or dew descends,
'T is nature's law that wine should flow
  To wet the lips of friends.
      Then once again, before we part,
        My empty glass shall ring ;
      And he that has the warmest heart
        Shall loudest laugh and sing.

They say we were not born to eat ;
  But gray-haired sages think

It means, — Be moderate in your meat,
  And partly live to drink ;
For baser tribes the rivers flow
  That know not wine or song ;
Man wants but little drink below,
  But wants that little strong.
      Then once again, etc.

If one bright drop is like the gem
  That decks a monarch's crown,
One goblet holds a diadem
  Of rubies melted down !
A fig for Cæsar's blazing brow,
  But, like the Egyptian queen,
Bid each dissolving jewel glow
  My thirsty lips between.
      Then once again, etc.

The Grecian's mound, the Roman's urn,
  Are silent when we call,
Yet still the purple grapes return
  To cluster on the wall ;
It was a bright Immortal's head
  They circled with the vine,
And o'er their best and bravest dead
  They poured the dark-red wine.
      Then once again, etc.

Methinks o'er every sparkling glass
  Young Eros waves his wings,
And echoes o'er its dimples pass
  From dead Anacreon's strings ;
And, tossing round its beaded brim
  Their locks of floating gold,
With bacchant dance and choral hymn
  Return the nymphs of old.
      Then once again, etc.

A welcome then to joy and mirth,
  From hearts as fresh as ours,
To scatter o'er the dust of earth
  Their sweetly mingled flowers ;
'T is Wisdom's self the cup that fills
  In spite of Folly's frown,
And Nature, from her vine-clad hills,
  That rains her life-blood down !

Then once again, before we part,
  My empty glass shall ring ;
And he that has the warmest heart
  Shall loudest laugh and sing.

SONG.

FOR A TEMPERANCE DINNER TO WHICH
LADIES WERE INVITED (NEW YORK
MERCANTILE LIBRARY ASSOCIATION,
NOV., 1842).

A HEALTH to dear woman ! She bids us
  untwine,
From the cup it encircles, the fast-cling-
  ing vine ;
But her cheek in its crystal with pleasure
  will glow,
And mirror its bloom in the bright wave
  below.

A health to sweet woman ! The days
  are no more
When she watched for her lord till the
  revel was o'er,
And smoothed the white pillow, and
  blushed when he came,
As she pressed her cold lips on his forehead of flame.

Alas for the loved one ! too spotless and
  fair
The joys of his banquet to chasten and
  share ;
Her eye lost its light that his goblet
  might shine,
And the rose of her cheek was dissolved
  in his wine.

Joy smiles in the fountain, health flows
  in the rills,
As their ribbons of silver unwind from
  the hills ;
They breathe not the mist of the baccha-
  nal's dream,
But the lilies of innocence float on their
  stream.

Then a health and a welcome to woman
  once more !
She brings us a passport that laughs at
  our door ;
It is written on crimson, — its letters
  are pearls, —
It is countersigned *Nature*. — So, room
  for the Girls !

A SENTIMENT.

THE pledge of Friendship ! it is still
  divine,
Though watery floods have quenched its
  burning wine ;
Whatever vase the sacred drops may
  hold,
The gourd, the shell, the cup of beaten
  gold,
Around its brim the hand of Nature
  throws
A garland sweeter than the banquet's
  rose.
Bright are the blushes of the vine-
  wreathed bowl,
Warm with the sunshine of Anacreon's
  soul,
But dearer memories gild the tasteless
  wave
That fainting Sidney perished as he gave.
'T is the heart's current lends the cup
  its glow,
Whate'er the fountain whence the
  draught may flow, —
The diamond dew-drops sparkling
  through the sand,
Scooped by the Arab in his sunburnt
  hand,
Or the dark streamlet oozing from the
  snow,
Where creep and crouch the shuddering
  Esquimaux ; —
Ay, in the stream that, ere again we
  meet,

Shall burst the pavement, glistening at
our feet,
And, stealing silent from its leafy
hills,
Thread all our alleys with its thousand
rills, —
In each pale draught if generous feeling
blend,
And o'er the goblet friend shall smile on
friend,
Even cold Cochituate every heart shall
warm,
And genial Nature still defy reform !

A RHYMED LESSON.[1]

(URANIA.)

YES, dear Enchantress, — wandering
far and long,
In realms unperfumed by the breath of
song,
Where flowers ill-flavored shed their
sweets around,
And bitterest roots invade the ungenial
ground,
Whose gems are crystals from the Epsom
mine,
Whose vineyards flow with antimonial
wine,
Whose gates admit no mirthful feature
in,
Save one gaunt mocker, the Sardonic
grin,
Whose pangs are real, not the woes of
rhyme
That blue-eyed misses warble out of
time ; —
Truant, not recreant to thy sacred claim,
Older by reckoning, but in heart the
same,

[1] This poem was delivered before the Boston
Mercantile Library Association, October 14,
1846.

Freed for a moment from the chains of
toil,
I tread once more thy consecrated soil ;
Here at thy feet my old allegiance own,
Thy subject still, and loyal to thy
throne !

My dazzled glance explores the crowded
hall ;
Alas, how vain to hope the smiles of all !
I know my audience. All the gay and
young
Love the light antics of a playful tongue ;
And these, remembering some expansive
line
My lips let loose among the nuts and
wine,
Are all impatience till the opening pun
Proclaims the witty shamfight is begun.
Two fifths at least, if not the total half,
Have come infuriate for an earthquake
laugh ;
I know full well what alderman has
tied
His red bandanna tight about his side ;
I see the mother, who, aware that
boys
Perform their laughter with superfluous
noise,
Beside her kerchief, brought an extra
one
To stop the explosions of her bursting
son ;
I know a tailor, once a friend of mine,
Expects great doings in the button
line ; —
For mirth's concussions rip the outward
case,
And plant the stitches in a tenderer
place.
I know my audience ; — these shall have
their due ;
A smile awaits them ere my song is
through !

I know myself.   Not servile for ap-
    plause,
My Muse permits no deprecating clause ;
Modest or vain, she will not be denied
One bold confession due to honest pride ;
And well she knows the drooping veil
    of song
Shall save her boldness from the cavil-
    ler's wrong.
Her sweeter voice the Heavenly Maid
    imparts
To tell the secrets of our aching hearts ;
For this, a suppliant, captive, prostrate,
    bound,
She kneels imploring at the feet of
    sound ;
For this, convulsed in thought's mater-
    nal pains,
She loads her arms with rhyme's re-
    sounding chains ;
Faint though the music of her fetters
    be,
It lends one charm ; — her lips are ever
    free !

Think not I come, in manhood's fiery
    noon,
To steal his laurels from the stage buf-
    foon ;
His sword of lath the harlequin may
    wield ;
Behold the star upon my lifted shield !
Though the just critic pass my humble
    name,
And sweeter lips have drained the cup
    of fame,
While my gay stanza pleased the ban-
    quet's lords,
The soul within was tuned to deeper
    chords !
Say, shall my arms, in other conflicts
    taught
To swing aloft the ponderous mace of
    thought,
Lift, in obedience to a school-girl's law,

Mirth's tinsel wand or laughter's tick-
    ling straw ?
Say, shall I wound with satire's rankling
    spear
The pure, warm hearts that bid me wel-
    come here ?
No ! while I wander through the land
    of dreams,
To strive with great and play with tri-
    fling themes,
Let some kind meaning fill the varied
    line ;
You have your judgment ; will you
    trust to mine ?

———

Between two breaths what crowded
    mysteries lie, —
The first short gasp, the last and long-
    drawn sigh !
Like phantoms painted on the magic
    slide,
Forth from the darkness of the past we
    glide,
As living shadows for a moment seen
In airy pageant on the eternal screen,
Traced by a ray from one unchanging
    flame,
Then seek the dust and stillness whence
    we came.

But whence and why, our trembling
    souls inquire,
Caught these dim visions their awaken-
    ing fire ?
O who forgets when first the piercing
    thought
Through childhood's musings found its
    way unsought ?
I AM ; — I LIVE.   The mystery and the
    fear
When the dread question, WHAT HAS
    BROUGHT ME HERE ?
Burst through life's twilight, as before
    the sun

Roll the deep thunders of the morning
    gun !

Are angel faces, silent and serene,
Bent on the conflicts of this little scene,
Whose dream-like efforts, whose unreal
    strife,
Are but the preludes to a larger life ?

    Or does life's summer see the end of
    all,
These leaves of being mouldering as they
    fall,
As the old poet vaguely used to deem,
As WESLEY questioned in his youthful
    dream ?
O could such mockery reach our souls
    indeed,
Give back the Pharaohs' or the Athe-
    nian's creed ;
Better than this a Heaven of man's
    device, —
The Indian's sports, the Moslem's para-
    dise !

    Or is our being's only end and aim
To add new glories to our Maker's name,
As the poor insect, shrivelling in the
    blaze,
Lends a faint sparkle to its streaming
    rays ?
Does earth send upwards to the Eternal's
    ear
The mingled discords of her jarring
    sphere
To swell his anthem, while creation
    rings
With notes of anguish from its shattered
    strings ?
Is it for this the immortal Artist means
These conscious, throbbing, agonized
    machines?

    Dark is the soul whose sullen creed
    can bind

In chains like these the all-embracing
    Mind ;
No ! two-faced bigot, thou dost ill re-
    prove
The sensual, selfish, yet benignant Jove,
And praise a tyrant throned in lonely
    pride,
Who loves himself, and cares for naught
    beside ;
Who gave thee, summoned from pri-
    meval night,
A thousand laws, and not a single
    right, —
A heart to feel, and quivering nerves to
    thrill,
The sense of wrong, the death-defying
    will ;
Who girt thy senses with this goodly
    frame,
Its earthly glories and its orbs of flame,
Not for thyself, unworthy of a thought,
Poor helpless victim of a life unsought,
But all for him, unchanging and su-
    preme,
The heartless centre of thy frozen
    scheme !

    Trust not the teacher with his lying
    scroll,
Who tears the charter of thy shuddering
    soul ;
The God of love, who gave the breath
    that warms
All living dust in all its varied forms,
Asks not the tribute of a world like this
To fill the measure of his perfect bliss.
Though winged with life through all its
    radiant shores,
Creation flowed with unexhausted stores
Cherub and seraph had not yet enjoyed ;
For this he called thee from the quick-
    ening void !
Nor this alone ; a larger gift was thine,
A mightier purpose swelled his vast de-
    sign ;

Thought,—conscience,—will,—to make
   them all thine own,
He rent a pillar from the eternal throne !

   Made in his image, thou must nobly
      dare
The thorny crown of sovereignty to
   share.
With eye uplifted, it is thine to view,
From thine own centre, Heaven's o'er-
   arching blue ;
So round thy heart a beaming circle lies
No fiend can blot, no hypocrite disguise ;
From all its orbs one cheering voice is
   heard,
Full to thine ear it bears the Father's
   word,
Now, as in Eden where his first-born
   trod :
" Seek thine own welfare, true to man
   and God ! "
   Think not too meanly of thy low es-
      tate ;
Thou hast a choice ; to choose is to cre-
   ate !
Remember whose the sacred lips that tell,
Angels approve thee when thy choice is
   well ;
Remember, One, a judge of righteous
   men,
Swore to spare Sodom if she held but
   ten !
Use well the freedom which thy Master
   gave,
(Think'st thou that Heaven can tolerate
   a slave ?)
And He who made thee to be just and
   true
Will bless thee, love thee, — ay, respect
   thee too !

   Nature has placed thee on a change-
      ful tide,
To breast its waves, but not without a
   guide ;

Yet, as the needle will forget its aim,
Jarred by the fury of the electric flame,
As the true current it will falsely feel,
Warped from its axis by a freight of steel;
So will thy CONSCIENCE lose its balanced
   truth,
If passion's lightning fall upon thy
   youth ;
So the pure effluence quit its sacred
   hold,
Girt round too deeply with magnetic
   gold.
   Go to yon tower, where busy science
      plies
Her vast antennæ, feeling through the
   skies ;
That little vernier on whose slender lines
The midnight taper trembles as it shines,
A silent index, tracks the planets' march
In all their wanderings through the ethe-
   real arch,
Tells through the mist where dazzled
   Mercury burns,
And marks the spot where Uranus re-
   turns.
   So, till by wrong or negligence effaced,
The living index which thy Maker traced
Repeats the line each starry Virtue draws
Through the wide circuit of creation's
   laws ;
Still tracks unchanged the everlasting
   ray
Where the dark shadows of temptation
   stray ;
But, once defaced, forgets the orbs of
   light,
And leaves thee wandering o'er the ex-
   panse of night.

   " What is thy creed ? " a hundred lips
      inquire ;
" Thou seekest God beneath what Chris-
   tian spire ? "
Nor ask they idly, for uncounted lies
Float upward on the smoke of sacrifice ;

When man's first incense rose above the
plain,
Of earth's two altars one was built by
Cain !

Uncursed by doubt, our earliest creed
we take ;
We love the precepts for the teacher's
sake ;
The simple lessons which the nursery
taught
Fell soft and stainless on the buds of
thought,
And the full blossom owes its fairest
hue
To those sweet tear-drops of affection's
dew.

Too oft the light that led our earlier
hours
Fades with the perfume of our cradle
flowers ;
The clear, cold question chills to frozen
doubt ;
Tired of beliefs, we dread to live without ;
O then, if Reason waver at thy side,
Let humbler Memory be thy gentle
guide ;
Go to thy birthplace, and, if faith was
there,
Repeat thy father's creed, thy mother's
prayer !

Faith loves to lean on Time's destroying arm,
And age, like distance, lends a double
charm ;
In dim cathedrals, dark with vaulted
gloom,
What holy awe invests the saintly
tomb !
There pride will bow, and anxious care
expand,
And creeping avarice come with open
hand ;
The gay can weep, the impious can adore,

From morn's first glimmerings on the
chancel floor,
Till dying sunset sheds his crimson
stains
Through the faint halos of the irised
panes.

Yet there are graves, whose rudely-
shapen sod
Bears the fresh footprints where the sex-
ton trod ;
Graves where the verdure has not dared
to shoot,
Where the chance wild-flower has not
fixed its root,
Whose slumbering tenants, dead without
a name,
The eternal record shall at length pro-
claim
Pure as the holiest in the long array
Of hooded, mitred, or tiaraed clay !

Come, seek the air ; some pictures we
may gain
Whose passing shadows shall not be in
vain ;
Not from the scenes that crowd the
stranger's soil,
Not from our own amidst the stir of
toil,
But when the Sabbath brings its kind
release,
And Care lies slumbering on the lap of
Peace.

The air is hushed ; the street is holy
ground ;
Hark ! The sweet bells renew their welcome sound ;
As one by one awakes each silent tongue,
It tells the turret whence its voice is
flung.

The Chapel, last of sublunary things
That stirs our echoes with the name of
Kings,

Whose bell, just glistening from the font
    and forge,
Rolled its proud requiem for the second
    George,
Solemn and swelling, as of old it rang,
Flings to the wind its deep, sonorous
    clang ; —
The simpler pile, that, mindful of the
    hour
When Howe's artillery shook its half-
    built tower,
Wears on its bosom, as a bride might do,
The iron breastpin which the "Rebels"
    threw,
Wakes the sharp echoes with the quiv-
    ering thrill
Of keen vibrations, tremulous and
    shrill ; —
Aloft, suspended in the morning's fire,
Crash the vast cymbals from the South-
    ern spire ; —
The Giant, standing by the elm-clad
    green,
His white lance lifted o'er the silent
    scene,
Whirling in air his brazen goblet round,
Swings from its brim the swollen floods
    of sound ; —
While, sad with memories of the olden
    time,
Throbs from his tower the Northern
    Minstrel's chime,
Faint, single tones, that spell their an-
    cient song,
But tears still follow as they breathe
    along.

Child of the soil, whom fortune sends
    to range
Where man and nature, faith and cus-
    toms change,
Borne in thy memory, each familiar tone
Mourns on the winds that sigh in every
    zone.

When Ceylon sweeps thee with her per-
    fumed breeze
Through the warm billows of the Indian
    seas ;
When — ship and shadow blended both
    in one —
Flames o'er thy mast the equatorial sun,
From sparkling midnight to refulgent
    noon
Thy canvas swelling with the still mon-
    soon ;
When through thy shrouds the wild tor-
    nado sings,
And thy poor seabird folds her tattered
    wings, —
Oft will delusion o'er thy senses steal,
And airy echoes ring the Sabbath peal !
Then, dim with grateful tears, in long
    array
Rise the fair town, the island-studded
    bay,
Home, with its smiling board, its cheer-
    ing fire,
The half-choked welcome of the expect-
    ing sire,
The mother's kiss, and, still if aught re-
    main,
Our whispering hearts shall aid the silent
    strain. —
Ah, let the dreamer o'er the taffrail
    lean
To muse unheeded, and to weep unseen ;
Fear not the tropic's dews, the evening's
    chills,
His heart lies warm among his triple
    hills !

Turned from her path by this deceit-
    ful gleam,
My wayward fancy half forgets her
    theme ;
See through the streets that slumbered
    in repose
The living current of devotion flows ;
Its varied forms in one harmonious band,

Age leading childhood by its dimpled
  hand,
Want, in the robe whose faded edges
  fall
To tell of rags beneath the tartan shawl,
And wealth, in silks that, fluttering to
  appear,
Lift the deep borders of the proud cash-
  mere.

  See, but glance briefly, sorrow-worn
    and pale,
Those sunken cheeks beneath the widow's
  veil;
Alone she wanders where with *him* she
  trod,
No arm to stay her, but she leans on
  God.
  While other doublets deviate here and
    there,
What secret handcuff binds that pretty
  pair?
Compactest couple! pressing side to
  side, —
Ah, the white bonnet that reveals the
  bride!
  By the white neckcloth, with its
    straitened tie,
The sober hat, the Sabbath-speaking
  eye,
Severe and smileless, he that runs may
  read
The stern disciple of Geneva's creed;
Decent and slow, behold his solemn
  march;
Silent he enters through yon crowded
  arch.
  A livelier bearing of the outward
    man,
The light-hued gloves, the undevout
  rattan,
Now smartly raised or half-profanely
  twirled, —
A bright, fresh twinkle from the week-
  day world, —

Tell their plain story; —yes, thine eyes
  behold
A cheerful Christian from the liberal fold.

  Down the chill street that curves in
    gloomiest shade
What marks betray yon solitary maid?
The cheek's red rose, that speaks of
  balmier air;
The Celtic hue that shades her braided
  hair;
The gilded missal in her kerchief tied;
Poor Nora, exile from Killarney's side!
  Sister in toil, though blanched by
    colder skies,
That left their azure in her downcast
  eyes,
See pallid Margaret, Labor's patient
  child,
Scarce weaned from home, the nursling
  of the wild,
Where white Katahdin o'er the horizon
  shines,
And broad Penobscot dashes through
  the pines.
Still, as she hastes, her careful fingers
  hold
The unfailing hymn-book in its cambric
  fold.
Six days at drudgery's heavy wheel she
  stands,
The seventh sweet morning folds her
  weary hands;
Yes, child of suffering, thou mayst well
  be sure
He who ordained the Sabbath loves the
  poor!

  This weekly picture faithful Memory
    draws,
Nor claims the noisy tribute of applause;
Faint is the glow such barren hopes can
  lend,
And frail the line that asks no loftier
  end.

Trust me, kind listener, I will yet
    beguile
Thy saddened features of the promised
    smile ;
This magic mantle thou must well
    divide,
It has its sable and its ermine side ;
Yet, ere the lining of the robe appears,
Take thou in silence what I give in
    tears.

Dear listening soul, this transitory
    scene
Of murmuring stillness, busily serene, —
This solemn pause, the breathing-space
    of man,
The halt of toil's exhausted caravan, —
Comes sweet with music to thy wearied
    ear ;
Rise with its anthems to a holier sphere !

Deal meekly, gently, with the hopes
    that guide
The lowliest brother straying from thy
    side ;
If right, they bid thee tremble for thine
    own,
If wrong, the verdict is for God alone !

What though the champions of thy
    faith esteem
The sprinkled fountain or baptismal
    stream ;
Shall jealous passions in unseemly strife
Cross their dark weapons o'er the waves
    of life ?

Let my free soul, expanding as it can,
Leave to his scheme the thoughtful
    Puritan ;
But Calvin's dogma shall my lips de-
    ride ?
In that stern faith my angel Mary
    died ; —

Or ask if mercy's milder creed can save,
Sweet sister, risen from thy new-made
    grave ?

True, the harsh founders of thy church
    reviled
That ancient faith, the trust of Erin's
    child ;
Must thou be raking in the crumbled
    past
For racks and fagots in her teeth to
    cast ?
See from the ashes of Helvetia's pile
The whitened skull of old Servetus
    smile !
Round her young heart thy "Romish
    Upas" threw
Its firm, deep fibres, strengthening as
    she grew ;
Thy sneering voice may call them
    " Popish tricks," —
Her Latin prayers, her dangling cruci-
    fix, —
But *De Profundis* blessed her father's
    grave ;
That "idol" cross her dying mother
    gave !
What if some angel looks with equal
    eyes
On her and thee, the simple and the
    wise,
Writes each dark fault against thy
    brighter creed,
And drops a tear with every foolish
    bead !

Grieve, as thou must, o'er history's
    reeking page ;
Blush for the wrongs that stain thy
    happier age ;
Strive with the wanderer from the
    better path,
Bearing thy message meekly, not in
    wrath ;

Weep for the frail that err, the weak
that fall,
Have thine own faith, — but hope and
pray for all!

Faith ; Conscience ; Love. A meaner
task remains,
And humbler thoughts must creep in
lowlier strains ;
Shalt thou be honest ? Ask the worldly
schools,
And all will tell thee knaves are busier
fools ;
Prudent ? Industrious ? Let not modern
pens
Instruct " Poor Richard's " fellow-citi-
zens.

Be firm ! one constant element in luck
Is genuine, solid, old Teutonic pluck ;
See yon tall shaft ; it felt the earth-
quake's thrill,
Clung to its base, and greets the sun-
rise still.

Stick to your aim ; the mongrel's hold
will slip,
But only crowbars loose the bulldog's
grip ;
Small as he looks, the jaw that never
yields
Drags down the bellowing monarch of
the fields !

Yet in opinions look not always back ;
Your wake is nothing, mind the coming
track ;
Leave what you 've done for what you
have to do ;
Don't be " consistent," but be simply
true.

Don't catch the fidgets ; you have
found your place
Just in the focus of a nervous race,
Fretful to change, and rabid to discuss,
Full of excitements, always in a fuss ;—
Think of the patriarchs ; then compare
as men
These lean-cheeked maniacs of the
tongue and pen !
Run, if you like, but try to keep your
breath ;
Work like a man, but don't be worked
to death ;
And with new notions, — let me change
the rule, —
Don't strike the iron till it 's slightly
cool.

Choose well your *set ;* our feeble na-
ture seeks
The aid of clubs, the countenance of
cliques ;
And with this object settle first of all
Your weight of metal and your size of
ball.
Track not the steps of such as hold you
cheap,
Too mean to prize, though good enough
to keep ;
The "real, genuine, no-mistake Tom
Thumbs "
Are little people fed on great men's
crumbs.
Yet keep no followers of that hateful
brood
That basely mingles with its wholesome
food
The tumid reptile, which, the poet said,
Doth wear a precious jewel in his head.

If the wild filly, " Progress," thou
wouldst ride,
Have young companions ever at thy
side ;
But, wouldst thou stride the stanch old
mare, " Success,"
Go with thine elders, though they please
thee less.

Shun such as lounge through after-
noons and eves,
And on thy dial write, "Beware of
thieves !"
Felon of minutes, never taught to feel
The worth of treasures which thy fingers
steal,
Pick my left pocket of its silver dime,
But spare the right, — it holds my
golden time !

Does praise delight thee ?   Choose
some *ultra* side ;
A sure old recipe, and often tried ;
Be its apostle, congressman, or bard,
Spokesman, or jokesman, only drive it
hard ;
But know the forfeit which thy choice
abides,
For on two wheels the poor reformer
rides,
One black with epithets the *anti* throws,
One white with flattery painted by the
pros.

Though books on MANNERS are not
out of print,
An honest tongue may drop a harmless
hint.
Stop not, unthinking, every friend
you meet,
To spin your wordy fabric in the street ;
While you are emptying your colloquial
pack,
The fiend *Lumbago* jumps upon his
back.
Nor cloud his features with the un-
welcome tale
Of how he looks, if haply thin and pale ;
Health is a subject for his child, his
wife,
And the rude office that insures his life.
Look in his face, to meet thy neigh-
bor's soul,
Not on his garments, to detect a hole ;

"How to observe," is what thy pages
show,
Pride of thy sex, Miss Harriet Mar-
tineau !
O, what a precious book the one would
be
That taught observers what they 're *not*
to see !

I tell in verse, — 't were better done
in prose, —
One curious trick that everybody knows ;
Once form this habit, and it 's very
strange
How long it sticks, how hard it is to
change.
Two friendly people, both disposed to
smile,
Who meet, like others, every little
while,
Instead of passing with a pleasant bow,
And "How d' ye do ?" or "How 's
your uncle now ?"
Impelled by feelings in their nature kind,
But slightly weak, and somewhat unde-
fined,
Rush at each other, make a sudden
stand,
Begin to talk, expatiate, and expand ;
Each looks quite radiant, seems ex-
tremely struck,
Their meeting so was such a piece of
luck ;
Each thinks the other thinks he 's
greatly pleased
To screw the vice in which they both
are squeezed ;
So there they talk, in dust, or mud, or
snow,
Both bored to death, and both afraid to
go !
Your hat once lifted, do not hang
your fire,
Nor, like slow Ajax, fighting still, retire ;

When your old castor on your crown
   you clap,
Go off ; you 've mounted your percussion
   cap.

   Some words on LANGUAGE may be
   well applied,
And take them kindly, though they
   touch your pride ;
Words lead to things ; a scale is more
   precise, —
Coarse speech, bad grammar, swearing,
   drinking, vice.
  Our cold Northeaster's icy fetter clips
The native freedom of the Saxon lips ;
See the brown peasant of the plastic
   South,
How all his passions play about his
   mouth!
With us, the feature that transmits the
   soul,
A frozen, passive, palsied breathing-hole.
The crampy shackles of the ploughboy's
   walk
Tie the small muscles when he strives to
   talk ;
Not all the pumice of the polished town
Can smooth this roughness of the barn-
   yard down ;
Rich, honored, titled, he betrays his race
By this one mark, — he 's awkward in
   the face ; —
Nature's rude impress, long before he knew
The sunny street that holds the sifted few.
  It can't be helped, though, if we 're
   taken young,
We gain some freedom of the lips and
   tongue ;
But school and college often try in vain
To break the padlock of our boyhood's
   chain :
One stubborn word will prove this axiom
   true, —
No quondam rustic can enunciate *view*.

  A few brief stanzas may be well em-
   ployed
To speak of errors we can all avoid.

  Learning condemns beyond the reach
   of hope
The careless lips that speak of sŏap for
   sōap ;
Her edict exiles from her fair abode
The clownish voice that utters rŏad for
   rōad :
Less stern to him who calls his cōat a
   cŏat,
And steers his bōat, believing it a
   bŏat,
She pardoned one, our classic city's boast,
Who said at Cambridge, mŏst instead of
   mōst,
But knit her brows and stamped her
   angry foot
To hear a Teacher call a rōot a rŏot.

  Once more ; speak clearly, if you speak
   at all ;
Carve every word before you let it
   fall ;
Don't, like a lecturer or dramatic star,
Try over hard to roll the British R ;
Do put your accents in the proper spot ;
Don't, — let me beg you, — don't say
   " How ? " for " What ? "
And, when you stick on conversation's
   burrs,
Don't strew your pathway with those
   dreadful *urs*.

  From little matters let us pass to
   less,
And lightly touch the mysteries of DRESS ;
The outward forms the inner man reveal, —
We guess the pulp before we cut the
   peel.

  I leave the broadcloth, — coats and
   all the rest, —

The dangerous waistcoat, called by cock-
    neys "vest,"
The things named "pants" in certain
    documents,
A word not made for gentlemen, but
    "gents";
One single precept might the whole con-
    dense:
Be sure your tailor is a man of sense;
But add a little care, a decent pride,
And always err upon the sober side.

Three pairs of boots one pair of feet de-
    mands,
If polished daily by the owner's hands;
If the dark menial's visit save from
    this,
Have twice the number, for he'll some-
    times miss.
One pair for critics of the nicer sex,
Close in the instep's clinging circum-
    flex,
Long, narrow, light; the Gallic boot of
    love,
A kind of cross between a boot and
    glove.
Compact, but easy, strong, substantial,
    square,
Let native art compile the medium pair.
The third remains, and let your tasteful
    skill
Here show some relics of affection still;
Let no stiff cowhide, reeking from the
    tan,
No rough caoutchouc, no deformed bro-
    gan,
Disgrace the tapering outline of your
    feet,
Though yellow torrents gurgle through
    the street.

Wear seemly gloves; not black, nor
    yet too light,
And least of all the pair that once was
    white;

Let the dead party where you told your
    loves
Bury in peace its dead bouquets and
    gloves;
Shave like the goat, if so your fancy bids,
But be a parent, — don't neglect your
    kids.

Have a good hat; the secret of your
    looks
Lives with the beaver in Canadian brooks;
Virtue may flourish in an old cravat,
But man and nature scorn the shocking
    hat.
Does beauty slight you from her gay
    abodes?
Like bright Apollo, you must take to
    Rhoades, —
Mount the new castor, — ice itself will
    melt;
Boots, gloves, may fail; the hat is al-
    ways felt!

Be shy of breastpins; plain, well-
    ironed white,
With small pearl buttons, — two of them
    in sight, —
Is always genuine, while your gems may
    pass,
Though real diamonds, for ignoble glass;
But spurn those paltry Cisatlantic lies,
That round his breast the shabby rustic
    ties;
Breathe not the name, profaned to hallow
    things
The indignant laundress blushes when
    she brings!

Our freeborn race, averse to every
    check,
Has tossed the yoke of Europe from its
    neck;
From the green prairie to the sea-girt
    town,
The whole wide nation turns its collars
    down.

The stately neck is manhood's manliest part ;
It takes the life-blood freshest from the heart ;
With short, curled ringlets close around it spread,
How light and strong it lifts the Grecian head !
Thine, fair Erechtheus of Minerva's wall ; —
Or thine, young athlete of the Louvre's hall,
Smooth as the pillar flashing in the sun
That filled the arena where thy wreaths were won, —
Firm as the band that clasps the antlered spoil,
Strained in the winding anaconda's coil !

I spare the contrast ; it were only kind
To be a little, nay, intensely blind :
Choose for yourself : I know it cuts your ear ;
I know the points will sometimes interfere ;
I know that often, like the filial John,
Whom sleep surprised with half his drapery on,
You show your features to the astonished town
With one side standing and the other down ; —
But, O my friend ! my favorite fellow-man !
If Nature made you on her modern plan,
Sooner than wander with your windpipe bare, —
The fruit of Eden ripening in the air, —
With that lean head-stalk, that protruding chin,
Wear standing collars, were they made of tin !

And have a neck-cloth, — by the throat of Jove !
Cut from the funnel of a rusty stove !

The long-drawn lesson narrows to its close,
Chill, slender, slow, the dwindled current flows ;
Tired of the ripples on its feeble springs,
Once more the Muse unfolds her upward wings.

Land of my birth, with this unhallowed tongue,
Thy hopes, thy dangers, I perchance had sung ;
But who shall sing, in brutal disregard
Of all the essentials of the "native bard"?
Lake, sea, shore, prairie, forest, mountain, fall,
His eye omnivorous must devour them all ;
The tallest summits and the broadest tides
His foot must compass with its giant strides,
Where Ocean thunders, where Missouri rolls,
And tread at once the tropics and the poles ;
His food all forms of earth, fire, water, air,
His home all space, his birthplace everywhere.

Some grave compatriot, having seen perhaps
The pictured page that goes in Worcester's Maps,
And read in earnest what was said in jest,
"Who drives fat oxen" — please to add the rest, —
Sprung the odd notion that the poet's dreams

Grow in the ratio of his hills and streams ;
And hence insisted that the aforesaid
    "bard,"
Pink of the future, — fancy's pattern-
    card, —
The babe of nature in the "giant West,"
Must be of course her biggest and her
    best.

  O when at length the expected bard
    shall come,
Land of our pride, to strike thine echoes
    dumb,
(And many a voice exclaims in prose
    and rhyme,
It 's getting late, and he 's behind his
    time,)
When all thy mountains clap their hands
    in joy,
And all thy cataracts thunder, "That 's
    the boy," —
Say if with him the reign of song shall
    end,
And Heaven declare its final dividend ?

  Be calm, dear brother ! whose impas-
    sioned strain
Comes from an alley watered by a drain ;
The little Mincio, dribbling to the Po,
Beats all the epics of the Hoang Ho ;
If loved in earnest by the tuneful maid,
Don't mind their nonsense, — never be
    afraid !

  The nurse of poets feeds her wingèd
    brood
By common firesides, on familiar food ;
In a low hamlet, by a narrow stream,
Where bovine rustics used to doze and
    dream,
She filled young William's fiery fancy full,
While old John Shakespeare talked of
    beeves and wool !

  No Alpine needle, with its climbing
    spire,

Brings down for mortals the Promethean
    fire;
If careless nature have forgot to frame
An altar worthy of the sacred flame.
  Unblest by any save the goatherd's
    lines,
Mont Blanc rose soaring through his
    "sea of pines" ;
In vain the rivers from their ice-caves
    flash ;
No hymn salutes them but the Ranz des
    Vaches,
Till lazy Coleridge, by the morning's
    light,
Gazed for a moment on the fields of
    white,
And lo, the glaciers found at length a
    tongue,
Mont Blanc was vocal, and Chamouni
    sung !

  Children of wealth or want, to each is
    given
One spot of green, and all the blue of
    heaven !
Enough, if these their outward shows
    impart ;
The rest is thine, — the scenery of the
    heart.

  If passion's hectic in thy stanzas glow,
Thy heart's best life-blood ebbing as
    they flow ;
If with thy verse thy strength and bloom
    distil,
Drained by the pulses of the fevered
    thrill ;
If sound's sweet effluence polarize thy
    brain,
And thoughts turn crystals in thy fluid
    strain, —
Nor rolling ocean, nor the prairie's
    bloom,
Nor streaming cliffs, nor rayless cavern's
    gloom,

Need'st thou, young poet, to inform thy
    line ;
Thy own broad signet stamps thy song
    divine !
    Let others gaze where silvery streams
    are rolled,
And chase the rainbow for its cup of
    gold ;
To thee all landscapes wear a heavenly
    dye,
Changed in the glance of thy prismatic
    eye ;
Nature evoked thee in sublimer throes,
For thee her inmost Arethusa flows, —
The mighty mother's living depths are
    stirred, —
Thou art the starred Osiris of the herd !

    A few brief lines ; they touch on
    solemn chords,
And hearts may leap to hear their hon-
    est words ;
Yet, ere the jarring bugle-blast is blown,
The softer lyre shall breathe its soothing
    tone.

    New England ! proudly may thy
    children claim
Their honored birthright by its hum-
    blest name !
Cold are thy skies, but, ever fresh and
    clear,
No rank malaria stains thine atmos-
    phere ;
No fungous weeds invade thy scanty
    soil,
Scarred by the ploughshares of unslum-
    bering toil.
Long may the doctrines by thy sages
    taught,
Raised from the quarries where their
    sires have wrought,
Be like the granite of thy rock-ribbed
    land, —
As slow to rear, as obdurate to stand :

And as the ice, that leaves thy crystal
    mine,
Chills the fierce alcohol in the Creole's
    wine,
So may the doctrines of thy sober school
Keep the hot theories of thy neighbors
    cool !

    If ever, trampling on her ancient path,
Cankered by treachery, or inflamed by
    wrath,
With smooth " Resolves," or with dis-
    cordant cries,
The mad Briareus of disunion rise,
Chiefs of New England ! by your sires'
    renown,
Dash the red torches of the rebel down !
Flood his black hearthstone till its
    flames expire,
Though your old Sachem fanned his
    council-fire !

    But if at last — her fading cycle
    run —
The tongue must forfeit what the arm
    has won,
Then rise, wild Ocean ! roll thy surging
    shock
Full on old Plymouth's desecrated rock !
Scale the proud shaft degenerate hands
    have hewn,
Where bleeding Valor stained the flowers
    of June !
Sweep in one tide her spires and turrets
    down,
And howl her dirge above Monadnock's
    crown !

    List not the tale ; the Pilgrim's hal-
    lowed shore,
Though strewn with weeds, is granite at
    the core ;
O rather trust that He who made her free
Will keep her true, as long as faith shall
    be !

Farewell! yet lingering through the destined hour,
Leave, sweet Enchantress, one memorial flower!

An Angel, floating o'er the waste of snow
That clad our Western desert, long ago,
(The same fair spirit, who, unseen by day,
Shone as a star along the Mayflower's way,)
Sent, the first herald of the Heavenly plan,
To choose on earth a resting-place for man, —
Tired with his flight along the unvaried field,
Turned to soar upwards, when his glance revealed
A calm, bright bay, enclosed in rocky bounds,
And at its entrance stood three sister mounds.

The Angel spake: "This threefold hill shall be
The home of Arts, the nurse of Liberty!
One stately summit from its shaft shall pour
Its deep-red blaze along the darkened shore;
Emblem of thoughts, that, kindling far and wide,
In danger's night shall be a nation's guide.
One swelling crest the citadel shall crown,
Its slanted bastions black with battle's frown,
And bid the sons that tread its scowling heights
Bare their strong arms for man and all his rights!
One silent steep along the northern wave
Shall hold the patriarch's and the hero's grave;

When fades the torch, when o'er the peaceful scene
The embattled fortress smiles in living green,
The cross of Faith, the anchor staff of Hope,
Shall stand eternal on its grassy slope;
There through all time shall faithful Memory tell,
'Here Virtue toiled, and Patriot Valor fell;
Thy free, proud fathers slumber at thy side;
Live as they lived, or perish as they died!'"

AN AFTER-DINNER POEM.[1]

(TERPSICHORE.)

In narrowest girdle, O reluctant Muse,
In closest frock and Cinderella shoes,
Bound to the foot-lights for thy brief display,
One zephyr step, and then dissolve away!

———

Short is the space that gods and men can spare
To Song's twin brother when she is not there.
Let others water every lusty line,
As Homer's heroes did their purple wine;
Pierian revellers! Know in strains like these
The native juice, the real honest squeeze, —
Strains that, diluted to the twentieth power,
In yon grave temple might have filled an hour.

[1] Read at the Annual Dinner of the Φ B K Society, at Cambridge, August 24, 1843.

Small room for Fancy's many-chorded
    lyre,
For Wit's bright rockets with their trains
    of fire,
For Pathos, struggling vainly to surprise
The iron tutor's tear-denying eyes,
For Mirth, whose finger with delusive
    wile
Turns the grim key of many a rusty
    smile,
For Satire, emptying his corrosive flood
On hissing Folly's gas-exhaling brood,
The pun, the fun, the moral and the
    joke,
The hit, the thrust, the pugilistic
    poke, —
Small space for these, so pressed by nig-
    gard Time,
Like that false matron, known to nursery
    rhyme, —
Insidious Morey, — scarce her tale begun,
Ere listening infants weep the story
    done.

O had we room to rip the mighty bags
That Time, the harlequin, has stuffed
    with rags !
Grant us one moment to unloose the
    strings,
While the old graybeard shuts his leather
    wings.
But what a heap of motley trash appears
Crammed in the bundles of successive
    years !
As the lost rustic on some festal day
Stares through the concourse in its vast
    array, —
Where in one cake a throng of faces
    runs,
All stuck together like a sheet of
    buns, —
And throws the bait of some unheeded
    name,
Or shoots a wink with most uncertain
    aim,

So roams my vision, wandering over all,
And strives to choose, but knows not
    where to fall.

Skins of flayed authors, — husks of dead
    reviews, —
The turn-coat's clothes, — the office-
    seeker's shoes, —
Scraps from cold feasts, where conversa-
    tion runs
Through mouldy toasts to oxidated puns,
And grating songs a listening crowd en-
    dures,
Rasped from the throats of bellowing
    amateurs ; —
Sermons, whose writers played such dan-
    gerous tricks
Their own heresiarchs called them here-
    tics
(Strange that one term such distant poles
    should link,
The Priestleyan's copper and the Pusey-
    an's zinc) ; —
Poems that shuffle with superfluous legs
A blindfold minuet over addled eggs,
Where all the syllables that end in éd,
Like old dragoons, have cuts across the
    head ; —
Essays so dark Champollion might de-
    spair
To guess what mummy of a thought was
    there,
Where our poor English, striped with for-
    eign phrase,
Looks like a Zebra in a parson's chaise ; —
Lectures that cut our dinners down to
    roots,
Or prove (by monkeys) men should stick
    to fruits ;
Delusive error, — as at trifling charge
Professor Gripes will certify at large ; —
Mesmeric pamphlets, which to facts ap-
    peal,
Each fact as slippery as a fresh-caught
    eel ; —

And figured heads, whose hieroglyphs
    invite
To wandering knaves that discount fools
    at sight ; —
Such things as these, with heaps of un-
    paid bills,
And candy puffs and homœopathic pills,
And ancient bell-crowns with contracted
    rim,
And bonnets hideous with expanded
    brim,
And coats whose memory turns the sar-
    tor pale,
Their sequels tapering like a lizard's
    tail ; —
How might we spread them to the smil-
    ing day,
And toss them, fluttering like the new-
    mown hay,
To laughter's light or sorrow's pitying
    shower,
Were these brief minutes lengthened to
    an hour.

The narrow moments fit like Sunday
    shoes,
How vast the heap, how quickly must
    we choose ;
A few small scraps from out his moun-
    tain mass
We snatch in haste, and let the vagrant
    pass.

This shrunken CRUST that Cerberus could
    not bite,
Stamped (in one corner) "Pickwick copy-
    right, "
Kneaded by youngsters, raised by flat-
    tery's yeast,
Was once a loaf, and helped to make a
    feast.
He for whose sake the glittering show
    appears
Has sown the world with laughter and
    with tears,

And they whose welcome wets the bump-
    er's brim
Have wit and wisdom, — for they all
    quote him.
So, many a tongue the evening hour pro-
    longs
With spangled speeches, — let alone the
    songs, —
Statesmen grow merry, lean attorneys
    laugh,
And weak teetotals warm to half and
    half,
And beardless Tullys, new to festive
    scenes,
Cut their first crop of youth's precocious
    greens,
And wits stand ready for impromptu
    claps,
With loaded barrels and percussion caps,
And Pathos, cantering through the mi-
    nor keys,
Waves all her onions to the trembling
    breeze ;
While the great Feasted views with si-
    lent glee
His scattered limbs in Yankee fricassee.

Sweet is the scene where genial friend-
    ship plays
The pleasing game of interchanging
    praise ;
Self-love, grimalkin of the human heart,
Is ever pliant to the master's art ;
Soothed with a word, she peacefully
    withdraws
And sheathes in velvet her obnoxious
    claws,
And thrills the hand that smooths her
    glossy fur
With the light tremor of her grateful
    pur.

But what sad music fills the quiet hall,
If on her back a feline rival fall ;

And O, what noises shake the tranquil
  house,
If old Self-interest cheats her of a mouse!

Thou, O my country, hast thy foolish
  ways,
Too apt to pur at every stranger's praise;
But, if the stranger touch thy modes or
  laws,
Off goes the velvet and out come the
  claws!
And thou, Illustrious! but too poorly
  paid
In toasts from Pickwick for thy great
  crusade,
Though, while the echoes labored with
  thy name,
The public trap denied thy little game,
Let other lips our jealous laws revile, —
The marble Talfourd or the rude Car-
  lyle, —
But on thy lids, which Heaven forbids
  to close
Where'er the light of kindly nature glows,
Let not the dollars that a churl denies
Weigh like the shillings on a dead man's
  eyes!
Or, if thou wilt, be more discreetly blind,
Nor ask to see all wide extremes com-
  bined.
Not in our wastes the dainty blossoms
  smile,
That crowd the gardens of thy scanty isle.
There white-cheeked Luxury weaves a
  thousand charms; —
Here sun-browned Labor swings his
  naked arms.
Long are the furrows he must trace be-
  tween
The ocean's azure and the prairie's green;
Full many a blank his destined realm
  displays,
Yet see the promise of his riper days:
Far through yon depths the panting
  engine moves,

His chariots ringing in their steel-shod
  grooves;
And Erie's naiad flings her diamond wave
O'er the wild sea-nymph in her distant
  cave!
While tasks like these employ his anxious hours,
What if his cornfields are not edged
  with flowers?
Though bright as silver the meridian
  beams
Shine through the crystal of thine English streams,
Turbid and dark the mighty wave is
  whirled
That drains our Andes and divides a
  world!

But lo! a PARCHMENT! Surely it would
  seem
The sculptured impress speaks of power
  supreme;
Some grave design the solemn page must
  claim
That shows so broadly an emblazoned
  name;
A sovereign's promise! Look, the lines
  afford
All Honor gives when Caution asks his
  word:
There sacred Faith has laid her snow-
  white hands,
And awful Justice knit her iron bands;
Yet every leaf is stained with treachery's
  dye,
And every letter crusted with a lie.
Alas! no treason has degraded yet
The Arab's salt, the Indian's calumet;
A simple rite, that bears the wanderer's
  pledge,
Blunts the keen shaft and turns the
  dagger's edge; —
While jockeying senates stop to sign
  and seal,
And freeborn statesmen legislate to steal.

Rise, Europe, tottering with thine Atlas load,
Turn thy proud eye to Freedom's blest abode,
And round her forehead, wreathed with heavenly flame,
Bind the dark garland of her daughter's shame!
Ye ocean clouds, that wrap the angry blast,
Coil her stained ensign round its haughty mast,
Or tear the fold that wears so foul a scar,
And drive a bolt through every blackened star!

Once more, — once only, — we must stop so soon, —
What have we here? A GERMAN-SILVER SPOON;
A cheap utensil, which we often see
Used by the dabblers in æsthetic tea,
Of slender fabric, somewhat light and thin,
Made of mixed metal, chiefly lead and tin;
The bowl is shallow, and the handle small,
Marked in large letters with the name JEAN PAUL.
Small as it is, its powers are passing strange,
For all who use it show a wondrous change;
And first, a fact to make the barbers stare,
It beats Macassar for the growth of hair;
See those small youngsters whose expansive ears
Maternal kindness grazed with frequent shears;
Each bristling crop a dangling mass becomes,
And all the spoonies turn to Absaloms!

Nor this alone its magic power displays,
It alters strangely all their works and ways;
With uncouth words they tire their tender lungs,
The same bald phrases on their hundred tongues;
"Ever" "The Ages" in their page appear,
"Alway" the bedlamite is called a "Seer";
On every leaf the "earnest" sage may scan,
Portentous bore! their "many-sided" man, —
A weak eclectic, groping vague and dim,
Whose every angle is a half-starved whim,
Blind as a mole and curious as a lynx,
Who rides a beetle, which he calls a "Sphinx."
And O what questions asked in club-foot rhyme
Of Earth the tongueless and the deaf-mute Time!
Here babbling "Insight" shouts in Nature's ears
His last conundrum on the orbs and spheres;
There Self-inspection sucks its little thumb,
With "Whence am I?" and "Wherefore did I come?"
Deluded infants! will they ever know
Some doubts must darken o'er the world below,
Though all the Platos of the nursery trail
Their "clouds of glory" at the go-cart's tail?
O might these couplets their attention claim,
That gain their author the Philistine's name;

(A stubborn race, that, spurning foreign law,
Was much belabored with an ass's jaw !)

Melodious Laura ! From the sad retreats
That hold thee, smothered with excess of sweets,
Shade of a shadow, spectre of a dream,
Glance thy wan eye across the Stygian stream !
The slip-shod dreamer treads thy fragrant halls,
The sophist's cobwebs hang thy roseate walls,
And o'er the crotchets of thy jingling tunes
The bard of mystery scrawls his crooked "runes."
Yes, thou art gone, with all the tuneful hordes
That candied thoughts in amber-colored words,
And in the precincts of thy late abodes
The clattering verse-wright hammers Orphic odes.
Thou, soft as zephyr, wast content to fly
On the gilt pinions of a balmy sigh ;
He, vast as Phœbus on his burning wheels,
Would stride through ether at Orion's heels ;
Thy emblem, Laura, was a perfume-jar,
And thine, young Orpheus, is a pewter star ;
The balance trembles, — be its verdict told
When the new jargon slumbers with the old !

———

Cease, playful goddess ! From thine airy bound
Drop like a feather softly to the ground ;
This light bolero grows a ticklish dance,
And there is mischief in thy kindling glance.
To-morrow bids thee, with rebuking frown,
Change thy gauze tunic for a home-made gown,
Too blest by fortune, if the passing day
Adorn thy bosom with its frail bouquet,
But O still happier if the next forgets
Thy daring steps and dangerous pirouettes !

MISCELLANEOUS POEMS.

FROM "THE COLLEGIAN," 1830, ILLUSTRATED ANNUALS, ETC.

Nescit vox missa reverti. — HORAT. *Ars Poetica.*

Ab iis quæ non adjuvant quam mollissime oportet pedem referre. — QUINTILIAN, L. VI. C. 4.

THE MEETING OF THE DRYADS.[1]

IT was not many centuries since,
  When, gathered on the moonlit green,
Beneath the Tree of Liberty,
  A ring of weeping sprites was seen.

The freshman's lamp had long been dim,
  The voice of busy day was mute,
And tortured Melody had ceased
  Her sufferings on the evening flute.

They met not as they once had met,
  To laugh o'er many a jocund tale :
But every pulse was beating low,
  And every cheek was cold and pale.

There rose a fair but faded one,
  Who oft had cheered them with her
    song ;
She waved a mutilated arm,
  And silence held the listening throng.

"Sweet friends," the gentle nymph be-
    gan,
  "From opening bud to withering leaf,
One common lot has bound us all,
  In every change of joy and grief.

[1] Written after a general pruning of the trees around Harvard College.

"While all around has felt decay,
  We rose in ever-living prime,
With broader shade and fresher green,
  Beneath the crumbling step of Time.

"When often by our feet has past
  Some biped, Nature's walking whim,
Say, have we trimmed one awkward
    shape,
  Or lopped away one crooked limb ?

"Go on, fair Science ; soon to thee
  Shall Nature yield her idle boast ;
Her vulgar fingers formed a tree,
  But thou hast trained it to a post.

"Go, paint the birch's silver rind,
  And quilt the peach with softer down ;
Up with the willow's trailing threads,
  Off with the sunflower's radiant crown !

"Go, plant the lily on the shore,
  And set the rose among the waves,
And bid the tropic bud unbind
  Its silken zone in arctic caves ;

"Bring bellows for the panting winds,
  Hang up a lantern by the moon,
And give the nightingale a fife,
  And lend the eagle a balloon !

"I cannot smile, — the tide of scorn,
  That rolled through every bleeding
        vein,
Comes kindling fiercer as it flows
  Back to its burning source again.

"Again in every quivering leaf
  That moment's agony I feel,
When limbs, that spurned the northern
        blast,
  Shrunk from the sacrilegious steel.

"A curse upon the wretch who dared
  To crop us with his felon saw!
May every fruit his lip shall taste
  Lie like a bullet in his maw.

"In every julep that he drinks,
  May gout, and bile, and headache be;
And when he strives to calm his pain,
  May colic mingle with his tea.

"May nightshade cluster round his path,
  And thistles shoot, and brambles
        cling;
May blistering ivy scorch his veins,
  And dogwood burn, and nettles sting.

"On him may never shadow fall,
  When fever racks his throbbing brow,
And his last shilling buy a rope
  To hang him on my highest bough!"

She spoke; — the morning's herald beam
  Sprang from the bosom of the sea,
And every mangled sprite returned
  In sadness to her wounded tree.[1]

THE MYSTERIOUS VISITOR.

THERE was a sound of hurrying feet,
  A tramp on echoing stairs,

[1] A little poem, on a similar occasion, may
be found in the works of Swift, from which,
perhaps, the idea was borrowed: although I
was as much surprised as amused to meet with
it some time after writing the preceding lines.

There was a rush along the aisles, —
  It was the hour of prayers.

And on, like Ocean's midnight wave,
  The current rolled along,
When, suddenly, a stranger form
  Was seen amidst the throng.

He was a dark and swarthy man,
  That uninvited guest;
A faded coat of bottle-green
  Was buttoned round his breast.

There was not one among them all
  Could say from whence he came;
Nor beardless boy, nor ancient man,
  Could tell that stranger's name.

All silent as the sheeted dead,
  In spite of sneer and frown,
Fast by a gray-haired senior's side
  He sat him boldly down.

There was a look of horror flashed
  From out the tutor's eyes;
When all around him rose to pray,
  The stranger did not rise!

A murmur broke along the crowd,
  The prayer was at an end;
With ringing heels and measured tread,
  A hundred forms descend.

Through sounding aisle, o'er grating
        stair,
  The long procession poured,
Till all were gathered on the seats
  Around the Commons board.

That fearful stranger! down he sat,
  Unasked, yet undismayed;
And on his lip a rising smile
  Of scorn or pleasure played.

He took his hat and hung it up,
  With slow but earnest air;
He stripped his coat from off his back,
  And placed it on a chair.

Then from his nearest neighbor's side
   A knife and plate he drew;
And, reaching out his hand again,
   He took his teacup too.

How fled the sugar from the bowl!
   How sunk the azure cream!
They vanished like the shapes that float
   Upon a summer's dream.

A long, long draught, — an outstretched
      hand, —
   And crackers, toast, and tea,
They faded from the stranger's touch,
   Like dew upon the sea.

Then clouds were dark on many a brow,
   Fear sat upon their souls,
And, in a bitter agony,
   They clasped their buttered rolls.

A whisper trembled through the
      crowd, —
   Who could the stranger be?
And some were silent, for they thought
   A cannibal was he.

What if the creature should arise, —
   For he was stout and tall, —
And swallow down a sophomore,
   Coat, crow's-foot, cap, and all!

All sullenly the stranger rose;
   They sat in mute despair;
He took his hat from off the peg,
   His coat from off the chair.

Four freshmen fainted on the seat,
   Six swooned upon the floor;
Yet on the fearful being passed,
   And shut the chapel door.

There is full many a starving man,
   That walks in bottle green,
But never more that hungry one
   In Commons-hall was seen.

Yet often at the sunset hour,
   When tolls the evening bell,
The freshman lingers on the steps,
   That frightful tale to tell.

THE TOADSTOOL.

THERE 's a thing that grows by the
     fainting flower,
And springs in the shade of the lady's
     bower;
The lily shrinks, and the rose turns pale,
When they feel its breath in the sum-
     mer gale,
And the tulip curls its leaves in pride,
And the blue-eyed violet starts aside;
But the lily may flaunt, and the tulip
     stare,
For what does the honest toadstool care?

She does not glow in a painted vest,
And she never blooms on the maiden's
     breast;
But she comes, as the saintly sisters do,
In a modest suit of a Quaker hue.
And, when the stars in the evening skies
Are weeping dew from their gentle eyes,
The toad comes out from his hermit cell,
The tale of his faithful love to tell.

O there is light in her lover's glance,
That flies to her heart like a silver lance;
His breeches are made of spotted skin,
His jacket is tight, and his pumps are
     thin;
In a cloudless night you may hear his
     song,
As its pensive melody floats along,
And, if you will look by the moonlight
     fair,
The trembling form of the toad is there.

And he twines his arms round her slen-
     der stem,
In the shade of her velvet diadem;

But she turns away in her maiden shame,
And will not breathe on the kindling
　　flame;
He sings at her feet through the live-
　　long night,
And creeps to his cave at the break of
　　light;
And whenever he comes to the air above,
His throat is swelling with baffled love.

THE SPECTRE PIG.

A BALLAD.

It was the stalwart butcher man,
　　That knit his swarthy brow,
And said the gentle Pig must die,
　　And sealed it with a vow.

And oh! it was the gentle Pig
　　Lay stretched upon the ground,
And ah! it was the cruel knife
　　His little heart that found.

They took him then, those wicked men,
　　They trailed him all along;
They put a stick between his lips,
　　And through his heels a thong;

And round and round an oaken beam
　　A hempen cord they flung,
And, like a mighty pendulum,
　　All solemnly he swung!

Now say thy prayers, thou sinful man,
　　And think what thou hast done,
And read thy catechism well,
　　Thou bloody-minded one;

For if his sprite should walk by night,
　　It better were for thee,
That thou wert mouldering in the
　　ground,
　　Or bleaching in the sea.

It was the savage butcher then,
　　That made a mock of sin,
And swore a very wicked oath,
　　He did not care a pin.

It was the butcher's youngest son, —
　　His voice was broke with sighs,
And with his pocket-handkerchief
　　He wiped his little eyes;

All young and ignorant was he,
　　But innocent and mild,
And, in his soft simplicity,
　　Out spoke the tender child:—

"O father, father, list to me;
　　The Pig is deadly sick,
And men have hung him by his heels,
　　And fed him with a stick."

It was the bloody butcher then,
　　That laughed as he would die,
Yet did he soothe the sorrowing child,
　　And bid him not to cry;—

"O Nathan, Nathan, what's a Pig,
　　That thou shouldst weep and wail?
Come, bear thee like a butcher's child,
　　And thou shalt have his tail!"

It was the butcher's daughter then,
　　So slender and so fair,
That sobbed as if her heart would break,
　　And tore her yellow hair;

And thus she spoke in thrilling tone, —
　　Fast fell the tear-drops big;—
"Ah! woe is me! Alas! Alas!
　　The Pig! The Pig! The Pig!"

Then did her wicked father's lips
　　Make merry with her woe,
And call her many a naughty name,
　　Because she whimpered so.

Ye need not weep, ye gentle ones,
  In vain your tears are shed,
Ye cannot wash his crimson hand,
  Ye cannot soothe the dead.

The bright sun folded on his breast
  His robes of rosy flame,
And softly over all the west
  The shades of evening came

He slept, and troops of murdered Pigs
  Were busy with his dreams;
Loud rang their wild, unearthly shrieks,
  Wide yawned their mortal seams.

The clock struck twelve; the Dead hath
      heard;
  He opened both his eyes,
And sullenly he shook his tail
  To lash the feeding flies.

One quiver of the hempen cord, —
  One struggle and one bound, —
With stiffened limb and leaden eye,
  The Pig was on the ground!

And straight towards the sleeper's house
  His fearful way he wended;
And hooting owl, and hovering bat,
  On midnight wing attended.

Back flew the bolt, up rose the latch,
  And open swung the door,
And little mincing feet were heard
  Pat, pat along the floor.

Two hoofs upon the sanded floor,
  And two upon the bed;
And they are breathing side by side,
  The living and the dead!

"Now wake, now wake, thou butcher
      man!
  What makes thy cheek so pale?
Take hold! take hold! thou dost not fear
  To clasp a spectre's tail?"

Untwisted every winding coil;
  The shuddering wretch took hold,
All like an icicle it seemed,
  So tapering and so cold.

"Thou com'st with me, thou butcher
      man!" —
  He strives to loose his grasp,
But, faster than the clinging vine,
  Those twining spirals clasp.

And open, open swung the door,
  And, fleeter than the wind,
The shadowy spectre swept before,
  The butcher trailed behind.

Fast fled the darkness of the night,
  And morn rose faint and dim;
They called full loud, they knocked full
      long,
  They did not waken him.

Straight, straight towards that oaken
      beam,
  A trampled pathway ran;
A ghastly shape was swinging there, —
  It was the butcher man.

TO A CAGED LION.

Poor conquered monarch! though that
      haughty glance
  Still speaks thy courage unsubdued
      by time,
And in the grandeur of thy sullen tread
  Lives the proud spirit of thy burning
      clime; —
Fettered by things that shudder at thy
      roar,
Torn from thy pathless wilds to pace
      this narrow floor!

Thou wast the victor, and all nature
      shrunk
  Before the thunders of thine awful
      wrath;

The steel-armed hunter viewed thee
   from afar,
   Fearless and trackless in thy lonely
      path !
The famished tiger closed his flaming
   eye,
And crouched and panted as thy step
   went by !

Thou art the vanquished, and insulting
   man
   Bars thy broad bosom as a sparrow's
      wing ;
His nerveless arms thine iron sinews
   bind,
   And lead in chains the desert's fallen
      king ;
Are these the beings that have dared to
   twine
Their feeble threads around those limbs
   of thine ?

So must it be ; the weaker, wiser race,
   That wields the tempest and that rides
      the sea,
Even in the stillness of thy solitude
   Must teach the lesson of its power to
      thee ;
And thou, the terror of the trembling
   wild,
Must bow thy savage strength, the mock-
   ery of a child !

THE STAR AND THE WATER-LILY.

THE sun stepped down from his golden
   throne,
   And lay in the silent sea,
And the Lily had folded her satin leaves,
   For a sleepy thing was she ;
What is the Lily dreaming of ?
   Why crisp the waters blue ?
See, see, she is lifting her varnished lid !
   Her white leaves are glistening
      through !

The Rose is cooling his burning cheek
   In the lap of the breathless tide ; —
The Lily hath sisters fresh and fair,
   That would lie by the Rose's side ;
He would love her better than all the rest,
   And he would be fond and true ; —
But the Lily unfolded her weary lids,
   And looked at the sky so blue.

Remember, remember, thou silly one,
   How fast will thy summer glide,
And wilt thou wither a virgin pale,
   Or flourish a blooming bride ?
" O the Rose is old, and thorny, and cold,
   And he lives on earth," said she ;
" But the Star is fair and he lives in
      the air,
   And he shall my bridegroom be."

But what if the stormy cloud should
   come,
   And ruffle the silver sea ?
Would he turn his eye from the distant
   sky,
   To smile on a thing like thee ?
O no, fair Lily, he will not send
   One ray from his far-off throne ;
The winds shall blow and the waves
   shall flow,
   And thou wilt be left alone.

There is not a leaf on the mountain-top
   Nor a drop of evening dew,
Nor a golden sand on the sparkling
   shore,
   Nor a pearl in the waters blue,
That he has not cheered with his fickle
   smile,
   And warmed with his faithless
      beam, —
And will he be true to a pallid flower,
   That floats on the quiet stream ?

Alas for the Lily ! she would not heed,
   But turned to the skies afar,

And bared her breast to the trembling
  ray
  That shot from the rising star ;
The cloud came over the darkened sky,
  And over the waters wide :
She looked in vain through the beating
  rain,
  And sank in the stormy tide.

ILLUSTRATION OF A PICTURE.

"A SPANISH GIRL IN REVERIE."

SHE twirled the string of golden beads,
  That round her neck was hung, —
My grandsire's gift ; the good old man
  Loved girls when he was young ;
And, bending lightly o'er the cord,
  And turning half away,
With something like a youthful sigh,
  Thus spoke the maiden gray : —

"Well, one may trail her silken robe,
  And bind her locks with pearls,
And one may wreathe the woodland rose
  Among her floating curls ;
And one may tread the dewy grass,
  And one the marble floor,
Nor half-hid bosom heave the less,
  Nor broidered corset more !

"Some years ago, a dark-eyed girl
  Was sitting in the shade, —
There's something brings her to my mind
  In that young dreaming maid, —
And in her hand she held a flower,
  A flower, whose speaking hue
Said, in the language of the heart,
  'Believe the giver true.'

"And, as she looked upon its leaves,
  The maiden made a vow
To wear it when the bridal wreath
  Was woven for her brow ;

She watched the flower, as, day by day,
  The leaflets curled and died ;
But he who gave it never came
  To claim her for his bride.

"O many a summer's morning glow
  Has lent the rose its ray,
And many a winter's drifting snow
  Has swept its bloom away ;
But she has kept that faithless pledge
  To this, her winter hour,
And keeps it still, herself alone,
  And wasted like the flower."

Her pale lip quivered, and the light
  Gleamed in her moistening eyes ; —
I asked her how she liked the tints
  In those Castilian skies ?
"She thought them misty, — 't was
    perhaps
  Because she stood too near" ;
She turned away, and as she turned
  I saw her wipe a tear.

A ROMAN AQUEDUCT.

THE sun-browned girl, whose limbs re-
  cline
  When noon her languid hand has laid
Hot on the green flakes of the pine,
  Beneath its narrow disk of shade ;

As, through the flickering noontide glare,
  She gazes on the rainbow chain
Of arches, lifting once in air
  The rivers of the Roman's plain ; —

Say, does her wandering eye recall
  The mountain-current's icy wave, —
Or for the dead one tear let fall,
  Whose founts are broken by their
    grave ?

From stone to stone the ivy weaves
  Her braided tracery's winding veil,

And lacing stalks and tangled leaves
    Nod heavy in the drowsy gale.

And lightly floats the pendent vine,
    That swings beneath her slender bow,
Arch answering arch, — whose rounded
        line
    Seems mirrored in the wreath below.

How patient Nature smiles at Fame !
    The weeds, that strewed the victor's
        way,
Feed on his dust to shroud his name,
    Green where his proudest towers decay.

See, through that channel, empty now,
    The scanty rain its tribute pours, —
Which cooled the lip and laved the brow
    Of conquerors from a hundred shores.

Thus bending o'er the nation's bier,
    Whose wants the captive earth sup-
        plied,
The dew of Memory's passing tear
    Falls on the arches of her pride !

FROM A BACHELOR'S PRIVATE JOURNAL.

Sweet Mary, I have never breathed
    The love it were in vain to name ;
Though round my heart a serpent
        wreathed,
    I smiled, or strove to smile, the same.

Once more the pulse of Nature glows
    With faster throb and fresher fire,
While music round her pathway flows,
    Like echoes from a hidden lyre.

And is there none with me to share
    The glories of the earth and sky ?
The eagle through the pathless air
    Is followed by one burning eye.

Ah no ! the cradled flowers may wake,
    Again may flow the frozen sea,
From every cloud a star may break, —
    There comes no second Spring to me.

Go, — ere the painted toys of youth
    Are crushed beneath the tread of years;
Ere visions have been chilled to truth,
    And hopes are washed away in tears.

Go, — for I will not bid thee weep, —
    Too soon my sorrows will be thine,
And evening's troubled air shall sweep
    The incense from the broken shrine.

If Heaven can hear the dying tone
    Of chords that soon will cease to thrill,
The prayer that Heaven has heard alone
    May bless thee when those chords are
        still.

LA GRISETTE.

Ah Clemence ! when I saw thee last
    Trip down the Rue de Seine,
And turning, when thy form had past,
    I said, "We meet again," —
I dreamed not in that idle glance
    Thy latest image came,
And only left to memory's trance
    A shadow and a name.

The few strange words my lips had taught
    Thy timid voice to speak,
Their gentler signs, which often brought
    Fresh roses to thy cheek,
The trailing of thy long loose hair
    Bent o'er my couch of pain,
All, all returned, more sweet, more fair ;
    O had we met again !

I walked where saint and virgin keep
    The vigil lights of Heaven,
I knew that thou hadst woes to weep,
    And sins to be forgiven ;

I watched where Genevieve was laid,
  I knelt by Mary's shrine,
Beside me low, soft voices prayed;
  Alas! but where was thine?

And when the morning sun was bright,
  When wind and wave were calm,
And flamed, in thousand-tinted light,
  The rose of Notre Dame,
I wandered through the haunts of men,
  From Boulevard to Quai,
Till, frowning o'er Saint Etienne,
  The Pantheon's shadow lay.

In vain, in vain; we meet no more,
  Nor dream what fates befall;
And long upon the stranger's shore
  My voice on thee may call,
When years have clothed the line in moss
  That tells thy name and days,
And withered, on thy simple cross,
  The wreaths of Père-la-Chaise!

OUR YANKEE GIRLS.

LET greener lands and bluer skies,
  If such the wide earth shows,
With fairer cheeks and brighter eyes,
  Match us the star and rose;
The winds that lift the Georgian's veil,
  Or wave Circassia's curls,
Waft to their shores the sultan's sail, —
  Who buys our Yankee girls?

The gay grisette, whose fingers touch
  Love's thousand chords so well;
The dark Italian, loving much,
  But more than *one* can tell;
And England's fair-haired, blue-eyed
    dame,
  Who binds her brow with pearls; —
Ye who have seen them, can they shame
  Our own sweet Yankee girls?

And what if court or castle vaunt
  Its children loftier born? —
Who heeds the silken tassel's flaunt
  Beside the golden corn?
They ask not for the dainty toil
  Of ribboned knights and earls,
The daughters of the virgin soil,
  Our freeborn Yankee girls!

By every hill whose stately pines
  Wave their dark arms above
The home where some fair being shines,
  To warm the wilds with love,
From barest rock to bleakest shore
  Where farthest sail unfurls,
That stars and stripes are streaming
    o'er, —
  God bless our Yankee girls!

L'INCONNUE.

Is thy name Mary, maiden fair?
  Such should, methinks, its music be;
The sweetest name that mortals bear
  Were best befitting thee;
And she to whom it once was given,
Was half of earth and half of heaven.

I hear thy voice, I see thy smile,
  I look upon thy folded hair;
Ah! while we dream not they beguile,
  Our hearts are in the snare;
And she who chains a wild bird's wing
Must start not if her captive sing.

So, lady, take the leaf that falls,
  To all but thee unseen, unknown;
When evening shades thy silent walls,
  Then read it all alone;
In stillness read, in darkness seal,
Forget, despise, but not reveal!

STANZAS.

STRANGE ! that one lightly whispered
     tone
     Is far, far sweeter unto me,
Than all the sounds that kiss the earth,
     Or breathe along the sea ;
But, lady, when thy voice I greet,
Not heavenly music seems so sweet.

I look upon the fair blue skies,
     And naught but empty air I see ;
But when I turn me to thine eyes,
     It seemeth unto me
Ten thousand angels spread their wings
Within those little azure rings.

The lily hath the softest leaf
     That ever western breeze hath fanned,
But thou shalt have the tender flower,
     So I may take thy hand ;
That little hand to me doth yield
More joy than all the broidered field.

O lady ! there be many things
     That seem right fair, below, above ;
But sure not one among them all
     Is half so sweet as love ; —
Let us not pay our vows alone,
But join two altars both in one.

LINES BY A CLERK.

OH ! I did love her dearly,
     And gave her toys and rings,
And I thought she meant sincerely,
     When she took my pretty things.
But her heart has grown as icy
     As a fountain in the fall,
And her love, that was so spicy,
     It did not last at all.

I gave her once a locket,
     It was filled with my own hair,
And she put it in her pocket
     With very special care.
But a jeweller has got it, —
     He offered it to me,
And another that is not it
     Around her neck I see.

For my cooings and my billings
     I do not now complain,
But my dollars and my shillings
     Will never come again ;
They were earned with toil and sorrow,
     But I never told her that,
And now I have to borrow,
     And want another hat.

Think, think, thou cruel Emma,
     When thou shalt hear my woe,
And know my sad dilemma,
     That thou hast made it so.
See, see my beaver rusty,
     Look, look upon this hole,
This coat is dim and dusty ;
     O let it rend thy soul !

Before the gates of fashion
     I daily bent my knee,
But I sought the shrine of passion,
     And found my idol, — thee.
Though never love intenser
     Had bowed a soul before it,
Thine eye was on the censer,
     And not the hand that bore it.

THE PHILOSOPHER TO HIS LOVE.

DEAREST, a look is but a ray
Reflected in a certain way ;
A word, whatever tone it wear,
Is but a trembling wave of air ;
A touch, obedience to a clause
In nature's pure material laws.

The very flowers that bend and meet,
In sweetening others, grow more sweet ;

The clouds by day, the stars by night,
Inweave their floating locks of light ;
The rainbow, Heaven's own forehead's
    braid,
Is but the embrace of sun and shade.

How few that love us have we found !
How wide the world that girds them
    round !
Like mountain streams we meet and part,
Each living in the other's heart,
Our course unknown, our hope to be
Yet mingled in the distant sea.

But Ocean coils and heaves in vain,
Bound in the subtle moonbeam's chain ;
And love and hope do but obey
Some cold, capricious planet's ray,
Which lights and leads the tide it charms
To Death's dark caves and icy arms.

Alas ! one narrow line is drawn,
That links our sunset with our dawn ;
In mist and shade life's morning rose,
And clouds are round it at its close ;
But ah ! no twilight beam ascends
To whisper where that evening ends.

Oh ! in the hour when I shall feel
Those shadows round my senses steal,
When gentle eyes are weeping o'er
The clay that feels their tears no more,
Then let thy spirit with me be,
Or some sweet angel, likest thee !

THE POET'S LOT.

WHAT is a poet's love ? —
    To write a girl a sonnet,
To get a ring, or some such thing,
    And fustianize upon it.

What is a poet's fame ? —
    Sad hints about his reason,

And sadder praise from garreteers,
    To be returned in season.

Where go the poet's lines ? —
    Answer, ye evening tapers !
Ye auburn locks, ye golden curls,
    Speak from your folded papers !

Child of the ploughshare, smile ;
    Boy of the counter, grieve not,
Though muses round thy trundle-bed
    Their broidered tissue weave not.

The poet's future holds
    No civic wreath above him ;
Nor slated roof, nor varnished chaise,
    Nor wife nor child to love him.

Maid of the village inn,
    Who workest woe on satin,
(The grass in black, the graves in green,
    The epitaph in Latin,)

Trust not to them who say,
    In stanzas, they adore thee ;
O rather sleep in churchyard clay,
    With urn and cherub o'er thee !

TO A BLANK SHEET OF PAPER.

WAN-VISAGED thing ! thy virgin leaf
    To me looks more than deadly pale,
Unknowing what may stain thee yet, —
    A poem or a tale.

Who can thy unborn meaning scan ?
    Can Seer or Sibyl read thee now ?
No, — seek to trace the fate of man
    Writ on his infant brow

Love may light on thy snowy cheek,
    And shake his Eden-breathing plumes ;
Then shalt thou tell how Lelia smiles,
    Or Angelina blooms.

Satire may lift his bearded lance,
   Forestalling Time's slow-moving
      scythe,
And, scattered on thy little field,
   Disjointed bards may writhe.

Perchance a vision of the night,
   Some grizzled spectre, gaunt and thin,
Or sheeted corpse, may stalk along,
   Or skeleton may grin !

If it should be in pensive hour
   Some sorrow-moving theme I try,
Ah, maiden, how thy tears will fall,
   For all I doom to die !

But if in merry mood I touch
   Thy leaves, then shall the sight of
      thee
Sow smiles as thick on rosy lips
   As ripples on the sea.

The Weekly press shall gladly stoop
   To bind thee up among its sheaves ;
The Daily steal thy shining ore,
   To gild its leaden leaves.

Thou hast no tongue, yet thou canst
     speak,
   Till distant shores shall hear the
     sound ;
Thou hast no life, yet thou canst breathe
   Fresh life on all around.

Thou art the arena of the wise,
   The noiseless battle-ground of fame ;
The sky where halos may be wreathed
   Around the humblest name.

Take, then, this treasure to thy trust,
   To win some idle reader's smile,
Then fade and moulder in the dust,
   Or swell some bonfire's pile.

TO THE PORTRAIT OF "A GENTLE-MAN."

IN THE ATHENÆUM GALLERY.

IT may be so, — perhaps thou hast
   A warm and loving heart ;
I will not blame thee for thy face,
   Poor devil as thou art.

That thing, thou fondly deem'st a nose,
   Unsightly though it be, —
In spite of all the cold world's scorn,
   It may be much to thee.

Those eyes, — among thine elder friends
   Perhaps they pass for blue, —
No matter, — if a man can see,
   What more have eyes to do ?

Thy mouth, — that fissure in thy face,
   By something like a chin, —
May be a very useful place
   To put thy victual in.

I know thou hast a wife at home,
   I know thou hast a child,
By that subdued, domestic smile
   Upon thy features mild.

That wife sits fearless by thy side,
   That cherub on thy knee ;
They do not shudder at thy looks,
   They do not shrink from thee.

Above thy mantel is a hook, —
   A portrait once was there ;
It was thine only ornament, —
   Alas ! that hook is bare.

She begged thee not to let it go,
   She begged thee all in vain ;
She wept, — and breathed a trembling
     prayer
   To meet it safe again.

It was a bitter sight to see
   That picture torn away ;
It was a solemn thought to think
   What all her friends would say !

And often in her calmer hours,
   And in her happy dreams,
Upon its long-deserted hook
   The absent portrait seems.

Thy wretched infant turns his head
   In melancholy wise,
And looks to meet the placid stare
   Of those unbending eyes.

I never saw thee, lovely one, —
   Perchance I never may ;
It is not often that we cross
   Such people in our way ;

But if we meet in distant years,
   Or on some foreign shore,
Sure I can take my Bible oath,
   I 've seen that face before.

THE BALLAD OF THE OYSTERMAN.

IT was a tall young oysterman lived by
   the river-side,
His shop was just upon the bank, his
   boat was on the tide ;
The daughter of a fisherman, that was so
   straight and slim,
Lived over on the other bank, right
   opposite to him.

It was the pensive oysterman that saw
   a lovely maid,
Upon a moonlight evening, a sitting in
   the shade ;
He saw her wave her handkerchief, as
   much as if to say,
"I 'm wide awake, young oysterman,
   and all the folks away."

Then up arose the oysterman, and to
   himself said he,
"I guess I 'll leave the skiff at home,
   for fear that folks should see ;
I read it in the story-book, that, for to
   kiss his dear,
Leander swam the Hellespont, — and I
   will swim this here."

And he has leaped into the waves, and
   crossed the shining stream,
And he has clambered up the bank, all
   in the moonlight gleam ;
O there were kisses sweet as dew, and
   words as soft as rain, —
But they have heard her father's step,
   and in he leaps again !

Out spoke the ancient fisherman, — "O
   what was that, my daughter?"
"'T was nothing but a pebble, sir, I
   threw into the water."
"And what is that, pray tell me, love,
   that paddles off so fast?"
"It 's nothing but a porpoise, sir, that 's
   been a swimming past."

Out spoke the ancient fisherman, —
   "Now bring me my harpoon !
I 'll get into my fishing-boat, and fix
   the fellow soon."
Down fell that pretty innocent, as falls
   a snow-white lamb,
Her hair drooped round her pallid
   cheeks, like seaweed on a clam.

Alas for those two loving ones ! she
   waked not from her swound,
And he was taken with the cramp, and
   in the waves was drowned ;
But Fate has metamorphosed them, in
   pity of their woe,
And now they keep an oyster-shop for
   mermaids down below.

A NOONTIDE LYRIC.

THE dinner-bell, the dinner-bell
  Is ringing loud and clear ;
Through hill and plain, through street
      and lane,
  It echoes far and near ;
From curtained hall and whitewashed
      stall,
  Wherever men can hide,
Like bursting waves from ocean caves,
  They float upon the tide.

I smell the smell of roasted meat !
  I hear the hissing fry !
The beggars know where they can go,
  But where, O where shall I ?
At twelve o'clock men took my hand,
  At two they only stare,
And eye me with a fearful look,
  As if I were a bear !

The poet lays his laurels down,
  And hastens to his greens ;
The happy tailor quits his goose,
  To riot on his beans ;
The weary cobbler snaps his thread,
  The printer leaves his pi ;
His very devil hath a home,
  But what, O what have I ?

Methinks I hear an angel voice,
  That softly seems to say :
" Pale stranger, all may yet be well,
  Then wipe thy tears away ;
Erect thy head, and cock thy hat,
  And follow me afar,
And thou shalt have a jolly meal,
  And charge it at the bar."

I hear the voice ! I go ! I go !
  Prepare your meat and wine !
They little heed their future need,
  Who pay not when they dine.

Give me to-day the rosy bowl,
  Give me one golden dream, —
To-morrow kick away the stool,
  And dangle from the beam !

THE HOT SEASON.

THE folks, that on the first of May
  Wore winter coats and hose,
Began to say, the first of June,
  " Good Lord ! how hot it grows ! "
At last two Fahrenheits blew up,
  And killed two children small,
And one barometer shot dead
  A tutor with its ball !

Now all day long the locusts sang
  Among the leafless trees ;
Three new hotels warped inside out,
  The pumps could only wheeze ;
And ripe old wine, that twenty years
  Had cobwebbed o'er in vain,
Came spouting through the rotten corks,
  Like Joly's best Champagne !

The Worcester locomotives did
  Their trip in half an hour ;
The Lowell cars ran forty miles
  Before they checked the power ;
Roll brimstone soon became a drug,
  And loco-focos fell ;
All asked for ice, but everywhere
  Saltpetre was to sell.

Plump men of mornings ordered tights,
  But, ere the scorching noons,
Their candle-moulds had grown as loose
  As Cossack pantaloons !
The dogs ran mad, — men could not try
  If water they would choose ;
A horse fell dead, — he only left
  Four red-hot, rusty shoes !

But soon the people could not bear
  The slightest hint of fire ;

Allusions to caloric drew
  A flood of savage ire ;
The leaves on heat were all torn out
  From every book at school,
And many blackguards kicked and
    caned,
  Because they said, "Keep cool ! "

The gas-light companies were mobbed,
  The bakers all were shot,
The penny press began to talk
Of Lynching Doctor Nott ;
And all about the warehouse steps
  Were angry men in droves,
Crashing and splintering through the
    doors
  To smash the patent stoves !

The abolition men and maids
  Were tanned to such a hue,
You scarce could tell them from their
    friends,
  Unless their eyes were blue ;
And, when I left, society
  Had burst its ancient guards,
And Brattle Street and Temple Place
  Were interchanging cards !

A PORTRAIT.

A STILL sweet, placid, moonlight face,
  And slightly nonchalant,
Which seems to claim a middle place
  Between one's love and aunt,
Where childhood's star has left a ray
  In woman's sunniest sky,
As morning dew and blushing day
  On fruit and blossom lie.

And yet, — and yet I cannot love
  Those lovely lines on steel ;
They beam too much of heaven above,
  Earth's darker shades to feel ;

Perchance some early weeds of care
  Around my heart have grown,
And brows unfurrowed seem not fair,
  Because they mock my own.

Alas ! when Eden's gates were sealed,
  How oft some sheltered flower
Breathed o'er the wanderers of the
    field,
  Like their own bridal bower ;
Yet, saddened by its loveliness,
  And humbled by its pride,
Earth's fairest child they could not
    bless, —
  It mocked them when they sighed.

AN EVENING THOUGHT.

WRITTEN AT SEA.

IF sometimes in the dark blue eye,
  Or in the deep red wine,
Or soothed by gentlest melody,
  Still warms this heart of mine,
Yet something colder in the blood,
  And calmer in the brain,
Have whispered that my youth's bright
    flood
  Ebbs, not to flow again.

If by Helvetia's azure lake,
  Or Arno's yellow stream,
Each star of memory could awake,
  As in my first young dream,
I know that when mine eye shall greet
  The hillsides bleak and bare,
That gird my home, it will not meet
  My childhood's sunsets there.

O when love's first, sweet, stolen kiss
  Burned on my boyish brow,
Was that young forehead worn as
    this ?
  Was that flushed cheek as now ?

Were that wild pulse and throbbing
heart
    Like these, which vainly strive,
In thankless strains of soulless art,
    To dream themselves alive ?

Alas ! the morning dew is gone,
    Gone ere the full of day ;
Life's iron fetter still is on,
    Its wreaths all torn away ;
Happy if still some casual hour
    Can warm the fading shrine,
Too soon to chill beyond the power
    Of love, or song, or wine !

THE WASP AND THE HORNET.

THE two proud sisters of the sea,
    In glory and in doom ! —
Well may the eternal waters be
    Their broad, unsculptured tomb !
The wind that rings along the wave,
    The clear, unshadowed sun,
Are torch and trumpet o'er the brave,
    Whose last green wreath is won !

No stranger-hand their banners furled,
    No victor's shout they heard ;
Unseen, above them ocean curled,
    Save by his own pale bird ;
The gnashing billows heaved and fell ;
    Wild shrieked the midnight gale ;
Far, far beneath the morning swell
    Were pennon, spar, and sail.

The land of Freedom ! Sea and shore
    Are guarded now, as when
Her ebbing waves to victory bore
    Fair barks and gallant men ;
O many a ship of prouder name
    May wave her starry fold,
Nor trail, with deeper light of fame,
    The paths they swept of old !

"QUI VIVE."

" *Qui vive !* "   The sentry's musket
        rings,
    The channelled bayonet gleams ;
High o'er him, like a raven's wings
The broad tricolored banner flings
Its shadow, rustling as it swings
    Pale in the moonlight beams ;
Pass on ! while steel-clad sentries keep
Their vigil o'er the monarch's sleep,
    Thy bare, unguarded breast
Asks not the unbroken, bristling zone
That girds yon sceptred trembler's
        throne ; —
    Pass on, and take thy rest !

" *Qui vive !* "   How oft the midnight
        air
    That startling cry has borne !
How oft the evening breeze has fanned
The banner of this haughty land,
O'er mountain snow and desert sand,
    Ere yet its folds were torn !
Through Jena's carnage flying red,
Or tossing o'er Marengo's dead,
    Or curling on the towers
Where Austria's eagle quivers yet,
And suns the ruffled plumage, wet
    With battle's crimson showers !

" *Qui vive !* "   And is the sentry's
        cry, —
    The sleepless soldier's hand, —
Are these — the painted folds that fly
And lift their emblems, printed high
On morning mist and sunset sky —
    The guardians of a land ?
No ! If the patriot's pulses sleep,
How vain the watch that hirelings
        keep, —
    The idle flag that waves,
When Conquest, with his iron heel,
Treads down the standards and the steel
    That belt the soil of slaves !

SONGS IN MANY KEYS.

THE piping of our slender, peaceful reeds
Whispers uncared for while the trumpets bray;
Song is thin air; our hearts' exulting play
Beats time but to the tread of marching deeds,
Following the mighty van that Freedom leads,
Her glorious standard flaming to the day!
The crimsoned pavement where a hero bleeds
Breathes nobler lessons than the poet's lay.
Strong arms, broad breasts, brave hearts, are better worth
Than strains that sing the ravished echoes dumb.
Hark! 't is the loud reverberating drum
Rolls o'er the prairied West, the rock-bound North:
The myriad-handed Future stretches forth
Its shadowy palms. Behold, we come, — we come!

Turn o'er these idle leaves. Such toys as these
Were not unsought for, as, in languid dreams,
We lay beside our lotus-feeding streams,
And nursed our fancies in forgetful ease.
It matters little if they pall or please,
Dropping untimely, while the sudden gleams
Glare from the mustering clouds whose blackness seems
Too swollen to hold its lightning from the trees.
Yet, in some lull of passion, when at last
These calm revolving moons that come and go —
Turning our months to years, they creep so slow —
Have brought us rest, the not unwelcome past
May flutter to thee through these leaflets, cast
On the wild winds that all around us blow.

MAY 1, 1861.

SONGS IN MANY KEYS.

I. — 1849 - 1856.

AGNES.

PART FIRST.

THE KNIGHT.

THE tale I tell is gospel true,
  As all the bookmen know,
And pilgrims who have strayed to view
  The wrecks still left to show.

The old, old story, — fair, and young,
  And fond, — and not too wise, —
That matrons tell, with sharpened
    tongue,
  To maids with downcast eyes.

Ah ! maidens err and matrons warn
  Beneath the coldest sky ;
Love lurks amid the tasselled corn
  As in the bearded rye !

But who would dream our sober sires
  Had learned the old world's ways,
And warmed their hearths with lawless
    fires
  In Shirley's homespun days ?

'T is like some poet's pictured trance
  His idle rhymes recite, —
This old New-England-born romance
  Of Agnes and the Knight ;

Yet, known to all the country round,
  Their home is standing still,
Between Wachuset's lonely mound
  And Shawmut's threefold hill.

— One hour we rumble on the rail,
  One half-hour guide the rein,
We reach at last, o'er hill and dale,
  The village on the plain.

With blackening wall and mossy roof,
  With stained and warping floor,
A stately mansion stands aloof
  And bars its haughty door.

This lowlier portal may be tried,
  That breaks the gable wall ;
And lo ! with arches opening wide,
  Sir Harry Frankland's hall !

'T was in the second George's day
  They sought the forest shade,
The knotted trunks they cleared away,
  The massive beams they laid,

They piled the rock-hewn chimney tall,
  They smoothed the terraced ground,
They reared the marble-pillared wall
  That fenced the mansion round.

Far stretched beyond the village bound
  The Master's broad domain ;

With page and valet, horse and hound,
  He kept a goodly train.

And, all the midland county through,
  The ploughman stopped to gaze
Whene'er his chariot swept in view
  Behind the shining bays,

With mute obeisance, grave and slow,
  Repaid by nod polite, —
For such the way with high and low
  Till after Concord fight.

Nor less to courtly circles known
  That graced the three-hilled town
With far-off splendors of the Throne,
  And glimmerings from the Crown ;

Wise Phipps, who held the seals of state
  For Shirley over sea ;
Brave Knowles, whose press-gang moved of late
  The King Street mob's decree ;

And judges grave, and colonels grand,
  Fair dames and stately men,
The mighty people of the land,
  The " World " of there and then.

'T was strange no Chloe's " beauteous Form,"
  And " Eyes' cœlestial Blew,"
This Strephon of the West could warm,
  No Nymph his Heart subdue !

Perchance he wooed as gallants use,
  Whom fleeting loves enchain,
But still unfettered, free to choose,
  Would brook no bridle-rein.

He saw the fairest of the fair,
  But smiled alike on all ;
No band his roving foot might snare,
  No ring his hand enthrall.

PART SECOND.

THE MAIDEN.

Why seeks the knight that rocky cape
  Beyond the Bay of Lynn ?
What chance his wayward course may shape
  To reach its village inn ?

No story tells ; whate'er we guess,
  The past lies deaf and still,
But Fate, who rules to blight or bless,
  Can lead us where she will.

Make way ! Sir Harry's coach and four,
  And liveried grooms that ride !
They cross the ferry, touch the shore
  On Winnisimmet's side.

They hear the wash on Chelsea Beach, —
  The level marsh they pass,
Where miles on miles the desert reach
  Is rough with bitter grass.

The shining horses foam and pant,
  And now the smells begin
Of fishy Swampscot, salt Nahant,
  And leather-scented Lynn.

Next, on their left, the slender spires,
  And glittering vanes, that crown,
The home of Salem's frugal sires,
  The old, witch-haunted town.

So onward, o'er the rugged way
  That runs through rocks and sand,
Showered by the tempest-driven spray,
  From bays on either hand,

That shut between their outstretched arms
  The crews of Marblehead,
The lords of ocean's watery farms,
  Who plough the waves for bread.

" She turned,—a reddening rose in bud." Page 91.

At last the ancient inn appears,
　The spreading elm below,
Whose flapping sign these fifty years
　Has seesawed to and fro.

How fair the azure fields in sight
　Before the low-browed inn !
The tumbling billows fringe with light
　The crescent shore of Lynn ;

Nahant thrusts outward through the
　　waves
　Her arm of yellow sand,
And breaks the roaring surge that braves
　The gauntlet on her hand ;

With eddying whirl the waters lock
　Yon treeless mound forlorn,
The sharp-winged sea-fowl's breeding-
　　rock,
　That fronts the Spouting Horn ;

Then free the white-sailed shallops glide,
　And wide the ocean smiles,
Till, shoreward bent, his streams divide
　The two bare Misery Isles.

The master's silent signal stays
　The wearied cavalcade ;
The coachman reins his smoking bays
　Beneath the elm-tree's shade.

A gathering on the village green !
　The cocked-hats crowd to see,
On legs in ancient velveteen,
　With buckles at the knee.

A clustering round the tavern-door
　Of square-toed village boys,
Still wearing, as their grandsires wore,
　The old-world corduroys !

A scampering at the "Fountain" inn, —
　A rush of great and small, —
With hurrying servants' mingled din
　And screaming matron's call !

Poor Agnes ! with her work half done
　They caught her unaware ;
As, humbly, like a praying nun,
　She knelt upon the stair ;

Bent o'er the steps, with lowliest mien
　She knelt, but not to pray, —
Her little hands must keep them clean,
　And wash their stains away.

A foot, an ankle, bare and white,
　Her girlish shapes betrayed, —
"Ha ! Nymphs and Graces !" spoke
　　the Knight ;
　"Look up, my beauteous Maid !"

She turned, — a reddening rose in bud,
　Its calyx half withdrawn, —
Her cheek on fire with damasked blood
　Of girlhood's glowing dawn !

He searched her features through and
　　through,
　As royal lovers look
On lowly maidens, when they woo
　Without the ring and book.

"Come hither, Fair one ! Here, my
　　Sweet !
　Nay, prithee, look not down !
Take this to shoe those little feet," —
　He tossed a silver crown.

A sudden paleness struck her brow, —
　A swifter flush succeeds ;
It burns her cheek ; it kindles now
　Beneath her golden beads.

She flitted, but the glittering eye
　Still sought the lovely face.
Who was she ? What, and whence ? and
　　why
　Doomed to such menial place ?

A skipper's daughter, — so they said, —
　Left orphan by the gale

That cost the fleet of Marblehead
   And Gloucester thirty sail.

Ah! many a lonely home is found
   Along the Essex shore,
That cheered its goodman outward
     bound,
   And sees his face no more!

"Not so," the matron whispered, —
   "sure
No orphan girl is she, —
The Surraige folk are deadly poor
   Since Edward left the sea,

"And Mary, with her growing brood,
   Has work enough to do
To find the children clothes and food
   With Thomas, John, and Hugh.

"This girl of Mary's, growing tall, —
   (Just turned her sixteenth year,) —
To earn her bread and help them all,
   Would work as housemaid here."

So Agnes, with her golden beads,
   And naught beside as dower,
Grew at the wayside with the weeds,
   Herself a garden-flower.

'T was strange, 't was sad, — so fresh, so
   fair!
   Thus Pity's voice began.
Such grace! an angel's shape and air!
   The half-heard whisper ran.

For eyes could see in George's time,
   As now in later days,
And lips could shape, in prose and
   rhyme,
   The honeyed breath of praise.

No time to woo! The train must go
   Long ere the sun is down,
To reach, before the night-winds blow,
   The many-steepled town.

'T is midnight, — street and square are
   still;
   Dark roll the whispering waves
That lap the piers beneath the hill
   Ridged thick with ancient graves.

Ah, gentle sleep! thy hand will smooth
   The weary couch of pain,
When all thy poppies fail to soothe
   The lover's throbbing brain!

'T is morn, — the orange-mantled sun
   Breaks through the fading gray,
And long and loud the Castle gun
   Peals o'er the glistening bay.

"Thank God 't is day!" With eager
   eye
   He hails the morning's shine : —
"If art can win, or gold can buy,
   The maiden shall be mine!"

PART THIRD.

THE CONQUEST.

"Who saw this hussy when she came?
   What is the wench, and who?"
They whisper. "*Agnes*, — is her name!
   Pray what has she to do?"

The housemaids parley at the gate,
   The scullions on the stair,
And in the footmen's grave debate
   The butler deigns to share.

Black Dinah, stolen when a child,
   And sold on Boston pier,
Grown up in service, petted, spoiled,
   Speaks in the coachman's ear:

"What, all this household at his will?
   And all are yet too few?
More servants, and more servants still, —
   This pert young madam too!"

"*Servant!* fine servant!" laughed aloud
   The man of coach and steeds ;
"She looks too fair, she steps too proud,
   This girl with golden beads !

"I tell you, you may fret and frown,
   And call her what you choose,
You 'll find my Lady in her gown,
   Your Mistress in her shoes!"

Ah, gentle maidens, free from blame,
   God grant you never know
The little whisper, loud with shame,
   That makes the world your foe !

Why tell the lordly flatterer's art,
   That won the maiden's ear, —
The fluttering of the frightened heart,
   The blush, the smile, the tear ?

Alas ! it were the saddening tale
   That every language knows, —
The wooing wind, the yielding sail,
   The sunbeam and the rose.

And now the gown of sober stuff
   Has changed to fair brocade,
With broidered hem, and hanging cuff,
   And flower of silken braid ;

And clasped around her blanching wrist
   A jewelled bracelet shines,
Her flowing tresses' massive twist
   A glittering net confines ;

And mingling with their truant wave
   A fretted chain is hung ;
But ah ! the gift her mother gave, —
   Its beads are all unstrung !

Her place is at the master's board,
   Where none disputes her claim ;
She walks beside the mansion's lord,
   His bride in all but name.

The busy tongues have ceased to talk,
   Or speak in softened tone,
So gracious in her daily walk
   The angel light has shown.

No want that kindness may relieve
   Assails her heart in vain,
The lifting of a ragged sleeve
   Will check her palfrey's rein.

A thoughtful calm, a quiet grace
   In every movement shown,
Reveal her moulded for the place
   She may not call her own.

And, save that on her youthful brow
   There broods a shadowy care,
No matron sealed with holy vow
   In all the land so fair !

PART FOURTH.

THE RESCUE.

A SHIP comes foaming up the bay,
   Along the pier she glides ;
Before her furrow melts away,
   A courier mounts and rides.

"Haste, Haste, post Haste !" the let-
     ters bear ;
   "Sir Harry Frankland, These."
Sad news to tell the loving pair !
   The knight must cross the seas.

"Alas ! we part !"—the lips that spoke
   Lost all their rosy red,
As when a crystal cup is broke,
   And all its wine is shed.

"Nay, droop not thus, — where'er," he
     cried,
   "I go by land or sea,
My love, my life, my joy, my pride,
   Thy place is still by me !"

Through town and city, far and wide,
  Their wandering feet have strayed,
From Alpine lake to ocean tide,
  And cold Sierra's shade.

At length they see the waters gleam
  Amid the fragrant bowers
Where Lisbon mirrors in the stream
  Her belt of ancient towers.

Red is the orange on its bough,
  To-morrow's sun shall fling
O'er Cintra's hazel-shaded brow
  The flush of April's wing.

The streets are loud with noisy mirth,
  They dance on every green ;
The morning's dial marks the birth
  Of proud Braganza's queen.

At eve beneath their pictured dome
  The gilded courtiers throng;
The broad moidores have cheated Rome
  Of all her lords of song.

Ah! Lisbon dreams not of the day —
  Pleased with her painted scenes —
When all her towers shall slide away
  As now these canvas screens!

The spring has passed, the summer fled,
  And yet they linger still,
Though autumn's rustling leaves have
    spread
  The flank of Cintra's hill.

The town has learned their Saxon name,
  And touched their English gold,
Nor tale of doubt nor hint of blame
  From over sea is told.

Three hours the first November dawn
  Has climbed with feeble ray
Through mists like heavy curtains drawn
  Before the darkened day.

How still the muffled echoes sleep!
  Hark! hark! a hollow sound, —
A noise like chariots rumbling deep
  Beneath the solid ground.

The channel lifts, the water slides
  And bares its bar of sand,
Anon a mountain billow strides
  And crashes o'er the land.

The turrets lean, the steeples reel
  Like masts on ocean's swell,
And clash a long discordant peal,
  The death-doomed city's knell.

The pavement bursts, the earth upheaves
  Beneath the staggering town !
The turrets crack — the castle cleaves —
  The spires come rushing down.

Around, the lurid mountains glow
  With strange unearthly gleams ;
While black abysses gape below,
  Then close in jagged seams.

The earth has folded like a wave,
  And thrice a thousand score,
Clasped, shroudless, in their closing
    grave,
  The sun shall see no more !

And all is over.   Street and square
  In ruined heaps are piled ;
Ah! where is she, so frail, so fair,
  Amid the tumult wild?

Unscathed, she treads the wreck-piled
    street,
  Whose narrow gaps afford
A pathway for her bleeding feet,
  To seek her absent lord.

A temple's broken walls arrest
  Her wild and wandering eyes ;
Beneath its shattered portal pressed,
  Her lord unconscious lies.

The power that living hearts obey
　　Shall lifeless blocks withstand?
Love led her footsteps where he lay, —
　　Love nerves her woman's hand :

One cry, — the marble shaft she grasps, —
　　Up heaves the ponderous stone :—
He breathes, — her fainting form he
　　　　clasps, —
　　Her life has bought his own !

PART FIFTH.

THE REWARD.

How like the starless night of death
　　Our being's brief eclipse,
When faltering heart and failing breath
　　Have bleached the fading lips !

She lives ! What guerdon shall repay
　　His debt of ransomed life ?
One word can charm all wrongs away, —
　　The sacred name of WIFE !

The love that won her girlish charms
　　Must shield her matron fame,
And write beneath the Frankland arms
　　The village beauty's name.

Go, call the priest ! no vain delay
　　Shall dim the sacred ring !
Who knows what change the passing day,
　　The fleeting hour, may bring ?

Before the holy altar bent,
　　There kneels a goodly pair ;
A stately man, of high descent,
　　A woman, passing fair.

No jewels lend the blinding sheen
　　That meaner beauty needs,
But on her bosom heaves unseen
　　A string of golden beads.

The vow is spoke, — the prayer is said, —
　　And with a gentle pride
The Lady Agnes lifts her head,
　　Sir Harry Frankland's bride.

No more her faithful heart shall bear
　　Those griefs so meekly borne, —
The passing sneer, the freezing stare,
　　The icy look of scorn ;

No more the blue-eyed English dames
　　Their haughty lips shall curl,
Whene'er a hissing whisper names
　　The poor New England girl.

But stay ! — his mother's haughty
　　　　brow, —
　　The pride of ancient race, —
Will plighted faith, and holy vow,
　　Win back her fond embrace ?

Too well she knew the saddening tale
　　Of love no vow had blest,
That turned his blushing honors pale
　　And stained his knightly crest.

They seek his Northern home, — alas :
　　He goes alone before ; —
His own dear Agnes may not pass
　　The proud, ancestral door.

He stood before the stately dame ;
　　He spoke ; she calmly heard,
But not to pity, nor to blame ;
　　She breathed no single word.

He told his love, — her faith betrayed ;
　　She heard with tearless eyes ;
Could she forgive the erring maid ?
　　She stared in cold surprise.

How fond her heart, he told, — how true;
　　The haughty eyelids fell ; —
The kindly deeds she loved to do ;
　　She murmured, "It is well."

But when he told that fearful day,
　　And how her feet were led
To where entombed in life he lay,
　　The breathing with the dead,

And how she bruised her tender breasts
　　Against the crushing stone,
That still the strong-armed clown pro-
　　　tests
　　No man can lift alone, —

O then the frozen spring was broke ;
　　By turns she wept and smiled ; —
"Sweet Agnes !" so the mother spoke,
　　"God bless my angel child !

"She saved thee from the jaws of
　　　death, —
　　'T is thine to right her wrongs ;
I tell thee, — I, who gave thee breath, —
　　To her thy life belongs !"

Thus Agnes won her noble name,
　　Her lawless lover's hand ;
The lowly maiden so became
　　A lady in the land !

PART SIXTH.

CONCLUSION.

THE tale is done ; it little needs
　　To track their after ways,
And string again the golden beads
　　Of love's uncounted days.

They leave the fair ancestral isle
　　For bleak New England's shore ;
How gracious is the courtly smile
　　Of all who frowned before !

Again through Lisbon's orange bowers
　　They watch the river's gleam,
And shudder as her shadowy towers
　　Shake in the trembling stream.

Fate parts at length the fondest pair ;
　　His cheek, alas ! grows pale ;
The breast that trampling death could
　　　spare
　　His noiseless shafts assail.

He longs to change the heaven of blue
　　For England's clouded sky, —
To breathe the air his boyhood knew ;
　　He seeks them but to die.

— Hard by the terraced hillside town,
　　Where healing streamlets run,
Still sparkling with their old renown, —
　　The "Waters of the Sun," —

The Lady Agnes raised the stone
　　That marks his honored grave,
And there Sir Harry sleeps alone
　　By Wiltshire Avon's wave.

The home of early love was dear ;
　　She sought its peaceful shade,
And kept her state for many a year,
　　With none to make afraid.

At last the evil days were come
　　That saw the red cross fall ;
She hears the rebels' rattling drum, —
　　Farewell to Frankland Hall !

— I tell you, as my tale began,
　　The Hall is standing still ;
And you, kind listener, maid or man,
　　May see it if you will.

The box is glistening huge and green,
　　Like trees the lilacs grow,
Three elms high-arching still are seen,
　　And one lies stretched below.

The hangings, rough with velvet flowers,
　　Flap on the latticed wall ;
And o'er the mossy ridge-pole towers
　　The rock-hewn chimney tall.

The doors on mighty hinges clash
  With massive bolt and bar,
The heavy English-moulded sash
  Scarce can the night-winds jar.

Behold the chosen room he sought
  Alone, to fast and pray,
Each year, as chill November brought
  The dismal earthquake day.

There hung the rapier blade he wore,
  Bent in its flattened sheath ;
The coat the shrieking woman tore
  Caught in her clenching teeth ; —

The coat with tarnished silver lace
  She snapped at as she slid,
And down upon her death-white face
  Crashed the huge coffin's lid.

A graded terrace yet remains ;
  If on its turf you stand
And look along the wooded plains
  That stretch on either hand,

The broken forest walls define
  A dim, receding view,
Where, on the far horizon's line,
  He cut his vista through.

If further story you shall crave,
  Or ask for living proof,
Go see old Julia, born a slave
  Beneath Sir Harry's roof.

She told me half that I have told,
  And she remembers well
The mansion as it looked of old
  Before its glories fell ; —

The box, when round the terraced square
  Its glossy wall was drawn ;
The climbing vines, the snow-balls fair,
  The roses on the lawn.

And Julia says, with truthful look
  Stamped on her wrinkled face,
That in her own black hands she took
  The coat with silver lace.

And you may hold the story light,
  Or, if you like, believe ;
But there it was, the woman's bite, —
  A mouthful from the sleeve.

Now go your ways ; — I need not tell
  The moral of my rhyme ;
But, youths and maidens, ponder well
  This tale of olden time !

THE PLOUGHMAN.

ANNIVERSARY OF THE BERKSHIRE AG-
RICULTURAL SOCIETY, OCT. 4, 1849.

CLEAR the brown path, to meet his coul-
    ter's gleam !
Lo ! on he comes, behind his smoking
    team,
With toil's bright dew-drops on his sun-
    burnt brow,
The lord of earth, the hero of the plough !

First in the field before the reddening
    sun,
Last in the shadows when the day is
    done,
Line after line, along the bursting sod,
Marks the broad acres where his feet
    have trod ;
Still, where he treads, the stubborn clods
    divide,
The smooth, fresh furrow opens deep and
    wide ;
Matted and dense the tangled turf up-
    heaves,
Mellow and dark the ridgy cornfield
    cleaves ;
Up the steep hillside, where the labor-
    ing train

Slants the long track that scores the
    level plain ;
Through the moist valley, clogged with
    oozing clay,
The patient convoy breaks its destined
    way ;
At every turn the loosening chains re-
    sound,
The swinging ploughshare circles glisten-
    ing round,
Till the wide field one billowy waste ap-
    pears,
And wearied hands unbind the panting
    steers.

These are the hands whose sturdy labor
    brings
The peasant's food, the golden pomp of
    kings ;
This is the page, whose letters shall be
    seen
Changed by the sun to words of living
    green ;
This is the scholar, whose immortal pen
Spells the first lesson hunger taught to
    men ;
These are the lines which heaven-com-
    manded Toil
Shows on his deed, — the charter of the
    soil !

O gracious Mother, whose benignant
    breast
Wakes us to life, and lulls us all to rest,
How thy sweet features, kind to every
    clime,
Mock with their smile the wrinkled front
    of time !
We stain thy flowers, — they blossom
    o'er the dead ;
We rend thy bosom, and it gives us
    bread ;
O'er the red field that trampling strife
    has torn,

Waves the green plumage of thy tasselled
    corn ;
Our maddening conflicts scar thy fairest
    plain,
Still thy soft answer is the growing grain.
Yet, O our Mother, while uncounted
    charms
Steal round our hearts in thine embrac-
    ing arms,
Let not our virtues in thy love decay,
And thy fond sweetness waste our
    strength away.

No ! by these hills, whose banners now
    displayed
In blazing cohorts Autumn has arrayed ;
By yon twin summits, on whose splin-
    tery crests
The tossing hemlocks hold the eagles'
    nests ;
By these fair plains the mountain circle
    screens,
And feeds with streamlets from its dark
    ravines, —
True to their home, these faithful arms
    shall toil
To crown with peace their own untainted
    soil ;
And, true to God, to freedom, to man-
    kind,
If her chained bandogs Faction shall
    unbind,
These stately forms, that bending even
    now
Bowed their strong manhood to the
    humble plough,
Shall rise erect, the guardians of the
    land,
The same stern iron in the same right
    hand,
Till o'er their hills the shouts of triumph
    run,
The sword has rescued what the plough-
    share won !

PICTURES FROM OCCASIONAL POEMS.

1850 - 56.

SPRING.

WINTER is past ; the heart of Nature
warms
Beneath the wrecks of unresisted storms ;
Doubtful at first, suspected more than
seen,
The southern slopes are fringed with
tender green ;
On sheltered banks, beneath the drip-
ping eaves,
Spring's earliest nurslings spread their
glowing leaves,
Bright with the hues from wider pic-
tures won,
White, azure, golden, — drift, or sky,
or sun, —
The snowdrop, bearing on her patient
breast
The frozen trophy torn from Winter's
crest ;
The violet, gazing on the arch of blue
Till her own iris wears its deepened hue ;
The spendthrift crocus, bursting through
the mould
Naked and shivering with his cup of gold.
Swelled with new life, the darkening
elm on high
Prints her thick buds against the spotted
sky ;
On all her boughs the stately chestnut
cleaves
The gummy shroud that wraps her
embryo leaves ;
The house-fly, stealing from his narrow
grave,
Drugged with the opiate that November
gave,
Beats with faint wing against the sunny
pane,
Or crawls, tenacious, o'er its lucid plain ;
From shaded chinks of lichen-crusted
walls,
In languid curves, the gliding serpent
crawls ;
The bog's green harper, thawing from
his sleep,
Twangs a hoarse note and tries a shortened leap ;
On floating rails that face the softening
noons
The still shy turtles range their dark
platoons,
Or, toiling aimless o'er the mellowing
fields,
Trail through the grass their tessellated
shields.

At last young April, ever frail and fair,
Wooed by her playmate with the golden
hair,
Chased to the margin of receding floods
O'er the soft meadows starred with open-
ing buds,
In tears and blushes sighs herself away,
And hides her cheek beneath the flowers
of May.

Then the proud tulip lights her beacon
blaze,
Her clustering curls the hyacinth displays ;

O'er her tall blades the crested fleur-de-
lis,
Like blue-eyed Pallas, towers erect and
free ;
With yellower flames the lengthened
sunshine glows,
And love lays bare the passion-breathing
rose ;
Queen of the lake, along its reedy verge
The rival lily hastens to emerge,
Her snowy shoulders glistening as she
strips,
Till morn is sultan of her parted lips.

Then bursts the song from every leafy
glade,
The yielding season's bridal serenade ;
Then flash the wings returning Summer
calls
Through the deep arches of her forest
halls, —
The bluebird, breathing from his azure
plumes
The fragrance borrowed where the myrtle
blooms ;
The thrush, poor wanderer, dropping
meekly down,
Clad in his remnant of autumnal brown ;
The oriole, drifting like a flake of fire
Rent by a whirlwind from a blazing
spire.
The robin, jerking his spasmodic throat,
Repeats, imperious, his *staccato* note ;
The crack-brained bobolink courts his
crazy mate,
Poised on a bulrush tipsy with his
weight ;
Nay, in his cage the lone canary sings,
Feels the soft air, and spreads his idle
wings.

Why dream I here within these caging
walls,
Deaf to her voice, while blooming Nature calls ;

Peering and gazing with insatiate looks
Through blinding lenses, or in wearying
books ?
Off, gloomy spectres of the shrivelled
past !
Fly with the leaves that fill the autumn
blast !
Ye imps of Science, whose relentless
chains
Lock the warm tides within these living
veins,
Close your dim cavern, while its captive
strays
Dazzled and giddy in the morning's
blaze !

THE STUDY.

YET in the darksome crypt I left so
late,
Whose only altar is its rusted grate, —
Sepulchral, rayless, joyless as it seems,
Shamed by the glare of May's refulgent
beams, —
While the dim seasons dragged their
shrouded train,
Its paler splendors were not quite in
vain.
From these dull bars the cheerful fire-
light's glow
Streamed through the casement o'er the
spectral snow ;
Here, while the night-wind wreaked its
frantic will
On the loose ocean and the rock-bound
hill,
Rent the cracked topsail from its quiver-
ing yard,
And rived the oak a thousand storms
had scarred,
Fenced by these walls the peaceful taper
shone,
Nor felt a breath to slant its trembling
cone.

Not all unblest the mild interior scene
When the red curtain spread its falling
    screen ;
O'er some light task the lonely hours
    were past,
And the long evening only flew too fast ;
Or the wide chair its leathern arms would
    lend
In genial welcome to some easy friend,
Stretched on its bosom with relaxing
    nerves,
Slow moulding, plastic, to its hollow
    curves ;
Perchance indulging, if of generous
    creed,
In brave Sir Walter's dream-compelling
    weed.
Or, happier still, the evening hour would
    bring
To the round table its expected ring,
And while the punch-bowl's sounding
    depths were stirred, —
Its silver cherubs smiling as they
    heard, —
Our hearts would open, as at evening's
    hour
The close-sealed primrose frees its hid-
    den flower.

Such the warm life this dim retreat
    has known,
Not quite deserted when its guests were
    flown ;
Nay, filled with friends, an unobtrusive
    set,
Guiltless of calls and cards and etiquette,
Ready to answer, never known to ask,
Claiming no service, prompt for every
    task.

On those dark shelves no housewife
    hand profanes,
O'er his mute files the monarch folio
    reigns ;

A mingled race, the wreck of chance
    and time,
That talk all tongues and breathe of
    every clime,
Each knows his place, and each may
    claim his part
In some quaint corner of his master's
    heart.
This old Decretal, won from Kloss's
    hoards,
Thick-leaved, brass-cornered, ribbed
    with oaken boards,
Stands the gray patriarch of the graver
    rows,
Its fourth ripe century narrowing to its
    close ;
Not daily conned, but glorious still to
    view,
With glistening letters wrought in red
    and blue.
There towers Stagira's all-embracing
    sage,
The Aldine anchor on his opening page ;
There sleep the births of Plato's heavenly
    mind,
In yon dark tomb by jealous clasps con-
    fined,
"Olim e libris" (dare I call it mine ?)
Of Yale's grave Head and Killingworth's
    divine !
In those square sheets the songs of Maro
    fill
The silvery types of smooth-leaved Bas-
    kerville ;
High over all, in close, compact array,
Their classic wealth the Elzevirs display.
In lower regions of the sacred space
Range the dense volumes of a humbler
    race ;
There grim chirurgeons all their mys-
    teries teach,
In spectral pictures, or in crabbed
    speech ;
Harvey and Haller, fresh from Nature's
    page,

Shoulder the dreamers of an earlier age,
Lully and Geber, and the learned crew
That loved to talk of all they could not
do.
Why count the rest, — those names of
later days
That many love, and all agree to
praise, —
Or point the titles, where a glance may
read
The dangerous lines of party or of creed?
Too well, perchance, the chosen list
would show
What few may care and none can claim
to know.
Each has his features, whose exterior seal
A brush may copy, or a sunbeam steal;
Go to his study, — on the nearest shelf
Stands the mosaic portrait of himself.

What though for months the tranquil
dust descends,
Whitening the heads of these mine ancient friends,
While the damp offspring of the modern
press
Flaunts on my table with its pictured
dress;
Not less I love each dull familiar face,
Nor less should miss it from the appointed place;
I snatch the book, along whose burning
leaves
His scarlet web our wild romancer
weaves,
Yet, while proud Hester's fiery pangs I
share,
My old MAGNALIA must be standing
there!

THE BELLS.

WHEN o'er the street the morning peal
is flung
From yon tall belfry with the brazen
tongue,
Its wide vibrations, wafted by the gale,
To each far listener tell a different tale.
The sexton, stooping to the quivering
floor
Till the great caldron spills its brassy
roar,
Whirls the hot axle, counting, one by
one,
Each dull concussion, till his task is
done.
Toil's patient daughter, when the wel-
come note
Clangs through the silence from the
steeple's throat,
Streams, a white unit, to the checkered
street,
Demure, but guessing whom she soon
shall meet;
The bell, responsive to her secret flame,
With every note repeats her lover's
name.
The lover, tenant of the neighboring
lane,
Sighing, and fearing lest he sigh in vain,
Hears the stern accents, as they come
and go,
Their only burden one despairing No!
Ocean's rough child, whom many a
shore has known
Ere homeward breezes swept him to his
own,
Starts at the echo as it circles round,
A thousand memories kindling with the
sound;
The early favorite's unforgotten charms,
Whose blue initials stain his tawny
arms;
His first farewell, the flapping canvas
spread,
The seaward streamers crackling over-
head,
His kind, pale mother, not ashamed to
weep
Her first-born's bridal with the haggard
deep,

While the brave father stood with tearless eye,
Smiling and choking with his last good-
by.

T is but a wave, whose spreading circle beats,
With the same impulse, every nerve it
meets,
Yet who shall count the varied shapes
that ride
On the round surge of that aerial tide !

O child of earth ! If floating sounds
like these
Steal from thyself their power to wound
or please,
If here or there thy changing will in-
clines,
As the bright zodiac shifts its rolling
signs,
Look at thy heart, and when its depths
are known
Then try thy brother's, judging by thine
own,
But keep thy wisdom to the narrower
range,
While its own standards are the sport of
change,
Nor count us rebels when we disobey
The passing breath that holds thy passion's sway.

NON-RESISTANCE.

PERHAPS too far in these considerate
days
Has patience carried her submissive
ways ;
Wisdom has taught us to be calm and
meek,
To take one blow, and turn the other
cheek ;
It is not written what a man shall do,
If the rude caitiff smite the other too !

Land of our fathers, in thine hour of
need
God help thee, guarded by the passive
creed !
As the lone pilgrim trusts to beads and
cowl,
When through the forest rings the gray
wolf's howl ;
As the deep galleon trusts her gilded
prow
When the black corsair slants athwart
her bow ;
As the poor pheasant, with his peaceful
mien,
Trusts to his feathers, shining golden-
green,
When the dark plumage with the crim-
son beak
Has rustled shadowy from its splintered
peak, —
So trust thy friends, whose babbling
tongues would charm
The lifted sabre from thy foeman's arm,
Thy torches ready for the answering peal
From bellowing fort and thunder-
freighted keel !

THE MORAL BULLY.

YON whey-faced brother, who delights
to wear
A weedy flux of ill-conditioned hair,
Seems of the sort that in a crowded
place
One elbows freely into smallest space ;
A timid creature, lax of knee and hip,
Whom small disturbance whitens round
the lip ;
One of those harmless spectacled ma-
chines,
The Holy-Week of Protestants convenes ;
Whom school-boys question if their walk
transcends
The last advices of maternal friends ;

Whom John, obedient to his master's
sign,
Conducts, laborious, up to *ninety-nine*,
While Peter, glistening with luxurious
scorn,
Husks his white ivories like an ear of
corn ;
Dark in the brow and bilious in the
cheek,
Whose yellowish linen flowers but once
a week,
Conspicuous, annual, in their threadbare
suits,
And the laced high-lows which they call
their boots
Well mayst thou *shun* that dingy front
severe,
But him, O stranger, him thou canst not
fear !

Be slow to judge, and slower to de-
spise,
Man of broad shoulders and heroic
size !
The tiger, writhing from the boa's rings,
Drops at the fountain where the cobra
stings.
In that lean phantom, whose extended
glove
Points to the text of universal love,
Behold the master that can tame thee
down
To crouch, the vassal of his Sunday
frown ;
His velvet throat against thy corded
wrist,
His loosened tongue against thy doubled
fist !

The MORAL BULLY, though he never
swears,
Nor kicks intruders down his entry
stairs,
Though meekness plants his backward-
sloping hat,

And non-resistance ties his white cravat,
Though his black broadcloth glories to
be seen
In the same plight with Shylock's gaber-
dine,
Hugs the same passion to his narrow
breast
That heaves the cuirass on the trooper's
chest,
Hears the same hell-hounds yelling in
his rear
That chase from port the maddened buc-
caneer,
Feels the same comfort while his acrid
words
Turn the sweet milk of kindness into
curds,
Or with grim logic prove, beyond debate,
That all we love is worthiest of our
hate,
As the scarred ruffian of the pirate's
deck,
When his long swivel rakes the staggering wreck !

Heaven keep us all !   Is every rascal
clown
Whose arm is stronger free to knock us
down ?
Has every scarecrow, whose cachectic
soul
Seems fresh from Bedlam, airing on pa-
role,
Who, though he carries but a doubtful
trace
Of angel visits on his hungry face,
From lack of marrow or the coins to
pay,
Has dodged some vices in a shabby
way,
The right to stick us with his cutthroat
terms,
And bait his homilies with his brother
worms ?

THE MIND'S DIET.

No life worth naming ever comes to
  good
If always nourished on the selfsame
  food ;
The creeping mite may live so if he please,
And feed on Stilton till he turns to cheese,
But cool Magendie proves beyond a
  doubt,
If mammals try it, that their eyes drop
  out.

No reasoning natures find it safe to
  feed,
For their sole diet, on a single creed ;
It spoils their eyeballs while it spares
  their tongues,
And starves the heart to feed the noisy
  lungs.

When the first larvæ on the elm are
  seen,
The crawling wretches, like its leaves,
  are green ;
Ere chill October shakes the latest down,
They, like the foliage, change their tint
  to brown ;
On the blue flower a bluer flower you spy,
You stretch to pluck it — 't is a butter-
  fly ;
The flattened tree-toads so resemble bark,
They 're hard to find as Ethiops in the
  dark ;
The woodcock, stiffening to fictitious
  mud,
Cheats the young sportsman thirsting for
  his blood ;
So by long living on a single lie,
Nay, on one truth, will creatures get its
  dye ;
Red, yellow, green, they take their sub-
  ject's hue. —
Except when squabbling turns them
  black and blue !

OUR LIMITATIONS.

WE trust and fear, we question and
  believe,
From life's dark threads a trembling
  faith to weave,
Frail as the web that misty night has
  spun,
Whose dew-gemmed awnings glitter in
  the sun.
While the calm centuries spell their lessons out,
Each truth we conquer spreads the realm
  of doubt ;
When Sinai's summit was Jehovah's
  throne,
The chosen Prophet knew his voice
  alone ;
When Pilate's hall that awful question
  heard,
The Heavenly Captive answered not a
  word.

Eternal Truth ! beyond our hopes and
  fears
Sweep the vast orbits of thy myriad
  spheres !
From age to age, while History carves
  sublime
On her waste rock the flaming curves of
  time,
How the wild swayings of our planet
  show
That worlds unseen surround the world
  we know.

THE OLD PLAYER.

THE curtain rose ; in thunders long
  and loud
The galleries rung ; the veteran actor
  bowed.
In flaming line the telltales of the stage
Showed on his brow the autograph of
  age ;

Pale, hueless waves amid his clustered
    hair,
And umbered shadows, prints of toil
    and care;
Round the wide circle glanced his vacant
    eye, —
He strove to speak, — his voice was but
    a sigh.

Year after year had seen its short-
    lived race
Flit past the scenes and others take their
    place;
Yet the old prompter watched his accents
    still,
His name still flaunted on the evening's
    bill.
Heroes, the monarchs of the scenic floor,
Had died in earnest and were heard no
    more;
Beauties, whose cheeks such roseate
    bloom o'erspread
They faced the footlights in unborrowed
    red,
Had faded slowly through successive
    shades
To gray duennas, foils of younger maids;
Sweet voices lost the melting tones that
    start
With Southern throbs the sturdy Saxon
    heart,
While fresh sopranos shook the painted
    sky
With their long, breathless, quivering
    locust-cry.
Yet there he stood, — the man of other
    days,
In the clear present's full, unsparing
    blaze,
As on the oak a faded leaf that clings
While a new April spreads its burnished
    wings.

How bright yon rows that soared in
    triple tier,

Their central sun the flashing chandelier!
How dim the eye that sought with
    doubtful aim
Some friendly smile it still might dare
    to claim!
How fresh these hearts! his own how
    worn and cold!
Such the sad thoughts that long-drawn
    sigh had told.
    No word yet faltered on his trembling
    tongue;
Again, again, the crashing galleries rung.
As the old guardsman at the bugle's blast
Hears in its strain the echoes of the past;
So, as the plaudits rolled and thundered
    round,
A life of memories startled at the sound.
    He lived again, — the page of earliest
    days, —
Days of small fee and parsimonious
    praise;
Then lithe young Romeo — hark that
    silvered tone,
From those smooth lips — alas! they
    were his own.
Then the bronzed Moor, with all his
    love and woe,
Told his strange tale of midnight melt-
    ing snow;
And dark-plumed Hamlet, with his
    cloak and blade,
Looked on the royal ghost, himself a
    shade.
All in one flash, his youthful memories
    came,
Traced in bright hues of evanescent
    flame,
As the spent swimmer's in the lifelong
    dream,
While the last bubble rises through the
    stream.

    Call him not old, whose visionary
    brain
Holds o'er the past its undivided reign.

For him in vain the envious seasons roll
Who bears eternal summer in his soul.
If yet the minstrel's song, the poet's lay,
Spring with her birds, or children at
their play,
Or maiden's smile, or heavenly dream
of art,
Stir the few life-drops creeping round
his heart,
Turn to the record where his years are
told, —
Count his gray hairs, — they cannot
make him old!
What magic power has changed the
faded mime?
One breath of memory on the dust of
time.
As the last window in the buttressed wall
Of some gray minster tottering to its fall,
Though to the passing crowd its hues
are spread,
A dull mosaic, yellow, green, and red,
Viewed from within, a radiant glory
shows
When through its pictured screen the
sunlight flows,
And kneeling pilgrims on its storied pane
See angels glow in every shapeless stain;
So streamed the vision through his
sunken eye,
Clad in the splendors of his morning sky.
All the wild hopes his eager boyhood
knew,
All the young fancies riper years proved
true,
The sweet, low-whispered words, the
winning glance
From queens of song, from Houris of
the dance,
Wealth's lavish gift, and Flattery's
soothing phrase,
And Beauty's silence when her blush
was praise,
And melting Pride, her lashes wet with
tears,

Triumphs and banquets, wreaths and
crowns and cheers,
Pangs of wild joy that perish on the
tongue,
And all that poets dream, but leave
unsung!

In every heart some viewless founts
are fed
From far-off hillsides where the dews
were shed;
On the worn features of the weariest face
Some youthful memory leaves its hidden
trace,
As in old gardens left by exiled kings
The marble basins tell of hidden springs,
But, gray with dust, and overgrown with
weeds,
Their choking jets the passer little heeds,
Till time's revenges break their seals
away,
And, clad in rainbow light, the waters
play.

Good night, fond dreamer! let the
curtain fall:
The world 's a stage, and we are players
all.
A strange rehearsal! Kings without
their crowns,
And threadbare lords, and jewel-wear-
ing clowns,
Speak the vain words that mock their
throbbing hearts,
As Want, stern prompter! spells them
out their parts.
The tinselled hero whom we praise and pay
Is twice an actor in a twofold play.
We smile at children when a painted
screen
Seems to their simple eyes a real scene;
Ask the poor hireling, who has left his
throne
To seek the cheerless home he calls his
own,

108   SONGS IN MANY KEYS.

Which of his double lives most real
    seems,
The world of solid fact or scenic dreams?
Canvas, or clouds, — the footlights, or
    the spheres, —
The play of two short hours, or seventy
    years?
    Dream on! Though Heaven may woo
        our open eyes,
Through their closed lids we look on
    fairer skies;
Truth is for other worlds, and hope for
    this;
The cheating future lends the present's
    bliss;
Life is a running shade, with fettered
    hands,
That chases phantoms over shifting
    sands;
Death a still spectre on a marble seat,
With ever clutching palms and shackled
    feet;
The airy shapes that mock life's slender
    chain,
The flying joys he strives to clasp in vain,
Death only grasps; to live is to pur-
    sue, —
    Dream on! there's nothing but illusion
        true!

THE ISLAND RUIN.

    YE that have faced the billows and
        the spray
Of good St. Botolph's island-studded
    bay,
As from the gliding bark your eye has
    scanned
The beaconed rocks, the wave-girt hills
    of sand,
Have ye not marked one elm-o'ershad-
    owed isle,
Round as the dimple chased in beauty's
    smile, —

A stain of verdure on an azure field,
Set like a jewel in a battered shield?
Fixed in the narrow gorge of Ocean's
    path,
Peaceful it meets him in his hour of
    wrath;
When the mailed Titan, scourged by
    hissing gales,
Writhes in his glistening coat of clash-
    ing scales;
The storm-beat island spreads its tran-
    quil green,
Calm as an emerald on an angry queen.
    So fair when distant should be fairer
        near;
A boat shall waft us from the out-
    stretched pier.
The breeze blows fresh; we reach the
    island's edge,
Our shallop rustling through the yield-
    ing sedge.
    No welcome greets us on the desert
        isle;
Those elms, far-shadowing, hide no
    stately pile:
Yet these green ridges mark an ancient
    road;
And lo! the traces of a fair abode;
The long gray line that marks a garden
    wall,
And heaps of fallen beams, — fire-
    branded all.

    Who sees unmoved, a ruin at his feet,
The lowliest home where human hearts
    have beat?
Its hearthstone, shaded with the bistre
    stain
A century's showery torrents wash in
    vain;
Its starving orchard, where the thistle
    blows
And mossy trunks still mark the broken
    rows;
Its chimney-loving poplar, oftenest seen

Next an old roof, or where a roof has
    been ;
Its knot-grass, plantain, — all the social
    weeds,
Man's mute companions, following where
    he leads ;
Its dwarfed, pale flowers, that show their
    straggling heads,
Sown by the wind from grass-choked
    garden-beds ;
Its woodbine, creeping where it used to
    climb ;
Its roses, breathing of the olden time ;
All the poor shows the curious idler sees,
As life's thin shadows waste by slow
    degrees,
Till naught remains, the saddening tale
    to tell,
Save home's last wrecks, — the cellar
    and the well !

    And whose the home that strews in
    black decay
The one green-glowing island of the bay ?
Some dark-browed pirate's, jealous of
    the fate
That seized the strangled wretch of
    " Nix's Mate" ?
Some forger's, skulking in a borrowed
    name,
Whom Tyburn's dangling halter yet
    may claim?
Some wan-eyed exile's, wealth and sor-
    row's heir,
Who sought a lone retreat for tears and
    prayer ?
Some brooding poet's, sure of deathless
    fame,
Had not his epic perished in the flame ?
Or some gray wooer's, whom a girlish
    frown
Chased from his solid friends and sober
    town ?
Or some plain tradesman's, fond of shade
    and ease,

Who sought them both beneath these
    quiet trees ?
Why question mutes no question can
    unlock,
Dumb as the legend on the Dighton rock?
One thing at least these ruined heaps
    declare, —
They were a shelter once ; a man lived
    there.

    But where the charred and crumbling
    records fail,
Some breathing lips may piece the half-
    told tale ;
No man may live with neighbors such
    as these,
Though girt with walls of rock and angry
    seas,
And shield his home, his children, or
    his wife,
His ways, his means, his vote, his creed,
    his life,
From the dread sovereignty of Ears and
    Eyes
And the small member that beneath
    them lies.
    They told strange things of that mys-
    terious man ;
Believe who will, deny them such as can ;
Why should we fret if every passing sail
Had its old seaman talking on the rail ?
The deep-sunk schooner stuffed with
    Eastern lime,
Slow wedging on, as if the waves were
    slime ;
The knife-edged clipper with her ruffled
    spars,
The pawing steamer with her mane of
    stars,
The bull-browed galliot butting through
    the stream,
The wide-sailed yacht that slipped along
    her beam,
The deck-piled sloops, the pinched che-
    bacco-boats,

The frigate, black with thunder-freighted
    throats,
All had their talk about the lonely man ;
And thus, in varying phrase, the story
    ran.
  His name had cost him little care to
    seek,
Plain, honest, brief, a decent name to
    speak,
Common, not vulgar, just the kind that
    slips
With least suggestion from a stranger's
    lips.
His birthplace England, as his speech
    might show,
Or his hale cheek, that wore the red-
    streak's glow ;
His mouth sharp-moulded ; in its mirth
    or scorn
There came a flash as from the milky corn,
When from the ear you rip the rustling
    sheath,
And the white ridges show their even
    teeth.
His stature moderate, but his strength
    confessed,
In spite of broadcloth, by his ample
    breast ;
Full-armed, thick-handed ; one that
    had been strong,
And might be dangerous still, if things
    went wrong.
He lived at ease beneath his elm-trees'
    shade,
Did naught for gain, yet all his debts
    were paid ;
Rich, so 't was thought, but careful of
    his store ;
Had all he needed, claimed to have no
    more.

  But some that lingered round the isle
    at night
Spoke of strange stealthy doings in their
    sight ;

Of creeping lonely visits that he made
To nooks and corners, with a torch and
    spade.
Some said they saw the hollow of a cave ;
One, given to fables, swore it was a grave ;
Whereat some shuddered, others boldly
    cried,
Those prowling boatmen lied, and knew
    they lied.
  They said his house was framed with
    curious cares,
Lest some old friend might enter un-
    awares ;
That on the platform at his chamber's
    door
Hinged a loose square that opened
    through the floor ;
Touch the black silken tassel next the
    bell,
Down, with a crash, the flapping trap-
    door fell ;
Three stories deep the falling wretch
    would strike,
To writhe at leisure on a boarder's pike.
  By day armed always ; double-armed
    at night,
His tools lay round him ; wake him
    such as might.
A carbine hung beside his India fan,
His hand could reach a Turkish ataghan ;
Pistols, with quaint-carved stocks and
    barrels gilt,
Crossed a long dagger with a jewelled
    hilt ;
A slashing cutlass stretched along the
    bed ; —
All this was what those lying boatmen
    said.
  Then some were full of wondrous sto-
    ries told
Of great oak chests and cupboards full of
    gold ;
Of the wedged ingots and the silver
    bars
That cost old pirates ugly sabre-scars ;

How his laced wallet often would dis-
gorge
The fresh-faced guinea of an English
George,
Or sweated ducat, palmed by Jews of
yore,
Or double Joe, or Portuguese moidore,
And how his finger wore a rubied ring
Fit for the white-necked play-girl of a
king.
But these fine legends, told with staring
eyes,
Met with small credence from the old
and wise.

Why tell each idle guess, each whisper
vain?
Enough : the scorched and cindered
beams remain.
He came, a silent pilgrim to the West,
Some old-world mystery throbbing in
his breast;
Close to the thronging mart he dwelt
alone ;
He lived ; he died.   The rest is all unknown.

Stranger, whose eyes the shadowy isle
survey,
As the black steamer dashes through
the bay,
Why ask his buried secret to divine?
He was thy brother; speak, and tell us
thine !

THE BANKER'S DINNER.

THE Banker's dinner is the stateliest
feast
The town has heard of for a year, at
least ;
The sparry lustres shed their broadest
blaze,
Damask and silver catch and spread the
rays ;

The florist's triumphs crown the daintier
spoil
Won from the sea, the forest, or the soil ;
The steaming hot-house yields its largest
pines,
The sunless vaults unearth their oldest
wines ;
With one admiring look the scene survey,
And turn a moment from the bright display.

Of all the joys of earthly pride or
power,
What gives most life, worth living, in
an hour?
When Victory settles on the doubtful
fight
And the last foeman wheels in panting
flight,
No thrill like this is felt beneath the
sun ;
Life's sovereign moment is a battle won.
But say what next?   To shape a Senate's
choice,
By the strong magic of the master's
voice ;
To ride the stormy tempest of debate
That whirls the wavering fortunes of the
state.
Third in the list, the happy lover's
prize
Is won by honeyed words from women's
eyes.
If some would have it first instead of
third,
So let it be, — I answer not a word.
The fourth, — sweet readers, let the
thoughtless half
Have its small shrug and inoffensive
laugh ;
Let the grave quarter wear its virtuous
frown,
The stern half-quarter try to scowl us
down ;

But the last eighth, the choice and
　　sifted few,
Will hear my words, and, pleased, con-
　　fess them true.

　　Among the great whom Heaven has
　　　made to shine,
How few have learned the art of arts, --
　　to dine!
Nature, indulgent to our daily need,
Kind-hearted mother! taught us all to
　　feed;
But the chief art, — how rarely Nature
　　flings
This choicest gift among her social
　　kings!
Say, man of truth, has life a brighter
　　hour
Than waits the chosen guest who knows
　　his power?
　　He moves with ease, itself an angel
　　　charm, —
Lifts with light touch my lady's jewelled
　　arm,
Slides to his seat, half leading and half
　　led,
Smiling but quiet till the grace is said,
Then gently kindles, while by slow de-
　　grees
Creep softly out the little arts that
　　please;
Bright looks, the cheerful language of
　　the eye,
The neat, crisp question and the gay
　　reply, —
Talk light and airy, such as well may
　　pass
Between the rested fork and lifted
　　glass;—
With play like this the earlier evening
　　flies,
Till rustling silks proclaim the ladies
　　rise.
　　His hour has come, — he looks along
　　　the chairs,

As the Great Duke surveyed his iron
　　squares.
— That's the young traveller, — isn't
　　much to show, —
Fast on the road, but at the table slow.
— Next him, — you see the author in
　　his look, —
His forehead lined with wrinkles like a
　　book, —
Wrote the great history of the ancient
　　Huns, —
Holds back to fire among the heavy
　　guns.
— O, there's our poet seated at his side,
Beloved of ladies, soft, cerulean-eyed.
Poets are prosy in their common talk,
As the fast trotters, for the most part,
　　walk.
— And there's our well-dressed gentle-
　　man, who sits,
By right divine, no doubt, among the
　　wits,
Who airs his tailor's patterns when he
　　walks,
The man that often speaks, but never
　　talks.
Why should he talk, whose presence
　　lends a grace
To every table where he shows his face?
He knows the manual of the silver fork,
Can name his claret — if he sees the
　　cork, —
Remark that "White-top" was consid-
　　ered fine,
But swear the "Juno" is the better
　　wine;—
Is not this talking? Ask Quintilian's
　　rules;
If they say No, the town has many fools.
— Pause for a moment, — for our eyes
　　behold
The plain unsceptred king, the man of
　　gold,
The thrice illustrious threefold million-
　　naire;

Mark his slow-creeping, dead, metallic
stare;
His eyes, dull glimmering, like the bal-
ance-pan
That weighs its guinea as he weighs his
man.
— Who's next? An artist, in a satin tie
Whose ample folds defeat the curious
eye.
— And there's the cousin, — must be
asked, you know, —
Looks like a spinster at a baby-show.
Hope he is cool, — they set him next
the door, —
And likes his place, between the gap
and bore.
— Next comes a Congress-man, distin-
guished guest!
We don't count him, — they asked him
with the rest;
And then some white cravats, with well-
shaped ties,
And heads above them which their
owners prize.

Of all that cluster round the genial
board,
Not one so radiant as the banquet's lord.
Some say they fancy, but they know not
why,
A shade of trouble brooding in his
eye,
Nothing, perhaps, — the rooms are over-
hot, —
Yet see his cheek, — the dull-red burn-
ing spot, —
Taste the brown sherry which he does
not pass, —
Ha! That is brandy; see him fill his
glass!
But not forgetful of his feasting
friends,
To each in turn some lively word he
sends;
See how he throws his baited lines about,

And plays his men as anglers play their
trout.

With the dry sticks all bonfires are
begun;
Bring the first fagot, proser number one!
A question drops among the listening
crew
And hits the traveller, pat on Tim-
buctoo.
We're on the Niger, somewhere near its
source, —
Not the least hurry, take the river's
course
Through Kissi, Foota, Kankan, Bamma-
koo,
Bambarra, Sego, so to Timbuctoo,
Thence down to Youri; — stop him if
we can,
We can't fare worse, — wake up the
Congress-man!
The Congress-man, once on his talking
legs,
Stirs up his knowledge to its thickest
dregs;
Tremendous draught for dining men to
quaff!
Nothing will choke him but a purpling
laugh.
A word, — a shout, — a mighty roar, —
't is done;
Extinguished; lassoed by a treacherous
pun.
A laugh is priming to the loaded soul;
The scattering shots become a steady
roll,
Broke by sharp cracks that run along
the line,
The light artillery of the talker's wine.
The kindling goblets flame with golden
dews,
The hoarded flasks their tawny fire dif-
fuse,
And the Rhine's breast-milk gushes cold
and bright,

Pale as the moon and maddening as her
 light ;
With crimson juice the thirsty southern
 sky
Sucks from the hills where buried armies
 lie,
So that the dreamy passion it imparts
Is drawn from heroes' bones and lovers'
 hearts.
 But lulls will come ; the flashing soul
  transmits
Its gleams of light in alternating fits.
The shower of talk that rattled down
 amain
Ends in small patterings like an April's
 rain ;
The voices halt ; the game is at a stand ;
Now for a solo from the master-hand !
 'T is but a story, — quite a simple
  thing, —
An *aria* touched upon a single string,
But every accent comes with such a
 grace
The stupid servants listen in their place,
Each with his waiter in his lifted hands,
Still as a well-bred pointer when he
 stands.
A query checks him : " Is he quite ex-
 act ? " —
(This from a grizzled, square-jawed man
 of fact.)
The sparkling story leaves him to his
 fate,
Crushed by a witness, smothered with
 a date,
As a swift river, sown with many a
 star,
Runs brighter, rippling on a shallow
 bar.
The smooth divine suggests a graver
 doubt ;
A neat quotation bowls the parson out ;
Then, sliding gayly from his own dis-
 play,
He laughs the learned dulness all away.

So, with the merry tale and jovial
 song,
The jocund evening whirls itself along,
Till the last chorus shrieks its loud *encore*,
And the white neckcloths vanish
 through the door.

 One savage word ! — The menials
  know its tone,
And slink away ; the master stands
 alone.
" Well played, by — " ; breathe not
 what were best unheard ;
His goblet shivers while he speaks the
 word, —
" If wine tells truth, — and so have said
 the wise, —
It makes me laugh to think how brandy
 lies !
Bankrupt to-morrow, — millionnaire to-
 day, —
The farce is over, — now begins the
 play ! "
 The spring he touches lets a panel
  glide ;
An iron closet lurks beneath the slide,
Bright with such treasures as a search
 might bring
From the deep pockets of a truant king.
Two diamonds, eyeballs of a God of
 bronze,
Bought from his faithful priest, a pious
 Bonze ;
A string of brilliants ; rubies, three or
 four ;
Bags of old coin and bars of virgin ore ;
A jewelled poniard and a Turkish knife,
Noiseless and useful if we come to strife.
 Gone ! As a pirate flies before the
  wind,
And not one tear for all he leaves be-
 hind !
From all the love his better years have
 known

Fled like a felon, — ah ! but not alone !
The chariot flashes through a lantern's
glare, —
O the wild eyes ! the storm of sable
hair !
Still to his side the broken heart will
cling, —
The bride of shame, the wife without
the ring :
Hark, the deep oath, — the wail of frenzied woe, —
Lost ! lost to hope of Heaven and peace
below !

He kept his secret ; but the seed of
crime
Bursts of itself in God's appointed time.
The lives he wrecked were scattered far
and wide ;
One never blamed nor wept, — she only
died.
None knew his lot, though idle tongues
would say
He sought a lonely refuge far away,
And there, with borrowed name and al-
tered mien,
He died unheeded, as he lived unseen.
The moral market had the usual chills
Of Virtue suffering from protested bills ;
The White Cravats, to friendship's mem-
ory true,
Sighed for the past, surveyed the future
too ;
Their sorrow breathed in one expressive
line, —
"Gave pleasant dinners ; who has got
his wine ?"

THE MYSTERIOUS ILLNESS.

WHAT ailed young Lucius ? Art had
vainly tried
To guess his ill, and found herself defied.
The Augur plied his legendary skill ;

Useless ; the fair young Roman lan-
guished still.
His chariot took him every cloudless
day
Along the Pincian Hill or Appian Way ;
They rubbed his wasted limbs with sul-
phurous oil,
Oozed from the far-off Orient's heated
soil ;
They led him tottering down the steamy
path
Where bubbling fountains filled the ther-
mal bath ;
Borne in his litter to Egeria's cave,
They washed him, shivering, in her icy
wave.
They sought all curious herbs and costly
stones,
They scraped the moss that grew on dead
men's bones,
They tried all cures the votive tablets
taught,
Scoured every place whence healing
drugs were brought,
O'er Thracian hills his breathless couriers
ran,
His slaves waylaid the Syrian caravan.
At last a servant heard a stranger
speak
A new chirurgeon's name ; a clever
Greek,
Skilled in his art ; from Pergamus he
came
To Rome but lately ; GALEN was the
name.
The Greek was called : a man with pier-
cing eyes,
Who must be cunning, and who might
be wise.
He spoke but little, — if they pleased,
he said,
He 'd wait awhile beside the sufferer's
bed.
So by his side he sat, serene and
calm,

His very accents soft as healing balm ;
Not curious seemed, but every movement
    spied,
His sharp eyes searching where they
    seemed to glide ;
Asked a few questions, — what he felt,
    and where?
"A pain just here," "A constant beat-
    ing there."
Who ordered bathing for his aches and
    ails ?
"Charmis, the water-doctor from Mar-
    seilles."
What was the last prescription in his
    case ?
"A draught of wine with powdered
    chrysoprase."
Had he no secret grief he nursed alone?
A pause ; a little tremor ; answer, —
    "None."
    Thoughtful, a moment, sat the cun-
    ning leech,
And muttered "Eros !" in his native
    speech.
    In the broad atrium various friends
    await
The last new utterance from the lips of
    fate ;
Men, matrons, maids, they talk the
    question o'er,
And, restless, pace the tessellated floor.
Not unobserved the youth so long had
    pined
By gentle-hearted dames and damsels
    kind ;
One with the rest, a rich Patrician's
    pride,
The lady Hermia, called "the golden-
    eyed";
The same the old Proconsul fain must
    woo,
Whom, one dark night, a masked sicarius
    slew ;
The same black Crassus over roughly
    pressed

To hear his suit, — the Tiber knows the
    rest.
(Crassus was missed next morning by his
    set ;
Next week the fishers found him in their
    net.)
She with the others paced the ample
    hall,
Fairest, alas ! and saddest of them all.
    At length the Greek declared, with
    puzzled face,
Some strange enchantment mingled in
    the case,
And naught would serve to act as counter-
    charm
Save a warm bracelet from a maiden's
    arm.
Not every maiden's, — many might be
    tried ;
Which not in vain, experience must de-
    cide.
Were there no damsels willing to at-
    tend
And do such service for a suffering friend ?
    The message passed among the waiting
    crowd,
First in a whisper, then proclaimed
    aloud.
Some wore no jewels ; some were disin-
    clined,
For reasons better guessed at than de-
    fined ;
Though all were saints, — at least pro-
    fessed to be, —
The list all counted, there were named
    but three.
    The leech, still seated by the patient's
    side,
Held his thin wrist, and watched him,
    eagle-eyed.
    Aurelia first, a fair-haired Tuscan girl,
Slipped off her golden asp, with eyes of
    pearl.
His solemn head the grave physician
    shook ;

The waxen features thanked her with a look.

Olympia next, a creature half divine,
Sprung from the blood of old Evander's line,
Held her white arm, that wore a twisted chain
Clasped with an opal-sheeny cymophane.
In vain, O daughter! said the baffled Greek.
The patient sighed the thanks he could not speak.

Last, Hermia entered; look, that sudden start!
The pallium heaves above his leaping heart;
The beating pulse, the cheek's rekindled flame,
Those quivering lips, the secret all proclaim.
The deep disease long throbbing in the breast,
The dread enchantment, all at once confessed!
The case was plain; the treatment was begun;
And Love soon cured the mischief he had done.

Young Love, too oft thy treacherous bandage slips
Down from the eyes it blinded to the lips!
Ask not the Gods, O youth, for clearer sight,
But the bold heart to plead thy cause aright.
And thou, fair maiden, when thy lovers sigh,
Suspect thy flattering ear, but trust thine eye;
And learn this secret from the tale of old:
No love so true as love that dies untold.

A MOTHER'S SECRET.

How sweet the sacred legend — if unblamed
In my slight verse such holy things are named —
Of Mary's secret hours of hidden joy,
Silent, but pondering on her wondrous boy!
Ave, Maria! Pardon, if I wrong
Those heavenly words that shame my earthly song!

The choral host had closed the Angel's strain
Sung to the listening watch on Bethlehem's plain,
And now the shepherds, hastening on their way,
Sought the still hamlet where the Infant lay.
They passed the fields that gleaning Ruth toiled o'er, —
They saw afar the ruined threshing-floor
Where Moab's daughter, homeless and forlorn,
Found Boaz slumbering by his heaps of corn;
And some remembered how the holy scribe,
Skilled in the lore of every jealous tribe,
Traced the warm blood of Jesse's royal son
To that fair alien, bravely wooed and won.

So fared they on to seek the promised sign,
That marked the anointed heir of David's line.
At last, by forms of earthly semblance led,
They found the crowded inn, the oxen's shed,
No pomp was there, no glory shone around

On the coarse straw that strewed the
reeking ground ;
One dim retreat a flickering torch be-
trayed, —
In that poor cell the Lord of Life was
laid !
  The wondering shepherds told their
breathless tale
Of the bright choir that woke the sleep-
ing vale ;
Told how the skies with sudden glory
flamed,
Told how the shining multitude pro-
claimed,
"Joy, joy to earth ! Behold the hal-
lowed morn !
In David's city Christ the Lord is born !
'Glory to God !' let angels shout on high,
'Good-will to men !' the listening earth
reply !"
  They spoke with hurried words and
accents wild ;
Calm in his cradle slept the heavenly
child.
No trembling word the mother's joy re-
vealed, —
One sigh of rapture, and her lips were
sealed ;
Unmoved she saw the rustic train depart,
But kept their words to ponder in her
heart.

  Twelve years had passed ; the boy was
fair and tall,
Growing in wisdom, finding grace with
all.
The maids of Nazareth, as they trooped
to fill
Their balanced urns beside the mountain rill,
The gathered matrons, as they sat and
spun,
Spoke in soft words of Joseph's quiet
son.
No voice had reached the Galilean vale

Of star-led kings, or awe-struck shep-
herd's tale ;
In the meek, studious child they only saw
The future Rabbi, learned in Israel's law.
  So grew the boy, and now the feast
was near
When at the Holy Place the tribes
appear.
Scarce had the home-bred child of
Nazareth seen
Beyond the hills that girt the village
green ;
Save when at midnight, o'er the starlit
sands,
Snatched from the steel of Herod's mur-
dering bands,
A babe, close folded to his mother's
breast,
Through Edom's wilds he sought the
sheltering West.
  Then Joseph spake : "Thy boy hath
largely grown ;
Weave him fine raiment, fitting to be
shown ;
Fair robes beseem the pilgrim, as the
priest :
Goes he not with us to the holy feast ?"
  And Mary culled the flaxen fibres
white ;
Till eve she spun ; she spun till morning light.
The thread was twined ; its parting
meshes through
From hand to hand her restless shuttle
flew,
Till the full web was wound upon the
beam ;
Love's curious toil, — a vest without a
seam !
  They reach the Holy Place, fulfil the
days
To solemn feasting given, and grateful
praise.
At last they turn, and far Moriah's
height

"Till eve she spun; she spun till morning light." Page 118.

Melts in the southern sky and fades
from sight.
All day the dusky caravan has flowed
In devious trails along the winding road;
(For many a step their homeward path
attends,
And all the sons of Abraham are as
friends.)
Evening has come, — the hour of rest
and joy, —
Hush! Hush! That whisper, — "Where
is Mary's boy?"
  O weary hour! O aching days that
passed
Filled with strange fears each wilder
than the last, —
The soldier's lance, the fierce centurion's
sword,
The crushing wheels that whirl some
Roman lord,
The midnight crypt that sucks the cap-
tive's breath,
The blistering sun on Hinnom's vale of
death!
  Thrice on his cheek had rained the
morning light;
Thrice on his lips the mildewed kiss of
night,
Crouched by a sheltering column's shin-
ing plinth,
Or stretched beneath the odorous tere-
binth.
  At last, in desperate mood, they
sought once more
The Temple's porches, searched in vain
before;
They found him seated with the ancient
men, —
The grim old rufflers of the tongue and
pen, —
Their bald heads glistening as they
clustered near,
Their gray beards slanting as they
turned to hear,
Lost in half-envious wonder and surprise

That lips so fresh should utter words so
wise.
  And Mary said, — as one who, tried
too long,
Tells all her grief and half her sense of
wrong, —
" What is this thoughtless thing which
thou hast done?
Lo, we have sought thee sorrowing, O
my son!"
  Few words he spake, and scarce of
filial tone,
Strange words, their sense a mystery
yet unknown;
Then turned with them and left the
holy hill,
To all their mild commands obedient
still.
  The tale was told to Nazareth's sober
men,
And Nazareth's matrons told it oft
again;
The maids retold it at the fountain's
side,
The youthful shepherds doubted or
denied;
It passed around among the listening
friends,
With all that fancy adds and fiction
lends,
Till newer marvels dimmed the young
renown
Of Joseph's son, who talked the Rabbis
down.
  But Mary, faithful to its lightest word,
Kept in her heart the sayings she had
heard,
Till the dread morning rent the Temple's veil,
And shuddering earth confirmed the
wondrous tale.

Youth fades; love droops; the leaves
of friendship fall:
A mother's secret hope outlives them all.

THE DISAPPOINTED STATESMAN.

Who of all statesmen is his country's
  pride,
Her councils' prompter and her leaders'
  guide ?
He speaks ; the nation holds its breath
  to hear ;
He nods, and shakes the sunset hemisphere.
Born where the primal fount of Nature
  springs
By the rude cradles of her throneless
  kings,
In his proud eye her royal signet flames,
By his own lips her Monarch she proclaims.

  Why name his countless triumphs,
    whom to meet
Is to be famous, envied in defeat ?
The keen debaters, trained to brawls
  and strife,
Who fire one shot, and finish with the
  knife,
Tried him but once, and, cowering in
  their shame,
Ground their hacked blades to strike at
  meaner game.
The lordly chief, his party's central stay,
Whose lightest word a hundred votes
  obey,
Found a new listener seated at his side,
Looked in his eye, and felt himself defied,
Flung his rash gauntlet on the startled
  floor,
Met the all-conquering, fought — and
  ruled no more.

  See where he moves, what eager
    crowds attend !
What shouts of thronging multitudes
  ascend !
If this is life, — to mark with every hour
The purple deepening in his robes of
  power,
To see the painted fruits of honor fall

Thick at his feet, and choose among
  them all,
To hear the sounds that shape his
  spreading name
Peal through the myriad organ-stops of
  fame,
Stamp the lone isle that spots the sea-
  man's chart,
And crown the pillared glory of the mart,
To count as peers the few supremely wise
Who mark their planet in the angels'
  eyes, —
If this is life —
        What savage man is he
Who strides alone beside the sounding
  sea ?
Alone he wanders by the murmuring
  shore,
His thoughts as restless as the waves
  that roar ;
Looks on the sullen sky as stormy-
  browed
As on the waves yon tempest-brooding
  cloud,
Heaves from his aching breast a wailing
  sigh,
Sad as the gust that sweeps the clouded
  sky.
Ask him his griefs ; what midnight de-
  mons plough
The lines of torture on his lofty brow ;
Unlock those marble lips, and bid them
  speak
The mystery freezing in his bloodless
  cheek.

  His secret ? Hid beneath a flimsy
    word ;
One foolish whisper that ambition heard ;
And thus it spake : " Behold yon gilded
  chair,
The world's one vacant throne, — thy
  place is there !"

  Ah, fatal dream ! What warning
    spectres meet
In ghastly circle round its shadowy seat !

Yet still the Tempter murmurs in his ear
The maddening taunt he cannot choose
   but hear :
" Meanest of slaves, by gods and men
   accurst,
He who is second when he might be first !
Climb with bold front the ladder's top-
   most round,
Or chain thy creeping footsteps to the
   ground !"
   Illustrious Dupe ! Have those majes-
   tic eyes
Lost their proud fire for such a vulgar
   prize ?
Art thou the last of all mankind to know
That party-fights are won by aiming low ?
Thou, stamped by Nature with her royal
   sign,
That party-hirelings hate a look like
   thine ?
Shake from thy sense the wild delusive
   dream !
Without the purple, art thou not su-
   preme ?
And soothed by love unbought, thy
   heart shall own
A nation's homage nobler than its throne !

THE SECRET OF THE STARS.

Is man's the only throbbing heart that
   hides
The silent spring that feeds its whispering tides ?
Speak from thy caverns, mystery-breed-
   ing Earth,
Tell the half-hinted story of thy birth,
And calm the noisy champions who have
   thrown
The book of types against the book of
   stone !

   Have ye not secrets, ye refulgent
   spheres,

No sleepless listener of the starlight
   hears ?
In vain the sweeping equatorial pries
Through every world-sown corner of the
   skies,
To the far orb that so remotely strays
Our midnight darkness is its noonday
   blaze ;
In vain the climbing soul of creeping
   man
Metes out the heavenly concave with a
   span,
Tracks into space the long-lost meteor's
   trail,
And weighs an unseen planet in the
   scale ;
Still o'er their doubts the waneyed
   watchers sigh,
And Science lifts her still unanswered
   cry :
" Are all these worlds, that speed their
   circling flight,
Dumb, vacant, soulless, — bawbles of
   the night ?
Warmed with God's smile and wafted
   by his breath,
To weave in ceaseless round the dance
   of Death ?
Or rolls a sphere in each expanding zone,
Crowned with a life as varied as our
   own ? "

   Maker of earth and stars ! If thou
   hast taught
By what thy voice hath spoke, thy hand
   hath wrought,
By all that Science proves, or guesses
   true,
More than thy Poet dreamed, thy prophet
   knew, —
The heavens still bow in darkness at thy
   feet,
And shadows veil thy cloud-pavilioned
   seat !
   Not for ourselves we ask thee to reveal

One awful word beneath the future's seal;
What thou shalt tell us, grant us strength
  to bear;
What thou withholdest is thy single
  care.
Not for ourselves; the present clings too
  fast,
Moored to the mighty anchors of the
  past;
But when, with angry snap, some cable
  parts,
The sound re-echoing in our startled
  hearts, —
When, through the wall that clasps the
  harbor round,
And shuts the raving ocean from its
  bound,
Shattered and rent by sacrilegious hands,
The first mad billow leaps upon the
  sands, —
Then to the Future's awful page we
  turn,
And what we question hardly dare to
  learn.

  Still let us hope! for while we seem
  to tread
The time-worn pathway of the nations
  dead,
Though Sparta laughs at all our warlike
  deeds,
And buried Athens claims our stolen
  creeds,
Though Rome, a spectre on her broken
  throne,
Beholds our eagle and recalls her own,
Though England fling her pennons on
  the breeze
And reign before us Mistress of the
  seas, —
While calm-eyed History tracks us circling round
Fate's iron pillar where they all were
  bound,
She sees new beacons crowned with
  brighter flame

Than the old watch-fires, like, but not
  the same!
Still in our path a larger curve she
  finds,
The spiral widening as the chain un-
  winds!
No shameless haste shall spot with ban-
  dit-crime
Our destined empire snatched before its
  time.
Wait, — wait, undoubting, for the winds
  have caught
From our bold speech the heritage of
  thought;
No marble form that sculptured truth
  can wear
Vies with the image shaped in viewless
  air;
And thought unfettered grows through
  speech to deeds,
As the broad forest marches in its
  seeds.
What though we perish ere the day is
  won?
Enough to see its glorious work begun!
The thistle falls before a trampling
  clown,
But who can chain the flying thistle-
  down?
Wait while the fiery seeds of freedom
  fly,
The prairie blazes when the grass is
  dry!
  What arms might ravish, leave to
  peaceful arts,
Wisdom and love shall win the roughest
  hearts;
So shall the angel who has closed for
  man
The blissful garden since his woes be-
  gan
Swing wide the golden portals of the
  West,
And Eden's secret stand at length con-
  fessed!

A POEM.

DEDICATION OF THE PITTSFIELD CEME-
TERY, SEPTEMBER 9, 1850.

ANGEL of Death! extend thy silent reign!
Stretch thy dark sceptre o'er this new
domain!
No sable car along the winding road
Has borne to earth its unresisting load;
No sudden mound has risen yet to show
Where the pale slumberer folds his arms
below;
No marble gleams to bid his memory live
In the brief lines that hurrying Time
can give;
Yet, O Destroyer! from thy shrouded
throne
Look on our gift; this realm is all thine
own!

Fair is the scene; its sweetness oft be-
guiled
From their dim paths the children of
the wild;
The dark-haired maiden loved its grassy
dells,
The feathered warrior claimed its wooded
swells,
Still on its slopes the ploughman's ridges
show
The pointed flints that left his fatal bow,
Chipped with rough art and slow bar-
barian toil, —
Last of his wrecks that strews the alien
soil!
Here spread the fields that heaped
their ripened store
Till the brown arms of Labor held no
more;
The scythe's broad meadow with its
dusky blush;
The sickle's harvest with its velvet flush;
The green-haired maize, her silken
tresses laid,
In soft luxuriance, on her harsh brocade;

The gourd that swells beneath her tossing plume;
The coarser wheat that rolls in lakes of
bloom, —
Its coral stems and milk-white flowers
alive
With the wide murmurs of the scattered
hive;
Here glowed the apple with the pencilled streak
Of morning painted on its southern
cheek;
The pear's long necklace strung with
golden drops,
Arched, like the banian, o'er its pillared
props;
Here crept the growths that paid the
laborer's care
With the cheap luxuries wealth con-
sents to spare;
Here sprang the healing herbs which
could not save
The hand that reared them from the
neighboring grave.

Yet all its varied charms, forever free
From task and tribute, Labor yields to
thee:
No more, when April sheds her fitful
rain,
The sower's hand shall cast its flying
grain;
No more, when Autumn strews the
flaming leaves,
The reaper's band shall gird its yellow
sheaves;
For thee alike the circling seasons flow
Till the first blossoms heave the latest
snow.
In the stiff clod below the whirling
drifts,
In the loose soil the springing herbage
lifts,
In the hot dust beneath the parching
weeds,

Life's withering flower shall drop its
  shrivelled seeds ;
Its germ entranced in thy unbreathing
  sleep
Till what thou sowest mightier angels
  reap !

Spirit of Beauty ! let thy graces blend
With loveliest Nature all that Art can
  lend.
Come from the bowers where Summer's
  life-blood flows
Through the red lips of June's half-open
  rose,
Dressed in bright hues, the loving sun-
  shine's dower ;
For tranquil Nature owns no mourning
  flower.
  Come from the forest where the beech's
  screen
Bars the fierce noonbeam with its flakes
  of green ;
Stay the rude axe that bares the shadowy
  plains,
Stanch the deep wound that dries the
  maple's veins.
  Come with the stream whose silver-
  braided rills
Fling their unclasping bracelets from the
  hills,
Till in one gleam, beneath the forest's
  wings,
Melts the white glitter of a hundred
  springs.
  Come from the steeps where look majestic forth
From their twin thrones the Giants of
  the North
On the huge shapes, that, crouching at
  their knees,
Stretch their broad shoulders, rough with
  shaggy trees.
Through the wide waste of ether, not in
  vain,

Their softened gaze shall reach our distant plain ;
There, while the mourner turns his aching eyes
On the blue mounds that print the bluer
  skies,
Nature shall whisper that the fading
  view
Of mightiest grief may wear a heavenly
  hue.

Cherub of Wisdom ! let thy marble page
Leave its sad lesson, new to every age ;
Teach us to live, not grudging every
  breath
To the chill winds that waft us on to
  death,
But ruling calmly every pulse it warms,
And tempering gently every word it
  forms.
Seraph of Love ! in heaven's adoring
  zone,
Nearest of all around the central throne,
While with soft hands the pillowed turf
  we spread
That soon shall hold us in its dreamless
  bed,
With the low whisper, — Who shall first
  be laid
In the dark chamber's yet unbroken
  shade ? —
Let thy sweet radiance shine rekindled
  here,
And all we cherish grow more truly dear.
Here in the gates of Death's o'erhanging
  vault,
O, teach us kindness for our brother's
  fault ;
Lay all our wrongs beneath this peaceful
  sod,
And lead our hearts to Mercy and its
  God.

FATHER of all ! in Death's relentless
  claim

We read thy mercy by its sterner name;
In the bright flower that decks the sol-
    emn bier,
We see thy glory in its narrowed sphere;
In the deep lessons that affliction draws,
We trace the curves of thy encircling
    laws ;
In the long sigh that sets our spirits free,
We own the love that calls us back to
    Thee !

Through the hushed street, along the
    silent plain,
The spectral future leads its mourning
    train,
Dark with the shadows of uncounted
    bands,
Where man's white lips and woman's
    wringing hands
Track the still burden, rolling slow be-
    fore,
That love and kindness can protect no
    more ;
The smiling babe that, called to mortal
    strife,
Shuts its meek eyes and drops its little
    life ;
The drooping child who prays in vain to
    live,
And pleads for help its parent cannot
    give ;
The pride of beauty stricken in its flower ;
The strength of manhood broken in an
    hour ;
Age in its weakness, bowed by toil and
    care,
Traced in sad lines beneath its silvered
    hair.

The sun shall set, and heaven's re-
    splendent spheres
Gild the smooth turf unhallowed yet by
    tears,
But ah ! how soon the evening stars will
    shed

Their sleepless light around the slum-
    bering dead !

Take them, O Father, in immortal
    trust !
Ashes to ashes, dust to kindred dust,
Till the last angel rolls the stone away,
And a new morning brings eternal day !

TO GOVERNOR SWAIN.

DEAR GOVERNOR, if my skiff might
    brave
The winds that lift the ocean wave,
The mountain stream that loops and
    swerves
Through my broad meadow's channelled
    curves
Should waft me on from bound to bound
To where the River weds the Sound,
The Sound should give me to the Sea,
That to the Bay, the Bay to Thee.

It may not be ; too long the track
To follow down or struggle back.
The sun has set on fair Naushon
Long ere my western blaze is gone ;
The ocean disk is rolling dark
In shadows round your swinging bark,
While yet the yellow sunset fills
The stream that scarfs my spruce-clad
    hills ;
The day-star wakes your island deer
Long ere my barnyard chanticleer ;
Your mists are soaring in the blue
While mine are sparks of glittering dew.

It may not be ; O would it might,
Could I live o'er that glowing night !
What golden hours would come to life,
What goodly feats of peaceful strife, —
Such jests, that, drained of every joke,
The very bank of language broke, —
Such deeds, that Laughter nearly died
With stitches in his belted side ;

While Time, caught fast in pleasure's
   chain,
His double goblet snapped in twain,
And stood with half in either hand, —
Both brimming full, — but not of sand !

It may not be ; I strive in vain
To break my slender household chain, —
Three pairs of little clasping hands,
One voice, that whispers, not commands.
Even while my spirit flies away,
My gentle jailers murmur nay ;
All shapes of elemental wrath
They raise along my threatened path ;
The storm grows black, the waters rise,
The mountains mingle with the skies,
The mad tornado scoops the ground,
The midnight robber prowls around, —
Thus, kissing every limb they tie,
They draw a knot and heave a sigh,
Till, fairly netted in the toil,
My feet are rooted to the soil.
Only the soaring wish is free ! —
And that, dear Governor, flies to thee !
   PITTSFIELD, 1851.

TO AN ENGLISH FRIEND.

THE seed that wasteful autumn cast
To waver on its stormy blast,
Long o'er the wintry desert tost,
Its living germ has never lost.
Dropped by the weary tempest's wing,
It feels the kindling ray of spring,
And, starting from its dream of death,
Pours on the air its perfumed breath.

So, parted by the rolling flood,
The love that springs from common
   blood
Needs but a single sunlit hour
Of mingling smiles to bud and flower ;
Unharmed its slumbering life has flown,
From shore to shore, from zone to
   zone,
Where summer's falling roses stain
The tepid waves of Pontchartrain,
Or where the lichen creeps below
Katahdin's wreaths of whirling snow.

Though fiery sun and stiffening cold
May change the fair ancestral mould,
No winter chills, no summer drains
The life-blood drawn from English
   veins,
Still bearing wheresoe'er it flows
The love that with its fountain rose,
Unchanged by space, unwronged by
   time,
From age to age, from clime to clime !
   1852.

VIGNETTES.

1853.

AFTER A LECTURE ON WORDSWORTH.

Come, spread your wings, as I spread
    mine,
    And leave the crowded hall
For where the eyes of twilight shine
    O'er evening's western wall.

These are the pleasant Berkshire hills,
    Each with its leafy crown;
Hark! from their sides a thousand rills
    Come singing sweetly down.

A thousand rills; they leap and shine,
    Strained through the shadowy nooks,
Till, clasped in many a gathering twine,
    They swell a hundred brooks.

A hundred brooks, and still they run
    With ripple, shade, and gleam,
Till, clustering all their braids in one,
    They flow a single stream.

A bracelet spun from mountain mist,
    A silvery sash unwound,
With ox-bow curve and sinuous twist
    It writhes to reach the Sound.

This is my bark, — a pygmy's ship;
    Beneath a child it rolls;
Fear not, — one body makes it dip,
    But not a thousand souls.

Float we the grassy banks between;
    Without an oar we glide;
The meadows, drest in living green,
    Unroll on either side.

— Come, take the book we love so well,
    And let us read and dream
We see whate'er its pages tell,
    And sail an English stream.

Up to the clouds the lark has sprung,
    Still trilling as he flies;
The linnet sings as there he sung;
    The unseen cuckoo cries,

And daisies strew the banks along,
    And yellow kingcups shine,
With cowslips, and a primrose throng,
    And humble celandine.

Ah foolish dream! when Nature nursed
    Her daughter in the West,
The fount was drained that opened first;
    She bared her other breast.

On the young planet's orient shore
    Her morning hand she tried;
Then turned the broad medallion o'er
    And stamped the sunset side.

Take what she gives, her pine's tall stem,
    Her elm with hanging spray;
She wears her mountain diadem
    Still in her own proud way.

Look on the forests' ancient kings,
    The hemlock's towering pride:
Yon trunk had thrice a hundred rings,
    And fell before it died.

Nor think that Nature saves her bloom
  And slights our grassy plain ;
For us she wears her court costume, —
  Look on its broidered train ; •

The lily with the sprinkled dots,
  Brands of the noontide beam ;
The cardinal, and the blood-red spots,
  Its double in the stream,

As if some wounded eagle's breast,
  Slow throbbing o'er the plain,
Had left its airy path impressed
  In drops of scarlet rain.

And hark ! and hark ! the woodland rings ;
  There thrilled the thrush's soul ;
And look ! that flash of flamy wings, —
  The fire-plumed oriole !

Above, the hen-hawk swims and swoops,
  Flung from the bright, blue sky ;
Below, the robin hops, and whoops
  His piercing, Indian cry.

Beauty runs virgin in the woods
  Robed in her rustic green,
And oft a longing thought intrudes,
  As if we might have seen

Her every finger's every joint
  Ringed with some golden line,
Poet whom Nature did anoint !
  Had our wild home been thine.

Yet think not so ; Old England's blood
  Runs warm in English veins ;
But wafted o'er the icy flood
  Its better life remains :

Our children know each wildwood smell,
  The bayberry and the fern,
The man who does not know them well
  Is all too old to learn.

Be patient !   On the breathing page
  Still pants our hurried past ;
Pilgrim and soldier, saint and sage, —
  The poet comes the last !

Though still the lark-voiced matins ring
  The world has known so long ;
The wood-thrush of the West shall sing
  Earth's last sweet even-song !

AFTER A LECTURE ON MOORE.

SHINE soft, ye trembling tears of light
  That strew the mourning skies ;
Hushed in the silent dews of night
  The harp of Erin lies.

What though her thousand years have
    past
  Of poets, saints, and kings, —
Her echoes only hear the last
  That swept those golden strings.

Fling o'er his mound, ye star-lit bowers,
  The balmiest wreaths ye wear,
Whose breath has lent your earth-born
    flowers
  Heaven's own ambrosial air.

Breathe, bird of night, thy softest tone,
  By shadowy grove and rill ;
Thy song will soothe us while we own
  That his was sweeter still.

Stay, pitying Time, thy foot for him
  Who gave thee swifter wings,
Nor let thine envious shadow dim
  The light his glory flings.

If in his cheek unholy blood
  Burned for one youthful hour,
'T was but the flushing of the bud
  That blooms a milk-white flower.

Take him, kind mother, to thy breast,
  Who loved thy smiles so well,
And spread thy mantle o'er his rest
  Of rose and asphodel.

— The bark has sailed the midnight sea,
  The sea without a shore,
That waved its parting sign to thee, —
  "A health to thee, Tom Moore!"

And thine, long lingering on the strand,
  Its bright-hued streamers furled,
Was loosed by age, with trembling hand,
  To seek the silent world.

Not silent! no, the radiant stars
  Still singing as they shine,
Unheard through earth's imprisoning
    bars,
  Have voices sweet as thine.

Wake, then, in happier realms above,
  The songs of bygone years,
Till angels learn those airs of love
  That ravished mortal ears!

AFTER A LECTURE ON KEATS.

"Purpureos spargam flores."

THE wreath that star-crowned Shelley
    gave
Is lying on thy Roman grave,
Yet on its turf young April sets
Her store of slender violets;
Though all the Gods their garlands
    shower,
I too may bring one purple flower.
— Alas! what blossom shall I bring,
That opens in my Northern spring?
The garden beds have all run wild,
So trim when I was yet a child;
Flat plantains and unseemly stalks
Have crept across the gravel walks;
The vines are dead, long, long ago,
The almond buds no longer blow.

No more upon its mound I see
The azure, plume-bound fleur-de-lis;
Where once the tulips used to show,
In straggling tufts the pansies grow;
The grass has quenched my white-rayed
    gem,
The flowering "Star of Bethlehem,"
Though its long blade of glossy green
And pallid stripe may still be seen.
Nature, who treads her nobles down,
And gives their birthright to the clown,
Has sown her base-born weedy things
Above the garden's queens and kings.
— Yet one sweet flower of ancient race
Springs in the old familiar place.
When snows were melting down the
    vale,
And Earth unlaced her icy mail,
And March his stormy trumpet blew,
And tender green came peeping through,
I loved the earliest one to seek
That broke the soil with emerald beak,
And watch the trembling bells so blue
Spread on the column as it grew.
Meek child of earth! thou wilt not shame
The sweet, dead poet's holy name;
The God of music gave thee birth,
Called from the crimson-spotted earth,
Where, sobbing his young life away,
His own fair Hyacinthus lay.
— The hyacinth my garden gave
Shall lie upon that Roman grave!

AFTER A LECTURE ON SHELLEY.

ONE broad, white sail in Spezzia's treach-
    erous bay;
  On comes the blast; too daring bark,
    beware!
The cloud has clasped her; lo! it melts
    away;
  The wide, waste waters, but no sail is
    there.

Morning : a woman looking on the sea;
  Midnight : with lamps the long veran-
  da burns;
Come, wandering sail, they watch, they
  burn for thee !
  Suns come and go, alas ! no bark
  returns.

And feet are thronging on the pebbly
  sands,
  And torches flaring in the weedy caves,
Where'er the waters lay with icy hands
  The shapes uplifted from their coral
  graves.

Vainly they seek ; the idle quest is o'er;
  The coarse, dark women, with their
  hanging locks,
And lean, wild children gather from the
  shore
  To the black hovels bedded in the
  rocks.

But Love still prayed, with agonizing
  wail,
  "One, one last look, ye heaving
  waters, yield !"
Till Ocean, clashing in his jointed mail,
  Raised the pale burden on his level
  shield.

Slow from the shore the sullen waves
  retire ;
  His form a nobler element shall
  claim ;
Nature baptized him in ethereal fire,
  And Death shall crown him with a
  wreath of flame.

Fade, mortal semblance, never to return ;
  Swift is the change within thy crimson
  shroud ;
Seal the white ashes in the peaceful urn ;
  All else has risen in yon silvery cloud.

Sleep where thy gentle Adonais lies,
  Whose open page lay on thy dying
  heart,
Both in the smile of those blue-vaulted
  skies,
  Earth's fairest dome of all divinest
  art.

Breathe for his wandering soul one passing sigh,
  O happier Christian, while thine eye
  grows dim, —
In all the mansions of the house on high,
  Say not that Mercy has not one for
  him !

AT THE CLOSE OF A COURSE OF LECTURES.

As the voice of the watch to the mariner's dream ;
As the footstep of Spring on the ice-
  girdled stream,
There comes a soft footstep, a whisper,
  to me, —
The vision is over, — the rivulet free !

We have trod from the threshold of tur-
  bulent March,
Till the green scarf of April is hung on
  the larch,
And down the bright hillside that wel-
  comes the day,
We hear the warm panting of beautiful
  May.

We will part before Summer has opened
  her wing,
And the bosom of June swells the bodice
  of Spring,
While the hope of the season lies fresh
  in the bud,
And the young life of Nature runs warm
  in our blood.

It is but a word, and the chain is unbound,
The bracelet of steel drops unclasped to
the ground;
No hand shall replace it, — it rests
where it fell, —
It is but one word that we all know too
well.

Yet the hawk with the wildness untamed in his eye,
If you free him, stares round ere he
springs to the sky;
The slave whom no longer his fetters
restrain
Will turn for a moment and look at his
chain.

Our parting is not as the friendship of
years,
That chokes with the blessing it speaks
through its tears;
We have walked in a garden, and, looking
around,
Have plucked a few leaves from the
myrtles we found.

But now at the gate of the garden we
stand,
And the moment has come for unclasping the hand;
Will you drop it like lead, and in silence
retreat
Like the twenty crushed forms from an
omnibus seat?

Nay! hold it one moment, — the last
we may share, —
I stretch it in kindness, and not for my
fare;
You may pass through the doorway in
rank or in file,
If your ticket from Nature is stamped
with a smile.

For the sweetest of smiles is the smile
as we part,
When the light round the lips is a ray
from the heart;
And lest a stray tear from its fountain
might swell,
We will seal the bright spring with a
quiet farewell.

THE HUDSON.

AFTER A LECTURE AT ALBANY.

'T WAS a vision of childhood that came
with its dawn,
Ere the curtain that covered life's day-
star was drawn;
The nurse told the tale when the shadows grew long,
And the mother's soft lullaby breathed
it in song.

" There flows a fair stream by the hills
of the west," —
She sang to her boy as he lay on her
breast;
" Along its smooth margin thy fathers
have played;
Beside its deep waters their ashes are
laid."

I wandered afar from the land of my
birth,
I saw the old rivers, renowned upon
earth,
But fancy still painted that wide-flow-
ing stream
With the many-hued pencil of infancy's
dream.

I saw the green banks of the castle-
crowned Rhine,
Where the grapes drink the moonlight
and change it to wine;

I stood by the Avon, whose waves as
    they glide
Still whisper his glory ¡who sleeps at
    their side.

But my heart would still yearn for the
    sound of the waves
That sing as they flow by my fore-
    fathers' graves ;
If manhood yet honors my cheek with a
    tear,

I care not who sees it, — no blush for it
    here !

Farewell to the deep-bosomed stream of
    the West !
I fling this loose blossom to float on its
    breast ;
Nor let the dear love of its children
    grow cold,
Till the channel is dry where its waters
    have rolled !
    December, 1854.

A POEM

FOR THE MEETING OF THE AMERICAN
MEDICAL ASSOCIATION AT NEW YORK,
MAY 5, 1853.

I HOLD a letter in my hand, —
    A flattering letter — more's the pity, —
By some contriving junto planned,
    And signed *per order of Committee ;*
It touches every tenderest spot, —
    My patriotic predilections,
My well - known — something — don't
    ask what,
    My poor old songs, my kind affec-
    tions.

They make a feast on Thursday next,
    And hope to make the feasters merry ;
They own they 're something more per-
    plexed
    For poets than for port and sherry ; —
They want the men of — (word torn
    out) ;
    Our friends will come with anxious
    faces
(To see our blankets off, no doubt,
    And trot us out and show our paces).

They hint that papers by the score
    Are rather musty kind of rations ;
They don't exactly mean a bore,
    But only trying to the patience ;
That such as — you know who I mean —
    Distinguished for their — what d' ye
    call 'em —
Should bring the dews of Hippocrene
    To sprinkle on the faces solemn.

— The same old story ; that 's the chaff
    To catch the birds that sing the dit-
    ties ;
Upon my soul, it makes me laugh
    To read these letters from Commit-
    tees !
They 're all *so* loving and *so* fair, —
    All for *your* sake such kind compunc-
    tion, --
'T would save your carriage half its wear
    To touch its wheels with such an unc-
    tion !

Why, who am I, to lift me here
    And beg such learned folk to listen, —
To ask a smile, or coax a tear
    Beneath these stoic lids to glisten ?

As well might some arterial thread
  Ask the whole frame to feel it gushing,
While throbbing fierce from heel to head
  The vast aortic tide was rushing.

As well some hair-like nerve might strain
  To set its special streamlet going,
While through the myriad-channelled brain
  The burning flood of thought was flowing;
Or trembling fibre strive to keep
  The springing haunches gathered shorter,
While the scourged racer, leap on leap,
  Was stretching through the last hot quarter!

Ah me! you take the bud that came
  Self-sown in your poor garden's borders,
And hand it to the stately dame
  That florists breed for, all she orders;
She thanks you — it was kindly meant—
  (*A pale affair, not worth the keeping,*)
Good morning; — and your bud is sent
  To join the tea-leaves used for sweeping.

Not always so, kind hearts and true, —
  For such I know are round me beating;
Is not the bud I offer you, —
  Fresh gathered for the hour of meeting, —
Pale though its outer leaves may be,
  Rose-red in all its inner petals,
Where the warm life we cannot see —
  The life of love that gave it — settles.

We meet from regions far away,
  Like rills from distant mountains streaming;

The sun is on Francisco's bay,
  O'er Chesapeake the lighthouse gleaming;
While summer girds the still bayou
  In chains of bloom, her bridal token,
Monadnock sees the sky grow blue,
  His crystal bracelet yet unbroken.

Yet Nature bears the selfsame heart
  Beneath her russet-mantled bosom,
As where with burning lips apart
  She breathes, and white magnolias blossom;
The selfsame founts her chalice fill
  With showery sunlight running over,
On fiery plain and frozen hill,
  On myrtle-beds and fields of clover.

I give you *Home!* its crossing lines
  United in one golden suture,
And showing every day that shines
  The present growing to the future, —
A flag that bears a hundred stars
  In one bright ring, with love for centre,
Fenced round with white and crimson bars,
  No prowling treason dares to enter!

O brothers, home may be a word
  To make affection's living treasure —
The wave an angel might have stirred —
  A stagnant pool of selfish pleasure;
HOME! It is where the day-star springs
  And where the evening sun reposes,
Where'er the eagle spreads his wings,
  From northern pines to southern roses!

A SENTIMENT.

A TRIPLE health to Friendship, Science, Art,
From heads and hands that own a common heart!

Each in its turn the others' willing
    slave, —
Each in its season strong to heal and save.

Friendship's blind service, in the hour
    of need,
Wipes the pale face — and lets the vic-
    tim bleed.
Science must stop to reason and explain ;
ART claps his finger on the streaming
    vein.

But Art's brief memory fails the hand
    at last ;
Then SCIENCE lifts the flambeau of the
    past.
When both their equal impotence de-
    plore, —
When Learning sighs, and Skill can do
    no more, —
The tear of FRIENDSHIP pours its heav-
    enly balm,
And soothes the pang no anodyne may
    calm !
May 1, 1855.

THE NEW EDEN.

MEETING OF THE BERKSHIRE HORTI-
CULTURAL SOCIETY, AT STOCKBRIDGE,
SEPT. 13, 1854.

SCARCE could the parting ocean close,
    Seamed by the Mayflower's cleaving
        bow,
When o'er the rugged desert rose
    The waves that tracked the Pilgrim's
        plough.

Then sprang from many a rock-strewn
    field
    The rippling grass, the nodding grain,
Such growths as English meadows yield
    To scanty sun and frequent rain.

But when the fiery days were done,
    And Autumn brought his purple haze,
Then, kindling in the slanted sun,
    The hillsides gleamed with golden
        maize.

The food was scant, the fruits were few :
    A red-streak glistening here and there ;
Perchance in statelier precincts grew
    Some stern old Puritanic pear.

Austere in taste, and tough at core,
    Its unrelenting bulk was shed,
To ripen in the Pilgrim's store
    When all the summer sweets were fled.

Such was his lot, to front the storm
    With iron heart and marble brow,
Nor ripen till his earthly form
    Was cast from life's autumnal bough.

— But ever on the bleakest rock
    We bid the brightest beacon glow,
And still upon the thorniest stock
    The sweetest roses love to blow.

So on our rude and wintry soil
    We feed the kindling flame of art,
And steal the tropic's blushing spoil
    To bloom on Nature's ice-clad heart.

See how the softening Mother's breast
    Warms to her children's patient
        wiles, —
Her lips by loving Labor pressed
    Break in a thousand dimpling smiles,

From when the flushing bud of June
    Dawns with its first auroral hue,
Till shines the rounded harvest-moon,
    And velvet dahlias drink the dew.

Nor these the only gifts she brings ;
    Look where the laboring orchard
        groans,
And yields its beryl-threaded strings
    For chestnut burs and hemlock cones.

Dear though the shadowy maple be,
  And dearer still the whispering pine,
Dearest yon russet-laden tree
  Browned by the heavy rubbing kine !

There childhood flung its rustling stone,
  There venturous boyhood learned to
    climb, —
How well the early graft was known
  Whose fruit was ripe ere harvest-time !

Nor be the Fleming's pride forgot,
  With swinging drops and drooping
    bells,
Freckled and splashed with streak and
    spot,
  On the warm-breasted, sloping swells;

Nor Persia's painted garden-queen, —
  Frail Houri of the trellised wall, —
Her deep-cleft bosom scarfed with
    green, —
  Fairest to see, and first to fall.

————

When man provoked his mortal doom,
  And Eden trembled as he fell,
When blossoms sighed their last per-
    fume,
  And branches waved their long fare-
    well,

One sucker crept beneath the gate,
  One seed was wafted o'er the wall,
One bough sustained his trembling
    weight ;
  These left the garden, — these were all.

And far o'er many a distant zone
  These wrecks of Eden still are flung :
The fruits that Paradise hath known
  Are still in earthly gardens hung.

Yes, by our own unstoried stream
  The pink-white apple-blossoms burst

That saw the young Euphrates gleam, —
  That Gihon's circling waters nursed.

For us the ambrosial pear displays
  The wealth its arching branches hold,
Bathed by a hundred summery days
  In floods of mingling fire and gold.

And here, where beauty's cheek of flame
  With morning's earliest beam is fed,
The sunset-painted peach may claim
  To rival its celestial red.

————

— What though in some unmoistened
    vale
  The summer leaf grow brown and sere,
Say, shall our star of promise fail
  That circles half the rolling sphere,

From beaches salt with bitter spray,
  O'er prairies green with softest rain,
And ridges bright with evening's ray,
  To rocks that shade the stormless
    main ?

If by our slender-threaded streams
  The blade and leaf and blossom die,
If, drained by noontide's parching
    beams,
  The milky veins of Nature dry,

See, with her swelling bosom bare,
  Yon wild-eyed Sister in the West, —
The ring of Empire round her hair,
  The Indian's wampum on her breast !

We saw the August sun descend,
  Day after day, with blood-red stain,
And the blue mountains dimly blend
  With smoke-wreaths from the burning
    plain ;

Beneath the hot Sirocco's wings
  We sat and told the withering hours,

Till Heaven unsealed its hoarded springs,
   And bade them leap in flashing showers.

Yet in our Ishmael's thirst we knew
   The mercy of the Sovereign hand
Would pour the fountain's quickening
     dew
   To feed some harvest of the land.

No flaming swords of wrath surround
   Our second Garden of the Blest ;
It spreads beyond its rocky bound,
   It climbs Nevada's glittering crest.

God keep the tempter from its gate !
   God shield the children, lest they fall
From their stern fathers' free estate, —
   Till Ocean is its only wall !

SEMICENTENNIAL CELEBRATION OF THE NEW ENGLAND SOCIETY,

NEW YORK, DEC. 22, 1855.

NEW ENGLAND, we love thee ; no time
   can erase
From the hearts of thy children the smile
   on thy face.
'T is the mother's fond look of affection
   and pride,
As she gives her fair son to the arms of
   his bride.

His bride may be fresher in beauty's
   young flower ;
She may blaze in the jewels she brings
   with her dower.
But passion must chill in Time's pitiless
   blast ;
The one that first loved us will love to
   the last.

You have left the dear land of the lake
   and the hill,
But its winds and its waters will talk
   with you still.

"Forget not," they whisper, "your love
   is our debt,"
And echo breathes softly, "We never
   forget."

The banquet's gay splendors are gleaming around,
But your hearts have flown back o'er the
   waves of the Sound ;
They have found the brown home where
   their pulses were born ;
They are throbbing their way through
   the trees and the corn.

There are roofs you remember, — their
   glory is fled ;
There are mounds in the churchyard, —
   one sigh for the dead.
There are wrecks, there are ruins, all
   scattered around ;
But Earth has no spot like that corner
   of ground.

Come, let us be cheerful, — remember
   last night,
How they cheered us, and — never mind
   — meant it all right ;
To-night, we harm nothing, — we love
   in the lump ;
Here 's a bumper to Maine, in the juice
   of the pump !

Here 's to all the good people, wherever
   they be,
Who have grown in the shade of the lib-
   erty-tree ;
We all love its leaves, and its blossoms
   and fruit,
But pray have a care of the fence round
   its root.

We should like to talk big ; it 's a kind
   of a right,
When the tongue has got loose and the
   waistband grown tight ;

But, as pretty Miss Prudence remarked
    to her beau,
On its own heap of compost, no biddy
    should crow.

Enough! There are gentlemen waiting
    to talk,
Whose words are to mine as the flower
    to the stalk.
Stand by your old mother whatever be-
    fall;
God bless all her children !   Good night
    to you all !

FAREWELL.

TO J. R. LOWELL.

FAREWELL, for the bark has her breast
    to the tide,
And the rough arms of Ocean are
    stretched for his bride;
The winds from the mountain stream
    over the bay;
One clasp of the hand, then away and
    away !

I see the tall mast as it rocks by the
    shore ;
The sun is declining, I see it once more ;
To-day like the blade in a thick-waving
    field,
To-morrow the spike on a Highlander's
    shield.

Alone, while the cloud pours its treach-
    erous breath,
With the blue lips all round her whose
    kisses are death ;
Ah, think not the breeze that is urging
    her sail
Has left her unaided to strive with the
    gale.

There are hopes that play round her,
    like fires on the mast,

That will light the dark hour till its
    danger has past;
There are prayers that will plead with
    the storm when it raves,
And whisper "Be still!" to the turbu-
    lent waves.

Nay, think not that Friendship has
    called us in vain
To join the fair ring ere we break it
    again ;
There is strength in its circle, — you
    lose the bright star,
But its sisters still chain it, though
    shining afar.

I give you one health in the juice of the
    vine,
The blood of the vineyard shall mingle
    with mine ;
Thus, thus let us drain the last dew-
    drops of gold,
As we empty our hearts of the blessings
    they hold.

April 29, 1855.

FOR THE MEETING OF THE BURNS CLUB.

1856.

THE mountains glitter in the snow
    A thousand leagues asunder;
Yet here, amid the banquet's glow,
    I hear their voice of thunder;
Each giant's ice-bound goblet clinks;
    A flowing stream is summoned;
Wachusett to Ben Nevis drinks;
    Monadnock to Ben Lomond !

Though years have clipped the eagle's
    plume
    That crowned the chieftain's bonnet,
The sun still sees the heather bloom,
    The silver mists lie on it;

With tartan kilt and philibeg,
  What stride was ever bolder
Than his who showed the naked leg
  Beneath the plaided shoulder?

The echoes sleep on Cheviot's hills,
  That heard the bugles blowing
When down their sides the crimson rills
  With mingled blood were flowing;
The hunts where gallant hearts were
    game,
  The slashing on the border,
The raid that swooped with sword and
    flame,
  Give place to "law and order."

Not while the rocking steeples reel
  With midnight tocsins ringing,
Not while the crashing war-notes peal,
  God sets his poets singing;
The bird is silent in the night,
  Or shrieks a cry of warning
While fluttering round the beacon-
    light, —
  But hear him greet the morning!

The lark of Scotia's morning sky!
  Whose voice may sing his praises?
With Heaven's own sunlight in his eye,
  He walked among the daisies,
Till through the cloud of fortune's wrong
  He soared to fields of glory;
But left his land her sweetest song
  And earth her saddest story.

'T is not the forts the builder piles
  That chain the earth together;
The wedded crowns, the sister isles,
  Would laugh at such a tether;
The kindling thought, the throbbing
    words,
  That set the pulses beating,
Are stronger than the myriad swords
  Of mighty armies meeting.

Thus while within the banquet glows,
  Without, the wild winds whistle,
We drink a triple health, — the Rose,
  The Shamrock, and the Thistle!
Their blended hues shall never fade
  Till War has hushed his cannon, —
Close-twined as ocean-currents braid
  The Thames, the Clyde, the Shannon!

ODE FOR WASHINGTON'S BIRTHDAY.

CELEBRATION OF THE MERCANTILE LI-
  BRARY ASSOCIATION, FEB. 22, 1856.

WELCOME to the day returning,
  Dearer still as ages flow,
While the torch of Faith is burning,
  Long as Freedom's altars glow!
See the hero whom it gave us
  Slumbering on a mother's breast;
For the arm he stretched to save us,
  Be its morn forever blest!

Hear the tale of youthful glory,
  While of Britain's rescued band
Friend and foe repeat the story,
  Spread his fame o'er sea and land,
Where the red cross, proudly streaming,
  Flaps above the frigate's deck,
Where the golden lilies, gleaming,
  Star the watch-towers of Quebec.

Look! The shadow on the dial
  Marks the hour of deadlier strife;
Days of terror, years of trial,
  Scourge a nation into life.
Lo, the youth, become her leader!
  All her baffled tyrants yield;
Through his arm the Lord hath freed
    her;
  Crown him on the tented field!

Vain is Empire's mad temptation!
  Not for him an earthly crown!

He whose sword hath freed a nation !
  Strikes the offered sceptre down.
See the throneless Conqueror seated,
  Ruler by a people's choice ;
See the Patriot's task completed ;
  Hear the Father's dying voice !

" By the name that you inherit,
  By the sufferings you recall,
Cherish the fraternal spirit ;
  Love your country first of all !
Listen not to idle questions
  If its bands may be untied ;
Doubt the patriot whose suggestions
  Strive a nation to divide ! "

Father ! We, whose ears have tingled
  With the discord-notes of shame, —
We, whose sires their blood have mingled
  In the battle's thunder-flame, —
Gathering, while this holy morning
  Lights the land from sea to sea,
Hear thy counsel, heed thy warning ;
  Trust us, while we honor thee !

BIRTHDAY OF DANIEL WEBSTER.

JANUARY 18, 1856.

WHEN life hath run its largest round
  Of toil and triumph, joy and woe,
How brief a storied page is found
  To compass all its outward show !

The world-tried sailor tires and droops ;
  His flag is rent, his keel forgot ;
His farthest voyages seem but loops
  That float from life's entangled knot.

But when within the narrow space
  Some larger soul hath lived and
    wrought,
Whose sight was open to embrace
  The boundless realms of deed and
    thought, —

When, stricken by the freezing blast,
  A nation's living pillars fall,
How rich the storied page, how vast,
  A word, a whisper, can recall !

No medal lifts its fretted face,
  Nor speaking marble cheats your eye,
Yet, while these pictured lines I trace,
  A living image passes by :

A roof beneath the mountain pines ;
  The cloisters of a hill-girt plain ;
The front of life's embattled lines ;
  A mound beside the heaving main.

These are the scenes : a boy appears ;
  Set life's round dial in the sun,
Count the swift arc of seventy years,
  His frame is dust ; his task is done.

Yet pause upon the noontide hour,
  Ere the declining sun has laid
His bleaching rays on manhood's power,
  And look upon the mighty shade.

No gloom that stately shape can hide,
  No change uncrown its brow ; behold !
Dark, calm, large-fronted, lightning-
    eyed,
  Earth has no double from its mould !

Ere from the fields by valor won
  The battle-smoke had rolled away,
And bared the blood-red setting sun,
  His eyes were opened on the day.

His land was but a shelving strip
  Black with the strife that made it free ;
He lived to see its banners dip
  Their fringes in the Western sea.

The boundless prairies learned his name,
  His words the mountain echoes knew,
The Northern breezes swept his fame
  From icy lake to warm bayou.

In toil he lived ; in peace he died ;
  When life's full cycle was complete,
Put off his robes of power and pride,
  And laid them at his Master's feet.

His rest is by the storm-swept waves
  Whom life's wild tempests roughly
    'tried,
Whose heart was like the streaming caves
  Of ocean, throbbing at his side.

Death's cold white hand is like the snow
  Laid softly on the furrowed hill,
It hides the broken seams below,
  And leaves the summit brighter
    still.

In vain the envious tongue upbraids ;
  His name a nation's heart shall keep
Till morning's latest sunlight fades
  On the blue tablet of the deep!

II. — 1857 - 1861.

THE VOICELESS.

WE count the broken lyres that rest
　　Where the sweet wailing singers
　　　slumber,
But o'er their silent sister's breast
　　The wild-flowers who will stoop to
　　　number?
A few can touch the magic string,
　　And noisy Fame is proud to win
　　　them : —
Alas for those that never sing,
　　But die with all their music in them !

Nay, grieve not for the dead alone
　　Whose song has told their hearts' sad
　　　story, —
Weep for the voiceless, who have known
　　The cross without the crown of glory !
Not where Leucadian breezes sweep
　　O'er Sappho's memory-haunted billow,
But where the glistening night-dews
　　weep
　　On nameless sorrow's churchyard pil-
　　　low.

O hearts that break and give no sign
　　Save whitening lip and fading tresses,
Till Death pours out his cordial wine
　　Slow-dropped from Misery's crushing
　　　presses, —
If singing breath or echoing chord
　　To every hidden pang were given,
What endless melodies were poured,
　　As sad as earth, as sweet as heaven !

THE TWO STREAMS.

BEHOLD the rocky wall
　　That down its sloping sides

Pours the swift rain-drops, blending, as
　　they fall,
　　In rushing river-tides !

Yon stream, whose sources run
　　Turned by a pebble's edge,
Is Athabasca, rolling toward the sun
　　Through the cleft mountain-ledge.

The slender rill had strayed,
　　But for the slanting stone,
To evening's ocean, with the tangled
　　braid
　　Of foam-flecked Oregon.

So from the heights of Will
　　Life's parting stream descends,
And, as a moment turns its slender rill,
　　Each widening torrent bends, —

From the same cradle's side,
　　From the same mother's knee, —
One to long darkness and the frozen tide,
　　One to the Peaceful Sea !

THE PROMISE.

NOT charity we ask,
　　Nor yet thy gift refuse ;
Please thy light fancy with the easy task
　　Only to look and choose.

The little-heeded toy
　　That wins thy treasured gold
May be the dearest memory, holiest joy,
　　Of coming years untold.

Heaven rains on every heart,
　　But there its showers divide,

The drops of mercy choosing as they part
    The dark or glowing side.

One kindly deed may turn
    The fountain of thy soul
To love's sweet day-star, that shall o'er
        thee burn
    Long as its currents roll !

The pleasures thou hast planned, —
    Where shall their memory be
When the white angel with the freezing
        hand
    Shall sit and watch by thee ?

Living, thou dost not live,
    If mercy's spring run dry ;
What Heaven has lent thee wilt thou
        freely give,
    Dying, thou shalt not die !

HE promised even so !
    To thee His lips repeat, —
Behold, the tears that soothed thy
        sister's woe
    Have washed thy Master's feet !

March 20, 1859.

AVIS.

I MAY not rightly call thy name, —
    Alas ! thy forehead never knew
The kiss that happier children claim,
    Nor glistened with baptismal dew.

Daughter of want and wrong and woe,
    I saw thee with thy sister-band,
Snatched from the whirlpool's narrowing
        flow
    By Mercy's strong yet trembling hand.

— "Avis !" — With Saxon eye and cheek,
    At once a woman and a child,
The saint uncrowned I came to seek
    Drew near to greet us, — spoke, and
        smiled.

God gave that sweet sad smile she wore
    All wrong to shame, all souls to win, —
A heavenly sunbeam sent before
    Her footsteps through a world of sin.

— "And who is Avis ?" — Hear the tale
    The calm - voiced matrons gravely
        tell, —
The story known through all the vale
    Where Avis and her sisters dwell.

With the lost children running wild,
    Strayed from the hand of human care,
They find one little refuse child
    Left helpless in its poisoned lair.

The primal mark is on her face, —
    The chattel-stamp, — the pariah-stain
That follows still her hunted race, —
    The curse without the crime of Cain.

How shall our smooth-turned phrase re-
        late
    The little suffering outcast's ail ?
Not Lazarus at the rich man's gate
    So turned the rose-wreathed revellers
        pale.

Ah, veil the living death from sight
    That wounds our beauty-loving eye !
The children turn in selfish fright,
    The white-lipped nurses hurry by.

Take her, dread Angel ! Break in love
    This bruisèd reed and make it thine ! —
No voice descended from above,
    But Avis answered, "She is mine."

The task that dainty menials spurn
    The fair young girl has made her own ;
Her heart shall teach, her hand shall
        learn
    The toils, the duties yet unknown.

So Love and Death in lingering strife
    Stand face to face from day to day,

Still battling for the spoil of Life
  While the slow seasons creep away.

Love conquers Death ; the prize is won ;
  See to her joyous bosom pressed
The dusky daughter of the sun, —
  The bronze against the marble breast !

Her task is done ; no voice divine
  Has crowned her deeds with saintly
    fame.
No eye can see the aureole shine
  That rings her brow with heavenly
    flame.

Yet what has holy page more sweet,
  Or what had woman's love more fair,
When Mary clasped her Saviour's feet
  With flowing eyes and streaming hair ?

Meek child of sorrow, walk unknown,
  The Angel of that earthly throng,
And let thine image live alone
  To hallow this unstudied song !

THE LIVING TEMPLE.

Not in the world of light alone,
Where God has built his blazing throne
Nor yet alone in earth below,
With belted seas that come and go,
And endless isles of sunlit green,
Is all thy Maker's glory seen :
Look in upon thy wondrous frame, —
Eternal wisdom still the same !

The smooth, soft air with pulse-like
    waves
Flows murmuring through its hidden
    caves,
Whose streams of brightening purple
    rush,
Fired with a new and livelier blush,
While all their burden of decay
The ebbing current steals away,

And red with Nature's flame they start
From the warm fountains of the heart.

No rest that throbbing slave may ask,
Forever quivering o'er his task,
While far and wide a crimson jet
Leaps forth to fill the woven net
Which in unnumbered crossing tides
The flood of burning life divides,
Then, kindling each decaying part,
Creeps back to find the throbbing heart.

But warmed with that unchanging flame
Behold the outward moving frame,
Its living marbles jointed strong
With glistening band and silvery thong,
And linked to reason's guiding reins
By myriad rings in trembling chains,
Each graven with the threaded zone
Which claims it as the master's own.

See how yon beam of seeming white
Is braided out of seven-hued light,
Yet in those lucid globes no ray
By any chance shall break astray.
Hark how the rolling surge of sound,
Arches and spirals circling round,
Wakes the hushed spirit through thine
    ear
With music it is heaven to hear.

Then mark the cloven sphere that holds
All thought in its mysterious folds.
That feels sensations faintest thrill,
And flashes forth the sovereign will ;
Think on the stormy world that dwells
Locked in its dim and clustering cells !
The lightning gleams of power it sheds
Along its hollow glassy threads !

O Father ! grant thy love divine
To make these mystic temples thine !
When wasting age and wearying strife
Have sapped the leaning walls of life,

When darkness gathers over all,
And the last tottering pillars fall,
Take the poor dust thy mercy warms,
And mould it into heavenly forms !

AT A BIRTHDAY FESTIVAL

TO J. R. LOWELL.

WE will not speak of years to-night, —
　For what have years to bring
But larger floods of love and light,
　And sweeter songs to sing ?

We will not drown in wordy praise
　The kindly thoughts that rise ;
If Friendship own one tender phrase,
　He reads it in our eyes.

We need not waste our school-boy art
　To gild this notch of Time ; —
Forgive me if my wayward heart
　Has throbbed in artless rhyme.

Enough for him the silent grasp
　That knits us hand in hand,
And he the bracelet's radiant clasp
　That locks our circling band.

Strength to his hours of manly toil !
　Peace to his starlit dreams !
Who loves alike the furrowed soil,
　The music-haunted streams !

Sweet smiles to keep forever bright
　The sunshine on his lips,
And faith that sees the ring of light
　Round nature's last eclipse !

February 22, 1859.

A BIRTHDAY TRIBUTE.

TO J. F. CLARKE.

WHO is the shepherd sent to lead,
　Through pastures green, the Master's
　　sheep ?

What guileless " Israelite indeed "
　The folded flock may watch and keep ?

He who with manliest spirit joins
　The heart of gentlest human mould,
With burning light and girded loins,
　To guide the flock, or watch the fold ;

True to all Truth the world denies,
　Not tongue-tied for its gilded sin ;
Not always right in all men's eyes,
　But faithful to the light within ;

Who asks no meed of earthly fame,
　Who knows no earthly master's call,
Who hopes for man, through guilt and
　　shame,
　Still answering, " God is over all " ;

Who makes another's grief his own,
　Whose smile lends joy a double cheer ;
Where lives the saint, if such be
　　known ? —
　Speak softly, — such an one is here !

O faithful shepherd ! thou hast borne
　The heat and burden of the day ;
Yet, o'er thee, bright with beams un-
　　shorn,
　The sun still shows thine onward way.

To thee our fragrant love we bring,
　In buds that April half displays,
Sweet first-born angels of the spring,
　Caught in their opening hymn of
　　praise.

What though our faltering accents fail,
　Our captives know their message well,
Our words unbreathed their lips exhale,
　And sigh more love than ours can tell.

April 4, 1860.

JAMES RUSSELL LOWELL.　Page 144.

THE GRAY CHIEF.

FOR THE MEETING OF THE MASSACHU-
SETTS MEDICAL SOCIETY, 1859.

'T is sweet to fight our battles o'er,
  And crown with honest praise
The gray old chief, who strikes no
    more
  The blow of better days.

Before the true and trusted sage
  With willing hearts we bend,
When years have touched with hallowing
    age
  Our Master, Guide, and Friend.

For all his manhood's labor past,
  For love and faith long tried,
His age is honored to the last,
  Though strength and will have died.

But when, untamed by toil and strife,
  Full in our front he stands,
The torch of light, the shield of life,
  Still lifted in his hands,

No temple, though its walls resound
  With bursts of ringing cheers,
Can hold the honors that surround
  His manhood's twice-told years !

THE LAST LOOK.

W. W. SWAIN.

BEHOLD — not him we knew !
This was the prison which his soul
    looked through,
  Tender, and brave, and true.

His voice no more is heard ;
And his dead name — that dear familiar
    word —
  Lies on our lips unstirred.

He spake with poet's tongue ;
Living, for him the minstrel's lyre was
    strung :
  He shall not die unsung !

Grief tried his love, and pain ;
And the long bondage of his martyr-
    chain
  Vexed his sweet soul, — in vain !

It felt life's surges break,
As, girt with stormy seas, his island
    lake,
  Smiling while tempests wake.

How can we sorrow more ?
Grieve not for him whose heart had
    gone before
  To that untrodden shore !

Lo, through its leafy screen,
A gleam of sunlight on a ring of green,
  Untrodden, half unseen !

Here let his body rest,
Where the calm shadows that his soul
    loved best
  May slide above his breast.

Smooth his uncurtained bed ;
And if some natural tears are softly shed,
  It is not for the dead.

Fold the green turf aright
For the long hours before the morning's
    light,
  And say the last Good Night !

And plant a clear white stone
Close by those mounds which hold his
    loved, his own, —
  Lonely, but not alone.

Here let him sleeping lie,
Till Heaven's bright watchers slumber
    in the sky
  And Death himself shall die !

NAUSHON, September 22, 1858.

IN MEMORY OF CHARLES WENTWORTH UPHAM, JR.

HE was all sunshine ; in his face
 The very soul of sweetness shone ;
Fairest and gentlest of his race ;
 None like him we can call our own.

Something there was of one that died
 In her fresh spring-time long ago,
Our first dear Mary, angel-eyed,
 Whose smile it was a bliss to know.

Something of her whose love imparts
 Such radiance to her day's decline,
We feel its twilight in our hearts
 Bright as the earliest morning-shine.

Yet richer strains our eye could trace
 That made our plainer mould more
  fair,
That curved the lip with happier grace,
 That waved the soft and silken hair.

Dust unto dust ! the lips are still
 That only spoke to cheer and bless ;
The folded hands lie white and chill
 Unclasped from sorrow's last caress.

Leave him in peace ; he will not heed
 These idle tears we vainly pour,
Give back to earth the fading weed
 Of mortal shape his spirit wore.

"Shall I not weep my heartstrings torn,
 My flower of love that falls half blown,
My youth uncrowned, my life forlorn,
 A thorny path to walk alone ? "

O Mary ! one who bore thy name,
 Whose Friend and Master was divine,
Sat waiting silent till He came,
 Bowed down in speechless grief like
  thine.

"Where have ye laid him ? " "Come,"
  they say,
 Pointing to where the loved one slept ;
Weeping, the sister led the way, —
 And, seeing Mary, " Jesus wept."

He weeps with thee, with all that mourn,
 And He shall wipe thy streaming eyes
Who knew all sorrows, woman-born, —
 Trust in his word ; thy dead shall rise !

April 15, 1860.

MARTHA.

DIED JANUARY 7, 1861.

SEXTON ! Martha 's dead and gone ;
 Toll the bell ! toll the bell !
Her weary hands their labor cease ;
Good night, poor Martha, — sleep in
  peace !
 Toll the bell !

Sexton ! Martha 's dead and gone ;
 Toll the bell ! toll the bell !
For many a year has Martha said,
" I 'm old and poor, — would I were
  dead ! "
 Toll the bell !

Sexton ! Martha 's dead and gone ;
 Toll the bell ! toll the bell !
She 'll bring no more, by day or night,
Her basket full of linen white.
 Toll the bell !

Sexton ! Martha 's dead and gone ;
 Toll the bell ! toll the bell !
'T is fitting she should lie below
A pure white sheet of drifted snow.
 Toll the bell !

Sexton ! Martha 's dead and gone ;
 Toll the bell ! toll the bell !

Sleep, Martha, sleep, to wake in light,
Where all the robes are stainless white.
    Toll the bell !

MEETING OF THE ALUMNI OF HAR-VARD COLLEGE.

1857.

I THANK you, MR. PRESIDENT, you 've
    kindly broke the ice ;
Virtue should always be the first, — I 'm
    only SECOND VICE —
(A vice is something with a screw that 's
    made to hold its jaw
Till some old file has played away upon
    an ancient saw).

Sweet brothers by the Mother's side,
    the babes of days gone by,
All nurslings of her Juno breasts whose
    milk is never dry,
We come again, like half-grown boys,
    and gather at her beck
About her knees, and on her lap, and
    clinging round her neck.

We find her at her stately door, and in
    her ancient chair,
Dressed in the robes of red and green
    she always loved to wear.
Her eye has all its radiant youth, her
    cheek its morning flame ;
We drop our roses as we go, hers flourish
    still the same.

We have been playing many an hour,
    and far away we 've strayed,
Some laughing in the cheerful sun, some
    lingering in the shade ;
And some have tired, and laid them down
    where darker shadows fall, —
Dear as her loving voice may be, they
    cannot hear its call.

What miles we 've travelled since we
    shook the dew-drops from our shoes

We gathered on this classic green, so
    famed for heavy dues !
How many boys have joined the game,
    how many slipped away,
Since we 've been running up and down,
    and having out our play !

One boy at work with book and brief,
    and one with gown and band,
One sailing vessels on the pool, one dig-
    ging in the sand,
One flying paper kites on change, one
    planting little pills, —
The seeds of certain annual flowers well
    known as little bills.

What maidens met us on our way, and
    clasped us hand in hand !
What cherubs, — not the legless kind,
    that fly, but never stand !
How many a youthful head we 've seen
    put on its silver crown !
What sudden changes back again to
    youth's empurpled brown !

But fairer sights have met our eyes, and
    broader lights have shone,
Since others lit their midnight lamps
    where once we trimmed our own ;
A thousand trains that flap the sky with
    flags of rushing fire,
And, throbbing in the Thunderer's hand,
    Thought's million-chorded lyre.

We 've seen the sparks of Empire fly
    beyond the mountain bars,
Till, glittering o'er the Western wave,
    they joined the setting stars ;
And ocean trodden into paths that
    trampling giants ford,
To find the planet's vertebræ and sink
    its spinal cord.

We 've tried reform, — and chloroform,
    — and both have turned our brain ;

When France called up the photograph,
  we roused the foe to pain ;
Just so those earlier sages shared the
  chaplet of renown, —
Hers sent a bladder to the clouds, ours
  brought their lightning down.

We 've seen the little tricks of life, its
  varnish and veneer,
Its stucco-fronts of character flake off
  and disappear,
We 've learned that oft the brownest
  hands will heap the biggest pile,
And met with many a " perfect brick "
  beneath a rimless " tile."

What dreams we 've had of deathless
  name, as scholars, statesmen, bards,
While Fame, the lady with the trump,
  held up her picture cards !
Till, having nearly played our game, she
  gayly whispered, " Ah !
I said you should be something grand, —
  you 'll soon be grandpapa."

Well, well, the old have had their day,
  the young must take their turn ;
There 's something always to forget, and
  something still to learn ;
But how to tell what 's old or young,
  the tap-root from the sprigs,
Since Florida revealed her fount to
  Ponce de Leon Twiggs ?

The wisest was a Freshman once, just
  freed from bar and bolt,
As noisy as a kettle-drum, as leggy as a
  colt ;
Don't be too savage with the boys, —
  the Primer does not say
The kitten ought to go to church because
  the cat doth prey.

The law of merit and of age is not the
  rule of three ;

Non constat that A. M. must prove as
  busy as A. B.
When Wise the father tracked the son,
  ballooning through the skies,
He taught a lesson to the old, — go thou
  and do like Wise !

Now then, old boys, and reverend youth,
  of high of low degree,
Remember how we only get one annual
  out of three,
And such as dare to simmer down three
  dinners into one
Must cut their salads mighty short, and
  pepper well with fun.

I 've passed my zenith long ago, it 's time
  for me to set ;
A dozen planets wait to shine, and I am
  lingering yet,
As sometimes in the blaze of day a milk-
  and-watery moon
Stains with its dim and fading ray the
  lustrous blue of noon.

Farewell ! yet let one echo rise to shake
  our ancient hall ;
God save the Queen, — whose throne is
  here, — the Mother of us all !
Till dawns the great commencement-day
  on every shore and sea,
And " Expectantur " all mankind, to
  take their last Degree !

THE PARTING SONG.

FESTIVAL OF THE ALUMNI, 1857.

THE noon of summer sheds its ray
  On Harvard's holy ground ;
The Matron calls, the sons obey,
  And gather smiling round.

CHORUS.

Then old and young together stand,
  The sunshine and the snow,

As heart to heart, and hand in hand,
  We sing before we go !

Her hundred opening doors have swung ;
  Through every storied hall
The pealing echoes loud have rung,
  "Thrice welcome one and all ! "
    Then old and young, etc.

We floated through her peaceful bay,
  To sail life's stormy seas ;
But left our anchor where it lay
  Beneath her green old trees.
    Then old and young, etc.

As now we lift its lengthening chain,
  That held us fast of old,
The rusted rings grow bright again, —
  Their iron turns to gold.
    Then old and young, etc.

Though scattered ere the setting sun,
  As leaves when wild winds blow,
Our home is here, are hearts are one,
  Till Charles forgets to flow.
    Then old and young, etc.

FOR THE MEETING OF THE NATIONAL SANITARY ASSOCIATION.

1860.

WHAT makes the Healing Art divine ?
  The bitter drug we buy and sell,
The brands that scorch, the blades that
    shine,
  The scars we leave, the " cures " we
    tell ?

Are these thy glories, holiest Art, —
  The trophies that adorn thee best, —
Or but thy triumph's meanest part, —
  Where mortal weakness stands con-
    fessed ?

We take the arms that Heaven supplies
  For Life's long battle with Disease,
Taught by our various need to prize
  Our frailest weapons, even these.

But ah ! when Science drops her shield —
  Its peaceful shelter proved in vain —
And bares her snow-white arm to wield
  The sad, stern ministry of pain ;

When shuddering o'er the fount of life,
  She folds her heaven-anointed wings,
To lift unmoved the glittering knife
  That searches all its crimson springs ;

When, faithful to her ancient lore,
  She thrusts aside her fragrant balm
For blistering juice, or cankering ore,
  And tames them till they cure or
    calm ;

When in her gracious hand are seen
  The dregs and scum of earth and seas,
Her kindness counting all things clean
  That lend the sighing sufferer ease ;

Though on the field that Death has won,
  She save some stragglers in retreat ;—
These single acts of mercy done
  Are but confessions of defeat.

What though our tempered poisons save
  Some wrecks of life from aches and
    ails ;
Those grand specifics Nature gave
  Were never poised by weights or
    scales !

God lent his creatures light and air,
  And waters open to the skies ;
Man locks him in a stifling lair,
  And wonders why his brother dies !

In vain our pitying tears are shed,
  In vain we rear the sheltering pile

Where Art weeds out from bed to bed
   The plagues we planted by the mile !

Be that the glory of the past ;
   With these our sacred toils begin :
So flies in tatters from its mast
   The yellow flag of sloth and sin,

And lo ! the starry folds reveal
   The blazoned truth we hold so dear :
To guard is better than to heal, —
   The shield is nobler than the spear !

FOR THE BURNS CENTENNIAL CELE-BRATION.

JANUARY 25, 1859.

His birthday. — Nay, we need not speak
   The name each heart is beating, —
Each glistening eye and flushing cheek
   In light and flame repeating !

We come in one tumultuous tide, —
   One surge of wild emotion, —
As crowding through the Frith of Clyde
   Rolls in the Western Ocean ;

As when yon cloudless, quartered moon
   Hangs o'er each storied river,
The swelling breasts of Ayr and Doon
   With sea-green wavelets quiver.

The century shrivels like a scroll, —
   The past becomes the present, —
And face to face, and soul to soul,
   We greet the monarch-peasant.

While Shenstone strained in feeble flights
   With Corydon and Phillis, —
While Wolfe was climbing Abraham's heights
   To snatch the Bourbon lilies, —

Who heard the wailing infant's cry,
   The babe beneath the sheeling,

Whose song to-night in every sky
   Will shake earth's starry ceiling, —

Whose passion-breathing voice ascends
   And floats like incense o'er us,
Whose ringing lay of friendship blends
   With labor's anvil chorus ?

We love him, not for sweetest song,
   Though never tone so tender ;
We love him, even in his wrong, —
   His wasteful self-surrender.

We praise him, not for gifts divine, —
   His Muse was born of woman, —
His manhood breathes in every line, —
   Was ever heart more human ?

We love him, praise him, just for this :
   In every form and feature,
Through wealth and want, through woe
      and bliss,
   He saw his fellow-creature !

No soul could sink beneath his love, —
   Not even angel blasted ;
No mortal power could soar above
   The pride that all outlasted !

Ay ! Heaven had set one living man
   Beyond the pedant's tether, —
His virtues, frailties, HE may scan,
   Who weighs them all together !

I fling my pebble on the cairn
   Of him, though dead, undying ;
Sweet Nature's nursling, bonniest bairn
   Beneath her daisies lying.

The waning suns, the wasting globe,
   Shall spare the minstrel's story, —
The centuries weave his purple robe,
   The mountain-mist of glory !

BOSTON COMMON. — THREE PICTURES.

FOR THE FAIR IN AID OF THE FUND
TO PROCURE BALL'S STATUE OF WASH-
INGTON.

1630.

ALL overgrown with bush and fern,
  And straggling clumps of tangled
    trees,
With trunks that lean and boughs that
    turn,
  Bent eastward by the mastering
    breeze, —
With spongy bogs that drip and fill
  A yellow pond with muddy rain,
Beneath the shaggy southern hill
  Lies wet and low the Shawmut plain.
And hark ! the trodden branches crack ;
  A crow flaps off with startled scream ;
A straying woodchuck canters back ;
  A bittern rises from the stream ;
Leaps from his lair a frightened deer ;
  An otter plunges in the pool ; —
Here comes old Shawmut's pioneer,
  The parson on his brindled bull !

1774.

THE streets are thronged with trampling
    feet,
  The northern hill is ridged with graves,
But night and morn the drum is beat
  To frighten down the " rebel knaves."
The stones of King Street still are red,
  And yet the bloody red-coats come :
I hear their pacing sentry's tread,
  The click of steel, the tap of drum,
And over all the open green,
  Where grazed of late the harmless
    kine,
The cannon's deepening ruts are seen,
  The war-horse stamps, the bayonets
    shine.
The clouds are dark with crimson rain
  Above the murderous hirelings' den,

And soon their whistling showers shall
    stain
  The pipe-clayed belts of Gage's men.

186 . . . .

AROUND the green, in morning light,
  The spired and palaced summits blaze,
And, sunlike, from her Beacon-height
  The dome-crowned city spreads her
    rays ;
They span the waves, they belt the plains,
  They skirt the roads with bands of
    white,
Till with a flash of gilded panes
  Yon farthest hillside bounds the sight.
Peace, Freedom, Wealth ! no fairer view,
  Though with the wild-bird's restless
    wings
We sailed beneath the noontide's blue
  Or chased the moonlight's endless
    rings !
Here, fitly raised by grateful hands
  His holiest memory to recall,
The Hero's, Patriot's image stands ;
  He led our sires who won them all !

November 14, 1859.

THE OLD MAN OF THE SEA.

A NIGHTMARE DREAM BY DAYLIGHT.

DO you know the Old Man of the Sea,
    of the Sea ?
  Have you met with that dreadful old
    man ?
If you have n't been caught, you will be,
    you will be ;
  For catch you he must and he can.

He does n't hold on by your throat, by
    your throat,
  As of old in the terrible tale ;
But he grapples you tight by the coat,
    by the coat,
  Till its buttons and button-holes fail.

There's the charm of a snake in his eye,
in his eye,
And a polypus-grip in his hands ;
You cannot go back, nor get by, nor get
by,
If you look at the spot where he
stands.

O, you're grabbed ! See his claw on
your sleeve, on your sleeve !
It is Sinbad's Old Man of the Sea !
You're a Christian, no doubt you be-
lieve, you believe :
You're a martyr, whatever you be !

— Is the breakfast-hour past ? They
must wait, they must wait,
While the coffee boils sullenly down,
While the Johnny-cake burns on the
grate, on the grate,
And the toast is done frightfully
brown.

— Yes, your dinner will keep ; let it
cool, let it cool,
And Madam may worry and fret,
And children half-starved go to school,
go to school ;
He can't think of sparing you yet.

— Hark ! the bell for the train ! "Come
along ! Come along !
For there isn't a second to lose."
"ALL ABOARD !" (He holds on.) "Fsht !
ding-dong ! Fsht ! ding-dong !" —
You can follow on foot, if you choose.

— There's a maid with a cheek like a
peach, like a peach,
That is waiting for you in the
church ; —
But he clings to your side like a leech,
like a leech,
And you leave your lost bride in the
lurch.

— There's a babe in a fit, — hurry
quick ! hurry quick !
To the doctor's as fast as you can !
The baby is off, while you stick, while
you stick,
In the grip of the dreadful Old Man !

— I have looked on the face of the Bore,
of the Bore ;
The voice of the Simple I know ;
I have welcomed the Flat at my door, at
my door ;
I have sat by the side of the Slow ;

I have walked like a lamb by the friend,
by the friend,
That stuck to my skirts like a bur ;
I have borne the stale talk without end,
without end,
Of the sitter whom nothing could stir :

But my hamstrings grow loose, and I
shake, and I shake,
At the sight of the dreadful Old Man ;
Yea, I quiver and quake, and I take,
and I take,
To my legs with what vigor I can !

O the dreadful Old Man of the Sea, of
the Sea !
He's come back like the Wandering
Jew !
He has had his cold claw upon me, upon
me, —
And be sure that he'll have it on you !

INTERNATIONAL ODE.

OUR FATHERS' LAND.[1]

God bless our Fathers' Land !
Keep her in heart and hand
One with our own !

[1] Sung in unison by twelve hundred chil-
dren of the public schools, at the visit of the
Prince of Wales to Boston, October 18, 1860.
Air, "God save the Queen."

From all her foes defend,
Be her brave People's Friend,
On all her realms descend,
Protect her Throne !

Father, with loving care
Guard Thou her kingdom's Heir,
Guide all his ways :
Thine arm his shelter be,
From him by land and sea
Bid storm and danger flee,
Prolong his days !

Lord, let War's tempest cease,
Fold the whole Earth in peace
Under thy wings !
Make all Thy nations one,
All hearts beneath the sun,
Till Thou shalt reign alone,
Great King of kings !

VIVE LA FRANCE!

A SENTIMENT OFFERED AT THE DINNER
TO H. I. H. THE PRINCE NAPOLEON, AT
THE REVERE HOUSE, SEPT. 25, 1861.

THE land of sunshine and of song !
Her name your hearts divine ;
To her the banquet's vows belong
Whose breasts have poured its
wine ;
Our trusty friend, our true ally
Through varied change and chance :
So, fill your flashing goblets high, —
I give you, VIVE LA FRANCE !

Above our hosts in triple folds
The selfsame colors spread,
Where Valor's faithful arm upholds
The blue, the white, the red ;
Alike each nation's glittering crest
Reflects the morning's glance, —
Twin eagles, soaring east and west :
Once more, then, VIVE LA FRANCE !

Sister in trial ! who shall count
Thy generous friendship's claim,
Whose blood ran mingling in the fount
That gave our land its name,
Till Yorktown saw in blended line
Our conquering arms advance,
And victory's double garlands twine
Our banners ?   VIVE LA FRANCE !

O land of heroes ! in our need
One gift from Heaven we crave
To stanch these wounds that vainly
bleed, —
The wise to lead the brave !
Call back one Captain of thy past
From glory's marble trance,
Whose name shall be a bugle-blast
To rouse us !   VIVE LA FRANCE !

Pluck Condé's baton from the trench,
Wake up stout Charles Martel,
Or find some woman's hand to clench
The sword of La Pucelle !
Give us one hour of old Turenne, —
One lift of Bayard's lance, —
Nay, call Marengo's Chief again
To lead us !   VIVE LA FRANCE !

Ah, hush ! our welcome Guest shall hear
But sounds of peace and joy ;
No angry echo vex thine ear,
Fair Daughter of Savoy !
Once more ! the land of arms and arts,
Of glory, grace, romance ;
Her love lies warm in all our hearts :
God bless her !   VIVE LA FRANCE !

BROTHER JONATHAN'S LAMENT FOR SISTER CAROLINE.

SHE has gone, — she has left us in passion and pride, —
Our stormy-browed sister, so long at our
side !

She has torn her own star from our firmament's glow,
And turned on her brother the face of a foe !

O Caroline, Caroline, child of the sun,
We can never forget that our hearts have been one, —
Our foreheads both sprinkled in Liberty's name,
From the fountain of blood with the finger of flame !

You were always too ready to fire at a touch ;
But we said, " She is hasty, — she does not mean much."
We have scowled, when you uttered some turbulent threat ;
But Friendship still whispered, " Forgive and forget !"

Has our love all died out ? Have its altars grown cold ?
Has the curse come at last which the fathers foretold ?
Then Nature must teach us the strength of the chain
That her petulant children would sever in vain.

They may fight till the buzzards are gorged with their spoil,
Till the harvest grows black as it rots in the soil,
Till the wolves and the catamounts troop from their caves,
And the shark tracks the pirate, the lord of the waves :

In vain is the strife ! When its fury is past,
Their fortunes must flow in one channel at last,

As the torrents that rush from the mountains of snow
Roll mingled in peace through the valleys below.

Our Union is river, lake, ocean, and sky :
Man breaks not the medal, when God cuts the die !
Though darkened with sulphur, though cloven with steel,
The blue arch will brighten, the waters will heal !

O Caroline, Caroline, child of the sun,
There are battles with Fate that can never be won !
The star-flowering banner must never be furled,
For its blossoms of light are the hope of the world !

Go, then, our rash sister ! afar and aloof,
Run wild in the sunshine away from our roof ;
But when your heart aches and your feet have grown sore,
Remember the pathway that leads to our door !

March 25, 1861.

UNDER THE WASHINGTON ELM, CAMBRIDGE.

April 27, 1861.

EIGHTY years have passed, and more,
Since under the brave old tree
Our fathers gathered in arms, and swore
They would follow the sign their banners bore,
And fight till the land was free.

Half of their work was done,
Half is left to do, —

Cambridge, and Concord, and Lexing-
    ton !
When the battle is fought and won,
    What shall be told of you ?

Hark !—'t is the south-wind moans,—
    Who are the martyrs down ?
Ah, the marrow was true in your chil-
    dren's bones
That sprinkled with blood the cursed
    stones
    Of the murder-haunted town !

What if the storm-clouds blow ?
    What if the green leaves fall ?
Better the crashing tempest's throe
Than the army of worms that gnawed
    below ;
    Trample them one and all !

Then, when the battle is won,
    And the land from traitors free,
Our children shall tell of the strife begun
When Liberty's second April sun
    Was bright on our brave old tree !

FREEDOM, OUR QUEEN.

LAND where the banners wave last in
    the sun,
Blazoned with star-clusters, many in one,
Floating o'er prairie and mountain and
    sea ;
Hark ! 't is the voice of thy children to
    thee !

Here at thine altar our vows we re-
    new
Still in thy cause to be loyal and
    true, —
True to thy flag on the field and the
    wave,
Living to honor it, dying to save !

Mother of heroes ! if perfidy's blight
Fall on a star in thy garland of light,
Sound but one bugle-blast ! Lo ! at the
    sign
Armies all panoplied wheel into line !

Hope of the world ! thou hast broken its
    chains, —
Wear thy bright arms while a tyrant
    remains,
Stand for the right till the nations shall
    own
Freedom their sovereign, with Law for
    her throne !

Freedom ! sweet Freedom ! our voices
    resound,
Queen by God's blessing, unsceptred, un-
    crowned !
Freedom, sweet Freedom, our pulses
    repeat,
Warm with her life-blood, as long as
    they beat !

Fold the broad banner-stripes over her
    breast, —
Crown her with star-jewels Queen of the
    West !
Earth for her heritage, God for her
    friend,
She shall reign over us, world without
    end !

ARMY HYMN.

"Old Hundred."

O LORD of Hosts ! Almighty King !
Behold the sacrifice we bring !
To every arm Thy strength impart,
Thy spirit shed through every heart !

Wake in our breasts the living fires,
The holy faith that warmed our sires ;
Thy hand hath made our Nation free ;
To die for her is serving Thee.

Be Thou a pillared flame to show
The midnight snare, the silent foe ;
And when the battle thunders loud,
Still guide us in its moving cloud.

God of all Nations ! Sovereign Lord !
In Thy dread name we draw the sword,
We lift the starry flag on high
That fills with light our stormy sky.

From treason's rent, from murder's stain,
Guard Thou its folds till Peace shall
    reign, —
Till fort and field, till shore and sea,
Join our loud anthem, PRAISE TO THEE!

PARTING HYMN.

" Dundee."

FATHER of Mercies, Heavenly Friend,
    We seek Thy gracious throne ;
To Thee our faltering prayers ascend,
    Our fainting hearts are known !

From blasts that chill, from suns that
    smite,
    From every plague that harms ;
In camp and march, in siege and fight,
    Protect our men-at-arms !

Though from our darkened lives they
    take
    What makes our life most dear,
We yield them for their country's sake
    With no relenting tear.

Our blood their flowing veins will shed,
    Their wounds our breasts will share ;
O, save us from the woes we dread,
    Or grant us strength to bear !

Let each unhallowed cause that brings
    The stern destroyer cease,
Thy flaming angel fold his wings,
    And seraphs whisper Peace !

Thine are the sceptre and the sword,
    Stretch forth Thy mighty hand, —
Reign Thou our kingless nation's Lord,
    Rule Thou our throneless land !

THE FLOWER OF LIBERTY.

WHAT flower is this that greets the morn,
Its hues from Heaven so freshly born ?
With burning star and flaming band
It kindles all the sunset land :
O tell us what its name may be, —
Is this the Flower of Liberty ?
    It is the banner of the free,
    The starry Flower of Liberty !

In savage Nature's far abode
Its tender seed our fathers sowed ;
The storm-winds rocked its swelling bud,
Its opening leaves were streaked with
    blood,
Till lo ! earth's tyrants shook to see
The full-blown Flower of Liberty !
    Then hail the banner of the free,
    The starry Flower of Liberty !

Behold its streaming rays unite,
One mingling flood of braided light, —
The red that fires the Southern rose,
With spotless white from Northern snows,
And, spangled o'er its azure, see
The sister Stars of Liberty !
    Then hail the banner of the free,
    The starry Flower of Liberty !

The blades of heroes fence it round,
Where'er it springs is holy ground ;
From tower and dome its glories spread ;
It waves where lonely sentries tread ;
It makes the land as ocean free,
And plants an empire on the sea !
    Then hail the banner of the free,
    The starry Flower of Liberty !

Thy sacred leaves, fair Freedom's flower,
Shall ever float on dome and tower,

To all their heavenly colors true,
In blackening frost or crimson dew, —
And God love us as we love thee,
Thrice holy Flower of Liberty!
    Then hail the banner of the free,
    The starry FLOWER OF LIBERTY!

THE SWEET LITTLE MAN.

DEDICATED TO THE STAY-AT-HOME
RANGERS.

Now, while our soldiers are fighting our
    battles,
    Each at his post to do all that he can,
Down among rebels and contraband
    chattels,
    What are you doing, my sweet little
    man?

All the brave boys under canvas are
    sleeping,
    All of them pressing to march with
    the van,
Far from the home where their sweet-
    hearts are weeping;
    What are you waiting for, sweet little
    man?

You with the terrible warlike mus-
    taches,
    Fit for a colonel or chief of a clan,
You with the waist made for sword-belts
    and sashes,
    Where are your shoulder-straps, sweet
    little man?

Bring him the buttonless garment of
    woman!
    Cover his face lest it freckle and tan;
Muster the Apron-string Guards on the
    Common,
    That is the corps for the sweet little
    man!

Give him for escort a file of young misses,
    Each of them armed with a deadly
    rattan;
They shall defend him from laughter
    and hisses,
    Aimed by low boys at the sweet little
    man.

All the fair maidens about him shall
    cluster,
    Pluck the white feathers from bonnet
    and fan,
Make him a plume like a turkey-wing
    duster, —
    That is the crest for the sweet little
    man!

O, but the Apron-string Guards are the
    fellows!
    Drilling each day since our troubles
    began, —
"Handle your walking-sticks!"
    "Shoulder umbrellas!"
    That is the style for the sweet little
    man.

Have we a nation to save? In the first
    place
    Saving ourselves is the sensible
    plan, —
Surely the spot where there's shooting's
    the worst place
Where I can stand, says the sweet little
    man.

Catch me confiding my person with
    strangers!
    Think how the cowardly Bull-Run-
    ners ran!
In the brigade of the Stay-at-home
    Rangers
    Marches my corps, says the sweet
    little man.

Such was the stuff of the Malakoff-
    takers,

Such were the soldiers that scaled
the Redan ;
Truculent housemaids and bloodthirsty
Quakers,
  Brave not the wrath of the sweet
  little man !

Yield him the sidewalk, ye nursery
maidens !
Sauve qui peut! Bridget, and right
about ! Ann ; —
Fierce as a shark in a school of men-
hadens,
  See him advancing, the sweet little
  man !

When the red flails of the battle-field's
threshers
  Beat out the continent's wheat from
  its bran,
While the wind scatters the chaffy
seceshers,
  What will become of our sweet little
  man ?

When the brown soldiers come back
from the borders,
  How will he look while his features
  they scan ?
How will he feel when he gets marching
orders,
  Signed by his lady love ? sweet little
  man !

Fear not for him, though the rebels expect him, —
  Life is too precious to shorten its span ;
Woman her broomstick shall raise to
protect him,
  Will she not fight for the sweet little
  man !

Now then, nine cheers for the Stay-at-
home Ranger !
  Blow the great fish-horn and beat the
  big pan !

First in the field that is farthest from
danger,
  Take your white-feather plume, sweet
  little man !

UNION AND LIBERTY.

FLAG of the heroes who left us their
glory,
Borne through their battle-fields' thunder and flame,
Blazoned in song and illumined in story,
  Wave o'er us all who inherit their
  fame !
    Up with our banner bright,
    Sprinkled with starry light,
    Spread its fair emblems from moun-
    tain to shore,
      While through the sounding sky
      Loud rings the Nation's cry, —
    UNION AND LIBERTY ! ONE EVER-
    MORE !

Light of our firmament, guide of our
Nation,
  Pride of her children, and honored
  afar,
Let the wide beams of thy full constel-
lation
  Scatter each cloud that would darken
  a star !
    Up with our banner bright, etc.

Empire unsceptred ! what foe shall assail
thee,
  Bearing the standard of Liberty's
  van ?
Think not the God of thy fathers shall
fail thee,
  Striving with men for the birthright
  of man !
    Up with our banner bright, etc.

Yet if, by madness and treachery
blighted,

Dawns the dark hour when the sword
thou must draw,
Then with the arms of thy millions
united,
Smite the bold traitors to Freedom
and Law !
Up with our banner bright, etc.

Lord of the Universe ! shield us and
guide us,
Trusting thee always, through shadow
and sun !

Thou hast united us, who shall divide
us ?
Keep us, O keep us the MANY IN
ONE !
Up with our banner bright,
Sprinkled with starry light,
Spread its fair emblems from moun-
tain to shore,
While through the sounding sky
Loud rings the Nation's cry, —
UNION AND LIBERTY ! ONE EVER-
MORE !

POEMS

FROM THE

AUTOCRAT OF THE BREAKFAST TABLE.

1857-1858.

THE CHAMBERED NAUTILUS.

This is the ship of pearl, which, poets
    feign,
    Sails the unshadowed main, —
    The venturous bark that flings
On the sweet summer wind its purpled
    wings
In gulfs enchanted, where the Siren
    sings,
    And coral reefs lie bare,
Where the cold sea-maids rise to sun
    their streaming hair.

Its webs of living gauze no more unfurl;
    Wrecked is the ship of pearl!
    And every chambered cell,
Where its dim dreaming life was wont to
    dwell,
As the frail tenant shaped his growing
    shell,
    Before thee lies revealed, —
Its irised ceiling rent, its sunless crypt
    unsealed!

Year after year beheld the silent toil
    That spread his lustrous coil;
    Still, as the spiral grew,
He left the past year's dwelling for the
    new,
Stole with soft step its shining archway
    through,
    Built up its idle door,
Stretched in his last-found home, and
    knew the old no more.

Thanks for the heavenly message brought
    by thee,
    Child of the wandering sea,
    Cast from her lap, forlorn!
From thy dead lips a clearer note is
    born
Than ever Triton blew from wreathéd
    horn!
    While on mine ear it rings,
Through the deep caves of thought I
    hear a voice that sings: —

Build thee more stately mansions, O my
    soul,
    As the swift seasons roll!
    Leave thy low-vaulted past!
Let each new temple, nobler than the
    last,
Shut thee from heaven with a dome more
    vast,
    Till thou at length art free,
Leaving thine outgrown shell by life's
    unresting sea!

SUN AND SHADOW.

As I look from the isle, o'er its billows
    of green,
    To the billows of foam-crested blue,
Yon bark, that afar in the distance is
    seen,
Half dreaming, my eyes will pursue :
Now dark in the shadow, she scatters
    the spray
    As the chaff in the stroke of the flail ;
Now white as the sea-gull, she flies on
    her way,
    The sun gleaming bright on her sail.

Yet her pilot is thinking of dangers to
    shun, —
    Of breakers that whiten and roar ;
How little he cares, if in shadow or sun
    They see him who gaze from the shore !
He looks to the beacon that looms from
    the reef,
    To the rock that is under his lee,
As he drifts on the blast, like a wind-
    wafted leaf,
    O'er the gulfs of the desolate sea.

Thus drifting afar to the dim-vaulted
    caves
    Where life and its ventures are laid,
The dreamers who gaze while we battle
    the waves
    May see us in sunshine or shade ;
Yet true to our course, though the
    shadows grow dark,
    We'll trim our broad sail as before,
And stand by the rudder that governs
    the bark,
    Nor ask how we look from the shore !

THE TWO ARMIES.

As Life's unending column pours,
    Two marshalled hosts are seen, —
Two armies on the trampled shores
    That Death flows black between.

One marches to the drum-beat's roll,
    The wide-mouthed clarion's bray,
And bears upon a crimson scroll,
    " Our glory is to slay."

One moves in silence by the stream,
    With sad, yet watchful eyes,
Calm as the patient planet's gleam
    That walks the clouded skies.

Along its front no sabres shine,
    No blood-red pennons wave ;
Its banner bears the single line,
    " Our duty is to save."

For those no death-bed's lingering shade ;
    At Honor's trumpet-call,
With knitted brow and lifted blade
    In Glory's arms they fall.

For these no clashing falchions bright,
    No stirring battle-cry ;
The bloodless stabber calls by night, —
    Each answers, " Here am I ! "

For those the sculptor's laurelled bust,
    The builder's marble piles,
The anthems pealing o'er their dust
    Through long cathedral aisles.

For these the blossom-sprinkled turf
    That floods the lonely graves
When Spring rolls in her sea-green surf
    In flowery-foaming waves.

Two paths lead upward from below,
    And angels wait above,
Who count each burning life-drop's flow,
    Each falling tear of Love.

Though from the Hero's bleeding breast
    Her pulses Freedom drew,
Though the white lilies in her crest
    Sprang from that scarlet dew, —

"Sun and shadow."   Page 162.

While Valor's haughty champions wait
  Till all their scars are shown,
Love walks unchallenged through the
    gate,
  To sit beside the Throne !

MUSA.

O MY lost beauty ! — hast thou folded
    quite
  Thy wings of morning light
  Beyond those iron gates
Where Life crowds hurrying to the hag-
    gard Fates,
And Age upon his mound of ashes waits
  To chill our fiery dreams,
Hot from the heart of youth plunged in
    his icy streams?

Leave me not fading in these weeds of
    care,
  Whose flowers are silvered hair !
  Have I not loved thee long,
Though my young lips have often done
    thee wrong,
And vexed thy heaven-tuned ear with
    careless song ?
  Ah, wilt thou yet return,
Bearing thy rose-hued torch, and bid
    thine altar burn ?

Come to me ! — I will flood thy silent
    shrine
  With my soul's sacred wine,
  And heap thy marble floors
As the wild spice-trees waste their fra-
    grant stores,
In leafy islands walled with madrepores
  And lapped in Orient seas,
When all their feathery palms toss,
    plume-like, in the breeze.

Come to me ! — thou shalt feed on hon-
    eyed words,
  Sweeter than song of birds ; —

No wailing bulbul's throat,
No melting dulcimer's melodious note
When o'er the midnight wave its mur-
    murs float,
  Thy ravished sense might soothe
With flow so liquid-soft, with strain so
    velvet-smooth.

Thou shalt be decked with jewels, like
    a queen,
  Sought in those bowers of green
  Where loop the clustered vines
And the close-clinging dulcamara[1]
    twines, —
Pure pearls of Maydew where the moon-
    light shines,
  And Summer's fruited gems,
And coral pendants shorn from Autumn's
    berried stems.

Sit by me drifting on the sleepy waves, —
  Or stretched by grass-grown graves,
  Whose gray, high-shouldered stones,
Carved with old names Life's time-worn
    roll disowns,
Lean, lichen-spotted, o'er the crumbled
    bones
  Still slumbering where they lay
While the sad Pilgrim watched to scare
    the wolf away.

Spread o'er my couch thy visionary
    wing !
  Still let me dream and sing, —
  Dream of that winding shore
Where scarlet cardinals bloom — for me
    no more, —
The stream with heaven beneath its
    liquid floor,
  And clustering nenuphars
Sprinkling its mirrored blue like golden-
    chaliced stars !

[1] The "bitter-sweet" of New England is the
Celastrus scandens, — "Bourreau des arbres"
of the Canadian French.

Come while their balms the linden-blos-
soms shed ! —
  Come while the rose is red, —
  While blue-eyed Summer smiles
On the green ripples round yon sunken
piles
Washed by the moon-wave warm from
Indian isles,
  And on the sultry air
The chestnuts spread their palms like
holy men in prayer !

O for thy burning lips to fire my brain
  With thrills of wild, sweet pain ! —
  On life's autumnal blast,
Like shrivelled leaves, youth's passion-
flowers are cast, —
Once loving thee, we love thee to the
last ! —
  Behold thy new-decked shrine,
And hear once more the voice that
breathed "Forever thine !"

A PARTING HEALTH.

TO J. L. MOTLEY.

YES, we knew we must lose him, —
though friendship may claim
To blend her green leaves with the laurels of fame ;
Though fondly, at parting, we call him
our own,
'T is the whisper of love when the bugle
has blown.

As the rider that rests with the spur on
his heel,
As the guardsman that sleeps in his
corselet of steel,
As the archer that stands with his shaft
on the string,
He stoops from his toil to the garland
we bring.

What pictures yet slumber unborn in
his loom,
Till their warriors shall breathe and
their beauties shall bloom,
While the tapestry lengthens the life-
glowing dyes
That caught from our sunsets the stain
of their skies !

In the alcoves of death, in the charnels
of time,
Where flit the gaunt spectres of passion
and crime,
There are triumphs untold, there are
martyrs unsung,
There are heroes yet silent to speak with
his tongue !

Let us hear the proud story which time
has bequeathed !
From lips that are warm with the free-
dom they breathed !
Let him summon its tyrants, and tell us
their doom,
Though he sweep the black past like
Van Tromp with his broom !

*   *   *

The dream flashes by, for the west-winds
awake
On pampas, on prairie, o'er mountain
and lake,
To bathe the swift bark, like a sea-
girdled shrine,
With incense they stole from the rose
and the pine.

So fill a bright cup with the sunlight
that gushed
When the dead summer's jewels were
trampled and crushed :
THE TRUE KNIGHT OF LEARNING, —
the world holds him dear, —
Love bless him, Joy crown him, God
speed his career !

1857.

WHAT WE ALL THINK.

THAT age was older once than now,
In spite of locks untimely shed,
Or silvered on the youthful brow ;
That babes make love and children
wed.

That sunshine had a heavenly glow,
Which faded with those "good old
days"
When winters came with deeper snow,
And autumns with a softer haze.

That — mother, sister, wife, or child —
The "best of women" each has
known.
Were school-boys ever half so wild ?
How young the grandpapas have
grown !

That *but for this* our souls were free,
And *but for that* our lives were blest ;
That in some season yet to be
Our cares will leave us time to rest.

Whene'er we groan with ache or pain, —
Some common ailment of the race, —
Though doctors think the matter
plain, —
That ours is "a peculiar case."

That when like babes with fingers burned
We count one bitter maxim more,
Our lesson all the world has learned,
And men are wiser than before.

That when we sob o'er fancied woes,
The angels hovering overhead
Count every pitying drop that flows,
And love us for the tears we shed.

That when we stand with tearless eye
And turn the beggar from our door,
They still approve us when we sigh,
"Ah, had I but *one thousand more !*"

Though temples crowd the crumbled
brink
O'erhanging truth's eternal flow,
Their tablets bold with *what we think*,
Their echoes dumb to *what we know ;*

That one unquestioned text we read,
All doubt beyond, all fear above,
Nor crackling pile nor cursing creed
Can burn or blot it : GOD IS LOVE !

SPRING HAS COME.

INTRA MUROS.

THE sunbeams, lost for half a year,
Slant through my pane their morning
rays ;
For dry northwesters cold and clear,
The east blows in its thin blue haze.

And first the snowdrop's bells are seen,
Then close against the sheltering wall
The tulip's horn of dusky green,
The peony's dark unfolding ball.

The golden-chaliced crocus burns ;
The long narcissus-blades appear ;
The cone-beaked hyacinth returns
To light her blue-flamed chandelier.

The willow's whistling lashes, wrung
By the wild winds of gusty March,
With sallow leaflets lightly strung,
Are swaying by the tufted larch.

The elms have robed their slender spray
With full-blown flower and embryo
leaf ;
Wide o'er the clasping arch of day
Soars like a cloud their hoary chief.

See the proud tulip's flaunting cup,
That flames in glory for an hour, —
Behold it withering, — then look up, —
How meek the forest monarch's flower!

When wake the violets, Winter dies ;
  When sprout the elm-buds, Spring is
    near ;
When lilacs blossom, Summer cries,
  " Bud, little roses ! Spring is here ! "

The windows blush with fresh bouquets,
  Cut with the May-dew on their lips ;
The radish all its bloom displays,
  Pink as Aurora's finger-tips.

Nor less the flood of light that showers
  On beauty's changed corolla-shades,—
The walks are gay as bridal bowers
  With rows of many-petalled maids.

The scarlet shell-fish click and clash
  In the blue barrow where they slide ;
The horseman, proud of streak and
    splash,
  Creeps homeward from his morning
    ride.

Here comes the dealer's awkward string,
  With neck in rope and tail in knot, —
Rough colts, with careless country-swing,
  In lazy walk or slouching trot.

————

Wild filly from the mountain-side,
  Doomed to the close and chafing thills,
Lend me thy long, untiring stride
  To seek with thee thy western hills !

I hear the whispering voice of Spring,
  The thrush's trill, the robin's cry,
Like some poor bird with prisoned wing
  That sits and sings, but longs to fly.

O for one spot of living green, —
  One little spot where leaves can
    grow, —
To love unblamed, to walk unseen,
  To dream above, to sleep below !

PROLOGUE.

A PROLOGUE ? Well, of course the ladies
  know ; —
I have my doubts. No matter, — here
  we go !
What is a Prologue ? Let our Tutor
  teach :
Pro means beforehand ; *logos* stands for
  speech.
'T is like the harper's prelude on the
  strings,
The prima donna's courtesy ere she
  sings : —
Prologues in metre are to other *pros*
As worsted stockings are to engine-hose.
"The world 's a stage," — as Shake-
  speare said, one day ;
The stage a world — was what he meant
  to say.
The outside world 's a blunder, that is
  clear ;
The real world that Nature meant is here.
Here every foundling finds its lost
  mamma ;
Each rogue, repentant, melts his stern
  papa ;
Misers relent, the spendthrift's debts
  are paid,
The cheats are taken in the traps they
  laid ;
One after one the troubles all are past
Till the fifth act comes right side up at
  last,
When the young couple, old folks,
  rogues, and all,
Join hands, *so* happy at the curtain's fall.
Here suffering virtue ever finds relief,
And black-browed ruffians always come
  to grief.
When the lorn damsel, with a frantic
  screech,
And cheeks as hueless as a brandy-peach,
Cries, "Help, kyind Heaven !" and
  drops upon her knees

On the green — baize, — beneath the (canvas) trees, —
See to her side avenging Valor fly : —
"Ha! Villain! Draw! Now, Terraitorr, yield or die!"
When the poor hero flounders in despair,
Some dear lost uncle turns up millionnaire,
Clasps the young scrapegrace with paternal joy,
Sobs on his neck, "*My boy!* MY BOY!! MY BOY!!!"

Ours, then, sweet friends, the real world to-night,
Of love that conquers in disaster's spite.
Ladies, attend! While woful cares and doubt
Wrong the soft passion in the world without,
Though fortune scowl, though prudence interfere,
One thing is certain : Love will triumph here!
Lords of creation, whom your ladies rule, —
The world's great masters, when you 're out of school, —
Learn the brief moral of our evening's play:
Man has his will, — but woman has her way!
While man's dull spirit toils in smoke and fire,
Woman's swift instinct threads the electric wire, —
The magic bracelet stretched beneath the waves
Beats the black giant with his score of slaves.
All earthly powers confess your sovereign art
But that one rebel, — woman's wilful heart.
All foes you master, but a woman's wit

Lets daylight through you ere you know you 're hit.
So, just to picture what her art can do,
Hear an old story, made as good as new.

Rudolph, professor of the headsman's trade,
Alike was famous for his arm and blade.
One day a prisoner Justice had to kill
Knelt at the block to test the artist's skill.
Bare-armed, swart-visaged, gaunt, and shaggy-browed,
Rudolph the headsman rose above the crowd.
His falchion lighted with a sudden gleam,
As the pike's armor flashes in the stream.
He sheathed his blade ; he turned as if to go ;
The victim knelt, still waiting for the blow.
"Why strikest not? Perform thy murderous act,"
The prisoner said. (His voice was slightly cracked.)
"Friend, I *have* struck," the artist straight replied ;
"Wait but one moment, and yourself decide."
He held his snuff-box, — "Now then, if you please!"
The prisoner sniffed, and, with a crashing sneeze,
Off his head tumbled, — bowled along the floor, —
Bounced down the steps ; — the prisoner said no more!
Woman! thy falchion is a glittering eye ;
If death lurk in it, O how sweet to die!
Thou takest hearts as Rudolph took the head ;
We die with love, and never dream we 're dead!

LATTER-DAY WARNINGS.

When legislators keep the law,
  When banks dispense with bolts and
    locks, —
When berries — whortle, rasp, and
    straw —
  Grow bigger *downwards* through the
    box, —

When he that selleth house or land
  Shows leak in roof or flaw in right, —
When haberdashers choose the stand
  Whose window hath the broadest
    light, —

When preachers tell us all they think,
  And party leaders all they mean, —
When what we pay for, that we drink,
  From real grape and coffee-bean, —

When lawyers take what they would
    give,
  And doctors give what they would
    take, —
When city fathers eat to live,
  Save when they fast for conscience'
    sake, —

When one that hath a horse on sale
  Shall bring his merit to the proof,
Without a lie for every nail
  That holds the iron on the hoof, —

When in the usual place for rips
  Our gloves are stitched with special
    care,
And guarded well the whalebone tips
  Where first umbrellas need repair, —

When Cuba's weeds have quite forgot
  The power of suction to resist,
And claret-bottles harbor not
  Such dimples as would hold your
    fist, —

When publishers no longer steal,
  And pay for what they stole before, —
When the first locomotive's wheel
  Rolls through the Hoosac tunnel's
    bore ; —

Till then let Cumming blaze away,
  And Miller's saints blow up the globe ;
But when you see that blessed day,
  Then order your ascension robe !

ALBUM VERSES.

When Eve had led her lord away,
  And Cain had killed his brother,
The stars and flowers, the poets say,
  Agreed with one another

To cheat the cunning tempter's art,
  And teach the race its duty,
By keeping on its wicked heart
  Their eyes of light and beauty.

A million sleepless lids, they say,
  Will be at least a warning ;
And so the flowers would watch by day,
  The stars from eve to morning.

On hill and prairie, field and lawn,
  Their dewy eyes upturning,
The flowers still watch from reddening
    dawn
  Till western skies are burning.

Alas ! each hour of daylight tells
  A tale of shame so crushing,
That some turn white as sea-bleached
    shells,
  And some are always blushing.

But when the patient stars look down
  On all their light discovers,
The traitor's smile, the murderer's frown,
  The lips of lying lovers,

They try to shut their saddening eyes,
    And in the vain endeavor
We see them twinkling in the skies,
    And so they wink forever.

A GOOD TIME GOING!

BRAVE singer of the coming time,
    Sweet minstrel of the joyous present,
Crowned with the noblest wreath of
    rhyme,
The holly-leaf of Ayrshire's peasant,
Good by! Good by! — Our hearts and
    hands,
    Our lips in honest Saxon phrases,
Cry, God be with him, till he stands
    His feet among the English daisies!

'T is here we part; — for other eyes
    The busy deck, the fluttering streamer,
The dripping arms that plunge and rise,
    The waves in foam, the ship in tremor,
The kerchiefs waving from the pier,
    The cloudy pillar gliding o'er him,
The deep blue desert, lone and drear,
    With heaven above and home before
    him!

His home! — the Western giant smiles,
    And twirls the spotty globe to find
    it; —
This little speck the British Isles?
    'T is but a freckle, — never mind it!
He laughs, and all his prairies roll,
    Each gurgling cataract roars and
    chuckles,
And ridges stretched from pole to pole
    Heave till they crack their iron
    knuckles!

But Memory blushes at the sneer,
    And Honor turns with frown defiant,
And Freedom, leaning on her spear,
    Laughs louder than the laughing
    giant:

"An islet is a world," she said,
    "When glory with its dust has
    blended,
And Britain keeps her noble dead
    Till earth and seas and skies are
    rended!"

Beneath each swinging forest-bough
    Some arm as stout in death reposes, —
From wave-washed foot to heaven-kissed
    brow
    Her valor's life-blood runs in roses;
Nay, let our brothers of the West
    Write smiling in their florid pages,
One half her soil has walked the rest
    In poets, heroes, martyrs, sages!

Hugged in the clinging billow's clasp,
    From sea-weed fringe to mountain
    heather,
The British oak with rooted grasp
    Her slender handful holds together; —
With cliffs of white and bowers of green,
    And Ocean narrowing to caress her,
And hills and threaded streams be-
    tween, —
    Our little mother isle, God bless her!

In earth's broad temple where we stand,
    Fanned by the eastern gales that
    brought us,
We hold the missal in our hand,
    Bright with the lines our Mother
    taught us.
Where'er its blazoned page betrays
    The glistening links of gilded fetters,
Behold, the half-turned leaf displays
    Her rubric stained in crimson letters!

Enough! To speed a parting friend
    'T is vain alike to speak and listen; —
Yet stay, — these feeble accents blend
    With rays of light from eyes that
    glisten.
Good by! once more, — and kindly tell

In words of peace the young world's
story, —
And say, besides, we love too well
Our mothers' soil, our fathers' glory!

THE LAST BLOSSOM.

THOUGH young no more, we still would
dream
Of beauty's dear deluding wiles ;
The leagues of life to graybeards seem
Shorter than boyhood's lingering miles.

Who knows a woman's wild caprice ?
It played with Goethe's silvered hair,
And many a Holy Father's "niece"
Has softly smoothed the papal chair.

When sixty bids us sigh in vain
To melt the heart of sweet sixteen,
We think upon those ladies twain
Who loved so well the tough old Dean.

We see the Patriarch's wintry face,
The maid of Egypt's dusky glow,
And dream that Youth and Age embrace,
As April violets fill with snow.

Tranced in her lord's Olympian smile
His lotus-loving Memphian lies, —
The musky daughter of the Nile,
With plaited hair and almond eyes.

Might we but share one wild caress
Ere life's autumnal blossoms fall,
And Earth's brown, clinging lips impress
The long cold kiss that waits us all !

My bosom heaves, remembering yet
The morning of that blissful day,
When Rose, the flower of spring, I met,
And gave my raptured soul away.

Flung from her eyes of purest blue,
A lasso, with its leaping chain,
Light as a loop of larkspurs, flew
O'er sense and spirit, heart and brain.

Thou com'st to cheer my waning age,
Sweet vision, waited for so long !
Dove that would seek the poet's cage
Lured by the magic breath of song !

She blushes ! Ah, reluctant maid,
Love's *drapeau rouge* the truth has
told !
O'er girlhood's yielding barricade
Floats the great Leveller's crimson
fold !

Come to my arms ! — love heeds not
years ;
No frost the bud of passion knows. —
Ha ! what is this my frenzy hears ?
A voice behind me uttered, — Rose !

Sweet was her smile, — but not for me ;
Alas ! when woman looks *too* kind,
Just turn your foolish head and see, —
Some youth is walking close behind !

CONTENTMENT.

"Man wants but little here below."

LITTLE I ask ; my wants are few ;
I only wish a hut of stone,
(A *very plain* brown stone will do,)
That I may call my own ; —
And close at hand is such a one,
In yonder street that fronts the sun.

Plain food is quite enough for me ;
Three courses are as good as ten ; —
If Nature can subsist on three,
Thank Heaven for three. Amen !
I always thought cold victual nice ; —
My *choice* would be vanilla-ice.

I care not much for gold or land ; —
Give me a mortgage here and there, —

Some good bank-stock, some note of
    hand,
    Or trifling railroad share, —
I only ask that Fortune send
A *little* more than I shall spend.

Honors are silly toys, I know,
    And titles are but empty names ;
I would, *perhaps*, be Plenipo, —
    But only near St. James ;
I 'm very sure I should not care
To fill our Gubernator's chair.

Jewels are bawbles ; 't is a sin
    To care for such unfruitful things ; —
One good-sized diamond in a pin, —
    Some, *not so large*, in rings, —
A ruby, and a pearl, or so,
Will do for me ; — I laugh at show.

My dame should dress in cheap attire ;
    (Good, heavy silks are never dear ;) —
I own perhaps I *might* desire
    Some shawls of true Cashmere, —
Some marrowy crapes of China silk,
Like wrinkled skins on scalded milk.

I would not have the horse I drive
    So fast that folks must stop and stare ;
An easy gait — two, forty-five —
    Suits me ; I do not care ; —
Perhaps, for just a *single spurt*,
Some seconds less would do no hurt.

Of pictures, I should like to own
    Titians and Raphaels three or four, —
I love so much their style and tone, —
    One Turner, and no more,
(A   landscape, — foreground   golden
        dirt, —
The sunshine painted with a squirt.)

Of books but few, — some fifty score
    For daily use, and bound for wear ;
The rest upon an upper floor ; —
    Some *little* luxury *there*

Of red morocco's gilded gleam,
And vellum rich as country cream.

Busts, cameos, gems, — such things as
    these,
    Which others often show for pride,
I value for their power to please,
        And selfish churls deride ; —
One Stradivarius, I confess,
Two Meerschaums, I would fain possess.

Wealth's wasteful tricks I will not learn
    Nor ape the glittering upstart fool ; —
Shall not carved tables serve my turn,
        But *all* must be of buhl ?
Give grasping pomp its double share, —
I ask but *one* recumbent chair.

Thus humble let me live and die,
    Nor long for Midas' golden touch ;
If Heaven more generous gifts deny,
        I shall not miss them *much*, —
Too grateful for the blessing lent
Of simple tastes and mind content !

ÆSTIVATION.

AN UNPUBLISHED POEM, BY MY LATE
            LATIN TUTOR.

IN candent ire the solar splendor flames ;
The foles, languescent, pend from arid
        rames ;
His humid front the cive, anheling,
        wipes,
And dreams of erring on ventiferous ripes.

How dulce to vive occult to mortal eyes,
Dorm on the herb with none to supervise,
Carp the suave berries from the crescent
        vine,
And bibe the flow from longicaudate
        kine !

To me, alas ! no verdurous visions come,
Save yon exiguous pool's conferva-
        scum, —

No concave vast repeats the tender hue
That laves my milk-jug with celestial
    blue !

Me wretched ! Let me curr to quercine
    shades !
Effund your albid hausts, lactiferous
    maids !
O, might I vole to some umbrageous
    clump, —
Depart, — be off, — excede, — evade, —
    erump !

THE DEACON'S MASTERPIECE;

OR, THE WONDERFUL "ONE-HOSS SHAY."

A LOGICAL STORY.

HAVE you heard of the wonderful one-
    hoss shay,
That was built in such a logical way
It ran a hundred years to a day,
And then, of a sudden, it —— ah, but
    stay,
I'll tell you what happened without delay,
Scaring the parson into fits,
Frightening people out of their wits, —
Have you ever heard of that, I say ?

Seventeen hundred and fifty-five.
Georgius Secundus was then alive, —
Snuffy old drone from the German hive.
That was the year when Lisbon-town
Saw the earth open and gulp her down,
And Braddock's army was done so brown,
Left without a scalp to its crown.
It was on the terrible Earthquake-day
That the Deacon finished the one-hoss
    shay.

Now in building of chaises, I tell you
    what,
There is always *somewhere* a weakest
    spot, —
In hub, tire, felloe, in spring or thill,

In panel, or crossbar, or floor, or sill,
In screw, bolt, thoroughbrace, — lurk-
    ing still,
Find it somewhere you must and will, —
Above or below, or within or without, —
And that's the reason, beyond a doubt,
That a chaise *breaks down*, but does n't
    wear out.

But the Deacon swore, (as Deacons do,
With an " I dew vum," or an " I tell
    yeou,")
He would build one shay to beat the
    taown
'n' the keounty 'n' all the kentry raoun' ;
It should be so built that it *couldn'* break
    daown :
— "Fur," said the Deacon, "'t's mighty
    plain
Thut the weakes' place mus' stan' the
    strain ;
'n' the way t' fix it, uz I maintain,
        Is only jest
T' make that place uz strong uz the rest."

So the Deacon inquired of the village
    folk
Where he could find the strongest oak,
That could n't be split nor bent nor
    broke, —
That was for spokes and floor and
    sills ;
He sent for lancewood to make the thills ;
The crossbars were ash, from the straight-
    est trees,
The panels of white-wood, that cuts like
    cheese,
But lasts like iron for things like these ;
The hubs of logs from the "Settler's
    ellum," —
Last of its timber, — they could n't sell
    'em,
Never an axe had seen their chips,
And the wedges flew from between their
    lips,

Their blunt ends frizzled like celery-
    tips;
Step and prop-iron, bolt and screw,
Spring, tire, axle, and linchpin too,
Steel of the finest, bright and blue;
Thoroughbrace bison-skin, thick and
    wide;
Boot, top, dasher, from tough old hide
Found in the pit when the tanner died.
That was the way he "put her
    through."—
"There!" said the Deacon, "naow
    she 'll dew!"

Do! I tell you, I rather guess
She was a wonder, and nothing less!
Colts grew horses, beards turned gray,
Deacon and deaconess dropped away,
Children and grandchildren—where
    were they?
But there stood the stout old one-hoss
    shay
As fresh as on Lisbon-earthquake-day!

EIGHTEEN HUNDRED;—it came and
    found
The Deacon's masterpiece strong and
    sound.
Eighteen hundred increased by ten;—
"Hahnsum kerridge" they called it
    then.
Eighteen hundred and twenty came;—
Running as usual; much the same.
Thirty and forty at last arrive,
And then come fifty, and FIFTY-FIVE.

Little of all we value here
Wakes on the morn of its hundredth year
Without both feeling and looking queer.
In fact, there 's nothing that keeps its
    youth,
So far as I know, but a tree and truth.
(This is a moral that runs at large;
Take it.—You 're welcome.—No extra
    charge.)

FIRST OF NOVEMBER,—the Earthquake-
    day—
There are traces of age in the one-hoss
    shay,
A general flavor of mild decay,
But nothing local, as one may say.
There could n't be,—for the Deacon's
    art
Had made it so like in every part
That there was n't a chance for one to
    start.
For the wheels were just as strong as the
    thills,
And the floor was just as strong as the
    sills,
And the panels just as strong as the floor,
And the whipple-tree neither less nor
    more,
And the back-crossbar as strong as the
    fore,
And spring and axle and hub *encore*.
And yet, *as a whole*, it is past a doubt
In another hour it will be *worn out!*

First of November, 'Fifty-five!
This morning the parson takes a drive.
Now, small boys, get out of the way!
Here comes the wonderful one-hoss shay,
Drawn by a rat-tailed, ewe-necked bay.
"Huddup!" said the parson.—Off
    went they.
The parson was working his Sunday's
    text,—
Had got to *fifthly*, and stopped per-
    plexed
At what the—Moses—was coming
    next.
All at once the horse stood still,
Close by the meet'n'-house on the hill.
—First a shiver, and then a thrill,
Then something decidedly like a spill,—
And the parson was sitting upon a rock,
At half past nine by the meet'n'-house
    clock,—
Just the hour of the Earthquake shock!

— What do you think the parson found,
When he got up and stared around ?
The poor old chaise in a heap or mound,
As if it had been to the mill and ground!
You see, of course, if you 're not a dunce,
How it went to pieces all at once, —
All at once, and nothing first, —
Just as bubbles do when they burst.

End of the wonderful one-hoss shay.
Logic is logic.   That 's all I say.

PARSON TURELL'S LEGACY.

OR, THE PRESIDENT'S OLD ARM-CHAIR.

A MATHEMATICAL STORY.

FACTS respecting an old arm-chair.
At Cambridge.   Is kept in the College
    there.
Seems but little the worse for wear.
That 's remarkable when I say
It was old in President Holyoke's day.
(One of his boys, perhaps you know,
Died, *at one hundred*, years ago.)
He took lodgings for rain or shine
Under green bed-clothes in '69.

Know old Cambridge? Hope you do.—
Born there ? Don't say so ! I was, too.
(Born in a house with a gambrel-roof,—
Standing still, if you must have proof.—
" Gambrel ?— Gambrel ? " — Let me beg
You 'll look at a horse's hinder leg, —
First great angle above the hoof, —
That 's the gambrel ; hence gambrel-
    roof.)
— Nicest place that ever was seen, —
Colleges red and Common green,
Sidewalks brownish with trees between.
Sweetest spot beneath the skies
When the canker-worms don't rise, —
When the dust, that sometimes flies
Into your mouth and ears and eyes,
In a quiet slumber lies,

Not in the shape of unbaked pies
Such as barefoot children prize.

A kind of harbor it seems to be,
Facing the flow of a boundless sea.
Rows of gray old Tutors stand
Ranged like rocks above the sand ;
Rolling beneath them, soft and green,
Breaks the tide of bright sixteen, —
One wave, two waves, three waves,
    four, —
Sliding up the sparkling floor :
Then it ebbs to flow no more,
Wandering off from shore to shore
With its freight of golden ore !
— Pleasant place for boys to play ; —
Better keep your girls away ;
Hearts get rolled as pebbles do
Which countless fingering waves pursue,
And every classic beach is strown
With heart-shaped pebbles of blood-red
    stone.

But this is neither here nor there ; —
I 'm talking about an old arm-chair.
You 've heard, no doubt, of PARSON
    TURELL ?
Over at Medford he used to dwell ;
Married one of the Mathers' folk ;
Got with his wife a chair of oak, —
Funny old chair with seat like wedge,
Sharp behind and broad front edge, —
One of the oddest of human things,
Turned all over with knobs and rings,—
But heavy, and wide, and deep, and
    grand, —
Fit for the worthies of the land, —
Chief Justice Sewall a cause to try in,
Or Cotton Mather to sit — and lie — in.
— Parson Turell bequeathed the same
To a certain student, — SMITH by name ;
These were the terms, as we are told :
" Saide Smith saide Chaire to have and
    holde ;
When he doth graduate, then to passe

To ye oldest Youth in ye Senior Classe.
On Payment of" — naming a certain
    sum) —
" By him to whom ye Chaire shall come;
He to ye oldest Senior next,
And soe forever," — (thus runs the
    text,) —
" But one Crown lesse then he gave to
    claime,
That being his Debte for use of same."

Smith transferred it to one of the
    BROWNS,
And took his money, — five silver
    crowns.
Brown delivered it up to MOORE,
Who paid, it is plain, not five, but four.
Moore made over the chair to LEE,
Who gave him crowns of silver three.
Lee conveyed it unto DREW,
And now the payment, of course, was two.
Drew gave up the chair to DUNN, —
All he got, as you see, was one.
Dunn released the chair to HALL,
And got by the bargain no crown at all.
— And now it passed to a second BROWN,
Who took it and likewise *claimed a
    crown.*
When *Brown* conveyed it unto WARE,
Having had one crown, to make it fair,
He paid him two crowns to take the
    chair ;
And *Ware*, being honest, (as all Wares
    be,)
He paid one POTTER, who took it, three.
Four got ROBINSON ; five got DIX ;
JOHNSON *primus* demanded six ;
And so the sum kept gathering still
Till after the battle of Bunker's Hill.

— When paper money became so
    cheap,
Folks would n't count it, but said "a
    heap,"
A certain RICHARDS, — the books de-
    clare, —

(A. M. in '90 ? I 've looked with care
Through the Triennial, — *name not
    there*,) —
This person, Richards, was offered then
Eightscore pounds, but would have
    ten ;
Nine, I think, was the sum he took, —
Not quite certain, — but see the book.
— By and by the wars were still,
But nothing had altered the Parson's
    will.
The old arm-chair was solid yet,
But saddled with such a monstrous
    debt !
Things grew quite too bad to bear,
Paying such sums to get rid of the
    chair !
But dead men's fingers hold awful tight,
And there was the will in black and
    white,
Plain enough for a child to spell.
What should be done no man could tell,
For the chair was a kind of nightmare
    curse,
And every season but made it worse.

As a last resort, to clear the doubt,
They got old GOVERNOR HANCOCK out.
The Governor came with his Light-
    horse Troop
And his mounted truckmen, all cock-a-
    hoop ;
Halberds glittered and colors flew,
French horns whinnied and trumpets
    blew,
The yellow fifes whistled between their
    teeth
And the bumble-bee bass-drums boomed
    beneath ;
So he rode with all his band,
Till the President met him, cap in hand.
— The Governor " hefted " the crowns,
    and said, —
" A will is a will, and the Parson 's
    dead."

The Governor hefted the crowns.   Said
he, —
"There is your p'int.   And here's my
fee.
These are the terms you must fulfil, —
On such conditions I BREAK THE
WILL !"
The Governor mentioned what these
should be.
(Just wait a minute and then you'll see.)
The President prayed.   Then all was
still,
And the Governor rose and BROKE THE
WILL !
— "About those conditions?"   Well,
now you go
And do as I tell you, and then you'll
know.
Once a year, on Commencement day,
If you'll only take the pains to stay,
You'll see the President in the CHAIR,
Likewise the Governor sitting there.
The President rises ; both old and young
May hear his speech in a foreign tongue,
The meaning whereof, as lawyers swear,

Is this : Can I keep this old arm-chair ?
And then his Excellency bows,
As much as to say that he allows.
The Vice-Gub. next is called by name ;
He bows like t' other, which means the
same.
And all the officers round 'em bow,
As much as to say that *they* allow.
And a lot of parchments about the chair
Are handed to witnesses then and there,
And then the lawyers hold it clear
That the chair is safe for another year.

God bless you, Gentlemen !   Learn to
give
Money to colleges while you live.
Don't be silly and think you'll try
To bother the colleges, when you die,
With codicil this, and codicil that,
That Knowledge may starve while Law
grows fat ;
For there never was pitcher that
would n't spill,
And there's always a flaw in a donkey's
will !

ODE FOR A SOCIAL MEETING.

WITH SLIGHT ALTERATIONS BY A TEETOTALER.

COME ! fill a fresh bumper, for why should we go
     logwood
While the ~~nectar~~ still reddens our cups as they flow ?
    decoction
Pour out the ~~rich juices~~ still bright with the sun,
     dye-stuff
Till o'er the brimmed crystal the ~~rubies~~ shall run.

     half-ripened apples
The ~~purple-globed clusters~~ their life-dews have bled ;
    taste   sugar of lead
How sweet is the ~~breath~~ of the ~~fragrance they shed~~ !
   rank poisons   wines ! ! !
For summer's ~~last roses~~ lie hid in the ~~wines~~
           stable-boys smoking long-nines
That were garnered by ~~maidens who laughed thro' the vines.~~

  scowl   howl   scoff   sneer
Then a ~~smile~~, and a ~~glass~~, and a ~~toast~~, and a ~~cheer~~,
    strychnine and whiskey, and ratsbane and beer
For ~~all the good wine, and we've some of it here~~ !
In cellar, in pantry, in attic, in hall,
   Down, down with the tyrant that masters us all !
~~Long live the gay servant that laughs for us all !~~

POEMS

FROM THE

PROFESSOR AT THE BREAKFAST TABLE.

1858 - 1859.

UNDER THE VIOLETS.

HER hands are cold ; her face is white ;
  No more her pulses come and go ;
Her eyes are shut to life and light ; —
  Fold the white vesture, snow on snow,
  And lay her where the violets blow.

But not beneath a graven stone,
  To plead for tears with alien eyes ;
A slender cross of wood alone
  Shall say, that here a maiden lies
  In peace beneath the peaceful skies.

And gray old trees of hugest limb
  Shall wheel their circling shadows
    round
To make the scorching sunlight dim
  That drinks the greenness from the
    ground,
  And drop their dead leaves on her
    mound.

When o'er their boughs the squirrels
    run,
  And through their leaves the robins
    call,
And, ripening in the autumn sun,
  The acorns and the chestnuts fall,
  Doubt not that she will heed them all.

For her the morning choir shall sing
  Its matins from the branches high,
And every minstrel-voice of Spring,
  That trills beneath the April sky,
  Shall greet her with its earliest cry.

When, turning round their dial-track,
  Eastward the lengthening shadows
    pass,
Her little mourners, clad in black,
  The crickets, sliding through the
    grass,
  Shall pipe for her an evening mass.

At last the rootlets of the trees
  Shall find the prison where she lies,
And bear the buried dust they seize
  In leaves and blossoms to the skies.
  So may the soul that warmed it rise !

If any, born of kindlier blood,
  Should ask, What maiden lies below ?
Say only this : A tender bud,
  That tried to blossom in the snow,
  Lies withered where the violets blow.

HYMN OF TRUST.

O LOVE Divine, that stooped to share
  Our sharpest pang, our bitterest tear,

On Thee we cast each earth-born care,
  We smile at pain while Thou art near!

Though long the weary way we tread,
  And sorrow crown each lingering year,
No path we shun, no darkness dread,
  Our hearts still whispering, Thou art
    near!

When drooping pleasure turns to grief,
  And trembling faith is changed to fear,
The murmuring wind, the quivering leaf,
  Shall softly tell us, Thou art near!

On Thee we fling our burdening woe,
  O Love Divine, forever dear,
Content to suffer while we know,
  Living and dying, Thou art near!

A SUN-DAY HYMN.

LORD of all being! throned afar,
Thy glory flames from sun and star;
Centre and soul of every sphere,
Yet to each loving heart how near!

Sun of our life, thy quickening ray
Sheds on our path the glow of day;
Star of our hope, thy softened light
Cheers the long watches of the night.

Our midnight is thy smile withdrawn;
Our noontide is thy gracious dawn;
Our rainbow arch thy mercy's sign;
All, save the clouds of sin, are thine!

Lord of all life, below, above,
Whose light is truth, whose warmth is
    love,
Before thy ever-blazing throne
We ask no lustre of our own.

Grant us thy truth to make us free,
And kindling hearts that burn for thee,
Till all thy living altars claim
One holy light, one heavenly flame!

THE CROOKED FOOTPATH.

AH, here it is! the sliding rail
  That marks the old remembered
    spot, —
The gap that struck our school-boy
    trail, —
  The crooked path across the lot.

It left the road by school and church,
  A pencilled shadow, nothing more,
That parted from the silver-birch
  And ended at the farm-house door.

No line or compass traced its plan;
  With frequent bends to left or right,
In aimless, wayward curves it ran,
  But always kept the door in sight.

The gabled porch, with woodbine
    green, —
  The broken millstone at the sill, —
Though many a rood might stretch be-
    tween,
  The truant child could see them still.

No rocks across the pathway lie, —
  No fallen trunk is o'er it thrown, —
And yet it winds, we know not why,
  And turns as if for tree or stone.

Perhaps some lover trod the way
  With shaking knees and leaping
    heart, —
And so it often runs astray
  With sinuous sweep or sudden start.

Or one, perchance, with clouded brain
  From some unholy banquet reeled, —
And since, our devious steps maintain
  His track across the trodden field.

Nay, deem not thus, — no earthborn will
  Could ever trace a faultless line;
Our truest steps are human still, —
  To walk unswerving were divine!

Truants from love, we dream of wrath ; —
  O, rather let us trust the more !
Through all the wanderings of the path,
  We still can see our Father's door !

IRIS, HER BOOK.

I PRAY thee by the soul of her that bore
    thee,
By thine own sister's spirit I implore
    thee,
Deal gently with the leaves that lie be-
    fore thee !

For Iris had no mother to infold her,
Nor ever leaned upon a sister's shoulder,
Telling the twilight thoughts that Na-
    ture told her.

She had not learned the mystery of
    awaking
Those chorded keys that soothe a sor-
    row's aching,
Giving the dumb heart voice, that else
    were breaking.

Yet lived, wrought, suffered. Lo, the
    pictured token !
Why should her fleeting day-dreams
    fade unspoken,
Like daffodils that die with sheaths un-
    broken ?

She knew not love, yet lived in maiden
    fancies, —
Walked simply clad, a queen of high
    romances,
And talked strange tongues with angels
    in her trances.

Twin-souled she seemed, a twofold na-
    ture wearing, —
Sometimes a flashing falcon in her dar-
    ing,
Then a poor mateless dove that droops
    despairing.

Questioning all things : Why her Lord
    had sent her ?
What were these torturing gifts, and
    wherefore lent her ?
Scornful as spirit fallen, its own tor-
    mentor.

And then all tears and anguish : Queen
    of Heaven,
Sweet Saints, and Thou by mortal sor-
    rows riven,
Save me ! O, save me ! Shall I die
    forgiven ?

And then —— Ah, God ! But nay, it
    little matters :
Look at the wasted seeds that autumn
    scatters,
The myriad germs that Nature shapes
    and shatters !

If she had —— Well ! She longed, and
    knew not wherefore.
Had the world nothing she might live
    to care for ?
No second self to say her evening prayer
    for ?

She knew the marble shapes that set
    men dreaming,
Yet with her shoulders bare and tresses
    streaming
Showed not unlovely to her simple
    seeming.

Vain ? Let it be so ! Nature was her
    teacher.
What if a lonely and unsistered creature
Loved her own harmless gift of pleasing
    feature,

Saying, unsaddened, — This shall soon
    be faded,
And double-hued the shining tresses
    braided,

And all the sunlight of the morning
   shaded?

—— This her poor book is full of saddest follies,
Of tearful smiles and laughing melan-
   cholies,
With summer roses twined and wintry
   hollies.

In the strange crossing of uncertain
   chances,
Somewhere, beneath some maiden's tear-
   dimmed glances
May fall her little book of dreams and
   fancies.

Sweet sister! Iris, who shall never
   name thee,
Trembling for fear her open heart may
   shame thee,
Speaks from this vision-haunted page
   to claim thee.

Spare her, I pray thee! If the maid is
   sleeping,
Peace with her! she has had her hour
   of weeping.
No more! She leaves her memory in
   thy keeping.

ROBINSON OF LEYDEN.

HE sleeps not here; in hope and prayer
   His wandering flock had gone before,
But he, the shepherd, might not share
   Their sorrows on the wintry shore.

Before the Speedwell's anchor swung,
   Ere yet the Mayflower's sail was
     spread,
While round his feet the Pilgrims clung,
   The pastor spake, and thus he said:—

"Men, brethren, sisters, children dear!
   God calls you hence from over sea;

Ye may not build by Haerlem Meer,
   Nor yet along the Zuyder-Zee.

"Ye go to bear the saving word
   To tribes unnamed and shores untrod:
Heed well the lessons ye have heard
   From those old teachers taught of God.

"Yet think not unto them was lent
   All light for all the coming days,
And Heaven's eternal wisdom spent
   In making straight the ancient ways:

"The living fountain overflows
   For every flock, for every lamb,
Nor heeds, though angry creeds oppose
   With Luther's dike or Calvin's dam."

He spake: with lingering, long embrace,
   With tears of love and partings fond,
They floated down the creeping Maas,
   Along the isle of Ysselmond.

They passed the frowning towers of Briel,
   The "Hook of Holland's" shelf of
     sand,
And grated soon with lifting keel
   The sullen shores of Fatherland.

No home for these!— too well they knew
   The mitred king behind the throne;—
The sails were set, the pennons flew,
   And westward ho! for worlds un-
     known.

— And these were they who gave us
   birth,
   The Pilgrims of the sunset wave,
Who won for us this virgin earth,
   And freedom with the soil they gave.

The pastor slumbers by the Rhine, —
   In alien earth the exiles lie, —
Their nameless graves our holiest shrine,
   His words our noblest battle-cry!

Still cry them, and the world shall hear,
  Ye dwellers by the storm-swept sea !
Ye *have* not built by Haerlem Meer,
  Nor on the land-locked Zuyder-Zee !

Ah, then beware of mortal pride !
  The smiling pride that calmly scorns
Those foolish fingers, crimson dyed
  In laboring on thy crown of thorns !

ST. ANTHONY THE REFORMER.

HIS TEMPTATION.

No fear lest praise should make us proud !
  We know how cheaply that is won ;
The idle homage of the crowd
  Is proof of tasks as idly done.

A surface-smile may pay the toil
  That follows still the conquering
      Right,
With soft, white hands to dress the spoil
  That sun-browned valor clutched in
      fight.

Sing the sweet song of other days,
  Serenely placid, safely true,
And o'er the present's parching ways
  The verse distils like evening dew.

But speak in words of living power, —
  They fall like drops of scalding rain
That plashed before the burning shower
  Swept o'er the cities of the plain !

Then scowling Hate turns deadly pale, —
  Then Passion's half-coiled adders
      spring,
And, smitten through their leprous mail,
  Strike right and left in hope to sting.

If thou, unmoved by poisoning wrath,
  Thy feet on earth, thy heart above,
Canst walk in peace thy kingly path,
  Unchanged in trust, unchilled in
      love, —

Too kind for bitter words to grieve,
  Too firm for clamor to dismay,
When Faith forbids thee to believe,
  And Meekness calls to disobey, —

THE OPENING OF THE PIANO.

In the little southern parlor of the house
    you may have seen
With the gambrel-roof, and the gable
    looking westward to the green,
At the side toward the sunset, with the
    window on its right,
Stood the London-made piano I am
    dreaming of to-night !

Ah me ! how I remember the evening
    when it came !
What a cry of eager voices, what a group
    of cheeks in flame,
When the wondrous box was opened
    that had come from over seas,
With its smell of mastic-varnish and
    its flash of ivory keys !

Then the children all grew fretful in the
    restlessness of joy ;
For the boy would push his sister, and
    the sister crowd the boy,
Till the father asked for quiet in his
    grave paternal way,
But the mother hushed the tumult with
    the words, "Now, Mary, play."

For the dear soul knew that music was
    a very sovereign balm ;
She had sprinkled it over Sorrow and
    seen its brow grow calm,
In the days of slender harpsichords with
    tapping tinkling quills,
Or carolling to her spinet with its thin
    metallic thrills.

So Mary, the household minstrel, who
    always loved to please,

Sat down to the new "Clementi," and
struck the glittering keys.
Hushed were the children's voices, and
every eye grew dim,
As, floating from lip and finger, arose
the "Vesper Hymn."

— Catharine, child of a neighbor, curly
and rosy-red,
(Wedded since, and a widow, — something like ten years dead,)
Hearing a gush of music such as none
before,
Steals from her mother's chamber and
peeps at the open door.

Just as the "Jubilate" in threaded
whisper dies,
"Open it! open it, lady!" the little
maiden cries,
(For she thought 't was a singing creature caged in a box she heard,)
"Open it! open it, lady! and let me
see the *bird!*"

MIDSUMMER.

HERE! sweep these foolish leaves away,
I will not crush my brains to-day!
Look! are the southern curtains drawn?
Fetch me a fan, and so begone!

Not that, — the palm-tree's rustling leaf
Brought from a parching coral-reef!
Its breath is heated; — I would swing
The broad gray plumes, — the eagle's
wing.

I hate these roses' feverish blood! —
Pluck me a half-blown lily-bud,
A long-stemmed lily from the lake,
Cold as a coiling water-snake.

Rain me sweet odors on the air,
And wheel me up my Indian chair,

And spread some book not overwise
Flat out before my sleepy eyes.

— Who knows it not, — this dead recoil
Of weary fibres stretched with toil, —
The pulse that flutters faint and low
When Summer's seething breezes blow!

O Nature! bare thy loving breast,
And give thy child one hour of rest, —
One little hour to lie unseen
Beneath thy scarf of leafy green!

So, curtained by a singing pine,
Its murmuring voice shall blend with
mine,
Till, lost in dreams, my faltering lay
In sweeter music dies away.

DE SAUTY.

AN ELECTRO–CHEMICAL ECLOGUE.

Professor.   *Blue-Nose.*

PROFESSOR.

TELL me, O Provincial! speak, Ceruleo-
Nasal!
Lives there one De Sauty extant now
among you,
Whispering Boanerges, son of silent
thunder,
    Holding talk with nations?

Is there a De Sauty ambulant on Tellus,
Bifid-cleft like mortals, dormient in
nightcap,
Having sight, smell, hearing, food-re-
ceiving feature
    Three times daily patent?

Breathes there such a being, O Ceruleo-
Nasal?
Or is he a *mythus,* — ancient word for
"humbug," —

Such as Livy told about the wolf that
wet-nursed
Romulus and Remus?

Was he born of woman, this alleged De
Sauty?
Or a living product of galvanic action,
Like the *acarus* bred in Crosse's flint-so-
lution?
Speak, thou Cyano-Rhinal!

BLUE-NOSE.

Many things thou askest, jackknife-
bearing stranger,
Much-conjecturing mortal, pork-and-
treacle-waster!
Pretermit thy whittling, wheel thine
ear-flap toward me,
Thou shalt hear them answered.

When the charge galvanic tingled
through the cable,
At the polar focus of the wire electric
Suddenly appeared a white-faced man
among us:
Called himself " DE SAUTY."

As the small opossum held in pouch
maternal
Grasps the nutrient organ whence the
term *mammalia*,
So the unknown stranger held the wire
electric,
Sucking in the current.

When the current strengthened, bloomed
the pale-faced stranger, —
Took no drink nor victual, yet grew fat
and rosy, —

And from time to time, in sharp articu-
lation,
Said, " *All right!* DE SAUTY."

From the lonely station passed the utterance, spreading
Through the pines and hemlocks to the
groves of steeples,
Till the land was filled with loud rever-
berations
Of " *All right!* DE SAUTY."

When the current slackened, drooped
the mystic stranger, —
Faded, faded, faded, as the stream grew
weaker, —
Wasted to a shadow, with a hartshorn
odor
Of disintegration.

Drops of deliquescence glistened on his
forehead,
Whitened round his feet the dust of
efflorescence,
Till one Monday morning, when the flow
suspended,
There was no De Sauty.

Nothing but a cloud of elements organic,
C. O. H. N. Ferrum, Chlor. Flu. Sil.
Potassa,
Calc. Sod. Phosph. Mag. Sulphur,
Mang. (?) Alumin. (?) Cuprum, (?)
Such as man is made of.

Born of stream galvanic, with it he had
perished!
There is no De Sauty now there is no
current!
Give us a new cable, then again we 'll
hear him
Cry, " *All right!* DE SAUTY."

POEMS

FROM THE

POET AT THE BREAKFAST TABLE.

1871-1872.

HOMESICK IN HEAVEN.

THE DIVINE VOICE.

Go seek thine earth-born sisters, — thus
the Voice
    That all obey, — the sad and silent
      three ;
These only, while the hosts of Heaven
rejoice,
    Smile never : ask them what their
      sorrows be :

And when the secret of their griefs they
tell,
    Look on them with thy mild, half-
      human eyes ;
Say what thou wast on earth ; thou
knowest well ;
    So shall they cease from unavailing
      sighs.

THE ANGEL.

— Why thus, apart, — the swift-winged
herald spake, —
    Sit ye with silent lips and unstrung
      lyres
While the trisagion's blending chords
awake
    In shouts of joy from all the heavenly
      choirs ?

THE FIRST SPIRIT.

— Chide not thy sisters, — thus the answer came ; —

Children of earth, our half-weaned
    nature clings
To earth's fond memories, and her whis-
    pered name
    Untunes our quivering lips, our sad-
      dened strings ;

For there we loved, and where we love
    is home,
    Home that our feet may leave, but not
      our hearts,
Though o'er us shine the jasper-lighted
    dome : —
    The chain may lengthen, but it never
      parts !

Sometimes a sunlit sphere comes rolling
    by,
    And then we softly whisper, — *can it
      be ?*
And leaning toward the silvery orb, we
    try
    To hear the music of its murmuring
      sea ;

To catch, perchance, some flashing
    glimpse of green,
    Or breathe some wild-wood fragrance,
      wafted through
The opening gates of pearl, that fold
    between
    The blinding splendors and the change-
      less blue.

THE ANGEL.

— Nay, sister, nay ! a single healing leaf
  Plucked from the bough of yon twelve-
    fruited tree,
Would soothe such anguish, — deeper
    stabbing grief
  Has pierced thy throbbing heart —

THE FIRST SPIRIT.

              — Ah, woe is me !

I from my clinging babe was rudely
  torn ;
  His tender lips a loveless bosom
    pressed ;
Can I forget him in my life new born ?
  O that my darling lay upon my breast !

THE ANGEL.

— And thou ? —

THE SECOND SPIRIT.

    I was a fair and youthful bride,
The kiss of love still burns upon my
  cheek,
He whom I worshipped, ever at my
  side, —
  Him through the spirit realm in vain
    I seek.

Sweet faces turn their beaming eyes on
  mine ;
  Ah ! not in these the wished-for look
    I read ;
Still for that one dear human smile I
  pine ;
  Thou and none other ! — is the lover's
    creed.

THE ANGEL.

— And whence *thy* sadness in a world
  of bliss
  Where never parting comes, nor
    mourner's tear ?
Art thou, too, dreaming of a mortal's kiss
  Amid the seraphs of the heavenly
    sphere ?

THE THIRD SPIRIT.

— Nay, tax not me with passion's wast-
  ing fire ;
  When the swift message set my spirit
    free,
Blind, helpless, lone, I left my gray-
  haired sire ;
  My friends were many, he had none
    save me.

I left him, orphaned, in the starless
  night ;
  Alas, for him no cheerful morning's
    dawn !
I wear the ransomed spirit's robe of
  white,
  Yet still I hear him moaning, *She is
    gone !*

THE ANGEL.

— Ye know me not, sweet sisters ? — All
  in vain
  Ye seek your lost ones in the shapes
    they wore ;
The flower once opened may not bud
  again,
  The fruit once fallen finds the stem
    no more.

Child, lover, sire, — yea, all things
  loved below, —
  Fair pictures damasked on a vapor's
    fold, —
Fade like the roseate flush, the golden
  glow,
  When the bright curtain of the day
    is rolled.

I was the babe that slumbered on *thy*
  breast.
— And, sister, mine the lips that called
  thee bride.
— Mine were the silvered locks *thy* hand
  caressed,
  That faithful hand, my faltering foot-
    step's guide !

Each changing form, frail vesture of
    decay,
  The soul unclad forgets it once hath
    worn,
Stained with the travel of the weary day,
  And shamed with rents from every
    wayside thorn.

To lie, an infant, in *thy* fond embrace, —
  To come with love's warm kisses back
    to *thee*, —
To show *thine* eyes thy gray-haired fa-
    ther's face,
  Not Heaven itself could grant; this
    may not be !

Then spread your folded wings, and
    leave to earth
  The dust once breathing ye have
    mourned so long,
Till Love, new risen, owns his heavenly
    birth,
  And sorrow's discords sweeten into
    song !

FANTASIA.

THE YOUNG GIRL'S POEM.

Kiss mine eyelids, beauteous Morn,
Blushing into life new-born !
Lend me violets for my hair,
And thy russet robe to wear,
And thy ring of rosiest hue
Set in drops of diamond dew !

Kiss my cheek, thou noontide ray,
From my Love so far away !
Let thy splendor streaming down
Turn its pallid lilies brown,
Till its darkening shades reveal
Where his passion pressed its seal !

Kiss my lips, thou Lord of light,
Kiss my lips a soft good-night !

Westward sinks thy golden car ;
Leave me but the evening star,
And my solace that shall be,
Borrowing all its light from thee !

AUNT TABITHA.

THE YOUNG GIRL'S POEM.

Whatever I do, and whatever I say,
Aunt Tabitha tells me that is n't the
    way ;
When *she* was a girl (forty summers ago)
Aunt Tabitha tells me they never did so.

Dear aunt ! If I only would take her
    advice !
But I like my own way, and I find it *so*
    nice !
And besides, I forget half the things I
    am told ;
But they all will come back to me —
    when I am old.

If a youth passes by, it may happen, no
    doubt,
He may chance to look in as I chance to
    look out ;
She would never endure an impertinent
    stare, —
It is *horrid*, she says, and I must n't sit
    there.

A walk in the moonlight has pleasures,
    I own,
But it is n't quite safe to be walking
    alone ;
So I take a lad's arm, — just for safety,
    you know, —
But Aunt Tabitha tells me *they* did n't
    do so.

How wicked we are, and how good they
    were then !
They kept at arm's length those detesta-
    ble men ;

What an era of virtue she lived in ! —
But stay —
Were the *men* all such rogues in Aunt
  Tabitha's day?

If the men *were* so wicked, I 'll ask my
  papa
How he dared to propose to my darling
  mamma ;
Was he like the rest of them ?   Good-
  ness !   Who knows ?
And what shall *I* say, if a wretch should
  propose ?

I am thinking if Aunt knew so little of
  sin,
What a wonder Aunt Tabitha's aunt
  must have been !
And her grand-aunt — it scares me —
  how shockingly sad
That we girls of to-day are so frightfully
  bad !

A martyr will save us, and nothing else
  can ;
Let *me* perish — to rescue some wretched
  young man !
Though when to the altar a victim I go,
Aunt Tabitha 'll tell me *she* never did so !

WIND-CLOUDS AND STAR-DRIFTS.

FROM THE YOUNG ASTRONOMER'S POEM.

I.

AMBITION.

ANOTHER clouded night ; the stars are
  hid,
The orb that waits my search is hid with
  them.
Patience !   Why grudge an hour, a
  month, a year,
To plant my ladder and to gain the
  round

That leads my footsteps to the heaven
  of fame,
Where waits the wreath my sleepless
  midnights won ?
Not the stained laurel such as heroes
  wear
That withers when some stronger conqueror's heel
Treads down their shrivelling trophies
  in the dust ;
But the fair garland whose undying
  green
Not time can change, nor wrath of gods
  or men !

With quickened heart-beats I shall
  hear the tongues
That speak my praise ; but better far
  the sense
That in the unshaped ages, buried deep
In the dark mines of unaccomplished
  time
Yet to be stamped with morning's royal
  die
And coined in golden days, — in those
  dim years
I shall be reckoned with the undying
  dead,
My name emblazoned on the fiery arch,
Unfading till the stars themselves shall
  fade.
Then, as they call the roll of shining
  worlds,
Sages of race unborn in accents new
Shall count me with the Olympian ones
  of old,
Whose glories kindle through the mid-
  night sky :
Here glows the God of Battles ; this
  recalls
The Lord of Ocean, and yon far-off sphere
The Sire of Him who gave his ancient
  name
To the dim planet with the wondrous
  rings ;

Here flames the Queen of Beauty's silver
    lamp,
And there the moon-girt orb of mighty
    Jove ;
But *this,* unseen through all earth's æons
    past,
A youth who watched beneath the west-
    ern star
Sought in the darkness, found, and
    shewed to men ;
Linked with his name thenceforth and
    evermore !
So shall that name be syllabled anew
In all the tongues of all the tribes of
    men :
I that have been through immemorial
    years
Dust in the dust of my forgotten time
Shall live in accents shaped of blood-
    warm breath,
Yea, rise in mortal semblance, newly
    born
In shining stone, in undecaying bronze,
And stand on high, and look serenely
    down
On the new race that calls the earth its
    own.

  Is this a cloud, that, blown athwart
    my soul,
Wears a false seeming of the pearly stain
Where worlds beyond the world their
    mingling rays
Blend in soft white, — a cloud that, born
    of earth,
Would cheat the soul that looks for light
    from heaven ?
Must every coral-insect leave his sign
On each poor grain he lent to build the
    reef,
As Babel's builders stamped their sun-
    burnt clay,
Or deem his patient service all in vain ?
What if another sit beneath the shade
Of the broad elm I planted by the way, —

What if another heed the beacon light
I set upon the rock that wrecked my
    keel, —
Have I not done my task and served my
    kind ?
Nay, rather act thy part, unnamed, un-
    known,
And let Fame blow her trumpet through
    the world
With noisy wind to swell a fool's re-
    nown,
Joined with some truth he stumbled
    blindly o'er,
Or coupled with some single shining
    deed
That in the great account of all his
    days
Will stand alone upon the bankrupt
    sheet
His pitying angel shows the clerk of
    Heaven.
The noblest service comes from nameless
    hands,
And the best servant does his work un-
    seen.
Who found the seeds of fire and made
    them shoot,
Fed by his breath, in buds and flowers
    of flame ?
Who forged in roaring flames the pon-
    derous stone,
And shaped the moulded metal to his
    need ?
Who gave the dragging car its rolling
    wheel,
And tamed the steed that whirls its
    circling round ?
All these have left their work and not
    their names, —
Why should I murmur at a fate like
    theirs ?
This is the heavenly light ; the pearly
    stain
Was but a wind-cloud drifting o'er the
    stars !

II.

REGRETS.

BRIEF glimpses of the bright celestial
    spheres,
False lights, false shadows, vague, un-
    certain gleams,
Pale vaporous mists, wan streaks of lurid
    flame,
The climbing of the upward-sailing
    cloud,
The sinking of the downward-falling
    star, —
All these are pictures of the changing
    moods
Borne through the midnight stillness of
    my soul.

Here am I, bound upon this pillared
    rock,
Prey to the vulture of a vast desire
That feeds upon my life. I burst my
    bands
And steal a moment's freedom from the
    beak,
The clinging talons and the shadowing
    plumes ;
Then comes the false enchantress, with
    her song ;
"Thou wouldst not lay thy forehead in
    the dust
Like the base herd that feeds and breeds
    and dies !
Lo, the fair garlands that I weave for
    thee,
Unchanging as the belt Orion wears,
Bright as the jewels of the seven-starred
    Crown,
The spangled stream of Berenice's hair ! "
And so she twines the fetters with the
    flowers
Around my yielding limbs, and the fierce
    bird
Stoops to his quarry, — then to feed his
    rage

Of ravening hunger I must drain my
    blood
And let the dew-drenched, poison-breed-
    ing night
Steal all the freshness from my fading
    cheek,
And leave its shadows round my cav-
    erned eyes.
All for a line in some unheeded scroll ;
All for a stone that tells to gaping
    clowns,
"Here lies a restless wretch beneath a
    clod
Where squats the jealous nightmare men
    call Fame ! "

I marvel not at him who scorns his
    kind
And thinks not sadly of the time fore-
    told
When the old hulk we tread shall be a
    wreck,
A slag, a cinder drifting through the
    sky
Without its crew of fools ! We live too
    long
And even so are not content to die,
But load the mould that covers up our
    bones
With stones that stand like beggars by
    the road
And show death's grievous wound and
    ask for tears ;
Write our great books to teach men who
    we are,
Sing our fine songs that tell in artful
    phrase
The secrets of our lives, and plead and
    pray
For alms of memory with the after time,
Those few swift seasons while the earth
    shall wear
Its leafy summers, ere its core grows cold
And the moist life of all that breathes
    shall die ;

Or as the new-born seer, perchance more
  wise,
Would have us deem, before its growing
  mass,
Pelted with star-dust, stoned with me-
  teor-balls,
Heats like a hammered anvil, till at last
Man and his works and all that stirred
  itself
Of its own motion, in the fiery glow
Turns to a flaming vapor, and our orb
Shines a new sun for earths that shall be
  born.

I am as old as Egypt to myself,
Brother to them that squared the pyra-
  mids
By the same stars I watch. I read the
  page
Where every letter is a glittering world,
With them who looked from Shinar's
  clay-built towers,
Ere yet the wanderer of the Midland
  sea
Had missed the fallen sister of the seven.
I dwell in spaces vague, remote, un-
  known,
Save to the silent few, who, leaving
  earth,
Quit all communion with their living
  time.
I lose myself in that ethereal void,
Till I have tired my wings and long to
  fill
My breast with denser air, to stand, to
  walk
With eyes not raised above my fellow-
  men.
Sick of my unwalled, solitary realm,
I ask to change the myriad lifeless
  worlds
I visit as mine own for one poor patch
Of this dull spheroid and a little breath
To shape in word or deed to serve my
  kind.

Was ever giant's dungeon dug so deep,
Was ever tyrant's fetter forged so strong,
Was e'er such deadly poison in the
  draught
The false wife mingles for the trusting
  fool,
As he whose willing victim is himself,
Digs, forges, mingles, for his captive
  soul ?

III.

SYMPATHIES.

THE snows that glittered on the disk of
  Mars
Have melted, and the planet's fiery orb
Rolls in the crimson summer of its year ;
But what to me the summer or the snow
Of worlds that throb with life in forms
  unknown,
If life indeed be theirs ; I heed not
  these.
My heart is simply human ; all my care
For them whose dust is fashioned like
  mine own ;
These ache with cold and hunger, live
  in pain,
And shake with fear of worlds more full
  of woe ;
There may be others worthier of my
  love,
But such I know not, save through these
  I know.

There are two veils of language, hid be-
  neath
Whose sheltering folds, we dare to be
  ourselves ;
And not that other self which nods and
  smiles
And babbles in our name ; the one is
  Prayer,
Lending its licensed freedom to the
  tongue

That tells our sorrows and our sins to
Heaven ;
The other, Verse, that throws its spangled
web
Around our naked speech and makes it
bold.
I, whose best prayer is silence ; sitting
dumb
In the great temple where I nightly
serve
Him who is throned in light, have dared
to claim
The poet's franchise, though I may not
hope
To wear his garland ; hear me while I
tell
My story in such form as poets use,
But breathed in fitful whispers, as the
wind
Sighs and then slumbers, wakes and
sighs again.

Thou Vision, floating in the breathless
air
Between me and the fairest of the stars,
I tell my lonely thoughts as unto thee.
Look not for marvels of the scholar's pen
In my rude measure ; I can only show
A slender-margined, unillumined page,
And trust its meaning to the flattering
eye
That reads it in the gracious light of
love.
Ah, wouldst thou clothe thyself in
breathing shape
And nestle at my side, my voice should
lend
Whate'er my verse may lack of tender
rhythm
To make thee listen.
                 I have stood entranced
When, with her fingers wandering o'er
the keys,
The white enchantress with the golden
hair

Breathed all her soul through some un-
valued rhyme ;
Some flower of song that long had lost
its bloom ;
Lo ! its dead summer kindled as she
sang !
The sweet contralto, like the ringdove's
coo,
Thrilled it with brooding, fond, caress-
ing tones,
And the pale minstrel's passion lived
again,
Tearful and trembling as a dewy rose
The wind has shaken till it fills the air
With light and fragrance.   Such the
wondrous charm
A song can borrow when the bosom
throbs
That lends it breath.
                 So from the poet's lips
His verse sounds doubly sweet, for none
like him
Feels every cadence of its wave-like
flow ;
He lives the passion over, while he reads,
That shook him as he sang his lofty
strain,
And pours his life through each resound-
ing line,
As ocean, when the stormy winds are
hushed,
Still rolls and thunders through his bil-
lowy caves.

IV.

MASTER AND SCHOLAR.

LET me retrace the record of the years
That made me what I am.   A man most
wise,
But overworn with toil and bent with
age,
Sought me to be his scholar, — me, run
wild

From books and teachers, — kindled in
my soul
The love of knowledge ; led me to his
tower,
Showed me the wonders of the midnight
realm
His hollow sceptre ruled, or seemed to
rule,
Taught me the mighty secrets of the
spheres,
Trained me to find the glimmering specks
of light
Beyond the unaided sense, and on my
chart
To string them one by one, in order due,
As on a rosary a saint his beads.
I was his only scholar ; I became
The echo to his thought ; whate'er he
knew
Was mine for asking ; so from year to
year
We wrought together, till there came a
time
When I, the learner, was the master
half
Of the twinned being in the dome-
crowned tower.

Minds roll in paths 'like planets ; they
revolve
This in a larger, that a narrower ring,
But round they come at last to that same
phase,
That selfsame light and shade they
showed before.
I learned his annual and his monthly
tale,
His weekly axiom and his daily phrase,
I felt them coming in the laden air,
And watched them laboring up to vocal
breath,
Even as the first-born at his father's
board
Knows ere he speaks the too familiar
jest

Is on its way, by some mysterious
sign
Forewarned, the click before the striking
bell.

He shrivelled as I spread my growing
leaves,
Till trust and reverence changed to pity-
ing care ;
He lived for me in what he once had
been,
But I for him, a shadow, a defence,
The guardian of his fame, his guide, his
staff,
Leaned on so long he fell if left alone.
I was his eye, his ear, his cunning
hand,
Love was my spur and longing after
fame,
But his the goading thorn of sleepless
age
That sees its shortening span, its length-
ening shades,
That clutches what it may with eager
grasp,
And drops at last with empty, out-
stretched hands.

All this he dreamed not. He would
sit him down
Thinking to work his problems as of
old,
And find the star he thought so plain a
blur,
The columned figures labyrinthine wilds
Without my comment, blind and sense-
less scrawls
That vexed him with their riddles ; he
would strive
And struggle for a while, and then his
eye
Would lose its light, and over all his
mind
The cold gray mist would settle ; and
erelong
The darkness fell, and I was left alone.

V.

ALONE.

ALONE ! no climber of an Alpine cliff,
No Arctic venturer on the waveless sea,
Feels the dread stillness round him as it
    chills
The heart of him who leaves the slum-
    bering earth
To watch the silent worlds that crowd
    the sky.

Alone ! And as the shepherd leaves his
    flock
To feed upon the hillside, he meanwhile
Finds converse in the warblings of the
    pipe
Himself has fashioned for his vacant
    hour,
So have I grown companion to myself,
And to the wandering spirits of the air
That smile and whisper round us in our
    dreams.
Thus have I learned to search if I may
    know
The whence and why of all beneath the
    stars
And all beyond them, and to weigh my
    life
As in a balance, — poising good and ill
Against each other, — asking of the
    Power
That flung me forth among the whirling
    worlds,
If I am heir to any inborn right,
Or only as an atom of the dust
That every wind may blow where'er it
    will.

VI.

QUESTIONING.

I AM not humble ; I was shown my
    place,
Clad in such robes as Nature had at
    hand ;
Took what she gave, not chose ; I know
    no shame,
No fear for being simply what I am.
I am not proud, I hold my every breath
At Nature's mercy.   I am as a babe
Borne in a giant's arms, he knows not
    where ;
Each several heart-beat, counted like the
    coin
A miser reckons, is a special gift
As from an unseen hand ; if that with-
    hold
Its bounty for a moment, I am left
A clod upon the earth to which I fall.

Something I find in me that well might
    claim
The love of beings in a sphere above
This doubtful twilight world of right
    and wrong ;
Something that shows me of the self-
    same clay
That creeps or swims or flies in humblest
    form.
Had I been asked, before I left my bed
Of shapeless dust, what clothing I would
    wear,
I would have said, More angel and less
    worm ;
But for their sake who are even such as I,
Of the same mingled blood, I would not
    choose
To hate that meaner portion of myself
Which makes me brother to the least of
    men.

I dare not be a coward with my lips
Who dare to question all things in my
    soul ;
Some men may find their wisdom on
    their knees,
Some prone and grovelling in the dust
    like slaves ;
Let the meek glowworm glisten in the
    dew ;

I ask to lift my taper to the sky
As they who hold their lamps above
    their heads,
Trusting the larger currents up aloft,
Rather than crossing eddies round their
    breast,
Threatening with every puff the flicker-
    ing blaze.

My life shall be a challenge, not a truce !
This is my homage to the mightier
    powers,
To ask my boldest question, undismayed
By muttered threats that some hysteric
    sense
Of wrong or insult will convulse the
    throne
Where wisdom reigns supreme ; and if I
    err,
They all must err who have to feel their
    way
As bats that fly at noon ; for what are we
But creatures of the night, dragged forth
    by day,
Who needs must stumble, and with
    stammering steps
Spell out their paths in syllables of pain ?

Thou wilt not hold in scorn the child
    who dares
Look up to Thee, the Father, — dares to
    ask
More than Thy wisdom answers. From
    Thy hand
The worlds were cast ; yet every leaflet
    claims
From that same hand its little shining
    sphere
Of star-lit dew ; thine image, the great
    sun,
Girt with his mantle of tempestuous
    flame,
Glares in mid-heaven ; but to his noon-
    tide blaze
The slender violet lifts its lidless eye,

And from his splendor steals its fairest
    hue,
Its sweetest perfume from his scorching
    fire.

VII.

WORSHIP.

From my lone turret as I look around
O'er the green meadows to the ring of
    blue,
From slope, from summit, and from
    half-hid vale
The sky is stabbed with dagger-pointed
    spires,
Their gilded symbols whirling in the
    wind,
Their brazen tongues proclaiming to
    the world,
" Here truth is sold, the only genuine
    ware ;
See that it has our trade-mark ! You
    will buy
Poison instead of food across the way,
The lies of —— " this or that, each sev-
    eral name
The standard's blazon and the battle-
    cry
Of some true-gospel faction, and again
The token of the Beast to all beside.
And grouped round each I see a hud-
    dling crowd
Alike in all things save the words they
    use ;
In love, in longing, hate and fear the
    same.

    Whom do we trust and serve ? We
    speak of one
And bow to many ; Athens still would
    find
The shrines of all she worshipped safe
    within
Our tall barbarian temples, and the
    thrones

That crowned Olympus mighty as of old.
The god of music rules the Sabbath
choir ;
The lyric muse must leave the sacred
nine
To help us please the dilettante's ear ;
Plutus limps homeward with us, as we
leave
The portals of the temple where we knelt
And listened while the god of eloquence
(Hermes of ancient days, but now dis-
guised
In sable vestments) with that other god
Somnus, the son of Erebus and Nox,
Fights in unequal contest for our souls ;
The dreadful sovereign of the under
world
Still shakes his sceptre at us, and we hear
The baying of the triple-throated hound';
Eros is young as ever, and as fair
The lovely Goddess born of ocean's foam.

These be thy gods, O Israel ! Who
is he,
The one ye name and tell us that ye
serve,
Whom ye would call me from my lonely
tower
To worship with the many - headed
throng ?
Is it the God that walked in Eden's grove
In the cool hour to seek our guilty sire ?
The God who dealt with Abraham as
the sons
Of that old patriarch deal with other
men ?
The jealous God of Moses, one who feels
An image as an insult, and is wroth
With him who made it and his child
unborn ?
The God who plagued his people for
the sin
Of their adulterous king, beloved of
him, —
The same who offers to a chosen few

The right to praise him in eternal song
While a vast shrieking world of endless
woe
Blends its dread chorus with their rap-
turous hymn ?
Is this the God ye mean, or is it he
Who heeds the sparrow's fall, whose
loving heart
Is as the pitying father's to his child,
Whose lesson to his children is " For-
give,"
Whose plea for all, "They know not
what they do " ?

VIII.

MANHOOD.

I CLAIM the right of knowing whom
I serve,
Else is my service idle ; He that asks
My homage asks it from a reasoning soul.
To crawl is not to worship ; we have
learned
A drill of eyelids, bended neck and knee,
Hanging our prayers on hinges, till we
ape
The flexures of the many-jointed worm.
Asia has taught her Allahs and salaams
To the world's children, — we have
grown to men !
We who have rolled the sphere beneath
our feet
To find a virgin forest, as we lay
The beams of our rude temple, first of all
Must frame its doorway high enough
for man
To pass unstooping ; knowing as we do
That He who shaped us last of living
forms
Has long enough been served by creep-
ing things,
Reptiles that left their footprints in
the sand
Of old sea-margins that have turned to
stone,

And men who learned their ritual ; we demand
To know him first, then trust him and then love
When we have found him worthy of our love,
Tried by our own poor hearts and not before ;
He must be truer than the truest friend,
He must be tenderer than a woman's love,
A father better than the best of sires ;
Kinder than she who bore us, though we sin
Oftener than did the brother we are told,
We — poor ill-tempered mortals — must forgive,
Though seven times sinning threescore times and ten.

This is the new world's gospel: Be ye men !
Try well the legends of the children's time ;
Ye are the chosen people, God has led
Your steps across the desert of the deep
As now across the desert of the shore ;
Mountains are cleft before you as the sea
Before the wandering tribe of Israel's sons ;
Still onward rolls the thunderous caravan,
Its coming printed on the western sky,
A cloud by day, by night a pillared flame ;
Your prophets are a hundred unto one
Of them of old who cried, "Thus saith the Lord " ;
They told of cities that should fall in heaps,
But yours of mightier cities that shall rise
Where yet the lonely fishers spread their nets,
Where hides the fox and hoots the midnight owl ;
The tree of knowledge in your garden grows
Not single, but at every humble door ;
Its branches lend you their immortal food,
That fills you with the sense of what ye are,
No servants of an altar hewed and carved
From senseless stone by craft of human hands,
Rabbi, or dervish, brahmin, bishop, bonze,
But masters of the charm with which they work
To keep your hands from that forbidden tree !
Ye that have tasted that divinest fruit,
Look on this world of yours with opened eyes !
Ye are as gods ! Nay, makers of your gods, —
Each day ye break an image in your shrine
And plant a fairer image where it stood :
Where is the Moloch of your fathers' creed,
Whose fires of torment burned for spanlong babes ?
Fit object for a tender mother's love !
Why not ? It was a bargain duly made
For these same infants through the surety's act
Intrusted with their all for earth and heaven,
By Him who chose their guardian, knowing well
His fitness for the task, — this, even this,
Was the true doctrine only yesterday
As thoughts are reckoned, — and to-day you hear
In words that sound as if from human tongues

Those monstrous, uncouth horrors of
    the past
That blot the blue of heaven and shame
    the earth
As would the saurians of the age of
    slime,
Awaking from their stony sepulchres
And wallowing hateful in the eye of
    day !

IX.

RIGHTS.

WHAT am I but the creature Thou hast
    made ?
What have I save the blessings Thou
    hast lent ?
What hope I but Thy mercy and Thy
    love ?
Who but myself shall cloud my soul with
    fear ?
Whose hand protect me from myself but
    Thine ?
    I claim the rights of weakness, I, the
    babe,
Call on my sire to shield me from the
    ills
That still beset my path, not trying me
With snares beyond my wisdom or my
    strength,
He knowing I shall use them to my
    harm,
And find a tenfold misery in the sense
That in my childlike folly I have sprung
The trap upon myself as vermin use
Drawn by the cunning bait to certain
    doom.
Who wrought the wondrous charm that
    leads us on
To sweet perdition, but the selfsame
    power
That set the fearful engine to destroy
His wretched offspring (as the Rabbis
    tell),

And hid its yawning jaws and treacher-
    ous springs
In such a show of innocent sweet flowers
It lured the sinless angels and they fell ?
    Ah ! He who prayed the prayer of
    all mankind
Summed in those few brief words the
    mightiest plea
For erring souls before the courts of
    heaven, —
Save us from being tempted, — lest we
    fall !

If we are only as the potter's clay
Made to be fashioned as the artist wills,
And broken into shards if we offend
The eye of Him who made us, it is well ;
Such love as the insensate lump of clay
That spins upon the swift-revolving
    wheel
Bears to the hand that shapes its growing
    form, —
Such love, no more, will be our hearts'
    return
To the great Master-workman for his
    care, —
Or would be, save that this, our breath-
    ing clay,
Is intertwined with fine innumerous
    threads
That make it conscious in its framer's
    hand ;
And this He must remember who has
    filled
These vessels with the deadly draught
    of life, —
Life, that means death to all it claims.
    Our love
Must kindle in the ray that streams
    from heaven,
A faint reflection of the light divine ;
The sun must warm the earth before the
    rose
Can show her inmost heart-leaves to the
    sun.

WIND-CLOUDS AND STAR-DRIFTS.

He yields some fraction of the Maker's
  right
Who gives the quivering nerve its sense
  of pain ;
Is there not something in the pleading
  eye
Of the poor brute that suffers, which ar-
  raigns
The law that bids it suffer ? Has it not
A claim for some remembrance in the
  book
That fills its pages with the idle words
Spoken of men ? Or is it only clay,
Bleeding and aching in the potter's hand,
Yet all his own to treat it as he will
And when he will to cast it at his feet,
Shattered, dishonored, lost forevermore ?
My dog loves me, but could he look be-
  yond
His earthly master, would his love ex-
  tend
To Him who — Hush ! I will not doubt
  that He
Is better than our fears, and will not
  wrong
The least, the meanest of created things !

He would not trust me with the small-
  est orb
That circles through the sky ; he would
  not give
A meteor to my guidance ; would not
  leave
The coloring of a cloudlet to my hand ;
He locks my beating heart beneath its
  bars
And keeps the key himself ; he meas-
  ures out
The draughts of vital breath that warm
  my blood,
Winds up the springs of instinct which
  uncoil,
Each in its season ; ties me to my home,
My race, my time, my nation, and my
  creed

So closely that if I but slip my wrist
Out of the band that cuts it to the bone,
Men say, "He hath a devil" ; he has lent
All that I hold in trust, as unto one
By reason of his weakness and his years
Not fit to hold the smallest shred in fee
Of those most common things he calls
  his own —
And yet — my Rabbi tells me — he has
  left
The care of that to which a million
  worlds
Filled with unconscious life were less
  than naught,
Has left that mighty universe, the Soul,
To the weak guidance of our baby hands,
Let the foul fiends have access at their
  will,
Taking the shape of angels, to our
  hearts, —
Our hearts already poisoned through and
  through
With the fierce virus of ancestral sin ;
Turned us adrift with our immortal
  charge,
To wreck ourselves in gulfs of endless woe.
If what my Rabbi tells me is the truth
Why did the choir of angels sing for joy ?
Heaven must be compassed in a narrow
  space,
And offer more than room enough for all
That pass its portals ; but the under-
  world,
The godless realm, the place where
  demons forge
Their fiery darts and adamantine chains,
Must swarm with ghosts that for a little
  while
Had worn the garb of flesh, and being
  heirs
Of all the dulness of their stolid sires,
And all the erring instincts of their
  tribe,
Nature's own teaching, rudiments of
  " sin,"

Fell headlong in the snare that could
  not fail
To trap the wretched creatures shaped
  of clay
And cursed with sense enough to lose
  their souls !
  Brother, thy heart is troubled at my
    word ;
Sister, I see the cloud is on thy brow.
He will not blame me, He who sends not
  peace,
But sends a sword, and bids us strike
  amain
At Error's gilded crest, where in the van
Of earth's great army, mingling with the
  best
And bravest of its leaders, shouting loud
The battle-cries that yesterday have
  led
The host of Truth to victory, but to-day
Are watchwords of the laggard and the
  slave,
He leads his dazzled cohorts. God has
  made
This world a strife of atoms and of
  spheres ;
With every breath I sigh myself away
And take my tribute from the wandering
  wind
To fan the flame of life's consuming fire ;
So, while my thought has life, it needs
  must burn,
And burning, set the stubble-fields
  ablaze,
Where all the harvest long ago was
  reaped
And safely garnered in the ancient barns,
But still the gleaners, groping for their
  food,
Go blindly feeling through the close-
  shorn straw,
While the young reapers flash their glit-
  tering steel
Where later suns have ripened nobler
  grain !

X.

TRUTHS.

THE time is racked with birth-pangs;
  every hour
Brings forth some gasping truth, and
  truth new-born
Looks a misshapen and untimely
  growth,
The terror of the household and its
  shame,
A monster coiling in its nurse's lap
That some would strangle, some would
  only starve ;
But still it breathes, and passed from
  hand to hand,
And suckled at a hundred half-clad
  breasts,
Comes slowly to its stature and its form,
Calms the rough ridges of its dragon-
  scales,
Changes to shining locks its snaky
  hair,
And moves transfigured into angel guise,
Welcomed by all that cursed its hour of
  birth,
And folded in the same encircling arms
That cast it like a serpent from their
  hold !

  If thou wouldst live in honor, die in
    peace,
Have the fine words the marble-workers
  learn
To carve so well, upon thy funeral-stone,
And earn a fair obituary, dressed
In all the many-colored robes of praise,
Be deafer than the adder to the cry
Of that same foundling truth, until it
  grows
To seemly favor, and at length has won
The smiles of hard-mouthed men and
  light-lipped dames ;
Then snatch it from its meagre nurse's
  breast,

Fold it in silk and give it food from
   gold ;
So shalt thou share its glory when at
   last
It drops its mortal vesture, and revealed
In all the splendor of its heavenly form,
Spreads on the startled air its mighty
   wings !

Alas ! how much that seemed immor-
   tal truth
That heroes fought for, martyrs died to
   save,
Reveals its earth-born lineage, growing
   old
And limping in its march, its wings un-
   plumed,
Its heavenly semblance faded like a
   dream !
Here in this painted casket, just un-
   sealed,
Lies what was once a breathing shape
   like thine,
Once loved as thou art loved ; there
   beamed the eyes
That looked on Memphis in its hour of
   pride,
That saw the walls of hundred-gated
   Thebes,
And all the mirrored glories of the Nile.
See how they toiled that all-consuming
   time
Might leave the frame immortal in its
   tomb ;
Filled it with fragrant balms and odor-
   ous gums
That still diffuse their sweetness through
   the air,
And wound and wound with patient fold
   on fold
The flaxen bands thy hand has rudely
   torn !
Perchance thou yet canst see the faded
   stain
Of the sad mourner's tear.

XI.

IDOLS.

But what is this ?
The sacred beetle, bound upon the breast
Of the blind heathen ! Snatch the curi-
   ous prize,
Give it a place among thy treasured
   spoils
Fossil and relic, — corals, encrinites,
The fly in amber and the fish in stone,
The twisted circlet of Etruscan gold,
Medal, intaglio, poniard, poison-ring,—
Place for the Memphian beetle with
   thine hoard !

Ah ! longer than thy creed has blest
   the world
This toy, thus ravished from thy broth-
   er's breast,
Was to the heart of Mizraim as divine,
As holy, as the symbol that we lay
On the still bosom of our white-robed
   dead,
And raise above their dust that all may
   know
Here sleeps an heir of glory. Loving
   friends,
With tears of trembling faith and chok-
   ing sobs,
And prayers to those who judge of mor-
   tal deeds,
Wrapped this poor image in the cere-
   ment's fold
That Isis and Osiris, friends of man,
Might know their own and claim the
   ransomed soul.

An idol ? Man was born to worship
   such !
An idol is an image of his thought ;
Sometimes he carves it out of gleaming
   stone,
And sometimes moulds it out of glittering gold,

Or rounds it in a mighty frescoed dome,
Or lifts it heavenward in a lofty spire,
Or shapes it in a cunning frame of words,
Or pays his priest to make it day by day ;
For sense must have its god as well as
  soul ;
A new-born Dian calls for silver shrines,
And Egypt's holiest symbol is our own,
The sign we worship as did they of old
When Isis and Osiris ruled the world.

Let us be true to our most subtle
  selves,
We long to have our idols like the rest.
Think ! when the men of Israel had
  their God
Encamped among them, talking with
  their chief,
Leading them in the pillar of the cloud
And watching o'er them in the shaft of
  fire,
They still must have an image ; still
  they longed
For somewhat of substantial, solid form
Whereon to hang their garlands, and to
  fix
Their wandering thoughts and gain a
  stronger hold
For their uncertain faith, not yet assured
If those same meteors of the day and
  night
Were not mere exhalations of the soil.
Are we less earthly than the chosen
  race ?
Are we more neighbors of the living God
Than they who gathered manna every
  morn,
Reaping where none had sown, and heard
  the voice
Of him who met the Highest in the
  mount,
And brought them tables, graven with
  His hand ?
Yet these must have their idol, brought
  their gold,

That star-browed Apis might be god
  again ;
Yea, from their ears the women brake
  the rings
That lent such splendors to the gypsy
  brown
Of sunburnt cheeks, — what more could
  woman do
To show her pious zeal ? They went
  astray,
But nature led them as it leads us all.
We too, who mock at Israel's golden
  calf
And scoff at Egypt's sacred scarabee,
Would have our amulets to clasp and
  kiss,
And flood with rapturous tears, and bear
  with us
To be our dear companions in the dust ;
Such magic works an image in our souls !

Man is an embryo ; see at twenty years
His bones, the columns that uphold his
  frame
Not yet cemented, shaft and capital,
Mere fragments of the temple incom-
  plete.
At twoscore, threescore, is he then full
  grown ?
Nay, still a child, and as the little maids
Dress and undress their puppets, so he
  tries
To dress a lifeless creed, as if it lived,
And change its raiment when the world
  cries shame !
We smile to see our little ones at play
So grave, so thoughtful, with maternal
  care
Nursing the wisps of rags they call their
  babes ; —
Does He not smile who sees us with the
  toys
We call by sacred names, and idly feign
To be what we have called them ? He
  is still

The Father of this helpless nursery-
  brood,
Whose second childhood joins so close
  its first,
That in the crowding, hurrying years
  between
We scarce have trained our senses to
  their task
Before the gathering mist has dimmed
  our eyes,
And with our hollowed palm we help
  our ear,
And trace with trembling hand our
  wrinkled names,
And then begin to tell our stories o'er,
And see — not hear — the whispering
  lips that say,
"You know——? Your father knew
  him. — This is he,
Tottering and leaning on the hireling's
  arm," —
And so, at length, disrobed of all that
  clad
The simple life we share with weed and
  worm,
Go to our cradles, naked as we came.

XII.

LOVE.

WHAT if a soul redeemed, a spirit that
  loved
While yet on earth and was beloved in
  turn,
And still remembered every look and
  tone
Of that dear earthly sister who was left
Among the unwise virgins at the gate, —
Itself admitted with the bridegroom's
  train, —
What if this spirit redeemed, amid the
  host
Of chanting angels, in some transient
  lull

Of the eternal anthem, heard the cry
Of its lost darling, whom in evil hour
Some wilder pulse of nature led astray
And left an outcast in a world of fire,
Condemned to be the sport of cruel
  fiends,
Sleepless, unpitying, masters of the skill
To wring the maddest ecstasies of pain
From worn-out souls that only ask to
  die, —
Would it not long to leave the bliss of
  Heaven, —
Bearing a little water in its hand
To moisten those poor lips that plead in
  vain
With Him we call our Father? Or is all
So changed in such as taste celestial joy
They hear unmoved the endless wail of
  woe;
The daughter in the same dear tones
  that hushed
Her cradled slumbers; she who once
  had held
A babe upon her bosom from its voice
Hoarse with its cry of anguish, yet the
  same?

No! not in ages when the Dreadful
  Bird
Stamped his huge footprints, and the
  Fearful Beast
Strode with the flesh about those fossil
  bones
We build to mimic life with pygmy
  hands, —
Not in those earliest days when men
  ran wild
And gashed each other with their knives
  of stone,
When their low foreheads bulged in
  ridgy brows
And their flat hands were callous in the
  palm
With walking in the fashion of their
  sires,

Grope as they might to find a cruel god
To work their will on such as human wrath
Had wrought its worst to torture, and had left
With rage unsated, white and stark and cold,
Could hate have shaped a demon more malign
Than him the dead men mummied in their creed
And taught their trembling children to adore !

Made in *his* image ! Sweet and gracious souls
Dear to my heart by nature's fondest names,
Is not your memory still the precious mould
That lends its form to Him who hears my prayer ?
Thus only I behold him, like to them,
Long-suffering, gentle, ever slow to wrath,
If wrath it be that only wounds to heal,
Ready to meet the wanderer ere he reach
The door he seeks, forgetful of his sin,
Longing to clasp him in a father's arms,
And seal his pardon with a pitying tear !

Four gospels tell their story to mankind,
And none so full of soft, caressing words
That bring the Maid of Bethlehem and her Babe
Before our tear-dimmed eyes, as his who learned
In the meek service of his gracious art
The tones which like the medicinal balms
That calm the sufferer's anguish, soothe our souls.
— O that the loving woman, she who sat
So long a listener at her Master's feet,
Had left us Mary's Gospel, — all she heard

Too sweet, too subtle for the ear of man !
Mark how the tender-hearted mothers read
The messages of love between the lines
Of the same page that loads the bitter tongue
Of him who deals in terror as his trade
With threatening words of wrath that scorch like flame !
They tell of angels whispering round the bed
Of the sweet infant smiling in its dream,
Of lambs enfolded in the Shepherd's arms,
Of Him who blessed the children ; of the land
Where crystal rivers feed unfading flowers,
Of cities golden-paved with streets of pearl,
Of the white robes the winged creatures wear,
The crowns and harps from whose melodious strings
One long, sweet anthem flows forevermore !
— We too had human mothers, even as Thou,
Whom we have learned to worship as remote
From mortal kindred, wast a cradled babe.
The milk of woman filled our branching veins,
She lulled us with her tender nursery-song,
And folded round us her untiring arms,
While the first unremembered twilight year
Shaped us to conscious being ; still we feel
Her pulses in our own, — too faintly feel ;
Would that the heart of woman warmed our creeds !

Not from the sad-eyed hermit's lonely
  cell,
Not from the conclave where the holy
  men
Glare on each other, as with angry eyes
They battle for God's glory and their
  own,
Till, sick of wordy strife, a show of
  hands
Fixes the faith of ages yet unborn, —
Ah, not from these the listening soul
  can hear
The Father's voice that speaks itself
  divine!
Love must be still our Master; till we
  learn
What he can teach us of a woman's
  heart,
We know not His, whose love embraces
  all.

EPILOGUE TO THE BREAKFAST-TABLE SERIES.

AUTOCRAT — PROFESSOR — POET.

AT A BOOKSTORE.

Anno Domini 1972.

A CRAZY bookcase, placed before
A low-price dealer's open door;
Therein arrayed in broken rows
A ragged crew of rhyme and prose,
The homeless vagrants, waifs and strays
Whose low estate this line betrays
(Set forth the lesser birds to lime)
*YOUR CHOICE AMONG THESE BOOKS, 1
  DIME!*

Ho! dealer; for its motto's sake
This scarecrow from the shelf I take;
Three starveling volumes bound in one,
Its covers warping in the sun.
Methinks it hath a musty smell,
I like its flavor none too well,
But Yorick's brain was far from dull,

Though Hamlet pah!'d, and dropped
  his skull.

Why, here comes rain! The sky grows
  dark, —
Was that the roll of thunder? Hark!
The shop affords a safe retreat,
A chair extends its welcome seat,
The tradesman has a civil look
(I 've paid, impromptu, for my book),
The clouds portend a sudden shower, —
I 'll read my purchase for an hour.

*   *   *

What have I rescued from the shelf?
A Boswell, writing out himself!
For though he changes dress and name,
The man beneath is still the same,
Laughing or sad, by fits and starts,
One actor in a dozen parts,
And whatsoe'er the mask may be,
The voice assures us, *This is he.*

I say not this to cry him down;
I find my Shakespeare in his clown,
His rogues the selfsame parent own;
Nay! Satan talks in Milton's tone!
Where'er the ocean inlet strays,
The salt sea wave its source betrays,
Where'er the queen of summer blows,
She tells the zephyr, "I 'm the rose!"

And his is not the playwright's page;
His table does not ape the stage;
What matter if the figures seen
Are only shadows on a screen,
He finds in them his lurking thought,
And on their lips the words he sought,
Like one who sits before the keys
And plays a tune himself to please.

And was he noted in his day?
Read, flattered, honored? Who shall
  say?
Poor wreck of time the wave has cast
To find a peaceful shore at last,

Once glorying in thy gilded name
And freighted deep with hopes of fame,
Thy leaf is moistened with a tear,
The first for many a long, long year !

For be it more or less of art
That veils the lowliest human heart
Where passion throbs, where friendship
    glows,
Where pity's tender tribute flows,
Where love has lit its fragrant fire,
And sorrow quenched its vain desire,
For me the altar is divine,
Its flame, its ashes, — all are mine !

And thou, my brother, as I look
And see thee pictured in thy book,

Thy years on every page confessed
In shadows lengthening from the west,
Thy glance that wanders, as it sought
Some freshly opening flower of thought,
Thy hopeful nature, light and free,
I start to find myself in thee !

*   *   *

Come, vagrant, outcast, wretch for-
    lorn
In leather jerkin stained and torn,
Whose talk has filled my idle hour
And made me half forget the shower,
I 'll do at least as much for you,
Your coat I 'll patch, your gilt renew,
Read you — perhaps — some other time.
Not bad, my bargain ! Price one dime !

YOUR CHOICE AMONG THESE BOOKS 1 DIME

" Come, vagrant, outcast, wretch forlorn." Page 206.

POEMS OF THE CLASS OF '29.

1851 - 1877.

BILL AND JOE.

COME, dear old comrade, you and I
Will steal an hour from days gone by,
The shining days when life was new,
And all was bright with morning dew,
The lusty days of long ago,
When you were Bill and I was Joe.

Your name may flaunt a titled trail
Proud as a cockerel's rainbow tail,
And mine as brief appendix wear
As Tam O'Shanter's luckless mare;
To-day, old friend, remember still
That I am Joe and you are Bill.

You 've won the great world's envied
    prize,
And grand you look in people's eyes,
With H O N. and L L. D.
In big brave letters, fair to see, —
Your fist, old fellow! off they go! —
How are you, Bill?   How are you, Joe?

You 've worn the judge's ermined robe;
You 've taught your name to half the
    globe;
You 've sung mankind a deathless strain;
You 've made the dead past live again:
The world may call you what it will,
But you and I are Joe and Bill.

The chaffing young folks stare and say
"See those old buffers, bent and gray, —
They talk like fellows in their teens!
Mad, poor old boys!   That 's what it
    means," —
And shake their heads; they little know
The throbbing hearts of Bill and Joe!—

How Bill forgets his hour of pride,
While Joe sits smiling at his side;
How Joe, in spite of time's disguise,
Finds the old schoolmate in his eyes, —
Those calm, stern eyes that melt and fill
As Joe looks fondly up at Bill.

Ah, pensive scholar, what is fame?
A fitful tongue of leaping flame;
A giddy whirlwind's fickle gust,
That lifts a pinch of mortal dust;
A few swift years, and who can show
Which dust was Bill and which was
    Joe?

The weary idol takes his stand,
Holds out his bruised and aching hand,
While gaping thousands come and go, —
How vain it seems, this empty show!
Till all at once his pulses thrill; —
'T is poor old Joe's "God bless you,
    Bill!"

And shall we breathe in happier spheres
The names that pleased our mortal ears;
In some sweet lull of harp and song
For earth-born spirits none too long,

Just whispering of the world below
Where this was Bill, and that was Joe?

No matter; while our home is here
No sounding name is half so dear;
When fades at length our lingering day,
Who cares what pompous tombstones
    say?
Read on the hearts that love us still,
Hic jacet Joe.   *Hic jacet* Bill.

1851.

A SONG OF "TWENTY-NINE."

The summer dawn is breaking
  On Auburn's tangled bowers,
The golden light is waking
  On Harvard's ancient towers;
    The sun is in the sky
    That must see us do or die,
  Ere it shine on the line
    Of the Class of '29.

At last the day is ended,
  The tutor screws no more,
By doubt and fear attended
  Each hovers round the door,
    Till the good old Præses cries,
    While the tears stand in his eyes,
  "You have passed, and are classed
    With the Boys of '29."

Not long are they in making
  The college halls their own,
Instead of standing shaking,
  Too bashful to be known;
    But they kick the Seniors' shins
    Ere the second week begins,
  When they stray in the way
    Of the Boys of '29.

If a jolly set is trolling
  The last *Der Freischutz* airs,
Or a "cannon bullet" rolling
  Comes bouncing down the stairs,

    The tutors looking out,
    Sigh, "Alas! there is no doubt,
  'T is the noise of the Boys
    Of the Class of '29."

Four happy years together,
  By storm and sunshine tried,
In changing wind and weather,
  They rough it side by side,
    Till they hear their Mother cry,
    "You are fledged, and you must fly,"
  And the bell tolls the knell
    Of the days of '29.

Since then in peace or trouble,
  Full many a year has rolled,
And life has counted double
  The days that then we told;
    Yet we 'll end as we 've begun,
    For though scattered, we are one,
  While each year sees us here,
    Round the board of '29.

Though fate may throw between us
  The mountains or the sea,
No time shall ever wean us,
  No distance set us free;
    But around the yearly board,
    When the flaming pledge is poured,
  It shall claim every name
    On the roll of '29.

To yonder peaceful ocean
  That glows with sunset fires,
Shall reach the warm emotion
  This welcome day inspires,
    Beyond the ridges cold
    Where a brother toils for gold,
  Till it shine through the mine
    Round the Boy of '29.

If one whom fate has broken
  Shall lift a moistened eye,
We 'll say, before he 's spoken —
  "Old Classmate, don't you cry!

Here, take the purse I hold,
  There 's a tear upon the gold —
It was mine — it is thine —
  A'n't we Boys of '29 ?"

As nearer still and nearer
  The fatal stars appear,
The living shall be dearer
  With each encircling year,
    Till a few old men shall say
    "We remember 't is the day —
Let it pass with a glass
  For the Class of '29."

As one by one is falling
  Beneath the leaves or snows,
Each memory still recalling
  The broken ring shall close,
    Till the nightwinds softly pass
    O'er the green and growing grass,
Where it waves on the graves
  Of the Boys of '29 !

1852.

QUESTIONS AND ANSWERS.

Where, O where are the visions of
    morning,
  Fresh as the dews of our prime ?
Gone, like tenants that quit without
    warning,
  Down the back entry of time.

Where, O where are life's lilies and roses,
  Nursed in the golden dawn's smile ?
Dead as the bulrushes round little Moses,
  On the old banks of the Nile.

Where are the Marys, and Anns, and
    Elizas,
  Loving and lovely of yore ?
Look in the columns of old Adver-
    tisers, —
  Married and dead by the score.

Where the gray colts and the ten-year-
    old fillies,
  Saturday's triumph and joy ?
Gone, like our friend ποδας ωκυς Achilles,
  Homer's ferocious old boy.

Die-away dreams of ecstatic emotion,
  Hopes like young eagles at play,
Vows of unheard-of and endless devotion,
  How ye have faded away !

Yet, though the ebbing of Time's mighty
    river
  Leave our young blossoms to die,
Let him roll smooth in his current for-
    ever,
  Till the last pebble is dry.

1853.

AN IMPROMPTU.

Not premeditated.

The clock has struck noon ; ere it thrice
    tell the hours
We shall meet round the table that
    blushes with flowers,
And I shall blush deeper with shame-
    driven blood
That I came to the banquet and brought
    not a bud.

Who cares that his verse is a beggar in
    art
If you see through its rags the full throb
    of his heart ?
Who asks if his comrade is battered and
    tanned
When he feels his warm soul in the clasp
    of his hand ?

No ! be it an epic, or be it a line,
The Boys will all love it because it is
    mine ;
I sung their last song on the morn of
    the day

That tore from their lives the last blos-
    som of May.

It is not the sunset that glows in the wine,
But the smile that beams over it, makes
    it divine ;
I scatter these drops, and behold, as
    they fall,
The day-star of memory shines through
    them all !

And these are the last ; they are drops
    that I stole
From a wine-press that crushes the life
    from the soul,
But they ran through my heart and they
    sprang to my brain
Till our twentieth sweet summer was
    smiling again !

1854.

THE OLD MAN DREAMS.

O FOR one hour of youthful joy !
    Give back my twentieth spring !
I 'd rather laugh, a bright-haired boy,
    Than reign, a gray-beard king.

Off with the spoils of wrinkled age !
    Away with Learning's crown !
Tear out life's Wisdom-written page,
    And dash its trophies down !

One moment let my life-blood stream
    From boyhood's fount of flame !
Give me one giddy, reeling dream
    Of life all love and fame !

My listening angel heard the prayer,
    And, calmly smiling, said,
" If I but touch thy silvered hair
    Thy hasty wish hath sped.

" But is there nothing in thy track,
    To bid thee fondly stay,
While the swift seasons hurry back
    To find the wished-for day ? "

" Ah, truest soul of womankind !
    Without thee what were life ?
One bliss I cannot leave behind :
    I 'll take — my — precious — wife ! "

— The angel took a sapphire pen
    And wrote in rainbow dew,
The man would be a boy again,
    And be a husband too !

" And is there nothing yet unsaid,
    Before the change appears ?
Remember, all their gifts have fled
    With those dissolving years."

" Why yes " ; for memory would recall
    My fond paternal joys ;
" I could not bear to leave them all —
    I 'll take — my — girl — and — boys."

The smiling angel dropped his pen, —
    " Why this will never do ;
The man would be a boy again,
    And be a father too ! "

And so I laughed, — my laughter woke
    The household with its noise, —
And wrote my dream, when morning
    broke,
    To please the gray-haired boys.

1855.

REMEMBER — FORGET.

AND what shall be the song to-night,
    If song there needs must be ?
If every year that brings us here
    Must steal an hour from me ?
Say, shall it ring a merry peal,
    Or heave a mourning sigh
O'er shadows cast, by years long past,
    On moments flitting by ?

Nay, take the first unbidden line
    The idle hour may send,
No studied grace can mend the face
    That smiles as friend on friend ;

The balsam oozes from the pine,
  The sweetness from the rose,
And so, unsought, a kindly thought
  Finds language as it flows.

The years rush by in sounding flight,
  I hear their ceaseless wings ;
Their songs I hear, some far, some near,
  And thus the burden rings :
"The morn has fled, the noon has past,
  The sun will soon be set,
The twilight fade to midnight shade ;
  Remember — and Forget ! "

Remember all that time has brought —
  The starry hope on high,
The strength attained, the courage gained,
  The love that cannot die.
Forget the bitter, brooding thought, —
  The word too harshly said,
The living blame love hates to name,
  The frailties of the dead !

We have been younger, so they say,
  But let the seasons roll,
He doth not lack an almanac,
  Whose youth is in his soul.
The snows may clog life's iron track,
  But does the axle tire,
While bearing swift through bank and
    drift
  The engine's heart of fire ?

I lift a goblet in my hand ;
  If good old wine it hold,
An ancient skin to keep it in,
  Is just the thing, we 're told.
We 're grayer than the dusty flask, —
  We 're older than our wine ;
Our corks reveal the " white top " seal,
  The stamp of '29.

Ah, Boys ! we clustered in the dawn,
  To sever in the dark ;
A merry crew, with loud halloo,
  We climbed our painted bark ;

We sailed her through the four years'
    cruise,
  We 'll sail her to the last,
Our dear old flag, though but a rag,
  Still flying on her mast.

So gliding on, each winter's gale
  Shall pipe us all on deck,
Till, faint and few, the gathering crew
  Creep o'er the parting wreck,
Her sails and streamers spread aloft
  To fortune's rain or shine,
Till storm or sun shall all be one,
  And down goes TWENTY-NINE !

1856.

OUR INDIAN SUMMER.

You 'll believe me, dear boys, 't is a
    pleasure to rise,
With a welcome like this in your dar-
    ling old eyes ;
To meet the same smiles and to hear
    the same tone,
Which have greeted me oft in the years
    that have flown.

Were I gray as the grayest old rat in
    the wall,
My locks would turn brown at the sight
    of you all ;
If my heart were as dry as the shell on
    the sand,
It would fill like the goblet I hold in
    my hand.

There are noontides of autumn when
    summer returns,
Though the leaves are all garnered and
    sealed in their urns,
And the bird on his perch that was
    silent so long,
Believes the sweet sunshine and breaks
    into song.

We have caged the young birds of our
  beautiful June;
Their plumes are still bright and their
  voices in tune;
One moment of sunshine from faces like
  these
And they sing as they sung in the
  green-growing trees.

The voices of morning! how sweet is
  their thrill
When the shadows have turned, and
  the evening grows still!
The text of our lives may get wiser with
  age,
But the print was so fair on its twentieth page!

Look off from your goblet and up from
  your plate;
Come, take the last journal, and glance
  at its date:
Then think what we fellows should say
  and should do,
If the 6 were a 9 and the 5 were a 2.

Ah, no! for the shapes that would meet
  with us here,
From the far land of shadows, are ever
  too dear!
Though youth flung around us its pride
  and its charms,
We should see but the comrades we
  clasped in our arms.

A health to our future — a sigh for our
  past,
We love, we remember, we hope to the
  last;
And for all the base lies that the
  almanacs hold,
While we've youth in our hearts we can
  never grow old!

1858.

MARE RUBRUM.

FLASH out a stream of blood-red wine,
  For I would drink to other days,
And brighter shall their memory shine,
  Seen flaming through its crimson
    blaze!
The roses die, the summers fade,
  But every ghost of boyhood's dream
By nature's magic power is laid
  To sleep beneath this blood-red
    stream!

It filled the purple grapes that lay,
  And drank the splendors of the sun,
Where the long summer's cloudless day
  Is mirrored in the broad Garonne;
It pictures still the bacchant shapes
  That saw their hoarded sunlight
    shed, —
The maidens dancing on the grapes, —
  Their milk-white ankles splashed with
    red.

Beneath these waves of crimson lie,
  In rosy fetters prisoned fast,
Those flitting shapes that never die, —
  The swift-winged visions of the past.
Kiss but the crystal's mystic rim
  Each shadow rends its flowery chain,
Springs in a bubble from its brim
  And walks the chambers of the brain.

Poor beauty! Time and fortune's wrong
  No shape nor feature may withstand;
Thy wrecks are scattered all along,
  Like emptied sea-shells on the sand;
Yet, sprinkled with this blushing rain,
  The dust restores each blooming girl,
As if the sea-shells moved again
  Their glistening lips of pink and pearl.

Here lies the home of school-boy life,
  With creaking stair and wind-swept
    hall,

And, scarred by many a truant knife,
  Our old initials on the wall;
Here rest, their keen vibrations mute,
  The shout of voices known so well,
The ringing laugh, the wailing flute,
  The chiding of the sharp-tongued bell.

Here, clad in burning robes, are laid
  Life's blossomed joys, untimely shed,
And here those cherished forms have strayed
  We miss awhile, and call them dead.
What wizard fills the wondrous glass?
  What soil the enchanted clusters grew?
That buried passions wake and pass
  In beaded drops of fiery dew?

Nay! take the cup of blood-red wine, —
  Our hearts can boast a warmer glow,
Filled from a vintage more divine,
  Calmed, but not chilled, by winter's snow!
To-night the palest wave we sip
  Rich as the priceless draught shall be
That wet the bride of Cana's lip, —
  The wedding wine of Galilee!

1859.

THE BOYS.

Has there any old fellow got mixed with the boys?
If there has, take him out, without making a noise.
Hang the Almanac's cheat and the Catalogue's spite!
Old time is a liar! We're twenty to-night!

We're twenty! We're twenty! Who says we are more?
He's tipsy, — young jackanapes! — show him the door!

"Gray temples at twenty?" — Yes! white if we please;
Where the snow-flakes fall thickest there's nothing can freeze!

Was it snowing I spoke of? Excuse the mistake!
Look close, — you will see not a sign of a flake!
We want some new garlands for those we have shed, —
And these are white roses in place of the red.

We've a trick, we young fellows, you may have been told,
Of talking (in public) as if we were old : —
That boy we call "Doctor," and this we call "Judge";
It's a neat little fiction, — of course it's all fudge.

That fellow's the "Speaker," — the one on the right;
"Mr. Mayor," my young one, how are you to-night?
That's our "Member of Congress," we say when we chaff;
There's the "Reverend" What's his name? — don't make me laugh.

That boy with the grave mathematical look
Made believe he had written a wonderful book,
And the Royal Society thought it was true!
So they chose him right in; a good joke it was, too!

There's a boy, we pretend, with a three-decker brain,
That could harness a team with a logical chain;

When he spoke for our manhood in syllabled fire,
We called him " The Justice," but now
he 's " The Squire."

And there 's a nice youngster of excel-
lent pith, —
Fate tried to conceal him by naming
him Smith ; *Rev. S. H. Smith*
But he shouted a song for the brave and
the free, —
Just read on his medal, " My country,"
" of thee ! "

You hear that boy laughing ? — You
think he 's all fun ;
But the angels laugh, too, at the good
he has done ;
The children laugh loud as they troop to
his call,
And the poor man that knows him laughs
loudest of all !

Yes, we 're boys, — always playing with
tongue or with pen, —
And I sometimes have asked, — Shall we
ever be men ?
Shall we always be youthful, and laughing, and gay,
Till the last dear companion drops smiling away ?

Then here 's to our boyhood, its gold and
its gray !
The stars of its winter, the dews of its
May !
And when we have done with our life-
lasting toys,
Dear Father, take care of thy children,
THE BOYS !

1860.

LINES.

I 'M ashamed, — that 's the fact, — it 's
a pitiful case, —

Won't any kind classmate get up in my
place ?
Just remember how often I 've risen before, —
I blush as I straighten my legs on the
floor !

There are stories, once pleasing, too many
times told, —
There are beauties once charming, too
fearfully old, —
There are voices we 've heard till we know
them so well,
Though they talked for an hour they 'd
have nothing to tell.

Yet, Classmates ! Friends ! Brothers !
dear blessed old boys !
Made one by a lifetime of sorrows and
joys,
What lips have such sounds as the poorest of these,
Though honeyed, like Plato's, by musical bees ?

What voice is so sweet and what greeting so dear
As the simple, warm welcome that waits
for us here ?
The love of our boyhood still breathes in
its tone,
And our hearts throb the answer, "He 's
one of our own ! "

Nay ! count not our numbers ; some
sixty we know,
But these are above, and those under the
snow ;
And thoughts are still mingled wherever
we meet
For those we remember with those that
we greet.

We have rolled on life's journey, — how
fast and how far !
One round of humanity's many-wheeled
car,

But up-hill and down-hill, through rat-
　　tle and rub,
Old, true Twenty-niners! we 've stuck
　　to our hub!

While a brain lives to think, or a bosom
　　to feel,
We will cling to it still like the spokes
　　of a wheel!
And age, as it chills us, shall fasten the
　　tire
That youth fitted round in his circle of
　　fire!

1861.

(JANUARY 3D.)

A VOICE OF THE LOYAL NORTH.

WE sing "Our Country's" song to-night
　　With saddened voice and eye;
Her banner droops in clouded light
　　Beneath the wintry sky.
We 'll pledge her once in golden wine
　　Before her stars have set:
Though dim one reddening orb may
　　shine,
　　We have a Country yet.

'T were vain to sigh o'er errors past,
　　The fault of sires or sons;
Our soldier heard the threatening blast,
　　And spiked his useless guns;
He saw the star-wreathed ensign fall,
　　By mad invaders torn;
But saw it from the bastioned wall
　　That laughed their rage to scorn!

What though their angry cry is flung
　　Across the howling wave, —
They smite the air with idle tongue
　　The gathering storm who brave;
Enough of speech! the trumpet rings;
　　Be silent, patient, calm, —
God help them if the tempest swings
　　The pine against the palm!

Our toilsome years have made us tame;
　　Our strength has slept unfelt;
The furnace-fire is slow to flame
　　That bids our ploughshares melt;
'T is hard to lose the bread they win
　　In spite of Nature's frowns, —
To drop the iron threads we spin
　　That weave our web of towns,

To see the rusting turbines stand
　　Before the emptied flumes,
To fold the arms that flood the land
　　With rivers from their looms, —
But harder still for those who learn
　　The truth forgot so long;
When once their slumbering passions
　　burn,
　　The peaceful are the strong!

The Lord have mercy on the weak,
　　And calm their frenzied ire,
And save our brothers ere they shriek,
　　"We played with Northern fire!"
The eagle hold his mountain height, —
　　The tiger pace his den!
Give all their country, each his right!
　　God keep us all! Amen!

1862.
*
J. D. R.   Jacob D. Russe

THE friends that are, and friends that
　　were,
　　What shallow waves divide!
I miss the form for many a year
　　Still seated at my side.

I miss him, yet I feel him still
　　Amidst our faithful band,
As if not death itself could chill
　　The warmth of friendship's hand.

His story other lips may tell, —
　　For me the veil is drawn;
I only know he loved me well,
　　He loved me — and is gone!

1862.

VOYAGE OF THE GOOD SHIP UNION.

'T IS midnight : through my troubled
          dream
  Loud wails the tempest's cry ;
Before the gale, with tattered sail,
  A ship goes plunging by.
What name ?   Where bound ? — The
          rocks around
  Repeat the loud halloo.
— The good ship Union, Southward
          bound :
  God help her and her crew !

And is the old flag flying still
  That o'er your fathers flew,
With bands of white and rosy light,
  And field of starry blue ?
— Ay ! look aloft ! its folds full oft
  Have braved the roaring blast,
And still shall fly when from the sky
  This black typhoon has past !

Speak, pilot of the storm-tost bark !
  May I thy peril share ?
— O landsman, these are fearful seas
  The brave alone may dare !
— Nay, ruler of the rebel deep,
  What matters wind or wave ?
The rocks that wreck your reeling deck
  Will leave me naught to save !

O landsman, art thou false or true ?
  What sign hast thou to show ?
— The crimson stains from loyal veins
  That hold my heart-blood's flow !
— Enough ! what more shall honor
          claim ?
  I know the sacred sign ;
Above thy head our flag shall spread,
  Our ocean path be thine !

The bark sails on ; the Pilgrim's Cape
  Lies low along her lee,

Whose headland crooks its anchor-flukes
  To lock the shore and sea.
No treason here ! it cost too dear
  To win this barren realm !
And true and free the hands must be
  That hold the whaler's helm !

Still on ! Manhattan's narrowing bay
  No Rebel cruiser scars ;
Her waters feel no pirate's keel
  That flaunts the fallen stars !
— But watch the light on yonder
          height, —
  Ay, pilot, have a care !
Some lingering cloud in mist may shroud
  The capes of Delaware !

Say, pilot, what this fort may be,
  Whose sentinels look down
From moated walls that show the sea
  Their deep embrasures' frown ?
The Rebel host claims all the coast,
  But these are friends, we know,
Whose footprints spoil the "sacred soil,"
  And this is ? —— Fort Monroe !

The breakers roar, — how bears the
          shore ?
  — The traitorous wreckers' hands
Have quenched the blaze that poured
          its rays
  Along the Hatteras sands.
— Ha ! say not so !   I see its glow !
  Again the shoals display
The beacon light that shines by night,
  The Union Stars by day !

The good ship flies to milder skies,
  The wave more gently flows,
The softening breeze wafts o'er the seas
  The breath of Beaufort's rose.
What fold is this the sweet winds kiss,
  Fair-striped and many-starred,
Whose shadow palls these orphaned
          walls,
  The twins of Beauregard ?

'What! heard you not Port Royal's doom?
  How the black war-ships came
And turned the Beaufort roses' bloom
  To redder wreaths of flame?
How from Rebellion's broken reed
  We saw his emblem fall,
As soon his curséd poison-weed
  Shall drop from Sumter's wall?

On! on! Pulaski's iron hail
  Falls harmless on Tybee!
The good ship feels the freshening gales,
  She strikes the open sea;
She rounds the point, she threads the keys
  That guard the Land of Flowers,
And rides at last where firm and fast
  Her own Gibraltar towers!

The good ship Union's voyage is o'er,
  At anchor safe she swings,
And loud and clear with cheer on cheer
  Her joyous welcome rings:
Hurrah! Hurrah! it shakes the wave,
  It thunders on the shore, —
One flag, one land, one heart, one hand,
  One Nation, evermore!

1863.

"CHOOSE YOU THIS DAY WHOM YE WILL SERVE."

YES, tyrants, you hate us, and fear while you hate
The self-ruling, chain-breaking, throne-shaking State!
The night-birds dread morning, — your instinct is true, —
The day-star of Freedom brings midnight for you!

Why plead with the deaf for the cause of mankind?
The owl hoots at noon that the eagle is blind!

We ask not your reasons, — 't were wasting our time, —
Our life is a menace, our welfare a crime!

We have battles to fight, we have foes to subdue, —
Time waits not for us, and we wait not for you!
The mower mows on, though the adder may writhe
And the copper-head coil round the blade of his scythe!

"No sides in this quarrel," your statesmen may urge,
Of school-house and wages with slave-pen and scourge! —
No sides in the quarrel! proclaim it as well
To the angels that fight with the legions of hell!

They kneel in God's temple, the North and the South,
With blood on each weapon and prayers in each mouth.
Whose cry shall be answered? Ye Heavens, attend
The lords of the lash as their voices ascend!

"O Lord, we are shaped in the image of Thee, —
Smite down the base millions that claim to be free,
And lend Thy strong arm to the soft-handed race
Who eat *not* their bread in the sweat of their face!"

So pleads the proud planter. What echoes are these?
The bay of his bloodhound is borne on the breeze,
And, lost in the shriek of his victim's despair,

His voice dies unheard. — Hear the Puritan's prayer !

" O Lord, that didst smother mankind
    in Thy flood,
The sun is as sackcloth, the moon is as
    blood,
The stars fall to earth as untimely are
    cast
The figs from the fig-tree that shakes in
    the blast !

" All nations, all tribes in whose nostrils
    is breath,
Stand gazing at Sin as she travails with
    Death !
Lord, strangle the monster that struggles to birth,
Or mock us no more with Thy 'Kingdom
    on Earth !'

" If Ammon and Moab must reign in the
    land
Thou gavest Thine Israel, fresh from
    Thy hand,
Call Baäl and Ashtaroth out of their
    graves
To be the new gods for the empire of
    slaves ! "

Whose God will ye serve, O ye rulers
    of men ?
Will ye build you new shrines in the
    slave-breeder's den ?
Or bow with the children of light, as
    they call
On the Judge of the Earth and the
    Father of All ?

Choose wisely, choose quickly, for time
    moves apace, —
Each day is an age in the life of our race !
Lord, lead them in love, ere they hasten
    in fear
From the fast-rising flood that shall girdle the sphere !

Frederick W. Crocker.

1864.

*

F. W. C.

FAST as the rolling seasons bring
    The hour of fate to those we love,
Each pearl that leaves the broken string
    Is set in Friendship's crown above.
As narrower grows the earthly chain,
    The circle widens in the sky ;
These are our treasures that remain,
    But those are stars that beam on high.

We miss — O, how we miss ! — *his* face, —
    With trembling accents speak his
        name.
Earth cannot fill his shadowed place
    From all her rolls of pride and fame ;
Our song has lost the silvery thread
    That carolled through his jocund lips ;
Our laugh is mute, our smile is fled,
    And all our sunshine in eclipse.

And what and whence the wondrous
        charm
    That kept his manhood boylike still, —
That life's hard censors could disarm
    And lead them captive at his will ?
His heart was shaped of rosier clay, —
    His veins were filled with ruddier
        fire, —
Time could not chill him, fortune sway,
    Nor toil with all its burdens tire.

His speech burst throbbing from its
        fount
    And set our colder thoughts aglow,
As the hot leaping geysers mount
    And falling melt the Iceland snow.
Some word, perchance, we counted
        rash, —
    Some phrase our calmness might disclaim,
Yet 't was the sunset's lightning's flash.
    No angry bolt, but harmless flame.

Man judges all, God knoweth each ;
  We read the rule, He sees the law ;
How oft his laughing children teach
  The truths his prophets never saw !
O friend, whose wisdom flowered in
  mirth,
    Our hearts are sad, our eyes are
    dim ;
He gave thy smiles to brighten earth, —
  We trust thy joyous soul to Him !

Alas ! — our weakness Heaven forgive !
  We murmur, even while we trust,
" How long earth's breathing burdens
  live,
    Whose hearts, before they die, are
    dust ! "
But thou ! — through grief's untimely
  tears
  We ask with half-reproachful sigh —
" Couldst thou not watch a few brief
  years
    Till Friendship faltered, 'Thou mayst
    die' ? "

Who loved our boyish years so well ?
  Who knew so well their pleasant
  tales,
And all those livelier freaks could tell
  Whose oft-told story never fails ?
In vain we turn our aching eyes, —
  In vain we stretch our eager hands, —
Cold in his wintry shroud he lies
  Beneath the dreary drifting sands !

Ah, speak not thus ! *He* lies not there !
  We see him, hear him as of old !
He comes ! he claims his wonted
  chair !
  His beaming face we still behold !
His voice rings clear in all our songs,
  And loud his mirthful accents rise ;
To us our brother's life belongs, —
  Dear friends, a classmate never dies !

1864.

THE LAST CHARGE.

Now, men of the North ! will you join
  in the strife
For country, for freedom, for honor, for
  life ?
The giant grows blind in his fury and
  spite, —
One blow on his forehead will settle the
  fight !

Flash full in his eyes the blue lightning
  of steel,
And stun him with cannon-bolts, peal
  upon peal !
Mount, troopers, and follow your game
  to its lair,
As the hound tracks the wolf and the
  beagle the hare !

Blow, trumpets, your summons, till slug-
  gards awake !
Beat, drums, till the roofs of the faint-
  hearted shake !
Yet, yet, ere the signet is stamped on
  the scroll,
Their names may be traced on the blood-
  sprinkled roll !

Trust not the false herald that painted
  your shield :
True honor *to-day* must be sought on the
  field !
Her scutcheon shows white with a blazon
  of red, —
The life-drop of crimson for liberty
  shed !

The hour is at hand, and the moment
  draws nigh ;
The dog-star of treason grows dim in
  the sky ;
Shine forth from the battle-cloud, light
  of the morn,

Call back the bright hour when the
    Nation was born !

The rivers of peace through our valleys
    shall run,
As the glaciers of tyranny melt in the
    sun ;
Smite, smite the proud parricide down
    from his throne, —
His sceptre once broken, the world is
    our own !

1865.

OUR OLDEST FRIEND.

I GIVE you the health of the oldest
    friend
That, short of eternity, earth can lend, —
A friend so faithful and tried and true
That nothing can wean him from me
    and you.

When first we screeched in the sudden
    blaze
Of the daylight's blinding and blasting
    rays,
And gulped at the gaseous, groggy air,
This old, old friend stood waiting there.

And when, with a kind of mortal strife,
We had gasped and choked into breath-
    ing life,
He watched by the cradle, day and night,
And held our hands till we stood upright.

From gristle and pulp our frames have
    grown
To stringy muscle and solid bone ;
While we were changing, he altered not ;
We might forget, but he never forgot.

He came with us to the college class, —
Little cared he for the steward's pass !
All the rest must pay their fee,
But the grim old dead-head entered free.

He stayed with us while we counted o'er
Four times each of the seasons four ;
And with every season, from year to year,
The dear name Classmate he made more
    dear.

He never leaves us, — he never will,
Till our hands are cold and our hearts
    are still ;
On birthdays, and Christmas, and New-
    Year's too,
He always remembers both me and you.

Every year this faithful friend
His little present is sure to send ;
Every year, wheresoe'er we be,
He wants a keepsake from you and me.

How he loves us ! he pats our heads,
And, lo ! they are gleaming with silver
    threads ;
And he 's always begging one lock of
    hair,
Till our shining crowns have nothing to
    wear.

At length he will tell us, one by one,
" My child, your labor on earth is done ;
And now you must journey afar to see
My elder brother, — Eternity !"

And so, when long, long years have
    passed,
Some dear old fellow will be the last, —
Never a boy alive but he
Of all our goodly company !

When he lies down, but not till then,
Our kind Class-Angel will drop the pen
That writes in the day-book kept above
Our lifelong record of faith and love.

So here 's a health in homely rhyme
To our oldest classmate, Father Time !
May our last survivor live to be
As bald and as wise and as tough as he!

1865.

SHERMAN 'S IN SAVANNAH.

A HALF-RHYMED IMPROMPTU.

LIKE the tribes of Israel,
Fed on quails and manna,
Sherman and his glorious band
Journeyed through the rebel land,
Fed from Heaven's all-bounteous hand,
Marching on Savannah!

As the moving pillar shone,
Streamed the starry banner
All day long in rosy light,
Flaming splendor all the night,
Till it swooped in eagle flight
Down on doomed Savannah!

Glory be to God on high!
Shout the loud Hosanna!
Treason's wilderness is past,
Canaan's shore is won at last,
Peal a nation's trumpet-blast, —
Sherman 's in Savannah!

Soon shall Richmond's tough old hide
Find a tough old tanner!
Soon from every rebel wall
Shall the rag of treason fall,
Till our banner flaps o'er all
As it crowns Savannah!

1866.

MY ANNUAL.

How long will this harp which you once
loved to hear
Cheat your lips of a smile or your eyes
of a tear?
How long stir the echoes it wakened of
old,
While its strings were unbroken, untar-
nished its gold?

Dear friends of my boyhood, my words
do you wrong;
The heart, the heart only, shall throb
in my song;
It reads the kind answer that looks from
your eyes, —
"We will bid our old harper play on
till he dies."

Though Youth, the fair angel that
looked o'er the strings,
Has lost the bright glory that gleamed
on his wings,
Though the freshness of morning has
passed from its tone,
It is still the old harp that was always
your own.

I claim not its music, — each note it
affords
I strike from your heart-strings, that
lend me its chords;
I know you will listen and love to the
last,
For it trembles and thrills with the
voice of your past.

Ah, brothers! dear brothers! the harp
that I hold
No craftsman could string and no artisan
mould;
He shaped it, He strung it, who fashioned the lyres
That ring with the hymns of the sera-
phim choirs.

Not mine are the visions of beauty it
brings,
Not mine the faint fragrance around it
that clings;
Those shapes are the phantoms of years
that are fled,
Those sweets breathe from roses your
summers have shed.

Each hour of the past lends its tribute
to this,
Till it blooms like a bower in the Garden of Bliss;
The thorn and the thistle may grow as
they will,
Where Friendship unfolds there is Paradise still.

The bird wanders careless while summer
is green,
The leaf-hidden cradle that rocked him
unseen ;
When Autumn's rude fingers the woods
have undressed,
The boughs may look bare, but they
show him his nest.

Too precious these moments ! the lustre
they fling
Is the light of our year, is the gem of
its ring,
So brimming with sunshine, we almost
forget
The rays it has lost, and its border of jet.

While round us the many-hued halo is
shed,
How dear are the living, how near are
the dead!
One circle, scarce broken, these waiting
below,
Those walking the shores where the
asphodels blow !

Not life shall enlarge it nor death shall
divide, —
No brother new-born finds his place at
my side ;
No titles shall freeze us, no grandeurs
infest,
His Honor, His Worship, are boys like
the rest.

Some won the world's homage, their
names we hold dear, —

But Friendship, not Fame, is the coun-
tersign here ;
Make room by the conqueror crowned
in the strife
For the comrade that limps from the
battle of life !

What tongue talks of battle ?   Too long
we have heard
In sorrow, in anguish, that terrible word;
It reddened the sunshine, it crimsoned
the wave,
It sprinkled our doors with the blood
of our brave.

Peace, Peace comes at last, with her
garland of white;
Peace broods in all hearts as we gather
to-night;
The blazon of Union spreads full in the
sun ;
We echo its words, — We are one !   We
are one !

1867.

ALL HERE.

IT is not what we say or sing,
    That keeps our charm so long un-
broken,
Though every lightest leaf we bring
    May touch the heart as friendship's
token ;
Not what we sing or what we say
    Can make us dearer to each other ;
We love the singer and his lay,
    But love as well the silent brother.

Yet bring whate'er your garden grows,
    Thrice welcome to our smiles and
praises;
Thanks for the myrtle and the rose,
    Thanks for the marigolds and daisies;
One flower erelong we all shall claim,
    Alas ! unloved of Amaryllis —

Nature's last blossom — need I name
  The wreath of threescore's silver lilies ?

How many, brothers, meet to-night
  Around our boyhood's covered embers?
Go read the treasured names aright
  The old triennial list remembers :
Though twenty wear the starry sign
  That tells a life has broke its tether,
The fifty-eight of 'twenty-nine —
  God bless THE BOYS ! — are all to-
    gether !

These come with joyous look and word,
  With friendly grasp and cheerful
    greeting, —
Those smile unseen, and move unheard,
  The angel guests of every meeting ;
They cast no shadow in the flame
  That flushes from the gilded lustre,
But count us — we are still the same ;
  One earthly band, one heavenly clus-
    ter !

Love dies not when he bows his head
  To pass beyond the narrow portals, —
The light these glowing moments shed
  Wakes from their sleep our lost im-
    mortals ;
They come as in their joyous prime,
  Before their morning days were num-
    bered, —
Death stays the envious hand of Time, —
  The eyes have not grown dim that
    slumbered !

The paths that loving souls have trod
  Arch o'er the dust where worldlings
    grovel
High as the zenith o'er the sod, —
  The cross above the Sexton's shovel !
We rise beyond the realms of day ;
  They seem to stoop from spheres of
    glory

With us one happy hour to stray,
  While youth comes back in song and
    story.

Ah ! ours is friendship true as steel
  That war has tried in edge and tem-
    per ;
It writes upon its sacred seal
  The priest's *ubique — omnes — sem-
    per !*
It lends the sky a fairer sun
  That cheers our lives with rays as
    steady
As if our footsteps had begun
  To print the golden streets already !

The tangling years have clinched its
    knot
  Too fast for mortal strength to sunder ;
The lightning bolts of noon are shot ;
  No fear of evening's idle thunder !
Too late ! too late ! — no graceless hand
  Shall stretch its cords in vain endeavor
To rive the close encircling band
  That made and keeps us one forever !

So when upon the fated scroll
  The falling stars have all descended,
And, blotted from the breathing roll,
  Our little page of life is ended,
We ask but one memorial line
  Traced on thy tablet, Gracious Mother :
" My children. Boys of '29.
  In pace. How they loved each other ! "

1868.

ONCE MORE.

" *Will I come ?* " That *is* pleasant ! I
  beg to inquire
If the gun that I carry has ever missed
  fire ?
And which was the muster-roll — mention but one —

That missed your old comrade who carries the gun ?

You see me as always, my hand on the lock,
The cap on the nipple, the hammer full cock ;
It is rusty, some tell me ; I heed not the scoff ;
It is battered and bruised, but it always goes off !

— "Is it loaded?" I 'll bet you ! What does n't it hold ?
Rammed full to the muzzle with memories untold ;
Why, it scares me to fire, lest the pieces should fly
Like the cannons that burst on the Fourth of July !

One charge is a remnant of College-day dreams
(Its wadding is made of forensics and themes) ;
Ah, visions of fame ! what a flash in the pan
As the trigger was pulled by each clever young man !

And love ! Bless my stars, what a cartridge is there !
With a wadding of rose-leaves and ribbons and hair, —
All crammed in one verse to go off at a shot !
— Were there ever such sweethearts ? Of course there were not !

And next, — what a load ! it will split the old gun, —
Three fingers, — four fingers, — five fingers of fun !
Come tell me, gray sages, for mischief and noise
Was there ever a lot like us fellows, "The Boys" ?

Bump ! bump ! down the staircase the cannon-ball goes, —
Aha, old Professor ! Look out for your toes !
Don't think, my poor Tutor, to *sleep* in your bed, —
Two "Boys"—'twenty-niners — room over your head !

Remember the nights when the tar-barrel blazed !
From red "Massachusetts" the war-cry was raised ;
And "Hollis" and "Stoughton" re-echoed the call ;
Till P—— poked his head out of Holworthy Hall !

Old P——, as we called him, — at fifty or so, —
Not exactly a bud, but not quite in full blow ;
In ripening manhood, suppose we should say,
Just nearing his prime, as we boys are to-day !

O, say, can you look through the vista of age
To the time when old Morse drove the regular stage?
When Lyon told tales of the long-vanished years,
And Lenox crept round with the rings in his ears ?

And dost thou, my brother, remember indeed
The days of our dealings with Willard and Read ?
When "Dolly" was kicking and running away,
And punch came up smoking on Fillebrown's tray ?

But where are the Tutors, my brother, O tell ! —

And where the Professors, remembered
   so well ?
The sturdy old Grecian of Holworthy
   Hall,
And Latin, and Logic, and Hebrew,
   and all ?

— " They are dead, the old fellows" (we
   called them so then,
Though we since have found out they
   were lusty young men).
— They are *dead*, do you tell me ? — but
   how do you know ?
You 've filled once too often.   I doubt if
   it 's so.

I 'm thinking.   I 'm thinking.   Is this
   'sixty-eight ?
It 's not quite so clear.   It admits of
   debate.
I *may* have been dreaming.   I rather
   incline
To think — yes, I 'm certain — it is
   'twenty-nine !

" By Zhorzhe ! " — as friend Sales is ac-
   customed to cry, —
You tell me they 're dead, but I know
   it 's a lie !
Is Jackson not President ? — What was
   't you said ?
It can't be ; you 're joking ; what, — all
   of 'em dead ?

Jim, — Harry, — Fred, — Isaac, — all
   gone from our side ?
They could n't have left us, — no, not if
   they tried.
— Look, — there 's our old Præses, —
   he can't find his text ;
— See, — P——rubs his leg, as he growls
   out, " *The next !* "

I told you 't was nonsense.   Joe, give
   us a song !

Go harness up " Dolly," and fetch her
   along ! —
Dead !   Dead !   You false graybeard, I
   swear they are not !
Hurrah for Old Hickory ! — O, I forgot !

Well, *one* we have with us (how could
   he contrive
To deal with us youngsters and still to
   survive ?)
Who wore for our guidance authority's
   robe, —
No wonder he took to the study of Job !

— And now as my load was uncommonly
   large,
Let me taper it off with a classical charge ;
When that has gone off, I shall drop my
   old gun —
And then stand at ease, for my service
   is done.

Bibamus   ad   Classem   vocatam   " The
   Boys"
Et   eorum   Tutorem   cui   nomen   est
   " Noyes" ;
Et floreant, valeant, vigeant tam,
Non Peircius ipse enumeret quam !

1869.

THE OLD CRUISER.

HERE 's the old cruiser, 'Twenty-nine,
Forty times she 's crossed the line ;
Same old masts and sails and crew,
Tight and tough and as good as new.

Into the harbor she bravely steers
Just as she 's done for these forty
   years,—
Over her anchor goes, splash and clang !
Down her sails drop, rattle and bang !

Comes a vessel out of the dock
Fresh and spry as a fighting-cock,

Feathered with sails and spurred with
    steam,
Heading out of the classic stream.

Crew of a hundred all aboard,
Every man as fine as a lord.
Gay they look and proud they feel,
Bowling along on even keel.

On they float with wind and tide, —
Gain at last the old ship's side;
Every man looks down in turn, —
Reads the name that's on her stern.

"Twenty-nine ! — *Diable* you say !
That was in Skipper Kirkland's day !
What was the Flying Dutchman's name?
This old rover must be the same.

" Ho ! you Boatswain that walks the
    deck,
How does it happen you're not a wreck?
One and another have come to grief,
How have you dodged by rock and reef?"

— Boatswain, lifting one knowing lid,
Hitches his breeches and shifts his quid :
"Hey? What is it? Who's come to
    grief?
Louder, young swab, I'm a little deaf."

"I say, old fellow, what keeps your boat
With all you jolly old boys afloat,
When scores of vessels as good as she
Have swallowed the salt of the bitter
    sea?

" Many a crew from many a craft
Goes drifting by on a broken raft
Pieced from a vessel that clove the brine
Taller and prouder than 'Twenty-nine.

" Some capsized in an angry breeze,
Some were lost in the narrow seas,
Some on snags and some on sands
Struck and perished and lost their hands.

" Tell us young ones, you gray old man,
What is your secret, if you can.
We have a ship as good as you,
Show us how to keep our crew."

So in his ear the youngster cries ;
Then the gray Boatswain straight re-
    plies : —
"All your crew be sure you know, —
Never let one of your shipmates go.

" If he leaves you, change your tack,
Follow him close and fetch him back ;
When you've hauled him in at last,
Grapple his flipper and hold him fast.

" If you've wronged him, speak him
    fair,
Say you're sorry and make it square ;
If he's wronged you, wink so tight
None of you see what's plain in sight.

"When the world goes hard and wrong,
Lend a hand to help him along ;
When his stockings have holes to darn,
Don't you grudge him your ball of yarn.

" Once in a twelvemonth, come what
    may,
Anchor your ship in a quiet bay,
Call all hands and read the log,
And give 'em a taste of grub and grog.

" Stick to each other through thick and
    thin ;
All the closer as age leaks in ;
Squalls will blow and clouds will frown,
But stay by your ship till you all go
    down !"

ADDED FOR THE ALUMNI MEETING,
JUNE 29, 1869.

So the gray Boatswain of 'Twenty-nine
Piped to " The Boys " as they crossed
    the line ;

Round the cabin sat thirty guests,
Babes of the nurse with a thousand
 breasts.

There were the judges, grave and grand,
Flanked by the priests on either hand ;
There was the lord of wealth untold,
And the dear good fellow in broadcloth
 old.

Thirty men, from twenty towns,
Sires and grandsires with silvered
 crowns, —
Thirty school-boys all in a row, —
Bens and Georges and Bill and Joe.

In thirty goblets the wine was poured,
But threescore gathered around the
 board, —
For lo ! at the side of every chair
A shadow hovered — we all were there !

1869.

HYMN FOR THE CLASS-MEETING.

Thou Gracious Power, whose mercy lends
The light of home, the smile of friends,
Our gathered flock thine arms infold
As in the peaceful days of old.

Wilt thou not hear us while we raise,
In sweet accord of solemn praise,
The voices that have mingled long
In joyous flow of mirth and song ?

For all the blessings life has brought,
For all its sorrowing hours have taught,
For all we mourn, for all we keep,
The hands we clasp, the loved that
 sleep ;

The noontide sunshine of the past,
These brief, bright moments fading fast,
The stars that gild our darkening years,
The twilight ray from holier spheres ;

We thank thee, Father ! let thy grace
Our narrowing circle still embrace,
Thy mercy shed its heavenly store,
Thy peace be with us evermore !

1870.

EVEN-SONG.

It may be, yes, it must be, Time that
 brings
  An end to mortal things,
That sends the beggar Winter in the
 train
  Of Autumn's burdened wain, —
Time, that is heir of all our earthly
 state,
  And knoweth well to wait
Till sea hath turned to shore and shore
 to sea,
  If so it need must be,
Ere he make good his claim and call his
 own
  Old empires overthrown, —
Time, who can find no heavenly orb too
 large
  To hold its fee in charge,
Nor any motes that fill its beam so
 small,
  But he shall care for all, —
It may be, must be, — yes, he soon
 shall tire
  This hand that holds the lyre.

Then ye who listened in that earlier day
  When to my careless lay
I matched its chords and stole their first-
 born thrill,
  With untaught rudest skill
Vexing a treble from the slender strings
  Thin as the locust sings
When the shrill-crying child of sum-
 mer's heat
  Pipes from its leafy seat,
The dim pavilion of embowering green

Beneath whose shadowy screen
The small sopranist tries his single note
  Against the song-bird's throat,
And all the echoes listen, but in vain ;
  They hear no answering strain, —
Then ye who listened in that earlier day
  Shall sadly turn away,

Saying, "The fire burns low, the hearth
    is cold
  That warmed our blood of old ;
Cover its embers and its half - burnt
    brands,
  And let us stretch our hands
Over a brighter and fresh-kindled flame ;
  Lo, this is not the same,
The joyous singer of our morning time,
  Flushed high with lusty rhyme !
Speak kindly, for he bears a human
    heart,
  But whisper him apart, —
Tell him the woods their autumn robes
    have shed
  And all their birds have fled,
And shouting winds unbuild the naked
    nests
  They warmed with patient breasts ;
Tell him the sky is dark, the summer
    o'er,
  And bid him sing no more !

Ah, welladay ! if words so cruel-kind
  A listening ear might find !
But who that hears the music in his soul
  Of rhythmic waves that roll
Crested with gleams of fire, and as they
    flow
  Stir all the deeps below
Till the great pearls no calm might ever
    reach
  Leap glistening on the beach, —
Who that has known the passion and
    the pain,
  The rush through heart and brain,
The joy so like a pang his hand is pressed

Hard on his throbbing breast,
When thou, whose smile is life and bliss
    and fame
  Hast set his pulse aflame,
Muse of the lyre ! can say farewell to
    thee ?
  Alas ! and must it be ?

In many a clime, in many a stately
    tongue,
  The mighty bards have sung ;
To these the immemorial thrones belong
  And purple robes of song ;
Yet the slight minstrel loves the slender
    tone
  His lips may call his own,
And finds the measure of the verse more
    sweet
  Timed by his pulse's beat,
Than all the hymnings of the laurelled
    throng.
  Say not I do him wrong,
For Nature spoils her warblers, — them
    she feeds
  In lotus-growing meads
And pours them subtle draughts from
    haunted streams
  That fill their souls with dreams.

Full well I know the gracious mother's
    wiles
  And dear delusive smiles !
No callow fledgling of her singing brood
  But tastes that witching food,
And hearing overhead the eagle's wing,
  And how the thrushes sing,
Vents his exiguous chirp, and from his
    nest
  Flaps forth — we know the rest.
I own the weakness of the tuneful
    kind,—
  Are not all harpers blind ?
I sang too early, must I sing too late ?
  The lengthening shadows wait
The first pale stars of twilight, — yet
  how sweet

The flattering whisper's cheat, —
" Thou hast the fire no evening chill
    can tame,
    Whose coals outlast its flame ! "

Farewell, ye carols of the laughing morn,
    Of earliest sunshine born !
The sower flings the seed and looks not
    back
    Along his furrowed track ;
The reaper leaves the stalks for other
    hands
    To gird with circling bands ;
The wind, earth's careless servant, truant-
    born,
    Blows clean the beaten corn
And quits the thresher's floor, and goes
    his way
    To sport with ocean's spray ;
The headlong-stumbling rivulet scram-
    bling down
    To wash the sea-girt town,
Still babbling of the green and billowy
    waste
    Whose salt he longs to taste,
Ere his warm wave its chilling clasp may
    feel
    Has twirled the miller's wheel.

The song has done its task that makes
    us bold
    With secrets else untold, —
And mine has run its errand ; through
    the dews
    I tracked the flying Muse ;
The daughter of the morning touched my
    lips
    With roseate finger-tips ;
Whether I would or would not, I must
    sing
    With the new choirs of spring ;
Now, as I watch the fading autumn day
    And trill my softened lay,
I think of all that listened, and of one
    For whom a brighter sun

Dawned at high summer's noon. Ah,
    comrades dear,
    Are not all gathered here ?
Our hearts have answered. — Yes ! they
    hear our call :
    All gathered here ! all ! all !

1871.

THE SMILING LISTENER.

PRECISELY. I see it. You all want to
    say
That a tear is too sad and a laugh is too
    gay ;
You could stand a faint smile, you could
    manage a sigh,
But you value your ribs, and you don't
    want to cry.

And why at our feast of the clasping of
    hands
Need we turn on the stream of our lach-
    rymal glands ?
Though we see the white breakers of age
    on our bow,
Let us take a good pull in the jolly-boat
    now !

It 's hard if a fellow cannot feel content
When a banquet like this does n't cost
    him a cent,
When his goblet and plate he may empty
    at will,
And our kind Class Committee will settle
    the bill.

And here 's your old friend the identical
    bard
Who has rhymed and recited you verse
    by the yard
Since the days of the empire of Andrew
    the First
Till you 're full to the brim and feel ready
    to burst,

It 's awful to think of, — how year after
 year
With his piece in his pocket he waits for
 you here ;
No matter who 's missing, there always
 is one
To lug out his manuscript, sure as a gun.

" Why won't he stop writing ? " Humanity cries :
The answer is briefly, " He can't if he
 tries ;
He has played with his foolish old feather
 so long,
That the goose-quill in spite of him
 cackles in song."

You have watched him with patience
 from morning to dusk
Since the tassel was bright o'er the green
 of the husk,
And now — it 's too bad — it 's a pitiful
 job —
He has shelled the ripe ear till he 's come
 to the cob.

I see one face beaming — it listens so
 well
There must be some music yet left in
 my shell —
The wine of my soul is not thick on the
 lees ;
One string is unbroken, one friend I can
 please !

Dear comrade, the sunshine of seasons
 gone by
Looks out from your tender and tear-
 moistened eye,
A pharos of love on an ice-girdled
 coast, —
Kind soul ! — Don't you hear me ? —
 He 's deaf as a post !

Can it be one of Nature's benevolent
 tricks

That you grow hard of hearing as I grow
 prolix ?
And that look of delight which would
 angels beguile
Is the deaf man's prolonged unintelligent
 smile ?

Ah ! the ear may grow dull, and the eye
 may wax dim,
But they still know a classmate — they
 can't mistake him ;
There is something to tell us, " That 's
 one of our band,"
Though we groped in the dark for a touch
 of his hand.

Well, Time with his snuffers is prowling
 about
And his shaky old fingers will soon snuff
 us out ;
There 's a hint for us all in each pendulum tick,
For we 're low in the tallow and long in
 the wick.

You remember Rossini — you 've been
 at the play ?
How his overture-endings keep crashing
 away
Till you think, " It 's all over — it can't
 but stop now —
That 's the screech and the bang of the
 final bow-wow."

And you find you 're mistaken ; there 's
 lots more to come,
More banging, more screeching of fiddle
 and drum,
Till when the last ending is finished and
 done,
You feel like a horse when the winning-
 post 's won.

So I, who have sung to you, merry or
 sad,

Since the days when they called me a
  promising lad,
Though I 've made you more rhymes
  than a tutor could scan,
Have a few more still left, like the razor-
  strop man.

Now pray don't be frightened— I 'm
  ready to stop
My galloping anapests' clatter and pop—
In fact, if you say so, retire from to-day
To the garret I left, on a poet's half-pay.

And yet — I can't help it — perhaps —
  who can tell ?
You might miss the poor singer you
  treated so well,
And confess you could stand him five
  minutes or so,
"It was so like old times we remember,
  you know."

'T is not that the music can signify
  much,
But then there are chords that awake
  with a touch, —
And our hearts can find echoes of sorrow
  and joy
To the winch of the minstrel who hails
  from Savoy.

So this hand-organ tune that I cheerfully
  grind
May bring the old places and faces to
  mind,
And seen in the light of the past we recall
The flowers that have faded bloom fairest of all !

1872.

OUR SWEET SINGER.

Joseph Angier
J. A.

ONE memory trembles on our lips :
  It throbs in every breast ;

In tear-dimmed eyes, in mirth's eclipse,
  The shadow stands confessed.

O silent voice, that cheered so long
  Our manhood's marching day,
Without thy breath of heavenly song,
  How weary seems the way !

Vain every pictured phrase to tell
  Our sorrowing heart's desire ;
The shattered harp, the broken shell,
  The silent unstrung lyre ;

For youth was round us while he sang ;
  It glowed in every tone ;
With bridal chimes the echoes rang,
  And made the past our own.

O blissful dream ! Our nursery joys
  We know must have an end,
But love and friendship's broken toys
  May God's good angels mend !

The cheering smile, the voice of mirth
  And laughter's gay surprise
That please the children born of earth,
  Why deem that Heaven denies ?

Methinks in that refulgent sphere
  That knows not sun or moon,
An earth-born saint might long to hear
  One verse of " Bonny Doon " ;

Or walking through the streets of gold
  In Heaven's unclouded light,
His lips recall the song of old
  And hum " The sky is bright."

  *   *   *

And can we smile when thou art dead ?
  Ah, brothers, even so !
The rose of summer will be red,
  In spite of winter's snow.

Thou wouldst not leave us all in gloom
  Because thy song is still,
Nor blight the banquet-garland's bloom
  With grief's untimely chill.

The sighing wintry winds complain, —
  The singing bird has flown, —
Hark ! heard I not that ringing strain,
  That clear celestial tone ?

How poor these pallid phrases seem,
  How weak this tinkling line,
As warbles through my waking dream
  That angel voice of thine !

Thy requiem asks a sweeter lay ;
  It falters on my tongue ;
For all we vainly strive to say,
  Thou shouldst thyself have sung !

Horatius C. Merriam
Howard Sargent
Josiah Kendall Waite

1873.

*   *   *

H. C. M. H. S. J. K. W.

THE dirge is played, the throbbing
    death-peal rung ;
  The sad-voiced requiem sung
On each white urn where memory
    dwells
The wreath of rustling immortelles
  Our loving hands have hung,
And balmiest leaves have strown and ten-
    derest blossoms flung.

The birds that filled the air with songs
    have flown,
  The wintry blasts have blown,
And these for whom the voice of
    spring
Bade the sweet choirs their carols
    sing
  Sleep in those chambers lone
Where snows untrodden lie, unheard the
    night-winds moan.

We clasp them all in memory, as the
    vine
  Whose running stems intwine,
The marble shaft, and steal around,

  The lowly stone, the nameless
    mound ;
  With sorrowing hearts resign
Our brothers true and tried, and close
    our broken line.

How fast the lamps of life grow dim
    and die
  Beneath our sunset sky !
Still fading, as along our track
We cast our saddened glances back,
  And while we vainly sigh
The shadowy day recedes, the starry
    night draws nigh.

As when from pier to pier across the
    tide
  With even keel we glide,
The lights we left along the shore
Grow less and less, while more, yet
    more
  New vistas open wide
Of fair illumined streets and casements
    golden-eyed.

Each closing circle of our sunlit sphere
  Seems to bring Heaven more near :
Can we not dream that those we love
Are listening in the world above
  And smiling as they hear
The voices known so well of friends that
    still are dear ?

Does all that made us human fade away
  With this dissolving clay ?
Nay, rather deem the blessed isles
Are bright and gay with joyous
    smiles,
  That angels have their play,
And saints that tire of song may claim
    their holiday.

All else of earth may perish ; love alone
  Not Heaven shall find outgrown !
Are they not here, our spirit guests
With love still throbbing in their
    breasts ?

Once more let flowers be strown.
Welcome, ye shadowy forms, we count
　　you still our own !

1873.

WHAT I HAVE COME FOR.

I HAVE come with my verses — I think
　　I may claim
It is not the first time I have tried on
　　the same.
They were puckered in rhyme, they
　　were wrinkled in wit ;
But your hearts were so large that they
　　made them a fit.

I have come — not to tease you with
　　more of my rhyme,
But to feel as I did in the blessed old
　　time ;
I want to hear him with the Brobding-
　　nag laugh —
We count him at least as three men and
　　a half.

I have come to meet judges so wise and
　　so grand
That I shake in my shoes while they 're
　　shaking my hand ;
And the prince among merchants who
　　put back the crown
When they tried to enthrone him the
　　King of the Town.

I have come to see George — Yes, I
　　think there are four,
If they all were like these I could wish
　　there were more.
I have come to see one whom we used
　　to call "Jim,"
I want to see — O, don't I want to see
　　him ?

I have come to grow young — on my
　　word I declare

I have thought I detected a change in
　　my hair !
One hour with "The Boys" will restore
　　it to brown —
And a wrinkle or two I expect to rub
　　down.

Yes, that 's what I 've come for, as all
　　of us come ;
When I meet the dear Boys I could wish
　　I were dumb.
You asked me, you know, but it 's
　　spoiling the fun ;
I have told what I came for; my ditty
　　is done.

1874.

OUR BANKER.

OLD Time, in whose bank we deposit
　　our notes,
Is a miser who always wants guineas for
　　groats ;
He keeps all his customers still in arrears
By lending them minutes and charging
　　them years.

The twelvemonth rolls round and we
　　never forget
On the counter before us to pay him our
　　debt.
We reckon the marks he has chalked on
　　the door,
Pay up and shake hands and begin a
　　new score.

How long he will lend us, how much we
　　may owe,
No angel will tell us, no mortal may
　　know.
At fivescore, at fourscore, at threescore
　　and ten,
He may close the account with a stroke
　　of his pen.

This only we know,—amid sorrows and joys
Old Time has been easy and kind with "The Boys."
Though he must have and will have and does have his pay,
We have found him good-natured enough in his way.

He never forgets us, as others will do,—
I am sure he knows me, and I think he knows you,
For I see on your foreheads a mark that he lends
As a sign he remembers to visit his friends.

In the shape of a classmate (a wig on his crown,—
His day-book and ledger laid carefully down)
He has welcomed us yearly, a glass in his hand,
And pledged the good health of our brotherly band.

He's a thief, we must own, but how many there be
That rob us less gently and fairly than he:
He has stripped the green leaves that were over us all,
But they let in the sunshine as fast as they fall.

Young beauties may ravish the world with a glance
As they languish in song, as they float in the dance,—
They are grandmothers now we remember as girls,
And the comely white cap takes the place of the curls.

But the sighing and moaning and groaning are o'er,
We are pining and moping and sleepless no more,
And the hearts that were thumping like ships on the rocks
Beat as quiet and steady as meeting-house clocks.

The trump of ambition, loud sounding and shrill,
May blow its long blast, but the echoes are still,
The spring-tides are past, but no billow may reach
The spoils they have landed far up on the beach.

We see that Time robs us, we know that he cheats,
But we still find a charm in his pleasant deceits,
While he leaves the remembrance of all that was best,
Love, friendship, and hope, and the promise of rest.

Sweet shadows of twilight! how calm their repose,
While the dewdrops fall soft in the breast of the rose!
How blest to the toiler his hour of release
When the vesper is heard with its whisper of peace!

Then here's to the wrinkled old miser, our friend;
May he send us his bills to the century's end,
And lend us the moments no sorrow alloys,
Till he squares his account with the last of "The Boys."

1875.

FOR CLASS MEETING.

It is a pity and a shame — alas ! alas !
   I know it is,
To tread the trodden grapes again, but
   so it has been, so it is ;
The purple vintage long is past, with
   ripened clusters bursting so
They filled the wine-vats to the brim —
   't is strange you will be thirsting so !

Too well our faithful memory tells what
   might be rhymed or sung about,
For all have sighed and some have wept
   since last year's snows were flung
   about ;
The beacon flame that fired the sky, the
   modest ray that gladdened us,
A little breath has quenched their light,
   and deepening shades have saddened
   us.

No more our brother's life is ours for
   cheering or for grieving us,
One only sadness they bequeathed, the
   sorrow of their leaving us ;
Farewell ! Farewell ! — I turn the leaf
   I read my chiming measure in ;
Who knows but something still is there
   a friend may find a pleasure in ?

For who can tell by what he likes what
   other people's fancies are ?
How all men think the best of wives
   their own particular Nancies are ?
If what I sing you brings a smile, you
   will not stop to catechise,
Nor read Bœotia's lumbering line with
   nicely scanning Attic eyes.

Perhaps the alabaster box that Mary
   broke so lovingly,
While Judas looked so sternly on, the
   Master so approvingly,

Was not so fairly wrought as those that
   Pilate's wife and daughters had,
Or many a dame of Judah's line that
   drank of Jordan's waters had.

Perhaps the balm that cost so dear, as
   some remarked officially,
The precious nard that filled the room
   with fragrance so deliciously,
So oft recalled in storied page and sung
   in verse melodious,
The dancing girl had thought too cheap
   — that daughter of Herodias.

Where now are all the mighty deeds
   that Herod boasted loudest of ?
Where now the flashing jewelry the
   tetrarch's wife was proudest of ?
Yet still to hear how Mary loved, all
   tribes of men are listening,
And still the sinful woman's tears like
   stars in heaven are glistening.

'T is not the gift our hands have brought,
   the love it is we bring with it,
The minstrel's lips may shape the song,
   his heart in tune must sing with it ;
And so we love the simple lays, and
   wish we might have more of them
Our poet brothers sing for us — there
   must be half a score of them.

It may be that of fame and name our
   voices once were emulous, —
With deeper thoughts, with tenderer
   throbs their softening tones are
   tremulous ;
The dead seem listening as of old, ere
   friendship was bereft of them ;
The living wear a kinder smile, the remnant that is left of them.

Though on the once unfurrowed brows
   the harrow-teeth of Time may show,
Though all the strain of crippling years
   the halting feet of rhyme may show,

We look and hear with melting hearts,
    for what we all remember is
The morn of Spring, nor heed how chill
    the sky of gray November is.

Thanks to the gracious powers above
    from all mankind that singled us,
And dropped the pearl of friendship in
    the cup they kindly mingled us,
And bound us in a wreath of flowers
    with hoops of steel knit under it; —
Nor time, nor space, nor chance, nor
    change, nor death himself shall
    sunder it !

1876.

"AD AMICOS."

"Dumque virent genua
Et decet, obducta solvatur fronte senectus."

THE muse of boyhood's fervid hour
    Grows tame as skies get chill and hazy;
Where once she sought a passion-flower,
    She only hopes to find a daisy.
Well, who the changing world bewails ?
    Who asks to have it stay unaltered ?
Shall grown-up kittens chase their tails ?
    Shall colts be never shod or haltered ?

Are we "the boys" that used to make
    The tables ring with noisy follies ?
Whose deep-lunged laughter oft would
    shake
The ceiling with its thunder-volleys?
Are we the youths with lips unshorn,
    At beauty's feet unwrinkled suitors,
Whose memories reach tradition's
    morn —
    The days of prehistoric tutors ?

"The boys" we knew — but who are
    these
    Whose heads might serve for Plu-
    tarch's sages,

Or Fox's martyrs, if you please,
    Or hermits of the dismal ages ?
"The boys" we knew — can these be
    those?
    Their cheeks with morning's blush
    were painted;—
Where are the Harrys, Jims, and Joes
    With whom we once were well
    acquainted ?

If we are they, we 're not the same ;
    If they are we, why then they 're
    masking ;
Do tell us, neighbor What 's-your-name,
    Who are you ? — What 's the use of
    asking ?
You once were George, or Bill, or Ben ;
    There 's you, yourself — there 's you,
    that other —
I know you now — I knew you then —
    You used to be your younger brother !

You both are all our own to-day —
    But ah ! I hear a warning whisper;
Yon roseate hour that flits away
    Repeats the Roman's sad *paulisper*.
Come back ! come back ! we 've need of
    you
    To pay you for your word of warning;
We 'll bathe your wings in brighter dew
    Than ever wet the lids of morning !

Behold this cup; its mystic wine
    No alien's lip has ever tasted ;
The blood of friendship's clinging
    vine,
    Still flowing, flowing, yet unwasted ;
Old Time forgot his running sand
    And laid his hour-glass down to fill it,
And Death himself with gentle hand
    Has touched the chalice, not to spill
    it.

Each bubble rounding at the brim
    Is rainbowed with its magic story;

The shining days with age grown dim
  Are dressed again in robes of glory;
In all its freshness spring returns
    With song of birds and blossoms
      tender;
Once more the torch of passion burns,
    And youth is here in all its splen-
      dor!

Hope swings her anchor like a toy,
  Love laughs and shows the silver arrow
We knew so well as man and boy, —
    The shaft that stings through bone
      and marrow;
Again our kindling pulses beat,
  With tangled curls our fingers dally,
And bygone beauties smile as sweet
  As fresh-blown lilies of the valley.

O blessèd hour! we may forget
  Its wreaths, its rhymes, its songs, its
    laughter,
But not the loving eyes we met,
  Whose light shall gild the dim here-
    after.
How every heart to each grows warm!
  Is one in sunshine's ray? We share
  it.
Is one in sorrow's blinding storm?
  A look, a word, shall help him bear it.

"The boys" we were, "the boys" we 'll
  be
  As long as three, as two, are creep-
    ing;
Then here 's to him — ah! which is
  he? —
  Who lives till all the rest are sleep-
    ing;
A life with tranquil comfort blest,
  The young man's health, the rich
    man's plenty,
All earth can give that earth has best,
  And heaven at fourscore years and
    twenty.

1877.

HOW NOT TO SETTLE IT.

I LIKE, at times, to hear the steeples'
  chimes
  With sober thoughts impressively
    that mingle;
But sometimes, too, I rather like —
  don't you? —
  To hear the music of the sleigh bells'
    jingle.

I like full well the deep resounding
  swell
  Of mighty symphonies with chords
    inwoven;
But sometimes, too, a song of Burns —
  don't you?
  After a solemn storm-blast of Beetho-
    ven.

Good to the heels the well-worn slipper
  feels
  When the tired player shuffles off the
    buskin;
A page of Hood may do a fellow good
  After a scolding from Carlyle or Rus-
    kin.

Some works I find, — say Watts upon
  the Mind, —
  No matter though at first they seemed
    amusing,
Not quite the same, but just a little tame
  After some five or six times' reperus-
    ing.

So, too, at times when melancholy
  rhymes
  Or solemn speeches sober down a din-
    ner,
I 've seen it, 's true, quite often, —
  have n't you? —
  The best-fed guests perceptibly grow
    thinner.

Better some jest (in proper terms ex-
pressed)
  Or story (strictly moral) even if musty,
Or song we sung when these old throats
were young, —
  Something to keep our souls from
getting rusty.

The poorest scrap from memory's ragged
lap
  Comes like an heirloom from a dear
dead mother —
Hush ! there 's a tear that has no business here,
  A half-formed sigh that ere its birth
we smother.

We cry, we laugh ; ah, life is half and
half,
  Now bright and joyous as a song of
Herrick's,
Then chill and bare as funeral-minded
Blair ;
  As fickle as a female in hysterics.

If I could make you cry I would n't try ;
  If you have hidden smiles I 'd like to
find them,
And that although, as well I ought to
know,
  The lips of laughter have a skull behind them.

Yet when I think we may be on the
brink
  Of having Freedom's banner to dis-
pose of,
All crimson-hued, because the Nation
would
  Insist on cutting its own precious
nose off,

I feel indeed as if we rather need
  A sermon such as preachers tie a text
on.

If Freedom dies because a ballot lies,
  She earns her grave ; 't is time to call
the sexton !

But if a fight can make the matter right,
  Here are we, classmates, thirty men
of mettle ;
We 're strong and tough, we 've lived
nigh long enough —
  What if the Nation gave it us to
settle ?

The tale would read like that illustrious
deed
  When Curtius took the leap the gap
that filled in,
Thus ; "Fivescore years, good friends,
as it appears,
  At last this people split on Hayes and
Tilden.

"One half cried, 'See ! the choice is
S. J. T. !'
  And one half swore as stoutly it was
t' other ;
Both drew the knife to save the Na-
tion's life
  By wholesale vivisection of each other.

"Then rose in mass that monumental
Class, —
  'Hold ! hold !' they cried, 'give us,
give us the daggers !'
'Content ! content !' exclaimed with
one consent
  The gaunt ex-rebels and the carpet-
baggers.

"Fifteen each side, the combatants
divide,
  So nicely balanced are their predilec-
tions ;
And first of all a tear-drop each lets fall,
  A tribute to their obsolete affections.

"Man facing man, the sanguine strife
        began,
    Jack, Jim and Joe against Tom, Dick
        and Harry,
Each several pair its own account to
        square,
    Till both were down or one stood soli-
        tary.

"And the great fight raged furious all
        the night
    Till every integer was made a fraction ;
Reader, wouldst know what history has
        to show
    As net result of the above transaction ?

"Whole coat-tails, four ; stray frag-
        ments, several score ;
    A heap of spectacles ; a deaf man's
        trumpet ;
Six lawyers' briefs ; seven pocket-hand-
        kerchiefs ;
    Twelve canes wherewith the owners
        used to stump it ;

"Odd rubber-shoes ; old gloves of dif-
        ferent hues ;
    Tax-bills, — unpaid, — and several
        empty purses ;
And, saved from harm by some protect-
        ing charm,
    A printed page with Smith's immortal
        verses ;

"Trifles that claim no very special
        name, —
    Some useful, others chiefly ornament-
        al ;
Pins, buttons, rings, and other trivial
        things,
    With various wrecks, capillary and
        dental.

"Also, one flag, — 't was nothing but a
        rag,

And what device it bore it little mat-
        ters ;
    Red, white, and blue, but rent all
        through and through,
' Union forever ' torn to shreds and
        tatters.

"They fought so well not one was left
        to tell
    Which got the largest share of cuts
        and slashes ;
When heroes meet, both sides are bound
        to beat ;
    They telescoped like cars in railroad
        smashes.

"So the great split that baffled human
        wit
    And might have cost the lives of
        twenty millions,
As all may see that know the rule of
        three,
    Was settled just as well by these
        civilians.

"As well. Just so. Not worse, not
        better. No,
    Next morning found the Nation still
        divided ;
Since all were slain, the inference is
        plain
    They left the point they fought for
        undecided."

        ————

If not quite true, as I have told it you, —
    This tale of mutual extermination,
To minds perplexed with threats of
        what comes next,
    Perhaps may furnish food for contem-
        plation.

To cut men's throats to help them count
        their votes
    Is asinine — nay, worse — ascidian
        folly ;

Blindness like that would scare the mole and bat,
And make the liveliest monkey melancholy.

I say once more, as I have said before,
If voting for our Tildens and our Hayeses
Means only fight, then, Liberty, good night!

Pack up your ballot-box and go to blazes!

Unfurl your blood-red flags, you murderous hags,
You *pétroleuses* of Paris, fierce and foamy;
We'll sell our stock in Plymouth's blasted rock,
Pull up our stakes and migrate to Dahomey!

SONGS OF MANY SEASONS.

1862 - 1874.

OPENING THE WINDOW.

THUS I lift the sash, so long
Shut against the flight of song ;
All too late for vain excuse, —
Lo, my captive rhymes are loose !

Rhymes that, flitting through my brain,
Beat against my window-pane,
Some with gayly colored wings,
Some, alas ! with venomed stings.

Shall they bask in sunny rays?
Shall they feed on sugared praise?
Shall they stick with tangled feet
On the critic's poisoned sheet?

Are the outside winds too rough?
Is the world not wide enough?
G o, my wingéd verse, and try, —
G o, like Uncle Toby's fly !

PROGRAMME.

READER — gentle — if so be
Such still live, and live for me,
Will it please you to be told
What my tenscore pages hold?

Here are verses that in spite
Of myself I needs must write,
Like the wine that oozes first
When the unsqueezed grapes have burst.

Here are angry lines, " too hard ! "
Says the soldier, battle-scarred.
Could I smile his scars away
I would blot the bitter lay,

Written with a knitted brow,
Read with placid wonder now.
Throbbed such passion in my heart?
— Did his wounds once really smart?

Here are varied strains that sing
All the changes life can bring,
Songs when joyous friends have met,
Songs the mourner's tears have wet.

See the banquet's dead bouquet,
Fair and fragrant in its day ;
Do they read the selfsame lines, —
He that fasts and he that dines?

Year by year, like milestones placed,
Mark the record Friendship traced.
Prisoned in the walls of time
Life has notched itself in rhyme :

As its seasons slid along,
Every year a notch of song,
From the June of long ago,
When the rose was full in blow,

Till the scarlet sage has come
And the cold chrysanthemum.
Read, but not to praise or blame ;
Are not all our hearts the same?

For the rest, they take their chance, —
Some may pay a passing glance;
Others, — well, they served a turn, —
Wherefore written, would you learn?

Not for glory, not for pelf,
Not, be sure, to please myself,
Not for any meaner ends, —
Always "by request of friends."

Here's the cousin of a king, —
Would I do the civil thing?
Here's the first-born of a queen;
Here's a slant-eyed Mandarin.

Would I polish off Japan?
Would I greet this famous man,
Prince or Prelate, Sheik or Shah? —
— Figaro çi and Figaro là!

Would I just this once comply? —
So they teased and teased till I

(Be the truth at once confessed)
Wavered — yielded — did my best.

Turn my pages, — never mind
If you like not all you find;
Think not all the grains are gold
Sacramento's sand-banks hold.

Every kernel has its shell,
Every chime its harshest bell,
Every face its weariest look,
Every shelf its emptiest book,

Every field its leanest sheaf,
Every book its dullest leaf,
Every leaf its weakest line, —
Shall it not be so with mine?

Best for worst shall make amends,
Find us, keep us, leave us friends
Till, perchance, we meet again.
Benedicite. — Amen!

October 7, 1874.

IN THE QUIET DAYS.

AN OLD-YEAR SONG.

As through the forest, disarrayed
By chill November, late I strayed,
A lonely minstrel of the wood
Was singing to the solitude:
I loved thy music, thus I said,
When o'er thy perch the leaves were
  spread ;
Sweet was thy song, but sweeter now
Thy carol on the leafless bough.
  Sing, little bird ! thy note shall cheer
  The sadness of the dying year.

When violets pranked the turf with blue
And morning filled their cups with dew,
Thy slender voice with rippling trill
The budding April bowers would fill,
Nor passed its joyous tones away
When April rounded into May ·
Thy life shall hail no second dawn, —
  Sing, little bird ! the spring is gone.

And I remember — well-a-day ! —
Thy full-blown summer roundelay,
As when behind a broidered screen
Some holy maiden sings unseen:
With answering notes the woodland
  rung,
And every tree-top found a tongue.
How deep the shade ! the groves how
  fair !
  Sing, little bird ! the woods are bare.

The summer's throbbing chant is done
And mute the choral antiphon ;
The birds have left the shivering pines

To flit among the trellised vines,
Or fan the air with scented plumes
Amid the love-sick orange-blooms,
And thou art here alone, — alone, —
  Sing, little bird ! the rest have flown.

The snow has capped yon distant hill,
At morn the running brook was still,
From driven herds the clouds that rise
Are like the smoke of sacrifice ;
Erelong the frozen sod shall mock
The ploughshare, changed to stubborn
  rock,
The brawling streams shall soon be
  dumb, —
  Sing, little bird ! the frosts have come.

Fast, fast the lengthening shadows
  creep,
The songless fowls are half asleep,
The air grows chill, the setting sun
May leave thee ere thy song is done,
The pulse that warms thy breast grow
  cold,
Thy secret die with thee, untold :
The lingering sunset still is bright, —
  Sing, little bird ! 't will soon be night.
1874.

DOROTHY Q.

A FAMILY PORTRAIT.

GRANDMOTHER's mother : her age, I
  guess,
Thirteen summers, or something less ;

Girlish bust, but womanly air ;
Smooth, square forehead with uprolled
    hair,
Lips that lover has never kissed ;
Taper fingers and slender wrist ;
Hanging sleeves of stiff brocade ;
So they painted the little maid.

On her hand a parrot green
Sits unmoving and broods serene.
Hold up the canvas full in view, —
Look ! there 's a rent the light shines
    through,
Dark with a century's fringe of dust, —
That was a Red-Coat's rapier-thrust !
Such is the tale the lady old,
Dorothy's daughter's daughter, told.

Who the painter was none may tell, —
One whose best was not over well ;
Hard and dry, it must be confessed,
Flat as a rose that has long been pressed ;
Yet in her cheek the hues are bright,
Dainty colors of red and white,
And in her slender shape are seen
Hint and promise of stately mien.

Look not on her with eyes of scorn, —
Dorothy Q. was a lady born !
Ay ! since the galloping Normans came,
England's annals have known her name ;
And still to the three-hilled rebel town
Dear is that ancient name's renown,
For many a civic wreath they won,
The youthful sire and the gray-haired
    son.

O Damsel Dorothy ! Dorothy Q. !
Strange is the gift that I owe to you ;
Such a gift as never a king
Save to daughter or son might bring, —
All my tenure of heart and hand,
All my title to house and land ;
Mother and sister and child and wife
And joy and sorrow and death and life !

What if a hundred years ago
Those close-shut lips had answered No,
When forth the tremulous question came
That cost the maiden her Norman name,
And under the folds that look so still
The bodice swelled with the bosom's
    thrill ?
Should I be I, or would it be
One tenth another, to nine tenths me ?

Soft is the breath of a maiden's YES :
Not the light gossamer stirs with less ;
But never a cable that holds so fast
Through all the battles of wave and
    blast,
And never an echo of speech or song
That lives in the babbling air so long !
There were tones in the voice that whis-
    pered then
You may hear to-day in a hundred men.

O lady and lover, how faint and far
Your images hover, — and here we are,
Solid and stirring in flesh and bone, —
Edward's and Dorothy's — all their
    own, —
A goodly record for Time to show
Of a syllable spoken so long ago ! —
Shall I bless you, Dorothy, or forgive
For the tender whisper that bade me
    live ?

It shall be a blessing, my little maid !
I will heal the stab of the Red-Coat's
    blade,
And freshen the gold of the tarnished
    frame,
And gild with a rhyme your household
    name ;
So you shall smile on us brave and bright
As first you greeted the morning's light,
And live untroubled by woes and fears
Through a second youth of a hundred
    years.

1871.

THE ORGAN-BLOWER.

DEVOUTEST of my Sunday friends,
The patient Organ-blower bends;
I see his figure sink and rise,
(Forgive me, Heaven, my wandering
    eyes !)
A moment lost, the next half seen,
His head above the scanty screen,
Still measuring out his deep salaams
Through quavering hymns and panting
    psalms.

No priest that prays in gilded stole,
To save a rich man's mortgaged soul;
No sister, fresh from holy vows,
So humbly stoops, so meekly bows;
His large obeisance puts to shame
The proudest genuflecting dame,
Whose Easter bonnet low descends
With all the grace devotion lends.

O brother with the supple spine,
How much we owe those bows of thine !
Without thine arm to lend the breeze,
How vain the finger on the keys !
Though all unmatched the player's skill,
Those thousand throats were dumb and
    still :
Another's art may shape the tone,
The breath that fills it is thine own.

Six days the silent Memnon waits
Behind his temple's folded gates;
But when the seventh day's sunshine
    falls
Through rainbowed windows on the
    walls,
He breathes, he sings, he shouts, he fills
The quivering air with rapturous thrills;
The roof resounds, the pillars shake,
And all the slumbering echoes wake !

The Preacher from the Bible-text
With weary words my soul has vexed
(Some stranger, fumbling far astray
To find the lesson for the day) ;

He tells us truths too plainly true,
And reads the service all askew, —
Why, why the — mischief — can't he
    look
Beforehand in the service-book ?

But thou, with decent mien and face,
Art always ready in thy place ;
Thy strenuous blast, whate'er the tune,
As steady as the strong monsoon ;
Thy only dread a leathery creak,
Or small residual extra squeak,
To send along the shadowy aisles
A sunlit wave of dimpled smiles.

Not all the preaching, O my friend,
Comes from the church's pulpit end !
Not all that bend the knee and bow
Yield service half so true as thou !
One simple task performed aright,
With slender skill, but all thy might,
Where honest labor does its best,
And leaves the player all the rest.

This many-diapasoned maze,
Through which the breath of being
    strays,
Whose music makes our earth divine,
Has work for mortal hands like mine.
My duty lies before me. Lo,
The lever there ! Take hold and blow !
And He whose hand is on the keys
Will play the tune as He shall please.

1872.

AT THE PANTOMIME.

THE house was crammed from roof to
    floor,
Heads piled on heads at every door ;
Half dead with August's seething heat
I crowded on and found my seat,
My patience slightly out of joint,
My temper short of boiling-point,
Not quite at *Hate mankind as such*,
Nor yet at *Love them overmuch*.

Amidst the throng the pageant drew
Were gathered Hebrews not a few,
Black-bearded, swarthy, — at their side
Dark, jewelled women, orient-eyed :
If scarce a Christian hopes for grace
Who crowds one in his narrow place
What will the savage victim do
Whose ribs are kneaded by a Jew ?

Next on my left a breathing form
Wedged up against me, close and warm ;
The beak that crowned the bistred face
Betrayed the mould of Abraham's race, —
That coal-black hair, that smoke-brown
          hue, —
Ah, cursèd, unbelieving Jew !
I started, shuddering, to the right,
And squeezed — a second Israelite !

Then woke the evil brood of rage
That slumber, tongueless, in their cage ;
I stabbed in turn with silent oaths
The hook-nosed kite of carrion clothes,
The snaky usurer, him that crawls
And cheats beneath the golden balls,
Moses and Levi, all the horde,
Spawn of the race that slew its Lord.

Up came their murderous deeds of old,
The grisly story Chaucer told,
And many an ugly tale beside
Of children caught and crucified ;
I heard the ducat-sweating thieves
Beneath the Ghetto's slouching eaves,
And, thrust beyond the tented green,
The lepers cry, "Unclean ! Unclean !"

The show went on, but, ill at ease,
My sullen eye it could not please,
In vain my conscience whispered,
          "Shame !
Who but their Maker is to blame ?"
I thought of Judas and his bribe,
And steeled my soul against their tribe :
My neighbors stirred ; I looked again
Full on the younger of the twain.

A fresh young cheek whose olive hue
The mantling blood shows faintly
          through ;
Locks dark as midnight, that divide
And shade the neck on either side ;
Soft, gentle, loving eyes that gleam
Clear as a starlit mountain stream ; —
So looked that other child of Shem,
The Maiden's Boy of Bethlehem !

— And thou couldst scorn the peerless
          blood
That flows unmingled from the Flood, —
Thy scutcheon spotted with the stains
Of Norman thieves and pirate Danes !
The New World's foundling, in thy pride
Scowl on the Hebrew at thy side,
And lo ! the very semblance there
The Lord of Glory deigned to wear !

I see that radiant image rise,
The flowing hair, the pitying eyes,
The faintly crimsoned cheek that shows
The blush of Sharon's opening rose, —
Thy hands would clasp his hallowed feet
Whose brethren soil thy Christian seat,
Thy lips would press his garment's hem
That curl in wrathful scorn for them !

A sudden mist, a watery screen,
Dropped like a veil before the scene ;
The shadow floated from my soul,
And to my lips a whisper stole, —
"Thy prophets caught the Spirit's flame,
From thee the Son of Mary came,
With thee the Father deigned to dwell, —
Peace be upon thee, Israel !"

18 —. Rewritten 1874.

AFTER THE FIRE.

WHILE far along the eastern sky
I saw the flags of Havoc fly,
As if his forces would assault
The sovereign of the starry vault

And hurl Him back the burning rain
That seared the cities of the plain,
I read as on a crimson page
The words of Israel's sceptred sage : —

For riches make them wings, and they
Do as an eagle fly away.

O vision of that sleepless night,
What hue shall paint the mocking light
That burned and stained the orient skies
Where peaceful morning loves to rise,
As if the sun had lost his way
And dawned to make a second day, —
Above how red with fiery glow,
How dark to those it woke below !

On roof and wall, on dome and spire,
Flashed the false jewels of the fire ;
Girt with her belt of glittering panes,
And crowned with starry-gleaming vanes,
Our northern queen in glory shone
With new-born splendors not her own,
And stood, transfigured in our eyes,
A victim decked for sacrifice !

The cloud still hovers overhead,
And still the midnight sky is red ;
As the lost wanderer strays alone
To seek the place he called his own,
His devious footprints sadly tell
How changed the pathways known so
    well ;
The scene, how new ! The tale, how old
Ere yet the ashes have grown cold !

Again I read the words that came
Writ in the rubric of the flame :
Howe'er we trust to mortal things,
Each hath its pair of folded wings ;
Though long their terrors rest unspread
Their fatal plumes are never shed ;
At last, at last, they stretch in flight,
And blot the day and blast the night !

Hope, only Hope, of all that clings
Around us, never spreads her wings ;
Love, though he break his earthly chain,
Still whispers he will come again ;
But Faith that soars to seek the sky
Shall teach our half-fledged souls to fly,
And find, beyond the smoke and flame,
The cloudless azure whence they came !
1872.

A BALLAD OF THE BOSTON TEA-PARTY.

No ! never such a draught was poured
    Since Hebe served with nectar
The bright Olympians and their Lord,
    Her over-kind protector, —
Since Father Noah squeezed the grape
    And took to such behaving
As would have shamed our grandsire ape
    Before the days of shaving, —
No ! ne'er was mingled such a draught
    In palace, hall, or arbor,
As freemen brewed and tyrants quaffed
    That night in Boston Harbor !
It kept King George so long awake
    His brain at last got addled,
It made the nerves of Britain shake,
    With sevenscore millions saddled ;
Before that bitter cup was drained,
    Amid the roar of cannon,
The Western war-cloud's crimson stained
    The Thames, the Clyde, the Shannon ;
Full many a six-foot grenadier
    The flattened grass had measured,
And many a mother many a year
    Her tearful memories treasured ;
Fast spread the tempest's darkening pall,
    The mighty realms were troubled,
The storm broke loose, but first of all
    The Boston teapot bubbled !

An evening party, — only that,
    No formal invitation,
No gold-laced coat, no stiff cravat,
    No feast in contemplation,

No silk-robed dames, no fiddling band,
  No flowers, no songs, no dancing, —
A tribe of Red men, axe in hand, —
  Behold the guests advancing !
How fast the stragglers join the throng,
  From stall and workshop gathered !
The lively barber skips along
  And leaves a chin half-lathered ;
The smith has flung his hammer down, —
  The horseshoe still is glowing ;
The truant tapster at the Crown
  Has left a beer-cask flowing ;
The cooper's boys have dropped the adze,
  And trot behind their master ;
Up run the tarry ship-yard lads, —
  The crowd is hurrying faster,
Out from the Millpond's purlieus gush
  The streams of white-faced millers,
And down their slippery alleys rush
  The lusty young Fort-Hillers ;
The ropewalk lends its 'prentice crew, —
  The tories seize the omen :
" Ay, boys, you 'll soon have work to do
  For England's rebel foemen,
'King Hancock,' Adams, and their gang,
  That fire the mob with treason, —
When these we shoot and those we
    hang
  The town will come to reason."

On — on to where the tea-ships ride !
  And now their ranks are forming, —
A rush, and up the Dartmouth's side
  The Mohawk band is swarming !
See the fierce natives ! What a glimpse
  Of paint and fur and feather,
As all at once the full-grown imps
  Light on the deck together !
A scarf the pigtail's secret keeps,
  A blanket hides the breeches, —
And out the curséd cargo leaps,
  And overboard it pitches !

O woman, at the evening board
  So gracious, sweet, and purring,

So happy while the tea is poured,
  So blest while spoons are stirring,
What martyr can compare with thee,
  The mother, wife, or daughter,
That night, instead of best Bohea,
  Condemned to milk and water !

Ah, little dreams the quiet dame
  Who plies with rock and spindle
The patient flax, how great a flame
  Yon little spark shall kindle !
The lurid morning shall reveal
  A fire no king can smother
Where British flint and Boston steel
  Have clashed against each other !
Old charters shrivel in its track,
  His Worship's bench has crumbled,
It climbs and clasps the union-jack,
  Its blazoned pomp is humbled,
The flags go down on land and sea
  Like corn before the reapers ;
So burned the fire that brewed the tea
  That Boston served her keepers !

The waves that wrought a century's
    wreck
  Have rolled o'er whig and tory ;
The Mohawks on the Dartmouth's deck
  Still live in song and story ;
The waters in the rebel bay
  Have kept the tea-leaf savor ;
Our old North-Enders in their spray
  Still taste a Hyson flavor ;
And Freedom's teacup still o'erflows
  With ever fresh libations,
To cheat of slumber all her foes
  And cheer the wakening nations !

1874.

NEARING THE SNOW-LINE.

SLOW toiling upward from the misty
    vale,
  I leave the bright enamelled zones
    below ;

" Nearing the snow-line."   Page 248

No more for me their beauteous bloom
shall glow,
Their lingering sweetness load the morning gale ;
Few are the slender flowerets, scentless,
pale,
That on their ice-clad stems all trembling blow
Along the margin of unmelting
snow ;
Yet with unsaddened voice thy verge I
hail,

White realm of peace above the flowering line ;
Welcome thy frozen domes, thy rocky
spires !
O'er thee undimmed the moon-girt
planets shine,
On thy majestic altars fade the fires
That filled the air with smoke of vain
desires,
And all the unclouded blue of heaven
is thine !

1870.

IN WAR TIME.

TO CANAAN.

A PURITAN WAR-SONG.

WHERE are you going, soldiers,
  With banner, gun, and sword ?
We 're marching South to Canaan
  To battle for the Lord !
What Captain leads your armies
  Along the rebel coasts ?
The Mighty One of Israel,
  His name is Lord of Hosts !
    To Canaan, to Canaan
    The Lord has led us forth,
    To blow before the heathen walls
    The trumpets of the North !

What flag is this you carry
  Along the sea and shore ?
The same our grandsires lifted up, —
  The same our fathers bore !
In many a battle's tempest
  It shed the crimson rain, —
What God has woven in his loom
  Let no man rend in twain !
    To Canaan, to Canaan
    The Lord has led us forth,
    To plant upon the rebel towers
    The banners of the North !

What troop is this that follows,
  All armed with picks and spades ?[1]
These are the swarthy bondsmen, —
  The iron-skin brigades !

[1] The captured slaves were at this time organized as pioneers.

They 'll pile up Freedom's breastwork,
  They 'll scoop out rebels' graves;
Who then will be their owner
  And march them off for slaves?
    To Canaan, to Canaan
    The Lord has led us forth,
    To strike upon the captive's chain
    The hammers of the North !

What song is this you 're singing?
  The same that Israel sung
When Moses led the mighty choir,
  And Miriam's timbrel rung !
To Canaan !   To Canaan !
  The priests and maidens cried :
To Canaan !   To Canaan !
  The people's voice replied.
    To Canaan, to Canaan
    The Lord has led us forth,
    To thunder through its adder dens
    The anthems of the North !

When Canaan's hosts are scattered,
  And all her walls lie flat,
What follows next in order?
  — The Lord will see to that !
We 'll break the tyrant's sceptre, —
  We 'll build the people's throne, —
When half the world is Freedom's,
  Then all the world's our own !
    To Canaan, to Canaan
    The Lord has led us forth,
    To sweep the rebel threshing-floors,
    A whirlwind from the North !

August 12, 1862.

"THUS SAITH THE LORD, I OFFER THEE THREE THINGS."

In poisonous dens, where traitors hide
  Like bats that fear the day,
While all the land our charters claim
Is sweating blood and breathing flame,
Dead to their country's woe and shame,
  The recreants whisper STAY!

In peaceful homes, where patriot fires
  On Love's own altars glow,
The mother hides her trembling fear,
The wife, the sister, checks a tear,
To breathe the parting word of cheer,
  Soldier of Freedom, Go!

In halls where Luxury lies at ease,
  And Mammon keeps his state,
Where flatterers fawn and menials
  crouch,
The dreamer, startled from his couch,
Wrings a few counters from his pouch,
  And murmurs faintly WAIT!

In weary camps, on trampled plains
  That ring with fife and drum,
The battling host, whose harness gleams
Along the crimson-flowing streams,
Calls, like a warning voice in dreams,
  We want you, Brother! COME!

Choose ye whose bidding ye will do, —
  To go, to wait, to stay!
Sons of the Freedom-loving town,
Heirs of the Fathers' old renown,
The servile yoke, the civic crown,
  Await your choice TO-DAY!

The stake is laid! O gallant youth
  With yet unsilvered brow,
If Heaven should lose and Hell should
  win,
On whom shall lie the mortal sin,
That cries aloud, *It might have been?*
  God calls you — answer NOW.

1862.

NEVER OR NOW.

AN APPEAL.

LISTEN, young heroes! your country is
  calling!
  Time strikes the hour for the brave
    and the true!
Now, while the foremost are fighting and
  falling,
  Fill up the ranks that have opened for
    you!

You whom the fathers made free and de-
  fended,
  Stain not the scroll that emblazons
    their fame!
You whose fair heritage spotless de-
  scended,
  Leave not your children a birthright
    of shame!

Stay not for questions while Freedom
  stands gasping!
  Wait not till Honor lies wrapped in
    his pall!
Brief the lips' meeting be, swift the
  hands' clasping, —
  " Off for the wars!" is enough for
    them all!

Break from the arms that would fondly
  caress you!
  Hark! 't is the bugle-blast, sabres are
    drawn!
Mothers shall pray for you, fathers shall
  bless you,
  Maidens shall weep for you when you
    are gone!

Never or now! cries the blood of a nation,
  Poured on the turf where the red rose
    should bloom;
Now is the day and the hour of salva-
  tion, —

Never or now ! peals the trumpet of
　　doom !

Never or now ! roars the hoarse-throated
　　cannon
　　Through the black canopy blotting
　　　the skies ;
Never or now ! flaps the shell-blasted
　　pennon
O'er the deep ooze where the Cumberland
　　lies !

From the foul dens where our brothers
　　are dying,
　　Aliens and foes in the land of their
　　　birth, —
From the rank swamps where our mar-
　　tyrs are lying
　　Pleading in vain for a handful of
　　　earth, —

From the hot plains where they perish
　　outnumbered,
　　Furrowed and ridged by the battle-
　　　field's plough,
Comes the loud summons ; too long you
　　have slumbered,
　　Hear the last Angel-trump, — Never
　　or Now !

1862.

ONE COUNTRY.

ONE country !　Treason's writhing asp
Struck madly at her girdle's clasp,
And Hatred wrenched with might and
　　main
To rend its welded links in twain,
While Mammon hugged his golden calf
Content to take one broken half,
While thankless churls stood idly by
And heard unmoved a nation's cry !

One country !　"Nay," — the tyrant
　　crew
Shrieked from their dens, — "it shall
　　be two !

Ill bodes to us this monstrous birth,
That scowls on all the thrones of earth,
Too broad yon starry cluster shines,
Too proudly tower the New-World
　　pines,
Tear down the ' banner of the free,'
And cleave their land from sea to sea !"

One country still, though foe and
　　"friend"
Our seamless empire strove to rend ;
Safe ! safe ! though all the fiends of hell
Join the red murderers' battle-yell !
What though the lifted sabres gleam,
The cannons frown by shore and stream, —
The sabres clash, the cannons thrill,
In wild accord, One country still !

One country ! in her stress and strain
We heard the breaking of a chain !
Look where the conquering Nation
　　swings
Her iron flail, — its shivered rings !
Forged by the rebels' crimson hand,
That bolt of wrath shall scourge the
　　land
Till Peace proclaims on sea and shore
One Country now and evermore !

1865.

GOD SAVE THE FLAG!

WASHED in the blood of the brave and
　　the blooming,
　　Snatched from the altars of insolent
　　foes,
Burning with star-fires, but never con-
　　suming,
　　Flash its broad ribbons of lily and
　　rose.

Vainly the prophets of Baal would rend
　　it,
　　Vainly his worshippers pray for its
　　fall ;

Thousands have died for it, millions defend it,
　　Emblem of justice and mercy to all :

Justice that reddens the sky with her terrors,
　　Mercy that comes with her white-handed train,
Soothing all passions, redeeming all errors,
　　Sheathing the sabre and breaking the chain.

Borne on the deluge of old usurpations,
　　Drifted our Ark o'er the desolate seas,
Bearing the rainbow of hope to the nations,
　　Torn from the storm-cloud and flung to the breeze !

God bless the Flag and its loyal defenders,
　　While its broad folds o'er the battle-field wave,
Till the dim star-wreath rekindle its splendors,
　　Washed from its stains in the blood of the brave !

1865.

HYMN

AFTER THE EMANCIPATION PROCLA-
MATION.

GIVER of all that crowns our days,
With grateful hearts we sing thy praise ;
Through deep and desert led by thee,
Our promised land at last we see.

Ruler of Nations, judge our cause !
If we have kept thy holy laws,

The sons of Belial curse in vain
The day that rends the captive's chain.

Thou God of vengeance ! Israel's Lord !
Break in their grasp the shield and sword,
And make thy righteous judgments known
Till all thy foes are overthrown !

Then, Father, lay thy healing hand
In mercy on our stricken land ;
Lead all its wanderers to the fold,
And be their Shepherd as of old.

So shall one Nation's song ascend
To thee, our Ruler, Father, Friend,
While Heaven's wide arch resounds again
With Peace on earth, good-will to men !

1865.

HYMN

FOR THE FAIR AT CHICAGO.

O GOD ! in danger's darkest hour,
　　In battle's deadliest field,
Thy name has been our Nation's tower,
　　Thy truth her help and shield.

Our lips should fill the air with praise,
　　Nor pay the debt we owe,
So high above the songs we raise
　　The floods of mercy flow.

Yet thou wilt hear the prayer we speak,
　　The song of praise we sing, —
Thy children, who thine altar seek
　　Their grateful gifts to bring.

Thine altar is the sufferer's bed,
　　The home of woe and pain,
The soldier's turfy pillow, red
　　With battle's crimson rain.

No smoke of burning stains the air,
  No incense-clouds arise ;
Thy peaceful servants, Lord, prepare
  A bloodless sacrifice.

Lo ! for our wounded brothers' need,
  We bear the wine and oil ;

For us they faint, for us they bleed,
  For them our gracious toil !

O Father, bless the gifts we bring !
  Cause thou thy face to shine,
Till every nation owns her King,
  And all the earth is thine.

1865.

SONGS OF WELCOME AND FAREWELL.

AMERICA TO RUSSIA.

AUGUST 5, 1866.

READ BY HON. G. V. FOX AT A DINNER GIVEN
TO THE MISSION FROM THE UNITED STATES,
ST. PETERSBURG.

THOUGH watery deserts hold apart
   The worlds of East and West,
Still beats the selfsame human heart
   In each proud Nation's breast.

Our floating turret tempts the main
   And dares the howling blast
To clasp more close the golden chain
   That long has bound them fast.

In vain the gales of ocean sweep,
   In vain the billows roar
That chafe the wild and stormy steep
   Of storied Elsinore.

She comes! She comes! her banners
      dip
   In Neva's flashing tide,
With greetings on her cannon's lip,
   The storm-god's iron bride!

Peace garlands with the olive-bough
   Her thunder-bearing tower,
And plants before her cleaving prow
   The sea-foam's milk-white flower.

No prairies heaped their garnered store
   To fill her sunless hold,
Not rich Nevada's gleaming ore
   Its hidden caves infold,

But lightly as the sea-bird swings
   She floats the depths above,
A breath of flame to lend her wings,
   Her freight a people's love!

When darkness hid the starry skies
   In war's long winter night,
One ray still cheered our straining eyes,
   The far-off Northern light!

And now the friendly rays return
   From lights that glow afar,
Those clustered lamps of Heaven that
      burn
   Around the Western Star.

A nation's love in tears and smiles
   We bear across the sea,
O Neva of the banded isles,
   We moor our hearts in thee!

WELCOME TO THE GRAND DUKE ALEXIS.

MUSIC HALL, DECEMBER 9, 1871.

SUNG TO THE RUSSIAN NATIONAL AIR BY THE
CHILDREN OF THE PUBLIC SCHOOLS.

SHADOWED so long by the storm-cloud
      of danger,
   Thou whom the prayers of an empire
      defend,
Welcome, thrice welcome! but not as a
      stranger,
   Come to the nation that calls thee its
      friend!

Bleak are our shores with the blasts of
    December,
  Fettered and chill is the rivulet's flow ;
Throbbing and warm are the hearts that
    remember
  Who was our friend when the world
    was our foe.

Look on the lips that are smiling to greet
    thee,
  See the fresh flowers that a people has
    strewn :
Count them thy sisters and brothers
    that meet thee ;
  Guest of the Nation, her heart is
    thine own !

Fires of the North, in eternal commun-
    ion,
  Blend your broad flashes with even-
    ing's bright star !
God bless the Empire that loves the
    Great Union ;
  Strength to her people ! Long life to
    the Czar !

AT THE BANQUET TO THE GRAND DUKE ALEXIS.

DECEMBER 9, 1871.

ONE word to the guest we have gathered
    to greet !
The echoes are longing that word to
    repeat, —
It springs to the lips that are waiting to
    part,
For its syllables spell themselves first in
    the heart.

Its accents may vary, its sound may be
    strange,
But it bears a kind message that noth-
    ing can change ;

The dwellers by Neva its meaning can
    tell,
For the smile, its interpreter, shows it
    full well.

That word ! How it gladdened the Pil-
    grim of yore,
As he stood in the snow on the desolate
    shore !
When the shout of the Sagamore startled
    his ear
In the phrase of the Saxon, 't was music
    to hear !

Ah, little could Samoset offer our sire, —
The cabin, the corn-cake, the seat by
    the fire ;
He had nothing to give, — the poor lord
    of the land, —
But he gave him a WELCOME, — his
    heart in his hand !

The tribe of the Sachem has melted
    away,
But the word that he spoke is remem-
    bered to-day,
And the page that is red with the record
    of shame
The tear-drops have whitened round
    Samoset's name.

The word that he spoke to the Pilgrim
    of old
May sound like a tale that has often
    been told ;
But the welcome we speak is as fresh as
    the dew, —
As the kiss of a lover, that always is new !

Ay, Guest of the Nation ! each roof is
    thine own
Through all the broad continent's star-
    bannered zone ;
From the shore where the curtain of
    morn is uprolled,

To the billows that flow through the gateway of gold.

The snow-crested mountains are calling aloud ;
Nevada to Ural speaks out of the cloud,
And Shasta shouts forth, from his throne in the sky,
To the storm-splintered summits, the peaks of Altai !

You must leave him, they say, till the summer is green !
Both shores are his home, though the waves roll between ;
And then we 'll return him, with thanks for the same,
As fresh and as smiling and tall as he came.

But ours is the region of Arctic delight ;
We can show him Auroras and pole-stars by night ;
There 's a Muscovy sting in the ice-tempered air,
And our firesides are warm and our maidens are fair.

The flowers are full blown in the garlanded hall, —
They will bloom round his footsteps wherever they fall ;
For the splendors of youth and the sunshine they bring
Make the roses believe 't is the summons of Spring.

One word of our language he needs must know well,
But another remains that is harder to spell ;
We shall speak it so ill, if he wishes to learn
How we utter *Farewell*, he will have to return !

AT THE BANQUET TO THE CHINESE EMBASSY.

AUGUST 21, 1868.

BROTHERS, whom we may not reach
Through the veil of alien speech,
Welcome ! welcome ! eyes can tell
What the lips in vain would spell, —
Words that hearts can understand,
Brothers from the Flowery Land !

We, the evening's latest born,
Hail the children of the morn !
We, the new creation's birth,
Greet the lords of ancient earth,
From their storied walls and towers
Wandering to these tents of ours !

Land of wonders, fair Cathay,
Who long hast shunned the staring day,
Hid in mists of poet's dreams
By thy blue and yellow streams, —
Let us thy shadowed form behold, —
Teach us as thou didst of old.

Knowledge dwells with length of days ;
Wisdom walks in ancient ways ;
Thine the compass that could guide
A nation o'er the stormy tide,
Scourged by passions, doubts, and fears,
Safe through thrice a thousand years !

Looking from thy turrets gray
Thou hast seen the world's decay, —
Egypt drowning in her sands, —
Athens rent by robbers' hands, —
Rome, the wild barbarian's prey,
Like a storm-cloud swept away :

Looking from thy turrets gray
Still we see thee.   Where are they ?
And lo ! a new-born nation waits,
Sitting at the golden gates
That glitter by the sunset sea, —
Waits with outspread arms for thee !

Open wide, ye gates of gold,
To the Dragon's banner-fold !
Builders of the mighty wall,
Bid your mountain barriers fall !
So may the girdle of the sun
Bind the East and West in one,

Till Mount Shasta's breezes fan
The snowy peaks of Ta Sieue-Shan, —
Till Erie blends its waters blue
With the waves of Tung-Ting-Hu, —
Till deep Missouri lends its flow
To swell the rushing Hoang-Ho !

AT THE BANQUET TO THE JAPANESE EMBASSY.

AUGUST 2, 1872.

WE welcome you, Lords of the Land of
the Sun !
The voice of the many sounds feebly
through one ;
Ah ! would 't were a voice of more musical tone,
But the dog-star is here, and the song-
birds have flown.

And what shall I sing that can cheat you
of smiles,
Ye heralds of peace from the Orient
isles ?
If only the Jubilee — Why did you
wait ?
You are welcome, but oh ! you 're a little too late !

We have greeted our brothers of Ireland
and France,
Round the fiddle of Strauss we have
joined in the dance,
We have lagered Herr Saro, that fine-
looking man,
And glorified Godfrey, whose name it is
Dan.

What a pity ! we 've missed it and you 've
missed it too,
We had a day ready and waiting for you ;
We 'd have shown you — provided, of
course, you had come—
You 'd have heard — no, you would n't,
because it was dumb.

And then the great organ ! The chorus's
shout !
Like the mixture teetotalers call, " Cold
without " —
A mingling of elements, strong, but not
sweet ;
And the drum, just referred to, that
" could n't be beat."

The shrines of our pilgrims are not like
your own,
Where white Fusiyama lifts proudly its
cone,
(The snow-mantled mountain we see on
the fan
That cools our hot cheeks with a breeze
from Japan.)

But ours the wide temple where worship
is free
As the wind of the prairie, the wave of
the sea ;
You may build your own altar wherever
you will,
For the roof of that temple is over you
still.

One dome overarches the star-bannered
shore ;
You may enter the Pope's or the Puritan's door,
Or pass with the Buddhist his gateway
of bronze,
For a priest is but Man, be he bishop or
bonze.

And the lesson we teach with the sword
and the pen

Is to all of God's children, "We also are
   men !
If you wrong us we smart, if you prick
   us we bleed,
If you love us, no quarrel with color or
   creed !"

You'll find us a well-meaning, free-
   spoken crowd,
Good-natured enough, but a little too
   loud, —
To be sure there is always a bit of a row
When we choose our Tycoon, and espe-
   cially now.

You'll take it all calmly, — we want
   you to see
What a peaceable fight such a contest
   can be,
And of one thing be certain, however it
   ends,
You will find that our voters have chosen
   your friends.

If the horse that stands saddled is first
   in the race,
You will greet your old friend with the
   weed in his face,
And if the white hat and the White
   House agree,
You'll find H. G. really as loving as he.

But O, what a pity — once more I must
   say —
That we could not have joined in a
   "Japanese day" !
Such greeting we give you to-night as
   we can ;
Long life to our brothers and friends of
   Japan !

The Lord of the mountain looks down
   from his crest
As the banner of morning unfurls in the
   West ;

The Eagle was always the friend of the
   Sun ;
You are welcome !— The song of the
   cage-bird is done.

BRYANT'S SEVENTIETH BIRTHDAY.

NOVEMBER 3, 1864.

O EVEN-HANDED Nature ! we confess
This life that men so honor, love, and
   bless
Has filled thine olden measure. Not the
   less

We count the precious seasons that remain ;
Strike not the level of the golden grain,
But heap it high with years, that earth
   may gain

What heaven can lose, — for heaven is
   rich in song :
Do not all poets, dying, still prolong
Their broken chants amid the seraph
   throng,

Where, blind no more, Ionia's bard is
   soon,
And England's heavenly minstrel sits
   between
The Mantuan and the wan-cheeked
   Florentine ?

— This was the first sweet singer in the
   cage
Of our close-woven life. A new-born
   age
Claims in his vesper song its heritage :

Spare us, O, spare us long our heart's
   desire !
Moloch, who calls our children through
   the fire,
Leaves us the gentle master of the lyre.

We count not on the dial of the sun
The hours, the minutes, that his sands
    have run ;
Rather, as on those flowers that one by
    one

From earliest dawn their ordered bloom
    display
Till evening's planet with her guiding
    ray
Leads in the blind old mother of the
    day,

We reckon by his songs, each song a
    flower,
The long, long daylight, numbering
    hour by hour,
Each breathing sweetness like a bridal
    bower.

His morning glory shall we e'er forget?
His noontide's full-blown lily coronet?
His evening primrose has not opened
    yet ;

Nay, even if creeping Time should hide
    the skies
In midnight from his century-laden
    eyes,
Darkened like his who sang of Paradise,

Would not some hidden song-bud open
    bright
As the resplendent cactus of the night
That floods the gloom with fragrance
    and with light ?

— How can we praise the verse whose
    music flows
With solemn cadence and majestic close,
Pure as the dew that filters through the
    rose ?

How shall we thank him that in evil
    days

He faltered never, — nor for blame, nor
    praise,
Nor hire, nor party, shamed his earlier
    lays ?

But as his boyhood was of manliest hue,
So to his youth his manly years were
    true,
All dyed in royal purple through and
    through !

He for whose touch the lyre of Heaven
    is strung
Needs not the flattering toil of mortal
    tongue :
Let not the singer grieve to die unsung !

Marbles forget their message to man-
    kind :
In his own verse the poet still we find,
In his own page his memory lives en-
    shrined,

As in their amber sweets the smothered
    bees, —
As the fair cedar, fallen before the
    breeze,
Lies self-embalmed amidst the moulder-
    ing trees.

— Poets, like youngest children, never
    grow
Out of their mother's fondness. Nature
    so
Holds their soft hands, and will not let
    them go,

Till at the last they track with even feet
Her rhythmic footsteps, and their pulses
    beat
Twinned with her pulses, and their lips
    repeat

The secrets she has told them, as their
    own :

Thus is the inmost soul of Nature known,
And the rapt minstrel shares her awful
    throne!

O lover of her mountains and her woods,
Her bridal chamber's leafy solitudes,
Where Love himself with tremulous
    step intrudes,

Her snows fall harmless on thy sacred
    fire:
Far be the day that claims thy sounding
    lyre
To join the music of the angel choir!

Yet, since life's amplest measure must
    be filled,
Since throbbing hearts must be forever
    stilled,
And all must fade that evening sunsets
    gild,

Grant, Father, ere he close the mortal
    eyes
That see a Nation's reeking sacrifice,
Its smoke may vanish from these black-
    ened skies!

Then, when his summons comes, since
    come it must,
And, looking heavenward with unfalter-
    ing trust,
He wraps his drapery round him for the
    dust,

His last fond glance will show him o'er
    his head
The Northern fires beyond the zenith
    spread
In lambent glory, blue and white and
    red, —

The Southern cross without its bleeding
    load,

The milky way of peace all freshly
    strowed,
And every white-throned star fixed in
    its lost abode!

AT A DINNER TO GENERAL GRANT.

JULY 31, 1865.

WHEN treason first began the strife
    That crimsoned sea and shore,
The Nation poured her hoarded life
    On Freedom's threshing-floor;
From field and prairie, east and west,
    From coast and hill and plain,
The sheaves of ripening manhood pressed
    Thick as the bearded grain.

Rich was the harvest; souls as true
    As ever battle tried;
But fiercer still the conflict grew,
    The floor of death more wide;
Ah, who forgets that dreadful day
    Whose blot of grief and shame
Four bitter years scarce wash away
    In seas of blood and flame?

Vain, vain the Nation's lofty boasts, —
    Vain all her sacrifice!
"Give me a man to lead my hosts,
    O God in heaven!" she cries.
While Battle whirls his crushing flail,
    And plies his winnowing fan, —
Thick flies the chaff on every gale, —
    She cannot find her man!

Bravely they fought who failed to win, —
    Our leaders battle-scarred, —
Fighting the hosts of hell and sin,
    But devils die always hard!
Blame not the broken tools of God
    That helped our sorest needs;
Through paths that martyr feet have trod
    The conqueror's steps he leads.

But now the heavens grow black with
　　doubt,
　　The ravens fill the sky,
"Friends" plot within, foes storm with-
　　out,
　　Hark, — that despairing cry,
"Where is the heart, the hand, the
　　brain
　　To dare, to do, to plan?"
The bleeding Nation shrieks in vain, —
　　She has not found her man!

A little echo stirs the air, —
　　Some tale, whate'er it be,
Of rebels routed in their lair
　　Along the Tennessee.
The little echo spreads and grows,
　　And soon the trump of Fame
Had taught the Nation's friends and
　　foes
　　The "man on horseback"'s name.

So well his warlike wooing sped,
　　No fortress might resist
His billets-doux of lisping lead,
　　The bayonets in his fist, —
With kisses from his cannons' mouth
　　He made his passion known
Till Vicksburg, vestal of the South,
　　Unbound her virgin zone.

And still where'er his banners led
　　He conquered as he came,
The trembling hosts of treason fled
　　Before his breath of flame,
And Fame's still gathering echoes grew
　　Till high o'er Richmond's towers
The starry fold of Freedom flew,
　　And all the land was ours.

Welcome from fields where valor fought
　　To feasts where pleasure waits;
A Nation gives you smiles unbought
　　At all her opening gates!

Forgive us when we press your hand, —
　　Your war-worn features scan, —
God sent you to a bleeding land;
　　Our Nation found its man!

AT A DINNER TO ADMIRAL FARRAGUT.

JULY 6, 1865.

Now, smiling friends and shipmates all,
　　Since half our battle's won,
A broadside for our Admiral!
　　— Load every crystal gun!
Stand ready till I give the word, —
　　— You won't have time to tire, —
And when that glorious name is heard,
　　Then hip! hurrah! and fire!

Bow foremost sinks the rebel craft, —
　　Our eyes not sadly turn
And see the pirates huddling aft
　　To drop their raft astern;
Soon o'er the sea-worm's destined prey
　　The lifted wave shall close, —
So perish from the face of day
　　All Freedom's banded foes!

But ah! what splendors fire the sky!
　　What glories greet the morn!
The storm-tost banner streams on high
　　Its heavenly hues new-born!
Its red fresh dyed in heroes' blood,
　　Its peaceful white more pure,
To float unstained o'er field and flood
　　While earth and seas endure!

All shapes before the driving blast
　　Must glide from mortal view;
Black roll the billows of the past
　　Behind the present's blue,
Fast, fast, are lessening in the light
　　The names of high renown, —
Van Tromp's proud besom fades from
　　sight,
　　And Nelson's half hull down!

Scarce one tall frigate walks the sea
  Or skirts the safer shores
Of all that bore to victory
  Our stout old Commodores ;
Hull, Bainbridge, Porter, — where are
  they ?
  The waves their answer roll,
" Still bright in memory's sunset ray, —
  God rest each gallant soul ! "

A brighter name must dim their light
  With more than noontide ray,
The Sea-King of the " River Fight,"
  The Conqueror of the Bay, —
Now then the broadside ! cheer on cheer
  To greet him safe on shore !
Health, peace, and many a bloodless year
  To fight his battles o'er !

A TOAST TO WILKIE COLLINS.

FEBRUARY 16, 1874.

THE painter's and the poet's fame
Shed their twinned lustre round his
  name,
To gild our story-teller's art,
Where each in turn must play his part.

What scenes from Wilkie's pencil sprung,
The minstrel saw but left unsung !
What shapes the pen of Collins drew,
No painter clad in living hue !

But on our artist's shadowy screen
A stranger miracle is seen
Than priest unveils or pilgrim seeks, —
The poem breathes, the picture speaks !

And so his double name comes true,
They christened better than they knew,
And Art proclaims him twice her son, —
Painter and poet, both in one !

TO H. W. LONGFELLOW.

BEFORE HIS DEPARTURE FOR EUROPE, MAY 27, 1868.

OUR Poet, who has taught the Western
  breeze
To waft his songs before him o'er the
  seas,
Will find them wheresoe'er his wanderings reach
Borne on the spreading tide of English
  speech
Twin with the rhythmic waves that kiss
  the farthest beach.

Where shall the singing bird a stranger
  be
That finds a nest for him in every tree ?
How shall he travel who can never go
Where his own voice the echoes do
  not know,
Where his own garden flowers no longer
  learn to grow ?

Ah, gentlest soul ! how gracious, how
  benign
Breathes through our troubled life that
  voice of thine,
Filled with a sweetness born of happier spheres,
That wins and warms, that kindles,
  softens, cheers,
That calms the wildest woe and stays
  the bitterest tears !

Forgive the simple words that sound
  like praise ;
The mist before me dims my gilded
  phrase ;
Our speech at best is half alive and
  cold,
And save that tenderer moments make
  us bold
Our whitening lips would close, their
  truest truth untold.

We who behold our autumn sun below
The Scorpion's sign, against the Archer's bow,
Know well what parting means of
friend from friend ;
After the snows no freshening dews
descend,
And what the frost has marred, the sunshine will not mend.

So we all count the months, the weeks,
the days,
That keep thee from us in unwonted
ways,
Grudging to alien hearths our widowed
time ;
And one has shaped a breath in artless
rhyme
That sighs, "We track thee still through
each remotest clime."

What wishes, longings, blessings,
prayers shall be
The more than golden freight that
floats with thee !
And know, whatever welcome thou
shalt find, —
Thou who hast won the hearts of half
mankind, —
The proudest, fondest love thou leavest
still behind !

TO CHRISTIAN GOTTFRIED EHREN-
BERG.

FOR HIS "JUBILÆUM" AT BERLIN,
NOVEMBER 5, 1868.

THOU who hast taught the teachers of
mankind
How from the least of things the
mightiest grow,
What marvel jealous Nature made thee
blind,
Lest man should learn what angels
long to know ?

Thou in the flinty rock, the river's flow,
In the thick-moted sunbeam's sifted
light
Hast trained thy downward-pointed tube
to show
Worlds within worlds unveiled to mortal sight,
Even as the patient watchers of the
night, —
The cyclope gleaners of the fruitful
skies, —
Show the wide misty way where heaven
is white
All paved with suns that daze our
wondering eyes.

Far o'er the stormy deep an empire lies,
Beyond the storied islands of the
blest,
That waits to see the lingering day-star
rise ;
The forest-cinctured Eden of the
West ;
Whose queen, fair Freedom, twines her
iron crest
With leaves from every wreath that
mortals wear,
But loves the sober garland ever best
That Science lends the sage's silvered
hair ; —
Science, who makes life's heritage more
fair,
Forging for every lock its mastering
key,
Filling with life and hope the stagnant
air,
Pouring the light of Heaven o'er land
and sea !
From her unsceptred realm we come to
thee,
Bearing our slender tribute in our
hands ;
Deem it not worthless, humble though
it be,
Set by the larger gifts of older lands :

The smallest fibres weave the strongest
bands, —
  In narrowest tubes the sovereign nerves
    are spun, —
A little cord along the deep sea-sands
  Makes the live thought of severed na-
    tions one :
Thy fame has journeyed westering with
the sun,
  Prairies and lone sierras know thy
    name
And the long day of service nobly done
  That crowns thy darkened evening
    with its flame !

One with the grateful world, we own thy
claim, —
  Nay, rather claim our right to join the
    throng

Who come with varied tongues, but
hearts the same,
  To hail thy festal morn with smiles
    and song ;
Ah, happy they to whom the joys be-
long
  Of peaceful triumphs that can never die
From History's record, — not of gilded
wrong,
  But golden truths that while the
    world goes by
With all its empty pageant, blazoned
high
  Around the Master's name forever
    shine !
So shines thy name illumined in the
sky, —
  Such joys, such triumphs, such re-
    membrance thine !

MEMORIAL VERSES.

FOR THE SERVICES IN MEMORY OF ABRAHAM LINCOLN.

CITY OF BOSTON, JUNE 1, 1865.

CHORAL: Luther's "Judgment Hymn."

O THOU of soul and sense and breath,
    The ever-present Giver,
Unto thy mighty Angel, Death,
    All flesh thou dost deliver ;
What most we cherish we resign,
For life and death alike are thine,
    Who reignest Lord forever !

Our hearts lie buried in the dust
    With him so true and tender,
The patriot's stay, the people's trust,
    The shield of the offender ;
Yet every murmuring voice is still,
As, bowing to thy sovereign will,
    Our best-loved we surrender.

Dear Lord, with pitying eye behold
    This martyr generation,
Which thou, through trials manifold,
    Art showing thy salvation !
O let the blood by murder spilt
Wash out thy stricken children's guilt
    And sanctify our nation !

Be thou thy orphaned Israel's friend,
    Forsake thy people never,
In One our broken Many blend,
    That none again may sever !
Hear us, O Father, while we raise
With trembling lips our song of praise,
    And bless thy name forever !

FOR THE COMMEMORATION SERVICES.

CAMBRIDGE, JULY 21, 1865.

FOUR summers coined their golden light
    in leaves,
    Four wasteful autumns flung them to
        the gale,
Four winters wore the shroud the tempest weaves,
    The fourth wan April weeps o'er hill
        and vale ;

And still the war-clouds scowl on sea
    and land,
    With the red gleams of battle staining
        through,
When lo ! as parted by an angel's
    hand,
    They open, and the heavens again are
        blue !

Which is the dream, the present or the
    past ?
    The night of anguish or the joyous
        morn ?
The long, long years with horrors overcast,
    Or the sweet promise of the day newborn ?

Tell us, O father, as thine arms infold
    Thy belted first-born in their fast embrace,
Murmuring the prayer the patriarch
    breathed of old, —
    " Now let me die, for I have seen thy
        face ! " *Gen. 46 : 30*
*Jacob or Israel said to
        Joseph.*

Tell us, O mother, — nay, thou canst
   not speak,
   But thy fond eyes shall answer,
      brimmed with joy, —
Press thy mute lips against the sun-
   browned cheek,
   Is this a phantom, — thy returning
      boy ?

Tell us, O maiden — Ah, what canst
   thou tell
   That Nature's record is not first to
      teach, —
The open volume all can read so well,
   With its twin rose-hued pages full of
      speech ?

And ye who mourn your dead, — how
   sternly true
   The crushing hour that wrenched their
      lives away,
Shadowed with sorrow's midnight veil
   for you,
   For them the dawning of immortal
      day !

Dream-like these years of conflict, not a
   dream !
   Death, ruin, ashes tell the awful tale,
Read by the flaming war-track's lurid
   gleam :
   No dream, but truth that turns the
      nations pale !

For on the pillar raised by martyr
   hands
   Burns the rekindled beacon of the
      right,
Sowing its seeds of fire o'er all the
   lands, —
   Thrones look a century older in its
      light !

Rome had her triumphs ; round the conqueror's car

The ensigns waved, the brazen clar-
   ions blew,
And o'er the reeking spoils of bandit
   war
   With outspread wings the cruel eagles
      flew ;

Arms, treasures, captives, kings in clank-
   ing chains
   Urged on by trampling cohorts bronzed
      and scarred,
And wild-eyed wonders snared on Lyb-
   ian plains,
   Lion and ostrich and camelopard.

Vain all that prætors clutched, that
   consuls brought
   When Rome's returning legions
      crowned their lord ;
Less than the least brave deed these
   hands have wrought,
   We clasp, unclinching from the bloody
      sword.

Theirs was the mighty work that seers
   foretold ;
   They know not half their glorious toil
      has won,
For this is Heaven's same battle, —
   joined of old
   When Athens fought for us at Mara-
      thon !

— Behold a vision none hath under-
   stood !
   The breaking of the Apocalyptic seal ;
Twice rings the summons. — Hail and
   fire and blood !
   Then the third angel blows his trum-
      pet-peal.

Loud wail the dwellers on the myrtled
   coasts,
   The green savannas swell the mad-
      dened cry,

And with a yell from all the demon hosts
   Falls the great star called Wormwood
      from the sky !

Bitter it mingles with the poisoned flow
   Of the warm rivers winding to the
      shore,
Thousands must drink the waves of
      death and woe,
   But the star Wormwood stains the
      heavens no more !

Peace smiles at last; the Nation calls
      her sons
   To sheathe the sword ; her battle-flag
      she furls,
Speaks in glad thunders from unshotted
      guns,
   No terror shrouded in the smoke-
      wreath's curls.

O ye that fought for Freedom, living,
      dead,
   One sacred host of God's anointed
      Queen,
For every holy drop your veins have shed
   We breathe a welcome to our bowers
      of green !

Welcome, ye living ! from the foeman's
      gripe
   Your country's banner it was yours
      to wrest, —
Ah, many a forehead shows the banner-
      stripe,
   And stars, once crimson, hallow many
      a breast.

And ye, pale heroes, who from glory's
      bed
   Mark when your old battalions form
      in line,
Move in their marching ranks with
      noiseless tread,
   And shape unheard the evening coun-
      tersign,

Come with your comrades, the returning
      brave ;
   Shoulder to shoulder they await you
      here ;
These lent the life their martyr-brothers
      gave, —
   Living and dead alike forever dear !

EDWARD EVERETT.

"OUR FIRST CITIZEN." [1]

WINTER's cold drift lies glistening o'er
      his breast ;
   For him no spring shall bid the leaf
      unfold :
What Love could speak, by sudden grief
      oppressed,
   What swiftly summoned Memory tell,
      is told.

Even as the bells, in one consenting
      chime,
   Filled with their sweet vibrations all
      the air,
So joined all voices, in that mournful
      time,
   His genius, wisdom, virtues, to de-
      clare.

What place is left for words of measured
      praise,
   Till calm-eyed History, with her iron
      pen,
Grooves in the unchanging rock the
      final phrase
   That shapes his image in the souls of
      men ?

Yet while the echoes still repeat his
      name,
   While countless tongues his full-orbed
      life rehearse,

[1] Read at the meeting of the Massachusetts
Historical Society, January 30, 1865.

Love, by his beating pulses taught, will claim
  The breath of song, the tuneful throb of verse, —

Verse that, in ever-changing ebb and flow,
  Moves, like the laboring heart, with rush and rest,
Or swings in solemn cadence, sad and slow,
  Like the tired heaving of a grief-worn breast.

— This was a mind so rounded, so complete;
  No partial gift of Nature in excess;
That, like a single stream where many meet,
  Each separate talent counted something less.

A little hillock, if it lonely stand,
  Holds o'er the fields an undisputed reign;
While the broad summit of the table-land
  Seems with its belt of clouds a level plain.

Servant of all his powers, that faithful slave,
  Unsleeping Memory, strengthening with his toils,
To every ruder task his shoulder gave,
  And loaded every day with golden spoils.

Order, the law of Heaven, was throned supreme
  O'er action, instinct, impulse, feeling, thought;
True as the dial's shadow to the beam,
  Each hour was equal to the charge it brought,

Too large his compass for the nicer skill
  That weighs the world of science grain by grain;
All realms of knowledge owned the mastering will
  That claimed the franchise of its whole domain.

Earth, air, sea, sky, the elemental fire,
  Art, history, song, — what meanings lie in each
Found in his cunning hand a stringless lyre,
  And poured their mingling music through his speech.

Thence flowed those anthems of our festal days,
  Whose ravishing division held apart
The lips of listening throngs in sweet amaze,
  Moved in all breasts the selfsame human heart.

Subdued his accents, as of one who tries
  To press some care, some haunting sadness down;
His smile half shadow; and to stranger eyes
  The kingly forehead wore an iron crown.

He was not armed to wrestle with the storm,
  To fight for homely truth with vulgar power;
Grace looked from every feature, shaped his form, —
  The rose of Academe, — the perfect flower!

Such was the stately scholar whom we knew
  In those ill days of soul-enslaving calm,

Before the blast of Northern vengeance
   blew
  Her snow-wreathed pine against the
    Southern palm.

Ah, God forgive us! did we hold too
   cheap
  The heart we might have known, but
    would not see,
And look to find the nation's friend
   asleep
  Through the dread hour of her Geth-
    semane?

That wrong is past; we gave him up to
   Death
  With all a hero's honors round his
    name;
As martyrs coin their blood, he coined
   his breath,
  And dimmed the scholar's in the
    patriot's fame.

So shall we blazon on the shaft we
   raise, —
  Telling our grief, our pride, to un-
    born years,—
"He who had lived the mark of all
   men's praise
  Died with the tribute of a Nation's
    tears."

SHAKESPEARE.

TERCENTENNIAL CELEBRATION.

APRIL 23, 1864.

"WHO claims our Shakespeare from
   that realm unknown,
  Beyond the storm-vexed islands of
    the deep,
Where Genoa's roving mariner was
   blown?
  Her twofold Saint's-day let our Eng-
    land keep;

Shall warring aliens share her holy
   task?"
  The Old World echoes ask.

O land of Shakespeare! ours with all
   thy past,
  Till these last years that make the
    sea so wide,
Think not the jar of battle's trumpet-
   blast
  Has dulled our aching sense to joyous
    pride
In every noble word thy sons bequeathed
  The air our fathers breathed!

War-wasted, haggard, panting from the
   strife,
  We turn to other days and far-off
    lands,
Live o'er in dreams the Poet's faded life,
  Come with fresh lilies in our fevered
    hands
To wreathe his bust, and scatter purple
   flowers, —
  Not his the need, but ours!

We call those poets who are first to
   mark
  Through earth's dull mist the coming
    of the dawn, —
Who see in twilight's gloom the first
   pale spark,
  While others only note that day is
    gone;
For him the Lord of light the curtain
   rent
  That veils the firmament.

The greatest for its greatness is half
   known,
  Stretching beyond our narrow quad-
    rant-lines, —
As in that world of Nature all outgrown
  Where Calaveras lifts his awful pines,

THE SHAKESPEARE BUST AT STRATFORD. Page 270

And cast from Mariposa's mountain-
wall
Nevada's cataracts fall.

Yet heaven's remotest orb is partly ours,
Throbbing its radiance like a beating
heart;
In the wide compass of angelic powers
The instinct of the blindworm has its
part;
So in God's kingliest creature we behold
The flower our buds infold.

With no vain praise we mock the stone-
carved name
Stamped once on dust that moved
with pulse and breath,
As thinking to enlarge that amplest
fame
Whose undimmed glories gild the
night of death:
We praise not star or sun; in these we
see
Thee, Father, only thee!

Thy gifts are beauty, wisdom, power,
and love:
We read, we reverence on this human
soul, —
Earth's clearest mirror of the light
above, —
Plain as the record on thy prophet's
scroll,
When o'er his page the effluent splendors poured,
Thine own, "Thus saith the Lord!"

This player was a prophet from on high,
Thine own elected. Statesman, poet,
sage,
For him thy sovereign pleasure passed
them by;
Sidney's fair youth, and Raleigh's
ripened age,

Spenser's chaste soul, and his imperial
mind
Who taught and shamed mankind.

Therefore we bid our hearts' Te Deum
rise,
Nor fear to make thy worship less divine,
And hear the shouted choral shake the
skies,
Counting all glory, power, and wisdom thine;
For thy great gift thy greater name
adore,
And praise thee evermore!

In this dread hour of Nature's utmost
need,
Thanks for these unstained drops of
freshening dew!
O, while our martyrs fall, our heroes
bleed,
Keep us to every sweet remembrance
true,
Till from this blood-red sunset springs
new-born
Our Nation's second morn!

IN MEMORY OF JOHN AND ROBERT WARE.

READ AT THE ANNUAL MEETING OF
THE MASSACHUSETTS MEDICAL SO-
CIETY, MAY 25, 1864.

No mystic charm, no mortal art,
Can bid our loved companions stay;
The bands that clasp them to our heart
Snap in death's frost and fall apart;
Like shadows fading with the day,
They pass away.

The young are stricken in their pride,
The old, long tottering, faint and fall;
Master and scholar, side by side,

Through the dark portals silent glide,
　　That open in life's mouldering wall
　　　And close on all.

Our friend's, our teacher's task was done,
　　When Mercy called him from on high;
A little cloud had dimmed the sun,
The saddening hours had just begun,
　　And darker days were drawing nigh:
　　　'T was time to die.

A whiter soul, a fairer mind,
　A life with purer course and aim,
A gentler eye, a voice more kind,
We may not look on earth to find.
　　The love that lingers o'er his name
　　　Is more than fame.

These blood-red summers ripen fast;
　The sons are older than the sires;
Ere yet the tree to earth is cast,
The sapling falls before the blast;
　　Life's ashes keep their covered fires, —
　　　Its flame expires.

Struck by the noiseless, viewless foe,
　　Whose deadlier breath than shot or
　　　shell
Has laid the best and bravest low,
His boy, all bright in morning's glow,
　　That high-souled youth he loved so
　　　well,
　　　　Untimely fell.

Yet still he wore his placid smile,
　　And, trustful in the cheering creed
That strives all sorrow to beguile,
Walked calmly on his way awhile:
　　Ah, breast that leans on breaking reed
　　　Must ever bleed!

So they both left us, sire and son,
　　With opening leaf, with laden bough:
The youth whose race was just begun,
The wearied man whose course was run,
　　Its record written on his brow,
　　　Are brothers now.

Brothers! — The music of the sound
　Breathes softly through my closing
　　strain;
The floor we tread is holy ground,
Those gentle spirits hovering round,
　　While our fair circle joins again
　　　　Its broken chain.

1864.

HUMBOLDT'S BIRTHDAY.

CENTENNIAL CELEBRATION, SEPTEM-
BER 14, 1869.

BONAPARTE, AUGUST 15, 1769. — HUM-
BOLDT, SEPTEMBER 14, 1769.

ERE yet the warning chimes of midnight
　　sound,
　　Set back the flaming index of the year,
Track the swift-shifting seasons in their
　　round
　　　Through fivescore circles of the swing-
　　　　ing sphere.

Lo, in yon islet of the midland sea
　　That cleaves the storm-cloud with its
　　　snowy crest,
The embryo-heir of Empires yet to be,
　　A month-old babe upon his mother's
　　　breast.

Those little hands that soon shall grow
　　so strong
　　In their rude grasp great thrones shall
　　　rock and fall,
Press her soft bosom, while a nursery
　　song
　　Holds the world's master in its slender
　　　thrall.

Look! a new crescent bends its silver
　　bow;
　　A new-lit star has fired the eastern
　　　sky;

Hark ! by the river where the lindens
    blow
  A waiting household hears an infant's
    cry.

This, too, a conqueror ! His the vast
    domain,
  Wider than widest sceptre-shadowed
    lands ;
Earth, and the weltering kingdom of the
    main
  Laid their broad charters in his royal
    hands.

His was no taper lit in cloistered cage,
  Its glimmer borrowed from the grove
    or porch ;
He read the record of the planet's page
  By Etna's glare and Cotopaxi's torch.

He heard the voices of the pathless
    woods ;
  On the salt steppes he saw the star-
    light shine ;
He scaled the mountain's windy soli-
    tudes,
  And trod the galleries of the breath-
    less mine.

For him no fingering of the love-strung
    lyre,
  No problem vague, by torturing school-
    men vexed ;
He fed no broken altar's dying fire,
  Nor skulked and scowled behind a
    Rabbi's text.

For God's new truth he claimed the
    kingly robe
  That priestly shoulders counted all
    their own,
Unrolled the gospel of the storied globe
  And led young Science to her empty
    throne.

While the round planet on its axle
    spins
  One fruitful year shall boast its double
    birth,
And show the cradles of its mighty
    twins,
  Master and Servant of the sons of
    earth.

Which wears the garland that shall never
    fade,
  Sweet with fair memories that can
    never die ?
Ask not the marbles where their bones
    are laid,
  But bow thine ear to hear thy brothers'
    cry : —

" Tear up the despot's laurels by the
    root,
  Like mandrakes, shrieking as they
    quit the soil !
Feed us no more upon the blood-red
    fruit
  That sucks its crimson from the heart
    of Toil !

" We claim the food that fixed our mor-
    tal fate, —
  Bend to our reach the long-forbidden
    tree !
The angel frowned at Eden's eastern
    gate, —
  Its western portal is forever free !

" Bring the white blossoms of the waning
    year,
  Heap with full hands the peaceful con-
    queror's shrine
Whose bloodless triumphs cost no suf-
    ferer's tear !
  Hero of knowledge, be our tribute
    thine ! "

POEM

AT THE DEDICATION OF THE HALLECK
MONUMENT, JULY 8, 1869.

SAY not the Poet dies !
Though in the dust he lies,
He cannot forfeit his melodious breath,
Unsphered by envious death !
Life drops the voiceless myriads from
its roll ;
Their fate he cannot share,
Who, in the enchanted air
Sweet with the lingering strains that
Echo stole,
Has left his dearer self, the music of his
soul !

We o'er his turf may raise
Our notes of feeble praise,
And carve with pious care for after
eyes
The stone with "Here he lies" ;
He for himself has built a nobler
shrine,
Whose walls of stately rhyme
Roll back the tides of time,
While o'er their gates the gleaming
tablets shine
That wear his name inwrought with
many a golden line !

Call not our Poet dead,
Though on his turf we tread !
Green is the wreath their brows so
long have worn, —
The minstrels of the morn,
Who, while the Orient burned with new-
born flame,
Caught that celestial fire
And struck a Nation's lyre !
These taught the western winds the
poet's name ;
Theirs the first opening buds, the maiden
flowers of fame !

Count not our Poet dead !
The stars shall watch his bed,
The rose of June its fragrant life renew
His blushing mound to strew,
And all the tuneful throats of summer
swell
With trills as crystal-clear
As when he wooed the ear
Of the young muse that haunts each
wooded dell,
With songs of that "rough land" he
loved so long and well !

He sleeps ; he cannot die !
As evening's long-drawn sigh,
Lifting the rose-leaves on his peaceful
mound,
Spreads all their sweets around,
So, laden with his song, the breezes
blow
From where the rustling sedge
Frets our rude ocean's edge
To the smooth sea beyond the peaks
of snow.
His soul the air enshrines and leaves but
dust below !

HYMN

FOR THE CELEBRATION AT THE LAY-
ING OF THE CORNER-STONE OF HAR-
VARD MEMORIAL HALL, CAMBRIDGE,
OCTOBER 6, 1870.

NOT with the anguish of hearts that are
breaking
Come we as mourners to weep for our
dead ;
Grief in our breasts has grown weary of
aching,
Green is the turf where our tears we
have shed.

While o'er their marbles the mosses are
creeping,

Stealing each name and its legend
away,
Give their proud story to Memory's
keeping,
Shrined in the temple we hallow to-
day.

Hushed are their battle-fields, ended
their marches,
Deaf are their ears to the drum-beat
of morn, —
Rise from the sod, ye fair columns and
arches !
Tell their bright deeds to the ages unborn !

Emblem and legend may fade from the
portal,
Keystone may crumble and pillar may
fall ;
They were the builders whose work is
immortal,
Crowned with the dome that is over
us all !

HYMN

FOR THE DEDICATION OF MEMORIAL
HALL AT CAMBRIDGE, JUNE 23, 1874.

WHERE, girt around by savage foes,
Our nurturing Mother's shelter rose,
Behold, the lofty temple stands,
Reared by her children's grateful hands !

Firm are the pillars that defy
The volleyed thunders of the sky ;
Sweet are the summer wreaths that
twine
With bud and flower our martyrs'
shrine.

The hues their tattered colors bore
Fall mingling on the sunlit floor

Till evening spreads her spangled pall,
And wraps in shade the storied hall.

Firm were their hearts in danger's
hour,
Sweet was their manhood's morning
flower,
Their hopes with rainbow hues were
bright, —
How swiftly winged the sudden night !

O Mother ! on thy marble page
Thy children read, from age to age,
The mighty word that upward leads
Through noble thought to nobler deeds.

TRUTH, heaven-born TRUTH, their fear-
less guide,
Thy saints have lived, thy heroes
died ;
Our love has reared their earthly shrine,
Their glory be forever thine !

HYMN

AT THE FUNERAL SERVICES OF CHARLES
SUMNER, APRIL 29, 1874.

SUNG BY MALE VOICES TO A NATIONAL AIR OF
HOLLAND.

ONCE more, ye sacred towers,
Your solemn dirges sound ;
Strew, loving hands, the April flowers,
Once more to deck his mound.
A nation mourns its dead,
Its sorrowing voices one,
As Israel's monarch bowed his head
And cried, " My son ! My son ! "

Why mourn for him ? — For him
The welcome angel came
Ere yet his eye with age was dim
Or bent his stately frame ;

His weapon still was bright,
His shield was lifted high
To slay the wrong, to save the right, —
What happier hour to die ?

Thou orderest all things well ;
Thy servant's work was done ;

He lived to hear Oppression's knell,
The shouts for Freedom won.
Hark ! from the opening skies
The anthem's echoing swell, —
"O   mourning Land, lift up thine
eyes !
God reigneth.   All is well !"

RHYMES OF AN HOUR.

ADDRESS

FOR THE OPENING OF THE FIFTH AVE-
NUE THEATRE, NEW YORK, DECEM-
BER 3, 1873.

HANG out our banners on the stately
tower !
It dawns at last — the long-expected
hour !
The steep is climbed, the star-lit summit won,
The builder's task, the artist's labor
done ;
Before the finished work the herald
stands,
And asks the verdict of your lips and
hands !

Shall rosy daybreak make us all for-
get
The golden sun that yester-evening
set ?
Fair was the fabric doomed to pass
away
Ere the last headaches born of New
Year's Day ;
With blasting breath the fierce destroyer
came
And wrapped the victim in his robes of
flame ;
The pictured sky with redder morning
blushed,
With scorching streams the naiad's foun-
tain gushed,
With kindling mountains glowed the
funeral pyre,

Forests ablaze and rivers all on fire, —
The scenes dissolved, the shrivelling curtain fell, —
Art spread her wings and sighed a long
farewell !

Mourn o'er the Player's melancholy
plight, —
Falstaff in tears, Othello deadly
white, —
Poor Romeo reckoning what his doublet
cost,
And Juliet whimpering for her dresses
lost, —
Their wardrobes burned, their salaries
all undrawn,
Their cues cut short, their occupation
gone !

"Lie there in dust," the red-winged
demon cried,
"Wreck of the lordly city's hope and
pride ! "
Silent they stand, and stare with vacant
gaze,
While o'er the embers leaps the fitful
blaze ;
When, lo ! a hand, before the startled
train,
Writes in the ashes, "It shall rise
again, —
Rise and confront its elemental foes ! "—
The word was spoken, and the walls
arose,
And ere the seasons round their brief
career

The new-born temple waits the unborn
    year.

Ours was the toil of many a weary
    day
Your smiles, your plaudits, only can
    repay;
We are the monarchs of the painted
    scenes,
You, you alone the real Kings and
    Queens!
Lords of the little kingdom where we
    meet,
We lay our gilded sceptres at your
    feet,
Place in your grasp our portal's silvered
    keys
With one brief utterance— *We have tried
    to please.*

Tell us, ye Sovereigns of the new do-
    main,
Are you content — or have we toiled in
    vain?

  With no irreverent glances look
    around
The realm you rule, for this is haunted
    ground!
Here stalks the Sorcerer, here the Fairy
    trips,
Here limps the Witch with malice-
    working lips,
The Graces here their snowy arms en-
    twine,
Here dwell the fairest sisters of the
    Nine, —
She who, with jocund voice and twink-
    ling eye,
Laughs at the brood of follies as they
    fly;
She of the dagger and the deadly
    bowl,
Whose charming horrors thrill the trem-
    bling soul;
She who, a truant from celestial spheres,

In mortal semblance now and then ap-
    pears,
Stealing the fairest earthly shape she
    can —
Sontag or Nilsson, Lind or Malibran;
With these the spangled houri of the
    dance, —
What shaft so dangerous as her melting
    glance,
As poised in air she spurns the earth
    below,
And points aloft her heavenly-minded
    toe!

  What were our life, with all its rents
    and seams,
Stripped of its purple robes, our waking
    dreams?
The poet's song, the bright romancer's
    page,
The tinselled shows that cheat us on
    the stage
Lead all our fancies captive at their will;
Three years or threescore, we are chil-
    dren still.
The little listener on his father's knee,
With wandering Sindbad ploughs the
    stormy sea,
With Gotham's sages hears the billows
    roll
(Illustrious trio of the venturous bowl,
Too early shipwrecked, for they died too
    soon
To see their offspring launch the great
    balloon);
Tracks the dark brigand to his moun-
    tain lair,
Slays the grim giant, saves the lady fair,
Fights all his country's battles o'er again
From Bunker's blazing height to
    Lundy's lane;
Floats with the mighty Captains as
    they sailed
Before whose flag the flaming red-cross
    paled,

And claims the oft-told story of the scars
Scarce yet grown white, that saved the stripes and stars !

Children of later growth, we love the PLAY,
We love its heroes, be they grave or gay,
From squeaking, peppery, devil-defying Punch
To roaring Richard with his camel-hunch ;
Adore its heroines, those immortal dames,
Time's only rivals, whom he never tames,
Whose youth, unchanging, lives while thrones decay
(Age spares the Pyramids — and Deja-zet);
The saucy-aproned, razor-tongued soubrette,
The blond-haired beauty with the eyes of jet,
The gorgeous Beings whom the viewless wires
Lift to the skies in strontian-crimsoned fires,
And all the wealth of splendor that awaits
The throng that enters those Elysian gates.

See where the hurrying crowd impatient pours,
With noise of trampling feet and flapping doors,
Streams to the numbered seat each pasteboard fits
And smooths its caudal plumage as it sits ;
Waits while the slow musicians saunter in,
Till the bald leader taps his violin ;
Till the old overture we know so well,

Zampa or Magic Flute or William Tell,
Has done its worst — then hark ! the tinkling bell !
The crash is o'er — the crinkling curtain furled,
And lo ! the glories of that brighter world !

Behold the offspring of the Thespian cart,
This full-grown temple of the magic art,
Where all the conjurors of illusion meet,
And please us all the more, the more they cheat.
These are the wizards and the witches too
Who win their honest bread by cheating you
With cheeks that drown in artificial tears
And lying skull-caps white with seventy years,
Sweet-tempered matrons changed to scolding Kates,
Maids mild as moonbeams crazed with murderous hates,
Kind, simple souls that stab and slash and slay
And stick at nothing, if it's in the play !

Would all the world told half as harmless lies !
Would all its real fools were half as wise
As he who blinks through dull Dundreary's eyes !
Would all the unhanged bandits of the age
Were like the peaceful ruffians of the stage !
Would all the cankers wasting town and state,
The mob of rascals, little thieves and great,

Dealers in watered milk and watered stocks,
Who lead us lambs to pasture on the rocks, —
Shepherds — Jack Sheppards — of their city flocks —
The rings of rogues that rob the luckless town,
Those evil angels creeping up and down
The Jacob's ladder of the treasury stairs, —
Not stage, but real Turpins and Macaires, —
Could doff, like us, their knavery with their clothes,
And find it easy as forgetting oaths !

Welcome, thrice welcome to our virgin dome,
The Muses' shrine, the Drama's new-found home !
Here shall the Statesman rest his weary brain,
The worn-out Artist find his wits again ;
Here Trade forget his ledger and his cares,
And sweet communion mingle Bulls and Bears ;
Here shall the youthful Lover, nestling near
The shrinking maiden, her he holds most dear,
Gaze on the mimic moonlight as it falls
On painted groves, on sliding canvas walls,
And sigh, "My angel ! What a life of bliss
We two could live in such a world as this !"
Here shall the tumid pedants of the schools,
The gilded boors, the labor-scorning fools,
The grass-green rustic and the smoke-dried wit,

Feel each in turn the stinging lash of wit,
And as it tingles on some tender part
Each find a balsam in his neighbor's smart ;
So every folly prove a fresh delight
As in the pictures of our play to-night.

Farewell ! The Players wait the Prompter's call ;
Friends, lovers, listeners ! Welcome one and all !

RIP VAN WINKLE, M. D.

AN AFTER-DINNER PRESCRIPTION TAKEN BY THE MASSACHUSETTS MEDICAL SOCIETY, AT THEIR MEETING HELD MAY 25, 1870.

CANTO FIRST.

OLD Rip Van Winkle had a grandson, Rip,
Of the paternal block a genuine chip;
A lazy, sleepy, curious kind of chap;
He, like his grandsire, took a mighty nap,
Whereof the story I propose to tell
In two brief cantos, if you listen well.

The times were hard when Rip to manhood grew ;
They always will be when there's work to do ;
He tried at farming — found it rather slow —
And then at teaching — what he did n't know ;
Then took to hanging round the tavern bars,
To frequent toddies and long-nine cigars,
Till Dame Van Winkle, out of patience, vexed
With preaching homilies, having for their text

A mop, a broomstick — aught that might
   avail
To point a moral or adorn a tale,
Exclaimed, "I have it! Now then,
   Mr. V.!
He's good for *something* — make him
   an M. D.!"

The die was cast; the youngster was
   content;
They packed his shirts and stockings,
   and he went.
How hard he studied it were vain to
   tell;
He drowsed through Wistar, nodded over
   Bell,
Slept sound with Cooper, snored aloud
   on Good;
Heard heaps of lectures — doubtless un-
   derstood —
A constant listener, for he did not fail
To carve his name on every bench and
   rail.

Months grew to years; at last he counted
   three,
And Rip Van Winkle found himself M. D.
Illustrious title! in a gilded frame
He set the sheepskin with his Latin
   name,
RIPUM VAN WINKLUM, QUEM we —
   SCIMUS — know
IDONEUM ESSE — to do so and so;
He hired an office; soon its walls dis-
   played
His new diploma and his stock in trade,
A mighty arsenal to subdue disease,
Of various names, whereof I mention
   these:
  Lancets and bougies, great and little
   squirt,
Rhubarb and Senna, Snakeroot, Thor-
   oughwort,
Ant. Tart., Vin. Colch., Pil. Cochiæ,
   and Black Drop,

Tinctures of Opium, Gentian, Henbane,
   Hop,
Pulv. Ipecacuanhæ, which for lack
Of breath to utter men call Ipecac,
Camphor and Kino, Turpentine, Tolu,
Cubebs, "Copeevy," Vitriol — white
   and blue,
Fennel and Flaxseed, Slippery Elm and
   Squill,
And roots of Sassafras, and "Sassaf'-
   rill,"
Brandy — for colics — Pinkroot, death
   on worms —
Valerian, calmer of hysteric squirms,
Musk, Assafœtida, the resinous gum
Named from its odor — well, it does
   smell some —
Jalap, that works not wisely, but too
   well,
Ten pounds of Bark and six of Calomel.

For outward griefs he had an ample
   store,
Some twenty jars and gallipots, or more;
Ceratum simplex — housewives oft com-
   pile
The same at home, and call it "wax
   and ile";
Unguentum Resinosum — change its
   name,
The "drawing salve" of many an an-
   cient dame;
Argenti Nitras, also Spanish flies,
Whose virtue makes the water-bladders
   rise —
(Some say that spread upon a toper's
   skin
They draw no water, only rum or gin) —
Leeches, sweet vermin! don't they
   charm the sick?
And Sticking-plaster — how it hates to
   stick!
Emplastrum Ferri — ditto *Picis*, Pitch;
Washes and Powders, Brimstone for the
   —— which,

Scabies or *Psora,* is thy chosen name
Since Hahnemann's goose-quill scratched
    thee into fame,
Proved thee the source of every name-
    less ill,
Whose sole specific is a moonshine pill,
Till saucy Science, with a quiet grin,
Held up the Acarus, crawling on a
    pin?
— Mountains have labored and have
    brought forth mice:
The Dutchman's theory hatched a brood
    of — twice
I 've wellnigh said them — words unfit-
    ting quite
For these fair precincts and for ears
    polite.

The surest foot may chance at last to
    slip,
And so at length it proved with Doctor
    Rip.
One full-sized bottle stood upon the shelf
Which held the medicine that he took
    himself;
Whate'er the reason, it must be confessed
He filled that bottle oftener than the
    rest;
What drug it held I don't presume to
    know —
The gilded label said "Elixir Pro."

One day the Doctor found the bottle
    full,
And, being thirsty, took a vigorous pull,
Put back the "Elixir" where 't was
    always found,
And had old Dobbin saddled and brought
    round.
— You know those old-time rhubarb-
    colored nags
That carried Doctors and their saddle-
    bags;
Sagacious beasts! they stopped at every
    place

Where blinds were shut — knew every
    patient's case —
Looked up and thought — the baby 's
    in a fit —
That won't last long — he 'll soon be
    through with it;
But shook their heads before the knock-
    ered door
Where some old lady told the story
    o'er
Whose endless stream of tribulation
    flows
For gastric griefs and peristaltic woes.

What jack-o'-lantern led him from
    his way,
And where it led him, it were hard to
    say —
Enough that wandering many a weary
    mile
Through paths the mountain sheep trod
    single file,
O'ercome by feelings such as patients
    know
Who dose too freely with "Elixir Pro.,"
He tumbl — dismounted, slightly in a
    heap,
And lay, promiscuous, lapped in balmy
    sleep.

Night followed night, and day suc-
    ceeded day,
But snoring still the slumbering Doctor
    lay.
Poor Dobbin, starving, thought upon
    his stall,
And straggled homeward, saddle-bags
    and all.
The village people hunted all around,
But Rip was missing, — never could be
    found.
"Drownded," they guessed; — for more
    than half a year
The pouts and eels *did* taste uncommon
    queer;

Some said of apple-brandy — other some
Found a strong flavor of New England
    rum.

— Why can't a fellow hear the fine
    things said
About a fellow when a fellow 's dead ?
The best of doctors — so the press de-
    clared —
A public blessing while his life was
    spared,
True to his country, bounteous to the
    poor,
In all things temperate, sober, just, and
    pure ;
The best of husbands ! echoed Mrs. Van,
And set her cap to catch another man.

— So ends this Canto — if it 's *quan-
    tum suff.*,
We 'll just stop here and say we 've had
    enough,
And leave poor Rip to sleep for thirty
    years ;
I grind the organ — if you lend your ears
To hear my second Canto, after that
We 'll send around the monkey with
    the hat.

CANTO SECOND.

So thirty years had past — but not a
    word
In all that time of Rip was ever heard ;
The world wagged on — it never does
    go back —
The widow Van was now the widow
    Mac —
France was an Empire — Andrew J. was
    dead,
And Abraham L. was reigning in his
    stead.
Four murderous years had passed in
    savage strife,
Yet still the rebel held his bloody knife.

— At last one morning — who forgets
    the day
When the black cloud of war dissolved
    away ?
The joyous tidings spread o'er land and
    sea,
Rebellion done for ! Grant has cap-
    tured Lee !
Up every flagstaff sprang the Stars and
    Stripes —
Out rushed the Extras wild with mam-
    moth types —
Down went the laborer's hod, the school-
    boy's book —
"Hooraw !" he cried, — "the rebel
    army 's took !"
Ah ! what a time ! the folks all mad
    with joy :
Each fond, pale mother thinking of her
    boy ;
Old gray-haired fathers meeting — Have
    — you — heard ?
And then a choke — and not another
    word ;
Sisters all smiling — maidens, not less
    dear,
In trembling poise between a smile and
    tear ;
Poor Bridget thinking how she 'll stuff
    the plums
In that big cake for Johnny when he
    comes ;
Cripples afoot ; rheumatics on the jump,
Old girls so loving they could hug the
    pump ;
Guns going bang ! from every fort and
    ship ;
They banged so loud at last they wak-
    ened Rip.

I spare the picture, how a man ap-
    pears
Who 's been asleep a score or two of
    years ;
You all have seen it to perfection done

By Joe Van Wink — I mean Rip Jeffer-
son.
Well, so it was ; old Rip at last came
back,
Claimed his old wife — the present
widow Mac —
Had his old sign regilded, and began
To practise physic on the same old plan.

Some weeks went by — it was not
long to wait —
And "please to call" grew frequent on
the slate.
He had, in fact, an ancient, mildewed
air,
A long gray beard, a plenteous lack of
hair —
The musty look that always recommends
Your good old Doctor to his ailing
friends.
— Talk of your science ! after all is said
There's nothing like a bare and shiny
head ;
Age lends the graces that are sure to
please ;
Folks want their Doctors mouldy, like
their cheese.

So Rip began to look at people's
tongues
And thump their briskets (called it
"sound their lungs"),
Brushed up his knowledge smartly as he
could,
Read in old Cullen and in Doctor Good.
The town was healthy ; for a month or
two
He gave the sexton little work to do.

About the time when dog-day heats
begin,
The summer's usual maladies set in ;
With autumn evenings dysentery came,
And dusky typhoid lit his smouldering
flame ;

The blacksmith ailed — the carpenter
was down,
And half the children sickened in the
town.
The sexton's face grew shorter than be-
fore —
The sexton's wife a brand-new bonnet
wore —
Things looked quite serious — Death had
got a grip
On old and young, in spite of Doctor
Rip.

And now the Squire was taken with
a chill —
Wife gave "hot-drops" — at night an
Indian pill ;
Next morning, feverish — bedtime, get-
ting worse —
Out of his head — began to rave and
curse ;
The Doctor sent for — double quick he
came :
Ant. Tart. gran. duo, and repeat the
same
If no et cetera.   Third day — nothing
new ;
Percussed his thorax till 't was black
and blue —
Lung-fever threatening — something of
the sort —
Out with the lancet — let him bleed —
a quart—
Ten leeches next — then blisters to his
side ;
Ten grains of calomel ; just then he
died.

The Deacon next required the Doctor's care —
Took cold by sitting in a draught of
air —
Pains in the back, but what the matter is
Not quite so clear, — wife calls it "rheu-
matiz,"

Rubs back with flannel — gives him
  something hot —
"Ah!" says the Deacon, "that goes
  nigh the spot."
Next day a *rigor* — "Run, my little
  man,
And say the Deacon sends for Doctor
  Van."
The Doctor came — percussion as before,
Thumping and banging till his ribs were
  sore —
"Right side the flattest" — then more
  vigorous raps —
"Fever — that's certain — pleurisy,
  perhaps.
A quart of blood will ease the pain, no
  doubt,
Ten leeches next will help to suck it out,
Then clap a blister on the painful part —
But first two grains of *Antimonium Tart.*
Last, with a dose of cleansing calomel
Unload the portal system — (that sounds
  well!)"

But when the selfsame remedies were
  tried,
As all the village knew, the Squire had
  died;
The neighbors hinted — this will never
  do,
He's killed the Squire — he'll kill the
  Deacon too."

— Now when a doctor's patients are per-
  plexed,
A *consultation* comes in order next —
You know what that is? In a certain
  place
Meet certain doctors to discuss a case
And other matters, such as weather,
  crops,
Potatoes, pumpkins, lager-beer, and
  hops.
For what's the use? — there's little to
  be said,

Nine times in ten your man's as good as
  dead;
At best a talk (the secret to disclose)
Where three men guess and *sometimes*
  one man knows.

The counsel summoned came without
  delay —
Young Doctor Green and shrewd old
  Doctor Gray —
They heard the story — "Bleed!" says
  Doctor Green,
"That's downright murder! cut his
  throat, you mean!
Leeches! the reptiles! Why, for pity's
  sake,
Not try an adder or a rattlesnake?
Blisters! Why bless you, they're against
  the law —
It's rank assault and battery if they
  draw!
Tartrate of Antimony! shade of Luke,
Stomachs turn pale at thought of such
  rebuke!
The portal system! What's the man
  about?
Unload your nonsense! Calomel's played
  out!
You've been asleep — you'd better sleep
  away
Till some one calls you."

          "Stop!" says Doctor Gray —
"The story is you slept for thirty
  years;
With brother Green, I own that it appears
You must have slumbered most amazing
  sound;
But sleep once more till thirty years
  come round,
You'll find the lancet in its honored
  place,
Leeches and blisters rescued from disgrace,

286   SONGS OF MANY SEASONS.

Your drugs redeemed from fashion's passing scorn,
And counted safe to give to babes unborn."

Poor sleepy Rip, M. M. S. S., M. D.,
A puzzled, serious, saddened man was he;
Home from the Deacon's house he plod-
ded slow
And filled one bumper of " Elixir Pro."
" Good by," he faltered, " Mrs. Van,
my dear!
I 'm going to sleep, but wake me once a
year;
I don't like bleaching in the frost and
dew,
I 'll take the barn, if all the same to you.
Just once a year — remember ! no mis-
take !
Cry, 'Rip Van Winkle ! time for you to
wake !'
Watch for the week in May when lay-
locks blow,
For then the Doctors meet, and I must
go."

Just once a year the Doctor's worthy
dame
Goes to the barn and shouts her hus-
band's name,
" Come, Rip Van Winkle !" (giving him
a shake)
" Rip ! Rip Van Winkle ! time for you
to wake !
Laylocks in blossom ! 't is the month of
May —
The Doctors' meeting is this blessed day,
And come what will, you know I heard
you swear
You 'd never miss it, but be always
there !"

And so it is, as every year comes round
Old Rip Van Winkle here is always
found.

You 'll quickly know him by his mil-
dewed air,
The hayseed sprinkled through his scanty
hair,
The lichens growing on his rusty suit —
I 've seen a toadstool sprouting on his
boot —
— Who says I lie ? Does any man pre-
sume ? —
Toadstool ? No matter — call it a mush-
room.
Where is his seat ? He moves it every
year ;
But look, you 'll find him — he is always
here —
Perhaps you 'll track him by a whiff you
know —
A certain flavor of " Elixir Pro."

Now, then, I give you — as you seem
to think
We can give toasts without a drop to
drink —
Health to the mighty sleeper — long
live he !
Our brother Rip, M. M. S. S., M. D. !

CHANSON WITHOUT MUSIC.

BY THE PROFESSOR EMERITUS OF DEAD
AND LIVE LANGUAGES.

Φ B K. — CAMBRIDGE, 1867.

You bid me sing, — can I forget
The classic ode of days gone by, —
How belle Fifine and jeune Lisette
Exclaimed, " Anacreōn, gerōn ei " ?
" Regardez donc," those ladies said, —
" You 're getting bald and wrinkled
too :
When summer's roses all are shed,
Love 's nullum ite, voyez-vous !"

In vain ce brave Anacreon's cry,
" Of Love alone my banjo sings "

(Erōta mounon).   " Etiam si, —
  Eh b'en ? " replied the saucy things, —
" Go find a maid whose hair is gray,
  And strike your lyre, — we sha' n't
    complain ;
But parce nobis, s'il vous plait, —
  Voilà Adolphe !   Voilà Eugène ! "

Ah, jeune Lisette !   Ah, belle Fifine !
  Anacreon's lesson all must learn ;
'O kairos oxūs ; Spring is green,
  But Acer Hyems waits his turn !
I hear you whispering from the dust,
" Tiens, mon cher, c'est toujours so, —
The brightest blade grows dim with rust,
  The fairest meadow white with snow ! "

— You do not mean it !   *Not* encore ?
  Another string of playday rhymes ?
You 've heard me — nonne est ? — before,
  Multoties, — more than twenty times ;
Non possum, — vraiment, — pas du tout,
  I cannot !   I am loath to shirk ;
But who will listen if I do,
  My memory makes such shocking
    work ?

Ginōsko.   Scio.   Yes, I 'm told
  Some ancients like my rusty lay,
As Grandpa Noah loved the old
  Red-sandstone march of Jubal's day.
I used to carol like the birds,
  But time my wits has quite unfixed,
Et quoad verba, — for my words, —
  Ciel ! Eheu ! Whe-ew ! — how they 're
    mixed !

Mehercle !   Zeu !   Diable ! how
  My thoughts were dressed when I was
    young,
But tempus fugit ! see them now
  Half clad in rags of every tongue !
O philoi, fratres, chers amis !
  I dare not court the youthful Muse,
For fear her sharp response should be,
  " Papa Anacreon, please excuse ! "

Adieu ! I 've trod my annual track
  How long ! — let others count the
    miles, —
And peddled out my rhyming pack
  To friends who always paid in smiles.
So, laissez-moi ! some youthful wit
  No doubt has wares he wants to show ;
And I am asking, " Let me sit,"
  Dum ille clamat, " Dos pou sto ! "

FOR THE CENTENNIAL DINNER

OF THE PROPRIETORS OF BOSTON PIER,
OR THE LONG WHARF, APRIL 16, 1873.

DEAR friends, we are strangers ; we
  never before
Have suspected what love to each other
  we bore ;
But each of us all to his neighbor is dear,
Whose heart has a throb for our time-
  honored pier.

As I look on each brother proprietor's
  face,
I could open my arms in a loving embrace ;
What wonder that feelings, undreamed
  of so long,
Should burst all at once in a blossom of
  song !

While I turn my fond glance on the monarch of piers,
Whose throne has stood firm through his
  eightscore of years,
My thought travels backward and reaches
  the day
When they drove the first pile on the
  edge of the bay.

See !   The joiner, the shipwright, the
  smith from his forge,
The redcoat, who shoulders his gun for
  King George,

The shopman, the 'prentice, the boys
from the lane,
The parson, the doctor with gold-headed
cane,

Come trooping down King Street, where
now may be seen
The pulleys and ropes of a mighty ma-
chine ;
The weight rises slowly ; it drops with
a thud ;
And, lo ! the great timber sinks deep in
the mud !

They are gone, the stout craftsmen that
hammered the piles,
And the square-toed old boys in the
three-cornered tiles ;
The breeches, the buckles, have faded
from view,
And the parson's white wig and the ribbon-tied queue.

The redcoats have vanished ; the last
grenadier
Stepped into the boat from the end of
our pier ;
They found that our hills were not easy
to climb,
And the order came, " Countermarch,
double-quick time ! "

They are gone, friend and foe, — an-
chored fast at the pier,
Whence no vessel brings back its pale
passengers here ;
But our wharf, like a lily, still floats on
the flood,
Its breast in the sunshine, its roots in
the mud.

Who — who that has loved it so long
and so well —
The flower of his birthright would barter
or sell ?

No : pride of the bay, while its ripples
shall run,
You shall pass, as an heirloom, from
father to son !

Let me part with the acres my grand-
father bought,
With the bonds that my uncle's kind
legacy brought,
With my bank-shares, — old " Union,"
whose ten per cent stock
Stands stiff through the storms as the
Eddystone rock ;

With my rights (or my wrongs) in the
" Erie," — alas !
With my claims on the mournful and
" Mutual Mass." ;
With my " Phil. Wil. and Balt.," with
my " C. B. and Q." ;
But I never, no never, will sell out of
you.

We drink to thy past and thy future to-
day,
Strong right arm of Boston, stretched
out o'er the bay.
May the winds waft the wealth of all
nations to thee,
And thy dividends flow like the waves
of the sea !

A POEM SERVED TO ORDER.

PHI BETA KAPPA, JUNE 26, 1873.

THE Caliph ordered up his cook,
And, scowling with a fearful look
    That meant, — We stand no gam-
    mon, —
" To-morrow, just at two," he said,
" Hassan, our cook, will lose his head,
    Or serve us up a salmon."

" Great Sire," the trembling *chef* replied,
" Lord of the Earth and all beside, .

Sun, Moon, and Stars, and so on —"
(Look in Eothen — there you 'll find
A list of titles.   Never mind,
   I have n't time to go on :)

"Great Sire," and so forth, thus he
     spoke,
"Your Highness must intend a joke ;
   It does n't stand to reason
For one to order salmon brought,
Unless that fish is sometimes caught,
   And also is in season.

"Our luck of late is shocking bad,
In fact, the latest catch we had
   (We kept the matter shady),
But, hauling in our nets, — alack !
We found no salmon, but a sack
   That held your honored Lady !"

— "Allah is great !" the Caliph said,
"My poor Zuleika, you are dead,
   I once took interest in you."
— "Perhaps, my Lord, you 'd like to
     know
We cut the lines and let her go."
   — "Allah be praised !   Continue."

— "It is n't hard one's hook to bait,
And, squatting down, to watch and wait,
   To see the cork go under ;
At last suppose you 've got your bite,
You twitch away with all your might, —
   You 've hooked an eel, by thunder !"

The Caliph patted Hassan's head :
"Slave, thou hast spoken well," he said,
   "And won thy master's favor.
Yes ; since what happened t' other morn
The salmon of the Golden Horn
   Might have a doubtful flavor.

"That last remark about the eel
Has also justice that we feel
   Quite to our satisfaction.
To-morrow we dispense with fish,

And, for the present, if you wish,
   You 'll keep your bulbous fraction."

"Thanks ! thanks !" the grateful *chef*
     replied,
His nutrient feature showing wide
   The gleam of arches dental :
"To cut my head off would n't pay,
I find it useful every day,
   As well as ornamental."

———

Brothers, I hope you will not fail
To see the moral of my tale
   And kindly to receive it.
You know your anniversary pie
Must have its crust, though hard and
     dry,
   And some prefer to leave it.

How oft before these youths were born
I 've fished in Fancy's Golden Horn
   For what the Muse might send me !
How gayly then I cast the line,
When all the morning sky was mine,
   And Hope her flies would lend me !

And now I hear our despot's call,
And come, like Hassan, to the hall, —
   If there 's a slave, I am one, —
My bait no longer flies, but worms !
I 've caught — Lord bless me ! how he
     squirms !
   An eel, and not a salmon !

THE FOUNTAIN OF YOUTH.

READ AT THE MEETING OF THE HAR-
   VARD ALUMNI ASSOCIATION, JUNE 25,
   1873.

THE fount the Spaniard sought in vain
   Through all the land of flowers
Leaps glittering from the sandy plain
   Our classic grove embowers ;

Here youth, unchanging, blooms and
    smiles,
  Here dwells eternal spring,
And warm from Hope's elysian isles
  The winds their perfume bring.

Here every leaf is in the bud,
  Each singing throat in tune,
And bright o'er evening's silver flood
  Shines the young crescent moon.
What wonder Age forgets his staff
  And lays his glasses down,
And gray-haired grandsires look and
    laugh
  As when their locks were brown !

With ears grown dull and eyes grown
    dim
  They greet the joyous day
That calls them to the fountain's brim
  To wash their years away.
What change has clothed the ancient
    sire
  In sudden youth ? For, lo !
The Judge, the Doctor, and the Squire
  Are Jack and Bill and Joe !

And be his titles what they will,
  In spite of manhood's claim
The graybeard is a school-boy still
  And loves his school-boy name ;
It calms the ruler's stormy breast
  Whom hurrying care pursues,
And brings a sense of peace and rest,
  Like slippers after shoes.

And what are all the prizes won
  To youth's enchanted view ?
And what is all the man has done
  To what the boy may do ?
O blessed fount, whose waters flow
  Alike for sire and son,
That melts our winter's frost and snow
  And makes all ages one !

I pledge the sparkling fountain's tide,
  That flings its golden shower
With age to fill and youth to guide,
  Still fresh in morning flower !
Flow on with ever-widening stream,
  In ever-brightening morn, —
Our story's pride, our future's dream,
  The hope of times unborn !

A HYMN OF PEACE.

SUNG AT THE "JUBILEE," JUNE 15,
1869, TO THE MUSIC OF KELLER'S
"AMERICAN HYMN."

ANGEL of Peace, thou hast wandered
    too long !
  Spread thy white wings to the sun-
    shine of love !
Come while our voices are blended in
    song, —
  Fly to our ark like the storm-beaten
    dove !
Fly to our ark on the wings of the
    dove, —
  Speed o'er the far-sounding billows of
    song,
Crowned with thine olive-leaf garland
    of love, —
  Angel of Peace, thou hast waited too
    long !

Brothers we meet, on this altar of thine
  Mingling the gifts we have gathered
    for thee,
Sweet with the odors of myrtle and pine,
  Breeze of the prairie and breath of
    the sea, —
Meadow and mountain and forest and
    sea !
  Sweet is the fragrance of myrtle and
    pine,
Sweeter the incense we offer to thee,
  Brothers once more round this altar
    of thine !

Angels of Bethlehem, answer the strain !
Hark ! a new birth-song is filling the
    sky ! —
Loud as the storm-wind that tumbles
    the main
Bid the full breath of the organ
    reply, —

Let the loud tempest of voices re-
    ply, —
Roll its long surge like the earth-
    shaking main !
Swell the vast song till it mounts to the
    sky ! —
Angels of Bethlehem, echo the strain !

ADDITIONAL POEMS.

TO 1878.

AT A MEETING OF FRIENDS.

AUGUST 29, 1859.

I REMEMBER — why yes ! God bless me !
  and was it so long ago?
I fear I 'm growing forgetful, as old folks
  do, you know ;
It must have been in 'forty — I would
  say 'thirty-nine —
We talked this matter over, I and a friend
  of mine.

He said "Well now, old fellow, I 'm
  thinking that you and I,
If we act like other people, shall be older
  by and by ;
What though the bright blue ocean is
  smooth as a pond can be,
There is always a line of breakers to
  fringe the broadest sea.

"We 're taking it mighty easy, but that
  is nothing strange,
For up to the age of thirty we spend our
  years like change ;
But creeping up towards the forties, as
  fast as the old years fill,
And Time steps in for payment, we seem
  to change a bill.

" — I know it, — I said, — old fellow ;
  you speak the solemn truth ;
A man can't live to a hundred and likewise keep his youth ;

But what if the ten years coming shall
  silver-streak my hair,
You know I shall then be forty ; of
  course I shall not care.

"At forty a man grows heavy and tired
  of fun and noise ;
Leaves dress to the five-and-twenties and
  love to the silly boys ;
No foppish tricks at forty, no pinching
  of waists and toes,
But high-low shoes and flannels and good
  thick worsted hose."

But one fine August morning I found
  myself awake :
My birthday : — By Jove, I 'm forty !
  Yes, forty, and no mistake !
Why this is the very milestone, I think
  I used to hold,
That when a fellow had come to, a fellow
  would then be old !

But that is the young folks' nonsense ;
  they 're full of their foolish stuff ;
A man 's in his prime at forty, — I see
  that plain enough ;
At *fifty* a man *is* wrinkled, and *may be*
  bald or gray ;
I call men old at fifty, in spite of all
  they say.

At last comes another August with mist
  and rain and shine ;

Its mornings are slowly counted and
    creep to twenty-nine,
And when on the western summits the
    fading light appears,
It touches with rosy fingers the last of
    my fifty years.

There have been both men and women
    whose hearts were firm and bold,
But there never was one of fifty that
    loved to say "I'm old";
So any elderly person that strives to
    shirk his years,
Make him stand up at a table and try
    him by his peers.

Now here I stand at fifty, my jury
    gathered round;
Sprinkled with dust of silver, but not
    yet silver-crowned,
Ready to meet your verdict, waiting to
    hear it told;
Guilty of fifty summers; speak! Is the
    verdict *old?*

No! say that his hearing fails him; say
    that his sight grows dim;
Say that he's getting wrinkled and weak
    in back and limb,
Losing his wits and temper, but plead-
    ing, to make amends,
The youth of his fifty summers he finds
    in his twenty friends.

A FAREWELL TO AGASSIZ.

How the mountains talked together,
Looking down upon the weather,
When they heard our friend had planned
    his
Little trip among the Andes!
How they'll bare their snowy scalps
To the climber of the Alps
When the cry goes through their passes,

"Here comes the great Agassiz!"
"Yes, I'm tall," says Chimborazo,
"But I wait for him to say so, —
That's the only thing that lacks, —
    he
Must see me, Cotopaxi!"
"Ay! ay!" the fire-peak thunders,
"And he must view my wonders!
I'm but a lonely crater
Till I have him for spectator!"
The mountain hearts are yearning,
The lava-torches burning,
The rivers bend to meet him,
The forests bow to greet him,
It thrills the spinal column
Of fossil fishes solemn,
And glaciers crawl the faster
To the feet of their old master!

Heaven keep him well and hearty,
Both him and all his party!
From the sun that broils and smites,
From the centipede that bites,
From the hail-storm and the thunder,
From the vampire and the condor,
From the gust upon the river,
From the sudden earthquake shiver,
From the trip of mule or donkey,
From the midnight howling monkey,
From the stroke of knife or dagger,
From the puma and the jaguar,
From the horrid boa-constrictor
That has scared us in the pictur',
From the Indians of the Pampas
Who would dine upon their grampas,
From every beast and vermin
That to think of sets us squirming,
From every snake that tries on
The traveller his p'ison,
From every pest of Natur',
Likewise the alligator,
And from two things left behind him, —
(Be sure they'll try to find him,)
The tax-bill and assessor, —
Heaven keep the great Professor!

LOUIS AGASSIZ.   Page 294.

A SEA DIALOGUE. 295

May he find, with his apostles,
That the land is full of fossils,
That the waters swarm with fishes
Shaped according to his wishes,
That every pool is fertile
In fancy kinds of turtle,
New birds around him singing,
New insects, never stinging,
With a million novel data
About the articulata,
And facts that strip off all husks
From the history of mollusks.

And when, with loud Te Deum,
He returns to his Museum,
May he find the monstrous reptile
That so long the land has kept ill
By Grant and Sherman throttled,
And by Father Abraham bottled,
(All specked and streaked and mottled
With the scars of murderous battles,
Where he clashed the iron rattles
That gods and men he shook at,)
For all the world to look at !

God bless the great Professor !
And Madam, too, God bless her !
Bless him and all his band,
On the sea and on the land,
Bless them head and heart and hand,
Till their glorious raid is o'er,
And they touch our ransomed shore !
Then the welcome of a nation,
With its shout of exultation,
Shall awake the dumb creation,
And the shapes of buried æons
Join the living creatures' pæans,
Till the fossil echoes roar ;
While the mighty megalosaurus
Leads the palæozoic chorus, —
God bless the great Professor,
And the land his proud possessor, —
Bless them now and evermore !

1865.

A SEA DIALOGUE.

Cabin Passenger.   *Man at Wheel.*

CABIN PASSENGER.

FRIEND, you seem thoughtful. I not
    wonder much
That he who sails the ocean should be sad.
I am myself reflective. — When I think
Of all this wallowing beast, the Sea, has
    sucked
Between his sharp, thin lips, the wedgy
    waves,
What heaps of diamonds, rubies, emer-
    alds, pearls ;
What piles of shekels, talents, ducats,
    crowns,
What bales of Tyrian mantles, Indian
    shawls,
Of laces that have blanked the weavers'
    eyes,
Of silken tissues, wrought by worm and
    man,
The half-starved workman, and the well-
    fed worm ;
What marbles, bronzes, pictures, parch-
    ments, books ;
What many-lobuled, thought-engender-
    ing brains ;
Lie with the gaping sea-shells in his
    maw, —
I, too, am silent ; for all language seems
A mockery, and the speech of man is
    vain.
O mariner, we look upon the waves
And they rebuke our babbling. "Peace!"
    they say, —
"Mortal, be still !" My noisy tongue
    is hushed,
And with my trembling finger on my lips
My soul exclaims in ecstasy —

MAN AT WHEEL.
                Belay!
CABIN PASSENGER.
Ah yes ! "Delay," — it calls, "not
    haste to break

The charm of stillness with an idle
  word !"
O mariner, I love thee, for thy thought
Strides even with my own, nay, flies be-
  fore.
Thou art a brother to the wind and
  wave ;
Have they not music for thine ear as
  mine,
When the wild tempest makes thy ship
  his lyre,
Smiting a cavernous basso from the
  shrouds
And climbing up his gamut through the
  stays,
Through buntlines, bowlines, ratlines,
  till it shrills
An alto keener than the locust sings,
And all the great Æolian orchestra
Storms out its mad sonata in the gale ?
Is not the scene a wondrous and —

MAN AT WHEEL.
                              Avast !

CABIN PASSENGER.

Ah yes, a vast, a vast and wondrous
  scene !
I see thy soul is open as the day
That holds the sunshine in its azure
  bowl
To all the solemn glories of the deep.
Tell me, O mariner, dost thou never feel
The grandeur of thine office, — to control
The keel that cuts the ocean like a knife
And leaves a wake behind it like a seam
In the great shining garment of the
  world ?

MAN AT WHEEL.

Belay y'r jaw, y' swab ! y' hoss-marine !
        (*To the Captain.*)

Ay, ay, Sir ! Stiddy, Sir ! Sou'wes'
  b' sou' !

November 10, 1864.

AT THE "ATLANTIC" DINNER.

DECEMBER 15, 1874.

I SUPPOSE it 's myself that you 're making
  allusion to
And bringing the sense of dismay and
  confusion to.
Of course *some* must speak, — they are
  always selected to,
But pray what 's the reason that I am
  expected to ?
I 'm not fond of wasting my breath as
  those fellows do
That want to be blowing forever as bellows do ;
Their legs are uneasy, but why will you
  jog any
That long to stay quiet beneath the mahogany ?

Why, why call *me* up with your battery
  of flatteries ?
You say "He writes poetry," — that 's
  what the matter is !
"It costs him no trouble — a pen full
  of ink or two
And the poem is done in the time of a
  wink or two ;
As for thoughts — never mind — take the
  ones that lie uppermost,
And the rhymes used by Milton and
  Byron and Tupper most ;
The lines come so easy ! at one end he
  jingles 'em,
At the other with capital letters he shin-
  gles 'em, —
Why, the thing writes itself, and before
  he 's half done with it
He hates to stop writing he has such
  good fun with it !"

Ah, that is the way in which simple ones
  go about
And draw a fine picture of things they
  don't know about !

We all know a kitten, but come to a catamount
The beast is a stranger when grown up to that amount,
(A stranger we rather prefer should n't visit us,
A *felis* whose advent is far from felicitous.)
The boy who can boast that his trap has just got a mouse
Must n't draw it and write underneath " hippopotamus " ;
Or say unveraciously, "this is an elephant " —
Don't think, let me beg, these examples irrelevant —
What they mean is just this — that a thing to be painted well
Should always be something with which we 're acquainted well.

You call on your victim for " things he has plenty of, —
Those copies of verses no doubt at least twenty of ;
His desk is crammed full, for he always keeps writing 'em
And reading to friends as his way of delighting 'em ! " —
I tell you this writing of verses means business, —
It makes the brain whirl in a vortex of dizziness :
You think they are scrawled in the languor of laziness —
I tell you they 're squeezed by a spasm of craziness,
A fit half as bad as the staggering vertigos
That seize a poor fellow and down in the dirt he goes !

And therefore it chimes with the word's etymology
That the sons of Apollo are great on apology,
For the writing of verse is a struggle mysterious
And the gayest of rhymes is a matter that 's serious.
For myself, I 'm relied on by friends in extremities,
And I don't mind so much if a comfort to them it is ;
'T is a pleasure to please, and the straw that can tickle us
Is a source of enjoyment though slightly ridiculous.

I am up for a — something — and since I 've begun with it,
I must give you a toast now before I have done with it.
Let me pump at my wits as they pumped the Cochituate
That moistened — it may be — the very last bit you ate.
— Success to our publishers, authors and editors ;
To our debtors good luck, — pleasant dreams to our creditors ;
May the monthly grow yearly, till all we are groping for
Has reached the fulfilment we 're all of us hoping for ;
Till the bore through the tunnel — it makes me let off a sigh
To think it may possibly ruin my prophecy —
Has been punned on so often 't will never provoke again
One mild adolescent to make the old joke again ;
Till abstinent, all-go-to-meeting society
Has forgotten the sense of the word inebriety ;
Till the work that poor Hannah and Bridget and Phillis do
The humanized, civilized female gorillas do ;

Till the roughs, as we call them, grown
    loving and dutiful,
Shall worship the true and the pure and
    the beautiful,
And, preying no longer as tiger and vul-
    ture do,
All read the "Atlantic" as persons of
    culture do !

"LUCY."

FOR HER GOLDEN WEDDING, OCTOBER
18, 1875.

"Lucy." — The old familiar name
    Is now, as always, pleasant,
Its liquid melody the same
    Alike in past or present ;
Let others call you what they will,
    I know you 'll let me use it ;
To me your name is Lucy still,
    I cannot bear to lose it.

What visions of the past return
    With Lucy's image blended !
What memories from the silent urn
    Of gentle lives long ended !
What dreams of childhood's fleeting
    morn,
    What starry aspirations,
That filled the misty days unborn
    With fancy's coruscations !

Ah, Lucy, life has swiftly sped
    From April to November ;
The summer blossoms all are shed
    That you and I remember ;
But while the vanished years we share
    With mingling recollections,
How all their shadowy features wear
    The hue of old affections !

Love called you. He who stole your
    heart
    Of sunshine half bereft us ;

Our household's garland fell apart
    The morning that you left us ;
The tears of tender girlhood streamed
    Through sorrow's opening sluices ;
Less sweet our garden's roses seemed,
    Less blue its flower-de-luces.

That old regret is turned to smiles,
    That parting sigh to greeting ;
I send my heart-throb fifty miles, —
    Through every line 't is beating ;
God grant you many and happy years,
    Till when the last has crowned you
The dawn of endless day appears,
    And Heaven is shining round you !

October 11, 1875.

HYMN.

FOR THE INAUGURATION OF THE STATUE
OF GOVERNOR ANDREW, HINGHAM,
OCTOBER 7, 1875.

BEHOLD the shape our eyes have known !
It lives once more in changeless stone ;
So looked in mortal face and form
Our guide through peril's deadly storm.

But hushed the beating heart we knew,
That heart so tender, brave, and true,
Firm as the rooted mountain rock,
Pure as the quarry's whitest block !

Not his beneath the blood-red star
To win the soldier's envied scar ;
Unarmed he battled for the right,
In Duty's never-ending fight.

Unconquered will, unslumbering eye,
Faith such as bids the martyr die,
The prophet's glance, the master's hand
To mould the work his foresight planned,

These were his gifts ; what Heaven had
    lent
For justice, mercy, truth, he spent,

First to avenge the traitorous blow,
And first to lift the vanquished foe.

Lo, thus he stood; in danger's strait
The pilot of the Pilgrim State!
Too large his fame for her alone, —
A nation claims him as her own!

A MEMORIAL TRIBUTE.

READ AT THE MEETING HELD AT MUSIC
HALL, FEBRUARY 8, 1876, IN MEMORY
OF DR. SAMUEL G. HOWE.

I.

LEADER of armies, Israel's God,
    Thy soldier's fight is won!
Master, whose lowly path he trod,
    Thy servant's work is done!

No voice is heard from Sinai's steep
    Our wandering feet to guide;
From Horeb's rock no waters leap;
    No Jordan's waves divide;

No prophet cleaves our western sky
    On wheels of whirling fire;
No shepherds hear the song on high
    Of heaven's angelic choir:

Yet here as to the patriarch's tent
    God's angel comes a guest;
He comes on heaven's high errand sent,
    In earth's poor raiment drest.

We see no halo round his brow
    Till love its own recalls,
And like a leaf that quits the bough,
    The mortal vesture falls.

In autumn's chill declining day,
    Ere winter's killing frost,
The message came; so passed away
    The friend our earth has lost.

Still, Father, in Thy love we trust;
    Forgive us if we mourn
The saddening hour that laid in dust
    His robe of flesh outworn.

II.

How long the wreck-strewn journey
        seems
    To reach the far-off past
That woke his youth from peaceful
        dreams
    With Freedom's trumpet-blast!

Along her classic hillsides rung
    The Paynim's battle-cry,
And like a red-cross knight he sprung
    For her to live or die.

No trustier service claimed the wreath
    For Sparta's bravest son;
No truer soldier sleeps beneath
    The mound of Marathon;

Yet not for him the warrior's grave
    In front of angry foes;
To lift, to shield, to help, to save,
    The holier task he chose.

He touched the eyelids of the blind,
    And lo! the veil withdrawn,
As o'er the midnight of the mind,
    He led the light of dawn.

He asked not whence the fountains roll
    No traveller's foot has found,
But mapped the desert of the soul
    Untracked by sight or sound.

What prayers have reached the sapphire
        throne,
    By silent fingers spelt,
For him who first through depths un-
        known
    His doubtful pathway felt,

Who sought the slumbering sense that lay
　　Close shut with bolt and bar,
And showed awakening thought the ray
　　Of reason's morning star !

Where'er he moved, his shadowy form
　　The sightless orbs would seek,
And smiles of welcome light and warm
　　The lips that could not speak.

No labored line, no sculptor's art,
　　Such hallowed memory needs ;
His tablet is the human heart,
　　His record loving deeds.

III.

The rest that earth denied is thine, —
　　Ah, is it rest ? we ask,
Or, traced by knowledge more divine,
　　Some larger, nobler task ?

Had but those boundless fields of blue
　　One darkened sphere like this ;
But what has heaven for thee to do
　　In realms of perfect bliss ?

No cloud to lift, no mind to clear,
　　No rugged path to smooth,
No struggling soul to help and cheer,
　　No mortal grief to soothe !

Enough ; is there a world of love,
　　No more we ask to know ;
The hand will guide thy ways above
　　That shaped thy task below.

JOSEPH WARREN, M. D.

Trained in the holy art whose lifted shield
Wards off the darts a never-slumbering foe,
By hearth and wayside lurking, waits to throw,
Oppression taught his helpful arm to wield
The slayer's weapon : on the murderous field
The fiery bolt he challenged laid him low,
Seeking its noblest victim.　Even so
The charter of a nation must be sealed !
The healer's brow the hero's honors crowned,
From lowliest duty called to loftiest deed.
Living, the oak-leaf wreath his temples bound ;
Dying, the conqueror's laurel was his meed,
Last on the broken ramparts' turf to bleed
Where Freedom's victory in defeat was found.

June 11, 1875.

GRANDMOTHER'S STORY OF BUNKER-HILL BATTLE.

AS SHE SAW IT FROM THE BELFRY.

'T is like stirring living embers when, at eighty, one remembers
All the achings and the quakings of "the times that tried men's souls" ;
When I talk of *Whig* and *Tory*, when I tell the *Rebel* story,
To you the words are ashes, but to me they 're burning coals.

I had heard the muskets' rattle of the April running battle ;
Lord Percy's hunted soldiers, I can see their red coats still ;
But a deadly chill comes o'er me, as the day looms up before me,
When a thousand men lay bleeding on the slopes of Bunker's Hill.

'T was a peaceful summer's morning,
   when the first thing gave us warning
Was the booming of the cannon from the
   river and the shore :
"Child," says grandma, "what's the
   matter, what is all this noise and
   clatter ?
Have those scalping Indian devils come
   to murder us once more ?"

Poor old soul ! my sides were shaking
   in the midst of all my quaking,
To hear her talk of Indians when the
   guns began to roar :
She had seen the burning village, and
   the slaughter and the pillage,
When the Mohawks killed her father
   with their bullets through his door.

Then I said, "Now, dear old granny,
   don't you fret and worry any,
For I'll soon come back and tell you
   whether this is work or play ;
There can't be mischief in it, so I won't
   be gone a minute " —
For a minute then I started. I was
   gone the livelong day.

No time for bodice-lacing or for looking-
   glass grimacing ;
Down my hair went as I hurried, tumbling half-way to my heels ;
God forbid your ever knowing, when
   there's blood around her flowing,
How the lonely, helpless daughter of a
   quiet household feels !

In the street I heard a thumping ; and
   I knew it was the stumping
Of the Corporal, our old neighbor, on
   that wooden leg he wore,
With a knot of women round him, — it
   was lucky I had found him,
So I followed with the others, and the
   Corporal marched before.

They were making for the steeple, — the
   old soldier and his people ;
The pigeons circled round us as we
   climbed the creaking stair,
Just across the narrow river — O, so
   close it made me shiver ! —
Stood a fortress on the hill-top that but
   yesterday was bare.

Not slow our eyes to find it ; well we
   knew who stood behind it,
Though the earthwork hid them from
   us, and the stubborn walls were
   dumb :
Here were sister, wife, and mother, looking wild upon each other,
And their lips were white with terror as
   they said, THE HOUR HAS COME !

The morning slowly wasted, not a morsel had we tasted,
And our heads were almost splitting
   with the cannons' deafening thrill,
When a figure tall and stately round
   the rampart strode sedately ;
It was PRESCOTT, one since told me ; he
   commanded on the hill.

Every woman's heart grew bigger when
   we saw his manly figure,
With the banyan buckled round it,
   standing up so straight and tall ;
Like a gentleman of leisure who is
   strolling out for pleasure,
Through the storm of shells and can-
   non-shot he walked around the wall.

At eleven the streets were swarming, for
   the red-coats' ranks were forming ;
At noon in marching order they were
   moving to the piers ;
How the bayonets gleamed and glistened,
   as we looked far down, and listened
To the trampling and the drum-beat of
   the belted grenadiers !

At length the men have started, with a cheer (it seemed faint-hearted),
In their scarlet regimentals, with their knapsacks on their backs,
And the reddening, rippling water, as after a sea-fight's slaughter,
Round the barges gliding onward blushed like blood along their tracks.

So they crossed to the other border, and again they formed in order;
And the boats came back for soldiers, came for soldiers, soldiers still:
The time seemed everlasting to us women faint and fasting, —
At last they 're moving, marching, marching proudly up the hill.

We can see the bright steel glancing all along the lines advancing —
Now the front rank fires a volley — they have thrown away their shot;
For behind their earthwork lying, all the balls above them flying,
Our people need not hurry; so they wait and answer not.

Then the Corporal, our old cripple (he would swear sometimes and tipple), —
He had heard the bullets whistle (in the old French war) before, —
Calls out in words of jeering, just as if they all were hearing, —
And his wooden leg thumps fiercely on the dusty belfry floor : —

"Oh! fire away, ye villains, and earn King George's shillin's,
But ye 'll waste a ton of powder afore a 'rebel' falls;
You may bang the dirt and welcome, they 're as safe as Dan'l Malcolm
Ten foot beneath the gravestone that you 've splintered with your balls!"

In the hush of expectation, in the awe and trepidation
Of the dread approaching moment, we are wellnigh breathless all;
Though the rotten bars are failing on the rickety belfry railing,
We are crowding up against them like the waves against a wall.

Just a glimpse (the air is clearer), they are nearer, — nearer, — nearer,
When a flash — a curling smoke-wreath — then a crash — the steeple shakes —
The deadly truce is ended; the tempest's shroud is rended;
Like a morning mist it gathered, like a thunder-cloud it breaks!

O the sight our eyes discover as the blue-black smoke blows over!
The red-coats stretched in windrows as a mower rakes his hay;
Here a scarlet heap is lying, there a headlong crowd is flying
Like a billow that has broken and is shivered into spray.

Then we cried, "The troops are routed! they are beat — it can't be doubted!
God be thanked, the fight is over!" —
Ah! the grim old soldier's smile!
"Tell us, tell us why you look so?" (we could hardly speak, we shook so), —
"Are they beaten? *Are* they beaten? ARE they beaten?" — "Wait a while."

O the trembling and the terror! for too soon we saw our error:
They are baffled, not defeated; we have driven them back in vain;
And the columns that were scattered, round the colors that were tattered,
Toward the sullen silent fortress turn their belted breasts again.

All at once, as we are gazing, lo the
    roofs of Charlestown blazing!
They have fired the harmless village;
    in an hour it will be down!
The Lord in heaven confound them,
    rain his fire and brimstone round
    them, —
The robbing, murdering red-coats, that
    would burn a peaceful town!

They are marching, stern and solemn;
    we can see each massive column
As they near the naked earth-mound
    with the slanting walls so steep.
Have our soldiers got faint-hearted, and
    in noiseless haste departed?
Are they panic-struck and helpless?
    Are they palsied or asleep?

Now! the walls they 're almost under!
    scarce a rod the foes asunder!
Not a firelock flashed against them! up
    the earthwork they will swarm!
But the words have scarce been spoken,
    when the ominous calm is broken,
And a bellowing crash has emptied all
    the vengeance of the storm!

So again, with murderous slaughter,
    pelted backwards to the water,
Fly Pigot's running heroes and the
    frightened braves of Howe;
And we shout, "At last they 're done
    for, it 's their barges they have run
    for:
They are beaten, beaten, beaten; and
    the battle 's over now!"

And we looked, poor timid creatures, on
    the rough old soldier's features,
Our lips afraid to question, but he knew
    what we would ask:
"Not sure," he said; "keep quiet, —
    once more, I guess, they 'll try it —
Here 's damnation to the cut-throats!"
    —— then he handed me his flask,

Saying, "Gal, you 're looking shaky;
    have a drop of old Jamaiky;
I 'm afeard there 'll be more trouble afore
    the job is done";
So I took one scorching swallow; dread-
    ful faint I felt and hollow,
Standing there from early morning when
    the firing was begun.

All through those hours of trial I had
    watched a calm clock dial,
As the hands kept creeping, creeping, —
    they were creeping round to four,
When the old man said, "They 're form-
    ing with their bagonets fixed for
    storming:
It 's the death-grip that 's a coming, —
    they will try the works once more."

With brazen trumpets blaring, the
    flames behind them glaring,
The deadly wall before them, in close
    array they come;
Still onward, upward toiling, like a
    dragon's fold uncoiling, —
Like the rattlesnake's shrill warning
    the reverberating drum!

Over heaps all torn and gory — shall I
    tell the fearful story,
How they surged above the breastwork,
    as a sea breaks over a deck;
How, driven, yet scarce defeated, our
    worn-out men retreated,
With their powder-horns all emptied,
    like the swimmers from a wreck?

It has all been told and painted; as for
    me, they say I fainted,
And the wooden-legged old Corporal
    stumped with me down the stair:
When I woke from dreams affrighted
    the evening lamps were lighted, —
On the floor a youth was lying; his
    bleeding breast was bare.

And I heard through all the flurry,
    "Send for WARREN! hurry! hurry!
Tell him here 's a soldier bleeding, and
    he 'll come and dress his wound!"
Ah, we knew not till the morrow told
    its tale of death and sorrow,
How the starlight found him stiffened
    on the dark and bloody ground.

Who the youth was, what his name was,
    where the place from which he
    came was,
Who had brought him from the battle,
    and had left him at our door,
He could not speak to tell us; but
    't was one of our brave fellows,
As the homespun plainly showed us
    which the dying soldier wore.

For they all thought he was dying, as
    they gathered round him crying, —
And they said, "O, how they 'll miss
    him!" and, "What *will* his mother
    do?"
Then, his eyelids just unclosing like a
    child's that has been dozing,
He faintly murmured, "Mother!" ——
    and — I saw his eyes were blue.

— "Why, grandma, how you 're wink-
    ing!" — Ah, my child, it sets me
    thinking
Of a story not like this one. Well, he
    somehow lived along;
So we came to know each other, and I
    nursed him like a — mother,
Till at last he stood before me, tall, and
    rosy-cheeked, and strong.

And we sometimes walked together in
    the pleasant summer weather;
— "Please to tell us what his name
    was?" — Just your own, my little
    dear, —

There 's his picture Copley painted : we
    became so well acquainted,
That — in short, that 's why I 'm grand-
    ma, and you children all are here!

OLD CAMBRIDGE.

JULY 3, 1875.

AND can it be you 've found a place
Within this consecrated space
    That makes so fine a show
For one of Rip Van Winkle's race?
    And is it really so?
Who wants an old receipted bill?
Who fishes in the Frog-pond still?
Who digs last year's potato hill? —
    That 's what he 'd like to know!

And were it any spot on earth
Save this dear home that gave him birth
    Some scores of years ago,
He had not come to spoil your mirth
    And chill your festive glow;
But round his baby-nest he strays,
With tearful eye the scene surveys,
His heart unchanged by changing
    days, —
    That 's what he 'd have you know.

Can you whose eyes not yet are dim
Live o'er the buried past with him,
    And see the roses blow
When white-haired men were Joe and
    Jim
    Untouched by winter's snow?
Or roll the years back one by one
As Judah's monarch backed the sun,
And see the century just begun? —
    That 's what he 'd like to know!

I come, but as the swallow dips,
Just touching with her feather-tips
    The shining wave below,

To sit with pleasure-murmuring lips
    And listen to the flow
Of Elmwood's sparkling Hippocrene,
To tread once more my native green,
To sigh unheard, to smile unseen, —
    That's what I'd have you know.

But since the common lot I've shared
(We all are sitting "unprepared,"
    Like culprits in a row,
Whose heads are down, whose necks are bared
    To wait the headsman's blow)
I'd like to shift my task to you,
By asking just a thing or two
About the good old times I knew, —
    Here's what I want to know :

The yellow meetin' house — can you tell
Just where it stood before it fell
    Prey of the vandal foe, —
Our dear old temple, loved so well
    By ruthless hands laid low ?
Where, tell me, was the Deacon's pew ?
Whose hair was braided in a queue ?
(For there were pig-tails not a few,) —
    That's what I'd like to know.

The bell — can you recall its clang ?
And how the seats would slam and bang ?
    The voices high and low ?
The basso's trump before he sang ?
    The viol and its bow ?
Where was it old Judge Winthrop sat ?
Who wore the last three-cornered hat ?
Was Israel Porter lean or fat ? —
    That's what I'd like to know.

Tell where the market used to be
That stood beside the murdered tree ?
    Whose dog to church would go ?
Old Marcus Reemie, who was he ?
    Who were the brothers Snow ?
Does not your memory slightly fail
About that great September gale

Whereof one told a moving tale,
    As Cambridge boys should know.

When Cambridge was a simple town,
Say just when Deacon William Brown
    (Last door in yonder row),
For honest silver counted down,
    His groceries would bestow ? —
For those were days when money meant
Something that jingled as you went, —
No hybrid like the nickel cent,
    I'd have you all to know,

But quarter, ninepence, pistareen,
And fourpence happennies in between
    All metal fit to show,
Instead of rags in stagnant green,
    The scum of debts we owe ;
How sad to think such stuff should be
Our Wendell's cure-all recipe, —
Not Wendell H., but Wendell P., —
    The one you all must know !

I question — but you answer not —
Dear me ! and have I quite forgot
    How fivescore years ago,
Just on this very blessed spot,
    The summer leaves below,
Before his homespun ranks arrayed
In green New England's elmbough shade
The great Virginian drew the blade
    King George full soon should know!

O George the Third ! you found it true
Our George was more than *double you*,
    For nature made him so.
Not much an empire's crown can do
    If brains are scant and slow, —
Ah, not like that his laurel crown
Whose presence gilded with renown
Our brave old Academic town,
    As all her children know !

So here we meet with loud acclaim
To tell mankind that here he came,
    With hearts that throb and glow ;

Ours is a portion of his fame
  Our trumpets needs must blow !
On yonder hill the Lion fell,
But here was chipped the eagle's shell, —
That little hatchet did it well,
  As all the world shall know !

WELCOME TO THE NATIONS.

PHILADELPHIA, JULY 4, 1876.

BRIGHT on the banners of lily and rose
  Lo ! the last sun of our century sets !
Wreath the black cannon that scowled
    on our foes,
  All but her friendships the nation for-
    gets !
All but her friends and their welcome
    forgets !
These are around her ; but where are
    her foes ?
  Lo, while the sun of her century sets,
  Peace with her garlands of lily and
    rose !

Welcome ! a shout like the war trumpet's
    swell
  Wakes the wild echoes that slumber
    around !
Welcome ! it quivers from Liberty's bell ;
  Welcome ! the walls of her temple re-
    sound !
  Hark ! the gray walls of her temple
    resound !
Fade the far voices o'er hillside and dell ;
  Welcome ! still whisper the echoes
    around ;
  Welcome ! still trembles on Liberty's
    bell !

Thrones of the continents ! isles of the
    sea !
  Yours are the garlands of peace we
    entwine ;
Welcome, once more, to the land of the
    free,

Shadowed alike by the palm and the
    pine ;
  Softly they murmur, the palm and the
    pine,
" Hushed is our strife, in the land of
    the free " ;
  Over your children their branches en-
    twine,
  Thrones of the continents ! isles of
    the sea !

A FAMILIAR LETTER.

TO SEVERAL CORRESPONDENTS.

YES, write, if you want to, there 's noth-
    ing like trying ;
  Who knows what a treasure your cas-
    ket may hold ?
I 'll show you that rhyming 's as easy as
    lying
  If you 'll listen to me while the art I
    unfold.

Here 's a book full of words ; one can
    choose as he fancies,
  As a painter his tint, as a workman
    his tool ;
Just think ! all the poems and plays and
    romances
  Were drawn out of this, like the fish
    from a pool !

You can wander at will through its syl-
    labled mazes,
  And take all you want, — not a cop-
    per they cost, —
What is there to hinder your picking
    out phrases
  For an epic as clever as " Paradise
    Lost " ?

Don't mind if the index of sense is at
    zero,

Use words that run smoothly, what-
    ever they mean ;
Leander and Lilian and Lillibullero
    Are much the same thing in the
    rhyming machine.

There are words so delicious their sweet-
    ness will smother
    That boarding-school flavor of which
    we 're afraid, —
There is "lush" is a good one, and
    "swirl" is another, —
    Put both in one stanza, its fortune is
    made.

With musical murmurs and rhythmical
    closes
    You can cheat us of smiles when you 've
    nothing to tell ;
You hand us a nosegay of milliner's roses,
    And we cry with delight, " O, how
    sweet they *do* smell ! "

Perhaps you will answer all needful con-
    ditions
    For winning the laurels to which you
    aspire,
By docking the tails of the two preposi-
    tions
    I' the style o' the bards you so greatly
    admire.

As for subjects of verse, they are only
    too plenty
    For ringing the changes on metrical
    chimes ;
A maiden, a moonbeam, a lover of twenty
    Have filled that great basket with
    bushels of rhymes.

Let me show you a picture — 't is far
    from irrelevant —
    By a famous old hand in the arts of
    design ;

'T is only a photographed sketch of an
    elephant, —
    The name of the draughtsman was
    Rembrandt of Rhine.

How easy ! no troublesome colors to lay
    on,
    It can't have fatigued him, — no, not
    in the least, —
A dash here and there with a hap-hazard
    crayon,
    And there stands the wrinkled-
    skinned, baggy-limbed beast.

Just so with your verse, — 't is as easy
    as sketching, —
    You can reel off a song without knit-
    ting your brow,
As lightly as Rembrandt a drawing or
    etching ;
    It is nothing at all, if you only know
    how.

Well ; imagine you 've printed your vol-
    ume of verses :
    Your forehead is wreathed with the
    garland of fame,
Your poems the eloquent school-boy re-
    hearses,
    Her album the school-girl presents for
    your name ;

Each morning the post brings you auto-
    graph letters ;
    You 'll answer them promptly, — an
    hour is n't much
For the honor of sharing a page with
    your betters,
    With magistrates, members of Con-
    gress, and such.

Of course you 're delighted to serve the
    committees
    That come with requests from the
    country all round ;

You would grace the occasion with poems
and ditties
 When they 've got a new schoolhouse,
or poorhouse, or pound.

With a hymn for the saints and a song
for the sinners,
 You go and are welcome wherever you
please ;
You 're a privileged guest at all manner
of dinners,
 You 've a seat on the platform among
the grandees.

At length your mere presence becomes
a sensation,
 Your cup of enjoyment is filled to its
brim
With the pleasure Horatian of digit-
monstration,
 As the whisper runs round of " That 's
he ! " or " That 's him ! "

But remember, O dealer in phrases sonorous,
 So daintily chosen, so tunefully
matched,
Though you soar with the wings of the
cherubim o'er us,
 The *ovum* was human from which you
were hatched.

No will of your own with its puny com-
pulsion
 Can summon the spirit that quickens
the lyre ;
It comes, if at all, like the Sibyl's con-
vulsion
 And touches the brain with a finger
of fire.

So perhaps, after all, it 's as well to be
quiet,
 If you 've nothing you think is worth
saying in prose,

As to furnish a meal of their cannibal
diet
 To the critics, by publishing, as you
propose.

But it 's all of no use, and I 'm sorry
I 've written, —
 I shall see your thin volume some day
on my shelf ;
For the rhyming tarantula surely has
bitten,
 And music must cure you, so pipe it
yourself.

UNSATISFIED.

" ONLY a housemaid ! " She looked
from the kitchen, —
 Neat was the kitchen and tidy was
she ;
There at her window a sempstress sat
stitching ;
 " Were I a sempstress, how happy
I 'd be ! "

" Only a Queen ! " She looked over the
waters, —
 Fair was her kingdom and mighty was
she ;
There sat an Empress, with Queens for
her daughters ;
 " Were I an Empress, how happy I 'd
be ! "

Still the old frailty they all of them trip
in !
 Eve in her daughters is ever the
same ;
Give her all Eden, she sighs for a
pippin ;
 Give her an Empire, she pines for a
name !

May 8, 1876.

HOW THE OLD HORSE WON THE BET.

DEDICATED BY A CONTRIBUTOR TO THE
COLLEGIAN, 1830, TO THE EDITORS OF
THE HARVARD ADVOCATE, 1876.

'T WAS on the famous trotting-ground,
The betting men were gathered round
From far and near; the "cracks" were there
Whose deeds the sporting prints declare:
The swift g. m., Old Hiram's nag,
The fleet s. h., Dan Pfeiffer's brag,
With these a third — and who is he
That stands beside his fast b. g.?
Budd Doble, whose catarrhal name
So fills the nasal trump of fame.
There too stood many a noted steed
Of Messenger and Morgan breed;
Green horses also, not a few;
Unknown as yet what they could do;
And all the hacks that know so well
The scourgings of the Sunday swell.

Blue are the skies of opening day;
The bordering turf is green with May;
The sunshine's golden gleam is thrown
On sorrel, chestnut, bay, and roan;
The horses paw and prance and neigh,
Fillies and colts like kittens play,
And dance and toss their rippled manes
Shining and soft as silken skeins;
Wagons and gigs are ranged about,
And fashion flaunts her gay turn-out;
Here stands — each youthful Jehu's dream —
The jointed tandem, ticklish team!
And there in ampler breadth expand
The splendors of the four-in-hand;
On faultless ties and glossy tiles
The lovely bonnets beam their smiles;
(The style 's the man, so books avow;
The style 's the woman, anyhow);
From flounces frothed with creamy lace
Peeps out the pug-dog's smutty face,

Or spaniel rolls his liquid eye,
Or stares the wiry pet of Skye —
O woman, in your hours of ease
So shy with us, so free with these!

"Come on! I 'll bet you two to one
I 'll make him do it!" "Will you!
Done!"

What was it who was bound to do?
I did not hear and can't tell you, —
Pray listen till my story 's through.

Scarce noticed, back behind the rest,
By cart and wagon rudely prest,
The parson's lean and bony bay
Stood harnessed in his one-horse shay—
Lent to his sexton for the day;
(A funeral — so the sexton said;
His mother's uncle's wife was dead.)

Like Lazarus bid to Dives' feast,
So looked the poor forlorn old beast;
His coat was rough, his tail was bare,
The gray was sprinkled in his hair;
Sportsmen and jockeys knew him not
And yet they say he once could trot
Among the fleetest of the town,
Till something cracked and broke him down, —
The steed's, the statesman's, common lot!
"And are we then so soon forgot?"
Ah me! I doubt if one of you
Has ever heard the name "Old Blue,"
Whose fame through all this region rung
In those old days when I was young!

"Bring forth the horse!" Alas! he showed
Not like the one Mazeppa rode;
Scant-maned, sharp-backed, and shaky-kneed,
The wreck of what was once a steed,
Lips thin, eyes hollow, stiff in joints;

Yet not without his knowing points.
The sexton laughing in his sleeve,
As if 't were all a make-believe,
Led forth the horse, and as he laughed
Unhitched the breeching from a shaft,
Unclasped the rusty belt beneath,
Drew forth the snaffle from his teeth,
Slipped off his head-stall, set him free
From strap and rein, — a sight to see !

So worn, so lean in every limb,
It can't be they are saddling him !
It is ! his back the pig-skin strides
And flaps his lank, rheumatic sides ;
With look of mingled scorn and mirth
They buckle round the saddle-girth ;
With horsey wink and saucy toss
A youngster throws his leg across,
And so, his rider on his back,
They lead him, limping, to the track,
Far up behind the starting-point,
To limber out each stiffened joint.

As through the jeering crowd he past,
One pitying look old Hiram cast ;
" Go it, ye cripple, while ye can ! "
Cried out unsentimental Dan ;
" A Fast-Day dinner for the crows ! "
Budd Doble's scoffing shout arose.

Slowly, as when the walking-beam
First feels the gathering head of steam,
With warning cough and threatening
    wheeze
The stiff old charger crooks his knees ;
At first with cautious step sedate,
As if he dragged a coach of state ;
He 's not a colt ; he knows full well
That time is weight and sure to tell ;
No horse so sturdy but he fears
The handicap of twenty years.

As through the throng on either hand
The old horse nears the judges' stand,
Beneath his jockey's feather-weight
He warms a little to his gait,

And now and then a step is tried
That hints of something like a stride.

" Go ! " — Through his ear the sum-
    mons stung
As if a battle-trump had rung ;
The slumbering instincts long un-
    stirred
Start at the old familiar word ;
It thrills like flame through every limb—
What mean his twenty years to him ?
The savage blow his rider dealt
Fell on his hollow flanks unfelt ;
The spur that pricked his staring hide
Unheeded tore his bleeding side ;
Alike to him are spur and rein, —
He steps a five-year-old again !

Before the quarter pole was past,
Old Hiram said, " He 's going fast."
Long ere the quarter was a half,
The chuckling crowd had ceased to
    laugh ;
Tighter his frightened jockey clung
As in a mighty stride he swung,
The gravel flying in his track,
His neck stretched out, his ears laid
    back,
His tail extended all the while
Behind him like a rat-tail file !
Off went a shoe, — away it spun,
Shot like a bullet from a gun ;
The quaking jockey shapes a prayer
From scraps of oaths he used to swear ;
He drops his whip, he drops his rein,
He clutches fiercely for a mane ;
He 'll lose his hold — he sways and
    reels —
He 'll slide beneath those trampling
    heels !
The knees of many a horseman quake,
The flowers on many a bonnet shake,
And shouts arise from left and right,
"Stick on ! Stick on ! " "Hould tight'
    Hould tight ! "

" Cling round his neck and don't let
    go —
" That pace can't hold—there ! steady !
    whoa ! "
But like the sable steed that bore
The spectral lover of Lenore,
His nostrils snorting foam and fire,
No stretch his bony limbs can tire ;
And now the stand he rushes by,
And " Stop him ! — stop him ! " is the
    cry.
Stand back ! he 's only just begun —
He 's having out three heats in one !

" Don't rush in front ! he 'll smash your
    brains ;
But follow up and grab the reins ! "
Old Hiram spoke.   Dan Pfeiffer heard,
And sprang impatient at the word ;
Budd Doble started on his bay,
Old Hiram followed on his gray,
And off they spring, and round they go,
The fast ones doing " all they know."
Look ! twice they follow at his heels,
As round the circling course he wheels,
And whirls with him that clinging boy
Like Hector round the walls of Troy ;
Still on, and on, the third time round !
They 're tailing off ! they 're losing
    ground !
Budd Doble's nag begins to fail !
Dan Pfeiffer's sorrel whisks his tail !
And see ! in spite of whip and shout,
Old Hiram's mare is giving out !
Now for the finish ! at the turn,
The old horse — all the rest astern —
Comes swinging in, with easy trot ;
By Jove ! he 's distanced all the lot !

That trot no mortal could explain ;
Some said, " Old Dutchman come
    again ! "
Some took his time, — at least they
    tried,
But what it was could none decide ;

One said he could n't understand
What happened to his second hand ;
One said 2. 10 ; *that* could n't be —
More like two twenty two or three ;
Old Hiram settled it at last ;
" The time was two — too dee-vel-ish
    fast ! "

The parson's horse had won the bet ;
It cost him something of a sweat ;
Back in the one-horse shay he went ;
The parson wondered what it meant,
And murmured, with a mild surprise
And pleasant twinkle of the eyes,
" That funeral must have been a trick,
Or corpses drive at double-quick ;
I should n't wonder, I declare,
If brother Murray made the prayer ! "

And this is all I have to say
About the parson's poor old bay,
The same that drew the one-horse
    shay.

Moral for which this tale is told :
A horse *can* trot, for all he 's old.

AN APPEAL FOR "THE OLD SOUTH."

" While stands the Coliseum, Rome shall
    stand ;
When falls the Coliseum, Rome shall fall."

FULL sevenscore years our city's pride —
    The comely Southern spire —
Has cast its shadow, and defied
    The storm, the foe, the fire ;
Sad is the sight our eyes behold ;
    Woe to the three-hilled town,
When through the land the tale is
    told—
    " The brave ' Old South ' is down ! "

Let darkness blot the starless dawn
    That hears our children tell,

" Here rose the walls, now wrecked and
        gone,
  Our fathers loved so well ;
Here, while his brethren stood aloof,
  The herald's blast was blown
That shook St. Stephen's pillared roof
  And rocked King George's throne !

" The home-bound wanderer of the main
  Looked from his deck afar,
To where the gilded, glittering vane
  Shone like the evening star,
And pilgrim feet from every clime
  The floor with reverence trod,
Where holy memories made sublime
  The shrine of Freedom's God ! "

The darkened skies, alas ! have seen
  Our monarch tree laid low,
And spread in ruins o'er the green,
  But Nature struck the blow ;
No scheming thrift its downfall planned,
  It felt no edge of steel,
No soulless hireling raised his hand
  The deadly stroke to deal.

In bridal garlands, pale and mute,
  Still pleads the storied tower ;
These are the blossoms, but the fruit
  Awaits the golden shower ;
The spire still greets the morning sun, —
  Say, shall it stand or fall ?
Help, ere the spoiler has begun !
  Help, each, and God help all !

THE FIRST FAN.

READ AT A MEETING OF THE BOSTON
BRIC-À-BRAC CLUB, FEBRUARY 21, 1877.

WHEN rose the cry " Great Pan is dead ! "
  And Jove's high palace closed its por-
        tal,
The fallen gods, before they fled,
  Sold out their frippery to a mortal.

" To whom ? " you ask.   I ask of you.
  The answer hardly needs suggestion ;
Of course it was the Wandering Jew, —
  How could you put me such a ques-
        tion ?

A purple robe, a little worn,
  The Thunderer deigned himself to
        offer ;
The   bearded   wanderer   laughed   in
        scorn, —
  You know he always was a scoffer.

" Vife shillins ! 't is a monstrous price ;
  Say two and six and further talk
        shun."
" Take it," cried Jove ; " we can't be
        nice, —
  'T would fetch twice that at Leonard's
        auction."

The ice was broken ; up they came,
  All sharp for bargains, god and god-
        dess,
Each ready with the price to name
  For robe or head-dress, scarf or bodice.

First Juno, out of temper, too, —
  Her   queenly   forehead   somewhat
        cloudy ;
Then Pallas in her stockings blue,
  Imposing, but a little dowdy.

The scowling queen of heaven unrolled
  Before the Jew a threadbare turban :
" Three shillings."   " One.   'T will suit
        some old
  Terrific feminine suburban."

But as for Pallas, — how to tell
  In seemly phrase a fact so shocking ?
She pointed, — pray excuse me, — well,
  She pointed to her azure stocking.

And if the honest truth were told,
  Its heel confessed the need of darning;

"Gods !" low-bred Vulcan cried, "be-
        hold !
    There ! that's what comes of too much
        larning ! "

Pale Proserpine came groping round,
    Her pupils dreadfully dilated
With too much living underground, —
    A residence quite overrated ;

"This kerchief's what you want, I
        know, —
    Don't cheat poor Venus of her ces-
        tus, —
You'll find it handy when you go
    To — you know where ; it's pure as-
        bestus."

Then Phœbus of the silver bow,
    And Hebe, dimpled as a baby,
And Dian with the breast of snow,
    Chaser and chased — and caught, it
        may be :

One took the quiver from her back,
    One held the cap he spent the night
        in,
And one a bit of *bric-à-brac*,
    Such as the gods themselves delight in.

Then Mars, the foe of human kind,
    Strode up and showed his suit of ar-
        mor ;
So none at last was left behind
    Save Venus, the celestial charmer.

Poor Venus !   What had she to sell ?
    For all she looked so fresh and jaunty,
Her wardrobe, as I blush to tell,
    Already seemed but quite too scanty.

Her gems were sold, her sandals gone, —
    She always would be rash and
        flighty, —
Her winter garments all in pawn,
    Alas for charming Aphrodite !

The lady of a thousand loves,
    The darling of the old religion,
Had only left of all the doves
    That drew her car one fan-tailed pig-
        eon.

How oft upon her finger-tips
    He perched, afraid of Cupid's arrow,
Or kissed her on the rosebud lips,
    Like Roman Lesbia's loving sparrow !

"My bird, I want your train," she cried ;
    "Come, don't let's have a fuss about
        it ;
I'll make it beauty's pet and pride,
    And you'll be better off without it.

"So vulgar !   Have you noticed, pray,
    An earthly belle or dashing bride walk,
And how her flounces track her way,
    Like slimy serpents on the sidewalk ?

"A lover's heart it quickly cools ;
    In mine it kindles up enough rage
To wring their necks.   How can such
        fools
    Ask men to vote for woman suffrage ?"

The goddess spoke, and gently stripped
    Her bird of every caudal feather ;
A strand of gold-bright hair she clipped,
    And bound the glossy plumes together,

And lo, the Fan ! for beauty's hand,
    The lovely queen of beauty made it ;
The price she named was hard to stand,
    But Venus smiled : the Hebrew paid it.

Jove, Juno, Venus, where are you ?
    Mars, Mercury, Phœbus, Neptune,
        Saturn ?
But o'er the world the Wandering Jew
    Has borne the Fan's celestial pattern.

So everywhere we find the Fan, —
    In lonely isles of the Pacific,

In farthest China and Japan, —
  Wherever suns are sudorific.

Nay, even the oily Esquimaux
  In summer court its cooling breezes, —
In fact, in every clime 't is so,
  No matter if it fries or freezes.

And since from Aphrodite's dove
  The pattern of the fan was given,
No wonder that it breathes of love
  And wafts the perfumed gales of
      heaven!

Before this new Pandora's gift
  In slavery woman's tyrant kept her,
But now he kneels her glove to lift, —
  The fan is mightier than the sceptre.

The tap it gives how arch and sly!
  The breath it wakes how fresh and
      grateful!
Behind its shield how soft the sigh!
  The whispered tale of shame how fate-
      ful!

Its empire shadows every throne
  And every shore that man is tost on;
It rules the lords of every zone,
  Nay, even the bluest blood of Boston!

But every one that swings to-night,
  Of fairest shape, from farthest region,
May trace its pedigree aright
  To Aphrodite's fan-tailed pigeon.

TO R. B. H.

AT THE DINNER TO THE PRESIDENT,
BOSTON, JUNE 26, 1877.

How to address him? awkward, it is
  true:
Call him "Great Father," as the Red
  Men do?
Borrow some title? this is not the place

That christens men Your Highness and
  Your Grace;
We tried such names as these awhile,
  you know,
But left them off a century ago.

His Majesty? We 've had enough of
  that:
Besides, that needs a crown; he wears
  a hat.
What if, to make the nicer ears content,
We say His Honesty, the President?

Sir, we believed you honest, truthful,
  brave,
When to your hands their precious trust
  we gave,
And we have found you better than we
  knew,
Braver, and not less honest, not less
  true!
So every heart has opened, every hand
Tingles with welcome, and through all
  the land
All voices greet you in one broad acclaim,
Healer of strife! Has earth a nobler
  name?

What phrases mean you do not need to
  learn;
We must be civil and they serve our
  turn:
"Your most obedient humble" means
  — means what?
Something the well-bred signer just is
  not.
Yet there are tokens, sir, you must believe;
There is one language never can deceive:
The lover knew it when the maiden
  smiled;
The mother knows it when she clasps
  her child;
Voices may falter, trembling lips turn
  pale,

Words grope and stumble; this will tell
their tale
Shorn of all rhetoric, bare of all pretence,
But radiant, warm, with Nature's eloquence.
Look in our eyes ! Your welcome waits
you there, —
North, South, East, West, from all and
everywhere !

"THE SHIP OF STATE."

A SENTIMENT.

THE Ship of State ! above her skies are
blue,
But still she rocks a little, it is true,
And there *are* passengers whose faces
white
Show they don't feel as happy as they
might ;
Yet on the whole her crew are quite
content,
Since its wild fury the typhoon has
spent,
And willing, if her pilot thinks it best,
To head a little nearer south by west.
And this they feel : the ship came too
near wreck,
In the long quarrel for the quarter-
deck,
Now when she glides serenely on her
way,
— The shallows past where dread explo-
sives lay, —
The stiff obstructive's churlish game to
try :
Let sleeping dogs and still torpedoes
lie !
And so I give you all the Ship of State ;
Freedom's last venture is her priceless
freight ;
God speed her, keep her, bless her, while
she steers
Amid the breakers of unsounded years ;

Lead her through danger's paths with
even keel,
And guide the honest hand that holds
her wheel !

WOODSTOCK, CONN., July 4, 1877.

A FAMILY RECORD.

WOODSTOCK, CONN., JULY 4, 1877.

NOT to myself this breath of vesper
song,
Not to these patient friends, this kindly
throng,
Not to this hallowed morning, though
it be
Our summer Christmas, Freedom's jubilee,
When every summit, topmast, steeple,
tower,
That owns her empire spreads her starry
flower,
Its blood-streaked leaves in heaven's
benignant dew
Washed clean from every crimson stain
they knew —
No, not to these the passing thrills belong
That steal my breath to hush themselves with song.
These moments all are memory's ; I
have come
To speak with lips that rather should
be dumb ;
For what are words ? At every step I
tread
The dust that wore the footprints of the
dead
But for whose life my life had never
known
This faded vesture which it calls its own.
Here sleeps my father's sire, and they
who gave
That earlier life here found their peaceful grave.

In days gone by I sought the hallowed
   ground ;
Climbed yon long slope ; the sacred spot
   I found
Where all unsullied lies the winter snow,
Where all ungathered Spring's pale vio-
   lets blow,
And tracked from stone to stone the
   Saxon name
That marks the blood I need not blush
   to claim,
Blood such as warmed the Pilgrim sons
   of toil,
Who held from God the charter of the
   soil.

  I come an alien to your hills and
   plains,
Yet feel your birthright tingling in my
   veins ;
Mine are this changing prospect's sun
   and shade,
In full-blown summer's bridal pomp
   arrayed ;
Mine these fair hillsides and the vales
   between ;
Mine the sweet streams that lend their
   brightening green ;
I breathed your air — the sunlit land-
   scape smiled ;
I touch your soil — it knows its chil-
   dren's child ;
Throned in my heart your heritage is
   mine ;
I claim it all by memory's right divine !
  Waking, I dream. Before my vacant
   eyes
In long procession shadowy forms arise ;
Far through the vista of the silent years
I see a venturous band ; the pioneers,
Who let the sunlight through the for-
   est's gloom,
Who bade the harvest wave, the garden
   bloom.
Hark ! loud resounds the bare-armed
   settler's axe, —

See where the stealthy panther left his
   tracks !
As fierce, as stealthy creeps the skulking foe
With stone - tipped shaft and sinew-
   corded bow ;
Soon shall he vanish from his ancient
   reign,
Leave his last cornfield to the coming
   train,
Quit the green margin of the wave he
   drinks,
For haunts that hide the wild-cat and
   the lynx.

  But who the Youth his glistening axe
   that swings
To smite the pine that shows a hundred
   rings ?
His features ? — something in his look
   I find
That calls the semblance of my race to
   mind.
His name ? — my own ; and that which
   goes before
The same that once the loved disciple
   bore.
Young, brave, discreet, the father of a line
Whose voiceless lives have found a voice
   in mine ;
Thinned by unnumbered currents though
   they be,
Thanks for the ruddy drops I claim from
   thee !

  The seasons pass ; the roses come and
   go ;
Snows fall and melt ; the waters freeze
   and flow ;
The boys are men ; the girls, grown tall
   and fair,
Have found their mates ; a gravestone
   here and there
Tells where the fathers lie ; the silvered
   hair

Of some bent patriarch yet recalls the
time
That saw his feet the northern hillside
climb,
A pilgrim from the pilgrims far away,
The godly men, the dwellers by the
bay.
On many a hearthstone burns the cheer-
ful fire ;
The schoolhouse porch, the heavenward
pointing spire .
Proclaim in letters every eye can read,
Knowledge and Faith, the new world's
simple creed.

Hush! 't is the Sabbath's silence-
stricken morn :
No feet must wander through the tasselled corn ;
No merry children laugh around the
door,
No idle playthings strew the sanded
floor ;
The law of Moses lays its awful ban
On all that stirs ; here comes the tith-
ing-man !

At last the solemn hour of worship
calls ;
Slowly they gather in the sacred walls ;
Man in his strength and age with
knotted staff,
And boyhood aching for its week-day
laugh,
The toil-worn mother with the child
she leads,
The maiden, lovely in her golden
beads, —
The popish symbols round her neck she
wears,
But on them counts her lovers, not her
prayers, —
Those youths in homespun suits and
ribboned queues,
Whose hearts are beating in the high-
backed pews.

The pastor rises ; looks along the seats

With searching eye ; each wonted face
he meets ;
Asks heavenly guidance ; finds the chapter's place
That tells some tale of Israel's stubborn
race ;
Gives out the sacred song ; all voices
join,
For no *quartette* extorts their scanty
coin ;
Then while both hands their black-
gloved palms display,
Lifts his gray head, and murmurs "Let
us pray !"

And pray he does ! as one that never
fears
To plead unanswered by the God that
hears ;
What if he dwells on many a fact as
though
Some things Heaven knew not which it
ought to know, —
Thanks God for all His favors past, and
yet,
Tells Him there 's something He must
not forget ;
Such are the prayers his people love to
hear, —
See how the Deacon slants his listening
ear !

What ! look once more ! Nay, surely
there I trace
The hinted outlines of a well-known
face !
Not those the lips for laughter to beguile,
Yet round their corners lurks an embryo
smile,
The same on other lips my childhood
knew
That scarce the Sabbath's mastery could
subdue.
Him too my lineage gives me leave to
claim, —
The good, grave man that bears the
Psalmist's name.

And still in ceaseless round the sea-
  sons passed ;
Spring piped her carol ; Autumn blew
  his blast ;
Babes waxed to manhood ; manhood
  shrunk to age ;
Life's worn-out players tottered off the
  stage ;
The few are many ; boys have grown to
  men
Since Putnam dragged the wolf from
  Pomfret's den ;
Our new-old Woodstock is a thriving
  town ;
Brave are her children ; faithful to the
  crown ;
Her soldiers' steel the savage redskin
  knows ;
Their blood has crimsoned his Canadian
  snows.
And now once more along the quiet vale
Rings the dread call that turns the
  mothers pale ;
Full well they know the valorous heat
  that runs
In every pulse-beat of their loyal sons ;
Who would not bleed in good King
  George's cause
When England's lion shows his teeth
  and claws ?
  With glittering firelocks on the vil-
    lage green
In proud array a martial band is seen ;
You know what names those ancient
  rosters hold, —
Whose belts were buckled when the
  drum-beat rolled, —
But mark their Captain ! tell us, who
  is he ?
On his brown face that same old look I
  see !
Yes ! from the homestead's still retreat
  he came,
Whose peaceful owner bore the Psalm-
  ist's name ;

The same his own. Well, Israel's glo-
  rious king
Who struck the harp could also whirl
  the sling, —
Breathe in his song a penitential sigh
And smite the sons of Amalek hip and
  thigh :
These shared their task ; one deaconed
  out the psalm,
One slashed the scalping hell-hounds of
  Montcalm ;
The praying father's pious work is done,
Now sword in hand steps forth the
  fighting son.
  On many a field he fought in wilds
  afar ;
See on his swarthy cheek the bullet's
  scar !
There hangs a murderous tomahawk ;
  beneath,
Without its blade, a knife's embroidered
  sheath ;
Save for the stroke his trusty weapon
  dealt
His scalp had dangled at their owner's
  belt ;
But not for him such fate ; he lived to see
The bloodier strife that made our nation
  free,
To serve with willing toil, with skilful
  hand,
The war-worn saviors of the bleeding
  land.
His wasting life to others' needs he
  gave, —
Sought rest in home and found it in the
  grave.
See where the stones life's brief memo-
  rials keep,
The tablet telling where he "fell on
  sleep," —
Watched by a winged cherub's rayless
  eye, —
A scroll above that says we all must
  die, —

Those saddening lines beneath, the
  "Night-Thoughts" lent:
So stands the Soldier's, Surgeon's monu-
  ment.
Ah! at a glance my filial eye divines
The scholar son in those remembered
  lines.

  The Scholar Son. His hand my foot-
    steps led.
No more the dim unreal past I tread.
O thou whose breathing form was once
  so dear,
Whose cheering voice was music to my
  ear,
Art thou not with me as my feet pursue
The village paths so well thy boyhood
  knew,
Along the tangled margin of the stream
Whose murmurs blended with thine in-
  fant dream,
Or climb the hill, or thread the wooded
  vale,
Or seek the wave where gleams yon dis-
  tant sail,
Or the old homestead's narrowed bounds
  explore,
Where sloped the roof that sheds the
  rains no more,
Where one last relic still remains to tell
Here stood thy home, — the memory-
  haunted well,
Whose waters quench a deeper thirst
  than thine,
Changed at my lips to sacramental
  wine, —

Art thou not with me, as I fondly trace
The scanty records of thine honored
  race,
Call up the forms that earlier years have
  known,
And spell the legend of each slanted
  stone?
  With thoughts of thee my loving
    verse began,
Not for the critic's curious eye to scan,
Not for the many listeners, but the
  few
Whose fathers trod the paths my fathers
  knew;
Still in my heart thy loved remembrance
  burns;
Still to my lips thy cherished name re-
  turns;
Could I but feel thy gracious presence
  near
Amid the groves that once to thee were
  dear!
Could but my trembling lips with mor-
  tal speech
Thy listening ear for one brief moment
  reach!
How vain the dream! The pallid voy-
  ager's track
No sign betrays; he sends no message
  back.
No word from thee since evening's
  shadow fell
On thy cold forehead with my long
  farewell, —
Now from the margin of the silent sea,
Take my last offering ere I cross to thee!

FIRST VERSES.

PHILLIPS ACADEMY, ANDOVER, MASS., 1824 OR 1825.

TRANSLATION FROM THE ÆNEID, — Book I.¹

THE god looked out upon the troubled deep
Waked into tumult from its placid sleep ;
The flame of anger kindles in his eye
As the wild waves ascend the lowering sky ;
He lifts his head above their awful height
And to the distant fleet directs his sight,
Now borne aloft upon the billow's crest,
Struck by the bolt or by the winds oppressed,
And well he knew that Juno's vengeful ire
Frowned from those clouds and sparkled in that fire.
On rapid pinions as they whistled by
He calls swift Zephyrus and Eurus nigh :
Is this your glory in a noble line
To leave your confines and to ravage mine ?
Whom I — but let these troubled waves subside —
Another tempest and I 'll quell your pride !
Go — bear our message to your master's ear,
That wide as ocean I am despot here ;
Let him sit monarch in his barren caves,
I wield the trident and control the waves !
　　He said, and as the gathered vapors break
The swelling ocean seemed a peaceful lake ;
To lift their ships the graceful nymphs essayed
And the strong trident lent its powerful aid ;
The dangerous banks are sunk beneath the main,
And the light chariot skims the unruffled plain.
As when sedition fires the public mind,
And maddening fury leads the rabble blind,
The blazing torch lights up the dread alarm,
Rage points the steel and fury nerves the arm,
Then, if some reverend sage appear in sight,
They stand — they gaze, and check their headlong flight, —
He turns the current of each wandering breast
And hushes every passion into rest, —
Thus by the power of his imperial arm
The boiling ocean trembled into calm ;
With flowing reins the father sped his way
And smiled serene upon rekindled day.

THE IRON GATE,

AND OTHER POEMS.

THE IRON GATE.

READ AT THE BREAKFAST GIVEN IN HONOR OF DR. HOLMES'S SEVENTIETH BIRTHDAY BY THE PUBLISHERS OF THE ATLANTIC MONTHLY, BOSTON, DECEMBER 3, 1879.

WHERE is this patriarch you are kindly
    greeting?
  Not unfamiliar to my ear his name,
Nor yet unknown to many a joyous
    meeting
  In days long vanished, — is he still
    the same,

Or changed by years, forgotten and for-
    getting,
  Dull-eared, dim-sighted, slow of
    speech and thought,
Still o'er the sad, degenerate present
    fretting,
  Where all goes wrong, and nothing
    as it ought?

Old age, the graybeard! Well, indeed,
    I know him, —
  Shrunk, tottering, bent, of aches and
    ills the prey;
In sermon, story, fable, picture, poem,
  Oft have I met him from my earliest
    day:

In my old Æsop, toiling with his bun-
    dle, —
  His load of sticks, — politely asking
    Death

Who comes when called for, — would
    he lug or trundle
  His fagot for him? — he was scant of
    breath.

And sad "Ecclesiastes, or the Preach-
    er," —
  Has he not stamped the image on my
    soul,
In that last chapter, where the worn-
    out Teacher
  Sighs o'er the loosened cord, the
    broken bowl?

Yes, long, indeed, I've known him at a
    distance,
  And now my lifted door-latch shows
    him here;
I take his shrivelled hand without re-
    sistance,
  And find him smiling as his step draws
    near.

What though of gilded baubles he be-
    reaves us,
  Dear to the heart of youth, to man-
    hood's prime;
Think of the calm he brings, the wealth
    he leaves us,
  The hoarded spoils, the legacies of
    time!

Altars once flaming, still with incense
    fragrant,
  Passion's uneasy nurslings rocked
    asleep,

Hope's anchor faster, wild desire less
    vagrant,
  Life's flow less noisy, but the stream
    how deep !

Still as the silver cord gets worn and
    slender,
  Its lightened task-work tugs with les-
    sening strain,
Hands get more helpful, voices, grown
    more tender,
  Soothe with their softened tones the
    slumberous brain.

Youth longs and manhood strives, but
    age remembers,
  Sits by the raked-up ashes of the
    past,
Spreads its thin hands above the whiten-
    ing embers
  That warm its creeping life-blood till
    the last.

Dear to its heart is every loving token
  That comes unbidden ere its pulse
    grows cold,
Ere the last lingering ties of life are
    broken,
  Its labors ended and its story told.

Ah, while around us rosy youth re-
    joices,
  For us the sorrow-laden breezes
    sigh,
And through the chorus of its jocund
    voices
  Throbs the sharp note of misery's
    hopeless cry.

As on the gauzy wings of fancy fly-
    ing
  From some far orb I track our watery
    sphere,
Home of the struggling, suffering,
    doubting, dying,
  The silvered globule seems a glisten-
    ing tear.

But Nature lends her mirror of illusion
  To win from saddening scenes our
    age-dimmed eyes,
And misty day-dreams blend in sweet
    confusion
  The wintry landscape and the sum-
    mer skies.

So when the iron portal shuts behind
    us,
  And life forgets us in its noise and
    whirl,
Visions that shunned the glaring noon-
    day find us,
  And glimmering starlight shows the
    gates of pearl.

— I come not here your morning hour
    to sadden,
  A limping pilgrim, leaning on his
    staff, —
I, who have never deemed it sin to
    gladden
  This vale of sorrows with a whole-
    some laugh.

If word of mine another's gloom has
    brightened,
  Through my dumb lips the heaven-
    sent message came ;
If hand of mine another's task has light-
    ened,
  It felt the guidance that it dares not
    claim.

But, O my gentle sisters, O my brothers,
  These thick-sown snow-flakes hint of
    toil's release ;
These feebler pulses bid me leave to
    others
  The tasks once welcome ; evening
    asks for peace.

Time claims his tribute ; silence now is
    golden ;
  Let me not vex the too long suffering
    lyre ;

Though to your love untiring still be-
  holden,
  The curfew tells me — cover up the
  fire.

And now with grateful smile and accents cheerful,
  And warmer heart than look or word
  can tell,
In simplest phrase — these traitorous
  eyes are tearful —
  Thanks, Brothers, Sisters — Children
  — and farewell !

VESTIGIA QUINQUE RETROR-
SUM.

AN ACADEMIC POEM.[1]

1829–1879.

WHILE fond, sad memories all around
  us throng
Silence were sweeter than the sweetest
  song ;
Yet when the leaves are green and
  heaven is blue,
The choral tribute of the grove is due,
And when the lengthening nights have
  chilled the skies,
We fain would hear the song-bird ere
  he flies,
And greet with kindly welcome, even
  as now,
The lonely minstrel on his leafless bough.

This is our golden year, — its golden
  day ;
Its bridal memories soon must pass
  away,
Soon shall its dying music cease to ring
And every year must loose some silver
  string,
Till the last trembling chords no longer
  thrill, —
Hands all at rest and hearts forever still.

[1] Read at the Commencement Dinner of the
Alumni of Harvard University, June 25, 1879.

A few gray heads have joined the
  forming line ;
We hear our summons, — " Class of
  'twenty-nine ! "
Close on the foremost, and, Alas, how
  few !
Are these " The Boys " our dear old
  Mother knew ?
Sixty brave swimmers. Twenty —
  something more —
Have passed the stream and reached
  this frosty shore !

How near the banks these fifty years
  divide
When memory crosses with a single
  stride !
'T is the first year of stern " Old Hick-
  ory " 's rule
When our good Mother lets us out of
  school,
Half glad, half sorrowing, it must be
  confessed,
To leave her quiet lap, her bounteous
  breast,
Armed with our dainty, ribbon-tied de-
  grees,
Pleased and yet pensive, exiles and
  A. B.'s.

Look back, O comrades, with your
  faded eyes,
And see the phantoms as I bid them
  rise.
Whose smile is that ? Its pattern Na-
  ture gave,
A sunbeam dancing in a dimpled wave ;
KIRKLAND alone such grace from
  Heaven could win,
His features radiant as the soul with-
  in ;
That smile would let him through Saint
  Peter's gate
While sad-eyed martyrs had to stand
  and wait.
Here flits mercurial *Farrar ;* standing
  there.

See mild, benignant, cautious, learned
 Ware,
And sturdy, patient, faithful, honest
 Hedge,
Whose grinding logic gave our wits their
 edge;
Ticknor, with honeyed voice and courtly
 grace;
And *Willard* larynxed like a double
 bass;
And *Channing* with his bland, superior
 look,
Cool as a moonbeam on a frozen brook,
While the pale student, shivering in his
 shoes,
Sees from his theme the turgid rhetoric
 ooze;
And the born soldier, fate decreed to
 wreak
His martial manhood on a class in
 Greek,
Popkin! How that explosive name re-
 calls
The grand old Busby of our ancient
 halls!
Such faces looked from Skippon's grim
 platoons,
Such figures rode with Ireton's stout
 dragoons;
He gave his strength to learning's gen-
 tle charms,
But every accent sounded " Shoulder
 arms!"

Names, — empty names! Save only
 here and there
Some white-haired listener, dozing in
 his chair,
Starts at the sound he often used to
 hear,
And upward slants his Sunday-sermon
 ear.

And we — our blooming manhood we
 regain;
Smiling we join the long Commencement train,

One point first battled in discussion
 hot, —
Shall we wear gowns? and settled: *We
 will not.*
How strange the scene, — that noisy
 boy-debate
Where embryo-speakers learn to rule
 the State!
This broad-browed youth,[1] sedate and
 sober-eyed,
Shall wear the ermined robe at Taney's
 side;
And he, the stripling,[2] smooth of face
 and slight,
Whose slender form scarce intercepts
 the light,
Shall rule the Bench where Parsons
 gave the law,
And sphynx-like sat uncouth, majestic
 Shaw!
Ah, many a star has shed its fatal ray
On names we loved — our brothers —
 where are they?
Nor these alone; our hearts in silence
 claim
Names not less dear, unsyllabled by
 fame.

How brief the space! and yet it sweeps
 us back
Far, far along our new-born history's
 track!
Five strides like this; — the Sachem
 rules the land;
The Indian wigwams cluster where we
 stand.

The second. — Lo! a scene of deadly
 strife —
A nation struggling into infant life;
Not yet the fatal game at Yorktown
 won
Where falling Empire fired its sunset
 gun.

[1] Benjamin Robbins Curtis.
[2] George Tyler Bigelow.

LANGDON sits restless in the ancient chair, —
Harvard's grave Head, — these echoes heard his prayer
When from yon mansion, dear to memory still,
The banded yeomen marched for Bunker's Hill.
Count on the grave triennial's thick-starred roll
What names were numbered on the lengthening scroll —
Not unfamiliar in our ears they ring —
Winthrop, Hale, Eliot, Everett, Dexter, Tyng.

Another stride. Once more at 'twenty-nine, —
GOD SAVE KING GEORGE, the Second of his line !
And is *Sir Isaac* living ? Nay, not so, —
He followed *Flamsteed* two short years ago, —
And what about the little hump-backed man
Who pleased the bygone days of good Queen Anne ?
What, *Pope?* another book he 's just put out —
" The Dunciad " — witty, but profane, no doubt.
Where 's *Cotton Mather* ? he was always here. —
And so he would be, but he died last year.
Who is this preacher our Northampton claims,
Whose rhetoric blazes with sulphureous flames
And torches stolen from Tartarean mines ?
Edwards, the salamander of divines.
A deep, strong nature, pure and unde-filed ;
Faith, firm as his who stabbed his sleeping child ;

Alas for him who blindly strays apart
And seeking God has lost his human heart !
Fall where they might, no flying cinders caught
These sober halls where WADSWORTH ruled and taught.

One footstep more ; the fourth receding stride
Leaves the round century on the nearer side.
GOD SAVE KING CHARLES ! God knows that pleasant knave
His grace will find it hard enough to save.
Ten years and more, and now the Plague, the Fire,
Talk of all tongues, at last begin to tire ;
One fear prevails, all other frights for-got, —
White lips are whispering, — hark ! *The popish Plot !*
Happy New England, from such troubles free
In health and peace beyond the stormy sea !
No Romish daggers threat her children's throats,
No gibbering nightmare mutters " *Titus Oates ;* "
Philip is slain, the Quaker graves are green,
Not yet the witch has entered on the scene ;
Happy our Harvard ; pleased her graduates four ;
URIAN OAKES the name their parchments bore.

Two centuries past, our hurried feet arrive
At the last footprint of the scanty five ;
Take the fifth stride ; our wandering eyes explore
A tangled forest on a trackless shore ;

Here, where we stand, the savage sor-
    cerer howls,
The wild cat snarls, the stealthy gray
    wolf prowls,
The slouching bear, perchance the tramp-
    ling moose
Starts the brown squaw and scares her
    red pappoose ;
At every step the lurking foe is near ;
His Demons reign ; God has no temple
    here !

Lift up your eyes ! behold these pic-
    tured walls ;
Look where the flood of western glory
    falls
Through the great sunflower disk of
    blazing panes
In ruby, saffron, azure, emerald stains ;
With reverent step the marble pavement
    tread
Where our proud Mother's martyr-roll
    is read ;
See the great halls that cluster, gather-
    ing round
This lofty shrine with holiest memories
    crowned ;
See the fair Matron in her summer
    bower ;
Fresh as a rose in bright perennial
    flower ;
Read on her standard, always in the
    van,
" TRUTH," — the one word that makes
    a slave a man ;
Think whose the hands that fed her
    altar-fires,
Then count the debt we owe our scholar-
    sires !

Brothers, farewell ! the fast declining
    ray
Fades to the twilight of our golden day ;
Some lesson yet our wearied brains may
    learn,
Some leaves, perhaps, in life's thin vol-
    ume turn.

How few they seem as in our waning
    age
We count them backwards to the title-
    page !
Oh let us trust with holy men of old
Not all the story here begun is told ;
So the tired spirit, waiting to be freed,
On life's last leaf with tranquil eye shall
    read
By the pale glimmer of the torch re-
    versed,
Not *Finis*, but *The End of Volume
    First !*

MY AVIARY.

THROUGH my north window, in the
    wintry weather, —
    My airy oriel on the river shore, —
I watch the sea-fowl as they flock to-
    gether
    Where late the boatman flashed his
    dripping oar.

The gull, high floating, like a sloop un-
    laden,
    Lets the loose water waft him as it
    will ;
The duck, round-breasted as a rustic
    maiden,
    Paddles and plunges, busy, busy still.

I see the solemn gulls in council sit-
    ting
    On some broad ice-floe, pondering long
    and late,
While overhead the home-bound ducks
    are flitting,
    And leave the tardy conclave in de-
    bate,

Those weighty questions in their breasts
    revolving
    Whose deeper meaning science never
    learns,

MY AVIARY.   Page 326.

Till at some reverend elder's look dis-
    solving,
  The speechless senate silently ad-
    journs.

But when along the waves the shrill
    north-easter
  Shrieks through the laboring coaster's
    shrouds "Beware!"
The pale bird, kindling like a Christmas
    feaster
  When some wild chorus shakes the
    vinous air,

Flaps from the leaden wave in fierce re-
    joicing,
  Feels heaven's dumb lightning thrill
    his torpid nerves,
Now on the blast his whistling plumage
    poising,
  Now wheeling, whirling in fantastic
    curves.

Such is our gull; a gentleman of leisure,
  Less fleshed than feathered; bagged
    you'll find him such;
His virtue silence; his employment
    pleasure;
  Not bad to look at, and not good for
    much.

What of our duck?   He has some high-
    bred cousins,
  His Grace the Canvas-back, My Lord
    the Brant, —
Anas and Anser, — both served up by
    dozens,
  At Boston's Rocher, half-way to Na-
    hant.

As for himself, he seems alert and thriv-
    ing, —
  Grubs up a living somehow — what,
    who knows?
Crabs? mussels? weeds? — Look quick!
    there's one just diving!
  Flop! Splash! his white breast glis-
    tens — down he goes!

And while he's under — just about a
    minute —
  I take advantage of the fact to
    say
His fishy carcase has no virtue in it
  The gunning idiot's worthless hire to
    pay.

He knows you! "sportsmen" from
    suburban alleys,
  Stretched under seaweed in the treach-
    erous punt;
Knows every lazy, shiftless lout that
    sallies
  Forth to waste powder — as he says,
    to "hunt."

I watch you with a patient satisfac-
    tion,
  Well pleased to discount your pre-
    destined luck;
The float that figures in your sly trans-
    action
  Will carry back a goose, but not a
    duck.

Shrewd is our bird; not easy to outwit
    him!
  Sharp is the outlook of those pin-head
    eyes;
Still, he is mortal and a shot may hit
    him,
  One cannot always miss him if he
    tries.

Look! there's a young one, dreaming
    not of danger;
  Sees a flat log come floating down
    the stream;
Stares undismayed upon the harmless
    stranger;
  Ah! were all strangers harmless as
    they seem!

Habet! a leaden shower his breast has
    shattered;
  Vainly he flutters, not again to
    rise;

His soft white plumes along the waves
   are scattered ;
  Helpless the wing that braved the
   tempest lies.

He sees his comrades high above him
   flying
  To seek their nests among the island
   reeds ;
Strong is their flight ; all lonely he is
   lying
  Washed by the crimsoned water as
   he bleeds.

O Thou who carest for the falling sparrow,
  Canst Thou the sinless sufferer's pang
   forget ?
Or is Thy dread account-book's page so
   narrow
  Its one long column scores Thy creatures' debt ?

Poor gentle guest, by nature kindly
   cherished,
  A world grows dark with thee in
   blinding death ;
One little gasp — thy universe has perished,
  Wrecked by the idle thief who stole
   thy breath !

Is this the whole sad story of creation,
  Lived by its breathing myriads o'er
   and o'er, —
One glimpse of day, then black annihi-
   lation, —
  A sunlit passage to a sunless shore ?

Give back our faith, ye mystery-solving
   lynxes !
  Robe us once more in heaven-aspiring
   creeds !
Happier was dreaming Egypt with her
   sphynxes,
  The stony convent with its cross and
   beads !

How often gazing where a bird reposes,
  Rocked on the wavelets, drifting with
   the tide,
I lose myself in strange metempsychosis
  And float a sea-fowl at a sea-fowl's
   side.

From rain, hail, snow in feathery mantle muffled,
  Clear-eyed, strong-limbed, with keen-
   est sense to hear
My mate soft murmuring, who, with
   plumes unruffled,
  Where'er I wander still is nestling
   near ;

The great blue hollow like a garment
   o'er me ;
  Space all unmeasured, unrecorded
   time ;
While seen with inward eye moves on
   before me
  Thought's pictured train in wordless
   pantomime.

— A voice recalls me. — From my window turning
  I find myself a plumeless biped still ;
No beak, no claws, no sign of wings
   discerning, —
  In fact with nothing bird-like but my
   quill.

ON THE THRESHOLD.

INTRODUCTION TO A COLLECTION OF
POEMS BY DIFFERENT AUTHORS.

An usher standing at the door
  I show my white rosette ;
A smile of welcome, nothing more,
  Will pay my trifling debt ;
Why should I bid you idly wait
Like lovers at the swinging gate ?

Can I forget the wedding guest ?
  The veteran of the sea ?

In vain the listener smites his breast, —
 "There was a ship," cries he!
Poor fasting victim, stunned and pale
He needs must listen to the tale.

He sees the gilded throng within,
 The sparkling goblets gleam,
The music and the merry din
 Through every window stream,
But there he shivers in the cold
Till all the crazy dream is told.

Not mine the graybeard's glittering eye
 That held his captive still
To hold my silent prisoners by
 And let me have my will;
Nay, I were like the three-years' child,
To think you could be so beguiled!

My verse is but the curtain's fold
 That hides the painted scene,
The mist by morning's ray unrolled
 That veils the meadow's green,
The cloud that needs must drift away
To show the rose of opening day.

See, from the tinkling rill you hear
 In hollowed palm I bring
These scanty drops, but ah, how near
 The founts that heavenward spring!
Thus, open wide the gates are thrown
And founts and flowers are all your
 own!

TO GEORGE PEABODY.

DANVERS, 1866.

BANKRUPT! our pockets inside out!
 Empty of words to speak his praises!
Worcester and Webster up the spout!
 Dead broke of laudatory phrases!
Yet why with flowery speeches tease,
 With vain superlatives distress him?
Has language better words than these?
 THE FRIEND OF ALL HIS RACE, GOD
 BLESS HIM!

A simple prayer — but words more
 sweet
 By human lips were never uttered,
Since Adam left the country seat
 Where angel wings around him flut-
 tered.
The old look on with tear-dimmed eyes
 The children cluster to caress him,
And every voice unbidden cries
 THE FRIEND OF ALL HIS RACE, GOD
 BLESS HIM!

AT THE PAPYRUS CLUB.

A LOVELY show for eyes to see
 I looked upon this morning —
A bright-hued, feathered company
 Of nature's own adorning;
But ah! those minstrels would not sing
 A listening ear while I lent —
The lark sat still and preened his
 wing —
 The nightingale was silent;
I longed for what they gave me not —
 Their warblings sweet and fluty,
But grateful still for all I got
 I thanked them for their beauty.

A fairer vision meets my view
 Of Claras, Margarets, Marys,
In silken robes of varied hue,
 Like bluebirds and canaries —
The roses blush, the jewels gleam,
 The silks and satins glisten,
The black eyes flash, the blue eyes
 beam,
 We look — and then we listen:
Behold the flock we cage to-night —
 Was ever such a capture?
To see them is a pure delight —
 To hear them — ah! what rapture!

Methinks I hear Delilah's laugh
 At Samson bound in fetters; —
" We captured!" shrieks each lovelier
 half,
 " Men think themselves our betters!

We push the bolt, we turn the key
  On warriors, poets, sages,
Too happy, all of them, to be
  Locked in our golden cages!"

Beware! the boy with bandaged eyes
  Has flung away his blinder;
He's lost his mother — so he cries —
  And here he knows he'll find her:
The rogue! 't is but a new device —
  Look out for flying arrows
Whene'er the birds of Paradise
  Are perched amid the sparrows!

FOR WHITTIER'S SEVENTIETH BIRTHDAY.

DECEMBER 17, 1877.

I BELIEVE that the copies of verses I've
  spun,
Like Scheherazade's tales, are a thousand and one, —
You remember the story, — those mornings in bed, —
'T was the turn of a copper, — a tale or
  a head.

A doom like Scheherazade's falls upon
  me
In a mandate as stern as the Sultan's
  decree:
I'm a florist in verse, and what *would*
  people say
If I came to a banquet without my bouquet?

It is trying, no doubt, when the com-
  pany knows
Just the look and the smell of each lily
  and rose,
The green of each leaf in the sprigs that
  I bring,
And the shape of the bunch and the
  knot of the string.

Yes, — " the style is the man," and the
  nib of one's pen
Makes the same mark at twenty, and
  three-score and ten;
It is so in all matters, if truth may be
  told;
Let one look at the cast he can tell you
  the mould.

How we all know each other! no use in
  disguise;
Through the holes in the mask comes
  the flash of the eyes;
We can tell by his — somewhat — each
  one of our tribe,
As we know the old hat which we cannot describe.

Though in Hebrew, in Sanscrit, in
  Choctaw you write,
Sweet singer who gave us the Voices of
  Night,
Though in buskin or slipper your song
  may be shod,
Or the velvety verse that Evangeline trod,

We shall say "You can't cheat us, —
  we know it is you,"
There is one voice like that, but there
  cannot be two,
Maëstro, whose chant like the dulcimer
  rings:
And the woods will be hushed while the
  nightingale sings.

And he, so serene, so majestic, so true,
Whose temple hypæthral the planets
  shine through,
Let us catch but five words from that
  mystical pen,
We should know our one sage from all
  children of men.

And he whose bright image no distance
  can dim,
Through a hundred disguises we can't
  mistake him,

Whose play is all earnest, whose wit is
    the edge
(With a beetle behind) of a sham-split-
    ting wedge.

Do you know whom we send you, Hidal-
    gos of Spain?
Do you know your old friends when you
    see them again?
Hosea was Sancho! you Dons of Ma-
    drid,
But Sancho that wielded the lance of
    the Cid!

And the wood-thrush of Essex, — you
    know whom I mean,
Whose song echoes round us while he
    sits unseen,
Whose heart-throbs of verse through
    our memories thrill
Like a breath from the wood, like a
    breeze from the hill,

So fervid, so simple, so loving, so pure,
We hear but one strain and our verdict
    is sure, —
Thee cannot elude us, — no further we
    search, —
'T is Holy George Herbert cut loose
    from his church!

We think it the voice of a seraph that
    sings, —
Alas! we remember that angels have
    wings, —
What story is this of the day of his
    birth?
Let him live to a hundred! we want
    him on earth!

One life has been paid him (in gold) by
    the sun;
One account has been squared and an-
    other begun;
But he never will die if he lingers below
Till we 've paid him in love half the
    balance we owe!

TWO SONNETS: HARVARD.[1]

"CHRISTO ET ECCLESIÆ."   1700.

To God's anointed and his chosen
    flock:
  So ran the phrase the black-robed
    conclave chose
  To guard the sacred cloisters that
    arose
Like David's altar on Moriah's rock.
Unshaken still those ancient arches
    mock
  The ram's-horn summons of the windy
    foes
  Who stand like Joshua's army while
    it blows
And wait to see them toppling with the
    shock.
Christ and the Church. *Their* church,
    whose narrow door
  Shut out the many, who if over bold
  Like hunted wolves were driven from
    the fold,
Bruised with the flails those godly zeal-
    ots bore,
  Mindful that Israel's altar stood of old
Where echoed once Araunah's thresh-
    ing-floor.

1643.   "VERITAS."   1878.

Truth: So the frontlet's older legend
    ran,
  On the brief record's opening page
    displayed;
  Not yet those clear-eyed scholars were
    afraid
Lest the fair fruit that wrought the woe
    of man
By far Euphrates, — where our sire
    began
  His search for truth, and seeking, was
    betrayed, —
  Might work new treason in their
    forest shade,

[1] At the meeting of the New York Harvard
Club, February 21, 1878.

Doubling the curse that brought life's
  shortened span.
Nurse of the future, daughter of the
  past,
  That stern phylactery best becomes
    thee now:
  Lift to the morning star thy marble
    brow!
Cast thy brave truth on every warring
  blast!
  Stretch thy white hand to that forbid-
    den bough,
And let thine earliest symbol be thy
    last!

THE LAST SURVIVOR.[1]

YES! the vacant chairs tell sadly we
  are going, going fast,
And the thought comes strangely o'er
  me who will live to be the last?
When the twentieth century's sunbeams
  climb the far-off eastern hill
With his ninety winters burdened will
  he greet the morning still?

Will he stand with Harvard's nurslings
  when they hear their mother's
  call
And the old and young are gathered in
  the many alcoved hall?
Will he answer to the summons when
  they range themselves in line
And the young mustachioed marshal
  calls out "Class of 29"?

Methinks I see the column as its lengthened ranks appear
In the sunshine of the morrow of the
  nineteen hundredth year;
Through the yard 't is creeping, winding, by the walls of dusky red —
What shape is that which totters at the
  long procession's head?

[1] Annual meeting of the Class of 1829, January 10, 1878.

Who knows this ancient graduate of
  fourscore years and ten, —
What place he held, what name he bore
  among the sons of men?
So speeds the curious question; its answer travels slow;
" 'T is the last of sixty classmates of
  seventy years ago."

His figure shows but dimly, his face I
  scarce can see, —
There 's something that reminds me, —
  it looks like — is it he?
He? Who? No voice may whisper
  what wrinkled brow shall claim
The wreath of stars that circles our last
  survivor's name.

Will he be some veteran minstrel, left
  to pipe in feeble rhyme
All the stories and the glories of our
  gay and golden time?
Or some quiet, voiceless brother in whose
  lonely loving breast
Fond memory broods in silence, like a
  dove upon her nest?

Will it be some old *Emeritus*, who taught
  so long ago
The boys that heard him lecture have
  heads as white as snow?
Or a pious, painful preacher, holding
  forth from year to year
Till his colleague got a colleague whom
  the young folks flocked to hear?

Will it be a rich old merchant in a
  square-tied white cravat,
Or select-man of a village in a pre-his-
  toric hat?
Will his dwelling be a mansion in a
  marble-fronted row,
Or a homestead by a hillside where the
  huckleberries grow?

I can see our one survivor, sitting lonely
  by himself, —

All his college text-books round him,
ranged in order on their shelf ;
There are classic "interliners" filled
with learning's choicest pith,
Each *cum notis variorum, quas recensuit
doctus* Smith ;

Physics, metaphysics, logic, mathemat-
ics — all the lot —
Every wisdom-crammed octavo he has
mastered and forgot,
With the ghosts of dead Professors
standing guard beside them all ;
And the room is full of shadows which
their lettered backs recall.

How the past spreads out in vision with
its far receding train,
Like a long embroidered arras in the
chambers of the brain,
From opening manhood's morning when
first we learned to grieve
To the fond regretful moments of our
sorrow saddened eve !

What early shadows darkened our idle
summer's joy
When death snatched roughly from us
that lovely bright-eyed boy ! [1]
The years move swiftly onwards ; the
deadly shafts fall fast, —
Till all have dropped around him — lo,
there he stands, — the last !

Their faces flit before him, some rosy-
hued and fair,
Some strong in iron manhood, some
worn with toil and care,
Their smiles no more shall greet him on
cheeks with pleasure flushed !
The friendly hands are folded, the pleasant voices hushed !

. . . . . .

[1] William Sturgis.

My picture sets me dreaming ; alas!
and can it be
Those two familiar faces we never more
may see ?
In every entering footfall I think them
drawing near,
With every door that opens I say, " At
last they're here ! "

The willow bends unbroken when angry tempests blow,
The stately oak is levelled and all its
strength laid low ;
So fell that tower of manhood, undaunted, patient, strong,
White with the gathering snow-flakes,
who faced the storm so long.[2]

And he,[3] — what subtle phrases their
varying light must blend
To paint as each remembers our many-
featured friend !
His wit a flash auroral that laughed in
every look,
His talk a sunbeam broken on the ripples of a brook,

Or, fed from thousand sources, a fountain's glittering jet,
Or careless handfuls scattered of diamond sparks unset,
Ah, sketch him, paint him, mould him
in every shape you will,
He was *himself* — the only — the one
unpictured still !

Farewell ! our skies are darkened and
yet the stars will shine,
We'll close our ranks together and still
fall into line
Till one is left, one only, to mourn for
all the rest ;
And Heaven bequeath their memories
to him who loves us best !

[2] Francis B. Crowninshield.
[3] George T. Davis.

THE ARCHBISHOP AND GIL BLAS.[1]

A MODERNIZED VERSION.

I DON'T think I feel much older; I'm
    aware I'm rather gray,
But so are many young folks; I meet
    'em every day.
I confess I'm more particular in what
    I eat and drink,
But one's taste improves with culture;
    that is all it means, I think.

Can you read as once you used to?
    Well, the printing is so bad,
No young folks' eyes can read it like the
    books that once we had.
Are you quite as quick of hearing? Please
    to say that once again.
Don't I use plain words, your Reverence?
    Yes, I often use a cane,

But it's not because I need it, — no,
    I always liked a stick;
And as one might lean upon it; 't is as
    well it should be thick.
Oh, I'm smart, I'm spry, I'm lively, —
    I can walk, yes, that I can,
On the days I feel like walking, just as
    well as you, young man!

*Don't you get a little sleepy after dinner
    every day?*
Well, I doze a little, sometimes, but that
    always was my way.
*Don't you cry a little easier than some
    twenty years ago?*
Well, my heart is very tender, but I
    think 't was always so.

*Don't you find it sometimes happens that
    you can't recall a name?*
Yes, — I know such lots of people, —
    but my memory's not to blame.

[1] Annual Meeting of the Class of 1829, January 6, 1879.

What! You think my memory's fail-
    ing! Why, it's just as bright
    and clear, —
I remember my great-grandma! She's
    been dead these sixty year!

Is your voice a little trembly? Well, it
    may be, now and then,
But I write as well as ever with a good
    old-fashioned pen;
It's the Gillotts make the trouble, —
    not at all my finger-ends, —
That is why my hand looks shaky when
    I sign for dividends.

Don't you stoop a little, walking? It's
    a way I've always had,
I have always been round-shouldered
    ever since I was a lad.
Don't you hate to tie your shoe-strings?
    Yes, I own it — that is true.
Don't you tell old stories over? I am not
    aware I do.

*Don't you stay at home of evenings?
    Don't you love a cushioned seat
In a corner, by the fireside, with your slip-
    pers on your feet?
Don't you wear warm fleecy flannels?
    Don't you muffle up your throat?
Don't you like to have one help you when
    you're putting on your coat?*

*Don't you like old books you've dogs-
    eared, you can't remember when?
Don't you call it late at nine o'clock and
    go to bed at ten?
How many cronies can you count of all
    you used to know
Who called you by your Christian name
    some fifty years ago?*

*How look the prizes to you that used to
    fire your brain?
You've reared your mound — how high is
    it above the level plain?*

*You've drained the brimming golden cup
    that made your fancy reel,*
*You've slept the giddy potion off, — now
    tell us how you feel!*

*You've watched the harvest ripening till
    every stem was cropped,*
*You've seen the rose of beauty fade till
    every petal dropped,*
*You've told your thought, you've done
    your task, you've tracked your dial
    round,*
— I backing down! Thank Heaven,
    not yet! I'm hale and brisk and
    sound,

And good for many a tussle, as you
    shall live to see;
My shoes are not quite ready yet, —
    don't think you're rid of me!
Old Parr was in his lusty prime when
    he was older far,
And where will you be if I live to beat
    old Thomas Parr?

*Ah well, — I know, — at every age life has
    a certain charm, —*
*You're going? Come, permit me, please,
    I beg you'll take my arm.*
I take your arm! Why take your arm?
    I'd thank you to be told
I'm old enough to walk alone, but not
    so *very* old!

THE SHADOWS.[1]

" How many have gone ? " was the ques-
    tion of old
    Ere Time our bright ring of its jewels
    bereft ;
Alas! for too often the death-bell has
    tolled,
    And the question we ask is, " How
    many are left ? "

[1] Annual Meeting of the Class of 1829, January 8, 1880.

Bright sparkled the wine ; there were
    fifty that quaffed ;
    For a decade had slipped and had
    taken but three.
How they frolicked and sung, how they
    shouted and laughed,
    Like a school full of boys from their
    benches set free !

There were speeches and toasts, there
    were stories and rhymes,
    The hall shook its sides with their
    merriment's noise ;
As they talked and lived over the col-
    lege-day times, —
    No wonder they kept their old name
    of " The Boys " !

The seasons moved on in their rhyth-
    mical flow
    With mornings like maidens that
    pouted or smiled,
With the bud and the leaf and the fruit
    and the snow,
    And the year - books of Time in his
    alcoves were piled.

There were *forty* that gathered where
    fifty had met ;
    Some locks had got silvered, some
    lives had grown sere,
But the laugh of the laughers was lusty
    as yet,
    And the song of the singers rose ring-
    ing and clear.

Still flitted the years ; there were *thirty*
    that came ;
    " The Boys " they were still and they
    answered their call ;
There were foreheads of care, but the
    smiles were the same
    And the chorus rang loud through
    the garlanded hall.

The hour-hand moved on, and they
    gathered again ;

There were *twenty* that joined in the
  hymn that was sung,
But ah ! for our song-bird we listened in
    vain, —
  The crystalline tones like a seraph's
    that rung !

How narrow the circle that holds us to-
    night !
  How many the loved ones that greet
    us no more,
As we meet like the stragglers that
    come from the fight,
  Like the mariners flung from a wreck
    on the shore !

We look through the twilight for those
    we have lost ;
  The stream rolls between us, and yet
    they seem near ;
Already outnumbered by those who
    have crossed,
  Our band is transplanted, its home is
    not here !

They smile on us still — is it only a
    dream ? —
  While fondly or proudly their names
    we recall —
They beckon — they come — they are
    crossing the stream —
  Lo ! the Shadows ! the Shadows !
    room — room for them all !

THE COMING ERA.

THEY tell us that the Muse is soon to
    fly hence,
  Leaving the bowers of song that were
    once dear,
Her robes bequeathing to her sister,
    Science,
  The groves of Pindus for the axe to
    clear.

Optics will claim the wandering eye of
    fancy,
  Physics will grasp imagination's
    wings,
Plain fact exorcise fiction's necromancy,
  The workshop hammer where the
    minstrel sings.

No more with laughter at Thalia's frolics
  Our eyes shall twinkle till the tears
    run down,
But in her place the lecturer on hy-
    draulics
  Spout forth his watery science to the
    town.

No more our foolish passions and affec-
    tions
  The tragic Muse with mimic grief
    shall try,
But, nobler far, a course of vivisec-
    tions
  Teach what it costs a tortured brute
    to die.

The unearthed monad, long in buried
    rocks hid,
  Shall tell the secret whence our being
    came ;
The chemist show us death is life's
    black oxide,
  Left when the breath no longer fans
    its flame.

Instead of cracked - brained poets in
    their attics
  Filling thin volumes with their flow-
    ery talk,
There shall be books of wholesome
    mathematics ;
  The tutor with his blackboard and his
    chalk.

No longer bards with madrigal and son-
    net
  Shall woo to moonlight walks the rib-
    boned sex,

But side by side the beaver and the bonnet
  Stroll, calmly pondering on some
  problem's x.

The sober bliss of serious calculation
  Shall mock the trivial joys that fancy
  drew,
And, oh, the rapture of a solved equa-
tion, —
  One self-same answer on the lips of
  two!

So speak in solemn tones our youthful
sages,
  Patient, severe, laborious, slow, ex-
  act,
As o'er creation's protoplasmic pages
  They browse and munch the thistle
  crops of fact.

And yet we've sometimes found it
rather pleasant
  To dream again the scenes that
  Shakespeare drew, —
To walk the hill-side with the Scottish
peasant
  Among the daisies wet with morn-
  ing's dew;

To leave awhile the daylight of the
real,
  Led by the guidance of the master's
  hand,
For the strange radiance of the far
ideal, —
  "The light that never was on sea or
  land."

Well, Time alone can lift the future's
curtain, —
  Science may teach our children all
  she knows,
But Love will kindle fresh young hearts,
'tis certain,
  And June will not forget her blushing rose.

And so, in spite of all that Time is
bringing, —
  Treasures of truth and miracles of art,
Beauty and Love will keep the poet singing,
  And song still live, the science of the
  heart.

IN RESPONSE.[1]

SUCH kindness! the scowl of a cynic
would soften,
  His pulse beat its way to some eloquent words,
Alas! my poor accents have echoed too
often,
  Like that Pinafore music you've
  some of you heard.

Do you know me, dear strangers — the
hundredth-time comer
  At banquets and feasts since the days
  of my Spring?
Ah! would I could borrow one rose of
my Summer,
  But this is a leaf of my Autumn I
  bring.

I look at your faces, — I'm sure there
are some from
  The three-breasted mother I count as
  my own;
You think you remember the place you
have come from,
  But how it has changed in the years
  that have flown!

Unaltered, 'tis true, is the hall we call
"Funnel,"
  Still fights the "Old South" in the
  battle for life,
But we've opened our door to the West
through the tunnel,
  And we've cut off Fort Hill with our
  Amazon knife.

[1] Breakfast at the Century Club, New York,
May, 1879.

You should see the new Westminster
    Boston has builded, —
  Its mansions, its spires, its museums
    of arts, —
You should see the great dome we have
    gorgeously gilded, —
  'T is the light of our eyes, 't is the
    joy of our hearts.

When first in his path a young asteroid
    found it,
  As he sailed through the skies with
    the stars in his wake,
He thought 't was the sun, and kept
    circling around it
  Till Edison signalled, " You 've made
    a mistake."

We are proud of our city, — her fast-
    growing figure,
  The warp and the woof of her brain
    and her hands, —
But we 're proudest of all that her heart
    has grown bigger,
  And warms with fresh blood as her
    girdle expands.

One lesson the rubric of conflict has
    taught her :
  Though parted awhile by war's earth-
    rending shock,
The lines that divide us are written in
    water,
  The love that unites us cut deep in
    the rock.

As well might the Judas of treason en-
    deavor
  To write his black name on the disk
    of the sun
As try the bright star-wreath that binds
    us to sever
  And blot the fair legend of " Many
    in One."

We love you, tall sister, the stately,
    the splendid, —

The banner of empire floats high on
    your towers,
Yet ever in welcome your arms are ex-
    tended, —
  We share in your splendors, your
    glory is ours.

Yes, Queen of the Continent ! All of
    us own thee, —
  The gold-freighted argosies flock at
    thy call,
The naiads, the sea-nymphs have met to
    enthrone thee,
  But the Broadway of one is the High-
    way of all !

— I thank you. Three words that can
    hardly be mended,
  Though phrases on phrases their elo-
    quence pile,
If you hear the heart's throb with their
    eloquence blended,
  And read all they mean in a sunshiny
    smile.

FOR THE MOORE CENTENNIAL CELEBRATION.

MAY 28, 1879.

I.

ENCHANTER of Erin, whose magic has
    bound us,
  Thy wand for one moment we fondly
    would claim,
Entranced while it summons the phan-
    toms around us
  That blush into life at the sound of
    thy name.

The tell-tales of memory wake from
    their slumbers, —
  I hear the old song with its tender re-
    frain, —
What passion lies hid in those honey-
    voiced numbers !
  What perfume of youth in each ex-
    quisite strain !

The home of my childhood comes back
　　as a vision, —
　Hark! Hark! A soft chord from its
　　song-haunted room, —
'T is a morning of May, when the air is
　　Elysian, —
　The syringa in bud and the lilac in
　　bloom, —

We are clustered around the "Clemen-
　　ti" piano, —
　There were six of us then, — there
　　are two of us now, —
She is singing, — the girl with the sil-
　　ver soprano, —
　How "The Lord of the Valley" was
　　false to his vow:

"Let Erin remember" the echoes are
　　calling:
　Through "The Vale of Avoca" the
　　waters are rolled:
"The Exile" laments while the night-
　　dews are falling:
　"The Morning of Life" dawns again
　　as of old.

But ah! those warm love-songs of fresh
　　adolescence!
　Around us such raptures celestial they
　　flung
That it seemed as if Paradise breathed
　　its quintessence
　Through the seraph-toned lips of the
　　maiden that sung!

Long hushed are the chords that my
　　boyhood enchanted
　As when the smooth wave by the an-
　　gel was stirred,
Yet still with their music is memory
　　haunted
　And oft in my dreams are their melo-
　　dies heard.

I feel like the priest to his altar return-
　　ing, —
　The crowd that was kneeling no
　　longer is there,
The flame has died down, but the brands
　　are still burning,
　And sandal and cinnamon sweeten the
　　air.

II.

The veil for her bridal young Summer
　　is weaving
　In her azure-domed hall with its tap-
　　estried floor,
And Spring the last tear-drop of May-
　　dew is leaving
　On the daisy of Burns and the sham-
　　rock of Moore.

How like, how unlike, as we view them
　　together,
　The song of the minstrels whose rec-
　　ord we scan, —
One fresh as the breeze blowing over
　　the heather, —
　One sweet as the breath from an oda-
　　lisque's fan!

Ah, passion can glow mid a palace's
　　splendor;
　The cage does not alter the song of
　　the bird;
And the curtain of silk has known whis-
　　pers as tender
　As ever the blossoming hawthorn has
　　heard.

No fear lest the step of the soft-slippered
　　Graces
　Should fright the young Loves from
　　their warm little nest,
For the heart of a queen, under jewels
　　and laces,
　Beats time with the pulse in the peas-
　　ant girl's breast!

Thrice welcome each gift of kind Nature's bestowing !
Her fountain heeds little the goblet we hold ;
Alike, when its musical waters are flowing,
The shell from the seaside, the chalice of gold.

The twins of the lyre to her voices had listened ;
Both laid their best gifts upon Liberty's shrine ;
For Coila's loved minstrel the holly-wreath glistened ;
For Erin's the rose and the myrtle entwine.

And while the fresh blossoms of summer are braided
For the sea-girdled, stream-silvered, lake-jewelled isle,
While her mantle of verdure is woven unfaded,
While Shannon and Liffey shall dimple and smile.

The land where the staff of Saint Patrick was planted,
Where the shamrock grows green from the cliffs to the shore,
The land of fair maidens and heroes undaunted,
Shall wreathe her bright harp with the garlands of Moore !

TO JAMES FREEMAN CLARKE.

APRIL 4, 1880.

I BRING the simplest pledge of love,
Friend of my earlier days ;
Mine is the hand without the glove,
The heart-beat, not the phrase.

How few still breathe this mortal air
We called by schoolboy names !
You still, whatever robe you wear,
To me are always James.

That name the kind apostle bore
Who shames the sullen creeds,
Not trusting less, but loving more,
And showing faith by deeds.

What blending thoughts our memories share !
What visions yours and mine
Of May-days in whose morning air
The dews were golden wine,

Of vistas bright with opening day,
Whose all-awakening sun
Showed in life's landscape, far away,
The summits to be won !

The heights are gained. — Ah, say not so
For him who smiles at time,
Leaves his tired comrades down below,
And only lives to climb !

His labors, — will they ever cease, —
With hand and tongue and pen ?
Shall wearied Nature ask release
At threescore years and ten ?

Our strength the clustered seasons tax,—
For him new life they mean ;
Like rods around the lictor's axe
They keep him bright and keen.

The wise, the brave, the strong, we know, —
We mark them here or there,
But he, — we roll our eyes, and lo !
We find him everywhere !

With truth's bold cohorts, or alone,
He strides through error's field ;
His lance is ever manhood's own,
His breast is woman's shield.

Count not his years while earth has
　　need
Of souls that Heaven inflames
With sacred zeal to save, to lead, —
Long live our dear Saint James !

WELCOME TO THE CHICAGO COMMERCIAL CLUB.

JANUARY 14, 1880.

CHICAGO sounds rough to the maker of
　　verse ;
One comfort we have — Cincinnati
　　sounds worse ;
If we only were licensed to say Chi-
　　cagó !
But Worcester and Webster won't let
　　us, you know.

No matter, we songsters must sing as
　　we can ;
We can make some nice couplets with
　　Lake Michigan,
And what more resembles a nightin-
　　gale's voice,
Than the oily trisyllable, sweet Illinois ?

Your waters are fresh, while our har-
　　bor is salt,
But we know you can't help it — it is n't
　　your fault ;
Our city is old and your city is new,
But the railroad men tell us we 're
　　greener than you.

You have seen our gilt dome, and no
　　doubt you 've been told
That the orbs of the universe round
　　it are rolled ;
But I 'll own it to you, and I ought to
　　know best,
That this is n't quite true of all stars of
　　the West.

You 'll go to Mount Auburn — we 'll
　　show you the track, —

And can stay there, — unless you pre-
　　fer to come back ;
And Bunker's tall shaft you can climb
　　if you will,
But you 'll puff like a paragraph prais-
　　ing a pill.

You must see — but you *have* seen —
　　our old Faneuil Hall,
Our churches, our school-rooms, our
　　sample-rooms, all ;
And, perhaps, though the idiots must
　　have their jokes,
You have found our good people much
　　like other folks.

There are cities by rivers, by lakes and
　　by seas,
Each as full of itself as a cheese-mite of
　　cheese ;
And a city will brag as a game-cock
　　will crow :
Don't your cockerels at home — just a
　　little, you know ?

But we 'll crow for you now — here 's a
　　health to the boys,
Men, maidens, and matrons of fair Illi-
　　nois,
And the rainbow of friendship that
　　arches its span
From the green of the sea to the blue
　　Michigan !

AMERICAN ACADEMY CENTEN-NIAL CELEBRATION.

MAY 26, 1880.

SIRE, son, and grandson ; so the century
　　glides ;
　　Three lives, three strides, three foot-
　　　prints in the sand ;
Silent as midnight's falling meteor
　　slides
　　Into the stillness of the far-off land ;
　　How dim the space its little arc has
　　　spanned !

See on this opening page the names re-
    nowned
    Tombed in these records on our dusty
        shelves,
Scarce on the scroll of living memory
        found,
    Save where the wan-eyed antiquarian
        delves;
    Shadows they seem; ah, what are we
        ourselves?

Pale ghosts of Bowdoin, Winthrop,
        Willard, West,
    Sages of busy brain and wrinkled
        brow,
Searchers of Nature's secrets uncon-
        fessed,
    Asking of all things Whence and
        Why and How —
    What problems meet your larger vis-
        ion now?

Has Gannett tracked the wild Aurora's
        path?
    Has Bowdoin found his all-surround-
        ing sphere?
What question puzzles ciphering Philo-
        math?
    Could Williams make the hidden
        causes clear
    Of the Dark Day that filled the land
        with fear?

Dear ancient schoolboys! Nature taught
        to them
    The simple lessons of the star and
        flower,
Showed them strange sights; how on a
        single stem, —
    Admire the marvels of Creative Pow-
        er! —
    Twin apples grew, one sweet, the
        other sour,

How from the hill-top where our eyes
        behold

In even ranks the plumed and ban-
        nered maize
Range its long columns, in the days of
        old
    The live volcano shot its angry
        blaze, —
    Dead since the showers of Noah's
        watery days;

How, when the lightning split the
        mighty rock,
    The spreading fury of the shaft was
        spent!
How the young scion joined the alien
        stock,
    And when and where the homeless
        swallows went
    To pass the winter of their discontent.

Scant were the gleanings in those years
        of dearth;
    No Cuvier yet had clothed the fossil
        bones
That slumbered, waiting for their sec-
        ond birth;
    No Lyell read the legend of the
        stones;
    Science still pointed to her empty
        thrones.

Dreaming of orbs to eyes of earth un-
        known,
    Herschel looked heavenwards in the
        starlight pale;
Lost in those awful depths he trod alone,
    Laplace stood mute before the lifted
        veil;
    While home-bred Humboldt trimmed
        his toy ship's sail.

No mortal feet these loftier heights had
        gained
    Whence the wide realms of Nature
        we descry;
In vain their eyes our longing fathers
        strained

To scan with wondering gaze the
summits high
That far beneath their children's foot-
paths lie.

Smile at their first small ventures as we
may,
The school - boy's copy shapes the
scholar's hand,
Their grateful memory fills our hearts
to-day;
Brave, hopeful, wise, this bower of
peace they planned,
While war's dread ploughshare scarred
the suffering land.

Child of our children's children yet unborn,
When on this yellow page you turn
your eyes,
Where the brief record of this May-day
morn
In phrase antique and faded letters lies,
How vague, how pale our flitting
ghosts will rise!

Yet in our veins the blood ran warm
and red,
For us the fields were green, the skies
were blue,
Though from our dust the spirit long
has fled,
We lived, we loved, we toiled, we
dreamed like you,
Smiled at our sires and thought how
much we knew.

Oh might our spirits for one hour return,
When the next century rounds its
hundredth ring,
All the strange secrets it shall teach to
learn,
To hear the larger truths its years
shall bring,
Its wiser sages talk, its sweeter minstrels sing!

THE SCHOOL - BOY.

READ AT THE CENTENNIAL CELEBRA-
TION OF THE FOUNDATION OF PHILLIPS
ACADEMY, ANDOVER.

1778–1878.

THESE hallowed precincts, long to mem-
ory dear,
Smile with fresh welcome as our feet
draw near;
With softer gales the opening leaves
are fanned,
With fairer hues the kindling flowers
expand,
The rose-bush reddens with the blush of
June,
The groves are vocal with their min-
strels' tune,
The mighty elm, beneath whose arching
shade
The wandering children of the forest
strayed,
Greets the bright morning in its bridal
dress,
And spreads its arms the gladsome
dawn to bless.
Is it an idle dream that nature shares
Our joys, our griefs, our pastimes, and
our cares?
Is there no summons when, at morning's
call,
The sable vestments of the darkness
fall?
Does not meek evening's low-voiced *Ave*
blend
With the soft vesper as its notes ascend?
Is there no whisper in the perfumed air
When the sweet bosom of the rose is
bare?
Does not the sunshine call us to rejoice?
Is there no meaning in the storm-cloud's
voice?
No silent message when from midnight
skies
Heaven looks upon us with its myriad
eyes?

Or shift the mirror; say our dreams diffuse
O'er life's pale landscape their celestial hues,
Lend heaven the rainbow it has never known,
And robe the earth in glories not its own,
Sing their own music in the summer breeze,
With fresher foliage clothe the stately trees,
Stain the June blossoms with a livelier dye
And spread a bluer azure on the sky, —
Blest be the power that works its lawless will
And finds the weediest patch an Eden still ;
No walls so fair as those our fancies build, —
No views so bright as those our visions gild !

So ran my lines, as pen and paper met,
The truant goose-quill travelling like Planchette;
Too ready servant, whose deceitful ways
Full many a slipshod line, alas ! betrays ;
Hence of the rhyming thousand not a few
Have builded worse — a great deal — than they knew.

What need of idle fancy to adorn
Our mother's birthplace on her birth-day morn ?
Hers are the blossoms of eternal spring,
From these green boughs her new-fledged birds take wing,
These echoes hear their earliest carols sung,
In this old nest the brood is ever young.
If some tired wanderer, resting from his flight,

Amid the gay young choristers alight,
These gather round him, mark his faded plumes
That faintly still the far-off grove perfumes,
And listen, wondering if some feeble note
Yet lingers, quavering in his weary throat :—
I, whose fresh voice yon red-faced temple knew,
What tune is left me, fit to sing to you ?
Ask not the grandeurs of a labored song,
But let my easy couplets slide along ;
Much could I tell you that you know too well ;
Much I remember, but I will not tell ;
Age brings experience; graybeards oft are wise,
But oh ! how sharp a youngster's ears and eyes !

My cheek was bare of adolescent down
When first I sought the academic town ;
Slow rolls the coach along the dusty road,
Big with its filial and parental load ;
The frequent hills, the lonely woods are past,
The school-boy's chosen home is reached at last.
I see it now, the same unchanging spot,
The swinging gate, the little garden plot,
The narrow yard, the rock that made its floor,
The flat, pale house, the knocker-garnished door,
The small, trim parlor, neat, decorous, chill,
The strange, new faces, kind, but grave and still ;
Two, creased with age, — or what I then called age, —

Life's volume open at its fiftieth page ;
One, a shy maiden's, pallid, placid, sweet
As the first snow-drop, which the sun-beams greet ;
One the last nursling's ; slight she was, and fair,
Her smooth white forehead warmed with auburn hair ;
Last came the virgin Hymen long had spared,
Whose daily cares the grateful house-hold shared,
Strong, patient, humble ; her substan-tial frame
Stretched the chaste draperies I forbear to name.
  Brave, but with effort, had the school-boy come
To the cold comfort of a stranger's home ;
How like a dagger to my sinking heart
Came the dry summons, " It is time to part ;
" Good - by ! " " Goo — ood - by ! " one fond maternal kiss. . . .
Homesick as death ! Was ever pang like this ? . . .
Too young as yet with willing feet to stray
From the tame fireside, glad to get away, —
Too old to let my watery grief appear,—
And what so bitter as a swallowed tear !
  One figure still my vagrant thoughts pursue ;
First boy to greet me, Ariel, where are you ?
Imp of all mischief, heaven alone knows how
You learned it all, — are you an angel now,
Or tottering gently down the slope of years,
Your face grown sober in the vale of tears ?

Forgive my freedom if you are breath-ing still ;
If in a happier world, I know you will.
You were a school-boy — what beneath the sun
So like a monkey ? I was also one.
  Strange, sure enough, to see what cu-rious shoots
The nursery raises from the study's roots !
In those old days the very, very good
Took up more room — a little — than they should ;
Something too much one's eyes encoun-tered then
Of serious youth and funeral - visaged men ;
The solemn elders saw life's mournful half, —
Heaven sent this boy, whose mission was to laugh,
Drollest of buffos, Nature's odd protest,
A catbird squealing in a blackbird's nest.
  Kind, faithful Nature ! While the sour-eyed Scot, —
Her cheerful smiles forbidden or for-got, —
Talks only of his preacher and his kirk,—
Hears five-hour sermons for his Sunday work, —
Praying and fasting till his meagre face
Gains its due length, the genuine sign of grace, —
An Ayrshire mother in the land of Knox
Her embryo poet in his cradle rocks ;—
Nature, long shivering in her dim eclipse,
Steals in a sunbeam to those baby lips ;
So to its home her banished smile re-turns,
And Scotland sweetens with the song of Burns !
  The morning came ; I reached the classic hall ;
A clock-face eyed me, staring from the wall ;

Beneath its hands a printed line I read :
YOUTH IS LIFE'S SEED–TIME : so the
    clock-face said :
Some took its counsel, as the sequel
    showed, —
Sowed, — their wild oats, — and reaped
    as they had sowed.

  How all comes back ! the upward
    slanting floor, —
The masters' thrones that flank the cen-
    tral door, —
The long, outstretching alleys that di-
    vide
The rows of desks that stand on either
    side, —
The staring boys, a face to every desk,
Bright, dull, pale, blooming, common,
    picturesque.

  Grave is the Master's look ; his fore-
    head wears
Thick rows of wrinkles, prints of worry-
    ing cares ;
Uneasy lie the heads of all that rule,
His most of all whose kingdom is a
    school.
Supreme he sits ; before the awful frown
That bends his brows the boldest eye
    goes down ;
Not more submissive Israel heard and
    saw
At Sinai's foot the Giver of the Law.

  Less stern he seems, who sits in equal
    state
On the twin throne and shares the em-
    pire's weight ;
Around his lips the subtle life that plays
Steals quaintly forth in many a jesting
    phrase ;
A lightsome nature, not so hard to
    chafe,
Pleasant when pleased ; rough-handled,
    not so safe ;
Some tingling memories vaguely I re-
    call,
But to forgive him.   God forgive us
    all !

One yet remains, whose well-remem-
    bered name
Pleads in my grateful heart its tender
    claim ;
His was the charm magnetic, the bright
    look
That sheds its sunshine on the dreariest
    book ;
A loving soul to every task he brought
That sweetly mingled with the lore he
    taught ;
Sprung from a saintly race that never
    could
From youth to age be anything but
    good,
His few brief years in holiest labors
    spent,
Earth lost too soon the treasure heaven
    had lent.
Kindest of teachers, studious to divine
Some hint of promise in my earliest
    line,
These faint and faltering words thou
    canst not hear
Throb from a heart that holds thy mem-
    ory dear.

  As to the traveller's eye the varied
    plain
Shows through the window of the flying
    train,
A mingled landscape, rather felt than
    seen,
A gravelly bank, a sudden flash of green,
A tangled wood, a glittering stream that
    flows
Through the cleft summit where the
    cliff once rose,
All strangely blended in a hurried
    gleam,
Rock, wood, waste, meadow, village,
    hill-side, stream, —
So, as we look behind us, life appears,
Seen through the vista of our bygone
    years.

  Yet in the dead past's shadow-filled
    domain,

Some vanished shapes the hues of life
    retain ;
Unbidden, oft, before our dreaming
    eyes
From the vague mists in memory's path
    they rise.
So comes his blooming image to my
    view,
The friend of joyous days when life
    was new,
Hope yet untamed, the blood of youth
    unchilled,
No blank arrear of promise unfulfilled,
Life's flower yet hidden in its sheltering
    fold,
Its pictured canvas yet to be unrolled.
His the frank smile I vainly look to
    greet,
His the warm grasp my clasping hand
    should meet ;
How would our lips renew their school-
    boy talk,
Our feet retrace the old familiar
    walk !
For thee no more earth's cheerful morn-
    ing shines
Through the green fringes of the tented
    pines ;
Ah me ! is heaven so far thou canst not
    hear,
Or is thy viewless spirit hovering near,
A fair young presence, bright with
    morning's glow,
The fresh-cheeked boy of fifty years
    ago ?
  Yes, fifty years, with all their circling
    suns,
Behind them all my glance reverted
    runs ;
Where now that time remote, its griefs,
    its joys,
Where are its gray - haired men, its
    bright-haired boys ?
Where is the patriarch time could hardly
    tire, —
The good old, wrinkled, immemorial
    " squire " ?

(An honest treasurer, like a black-
    plumed swan,
Not every day our eyes may look upon.)
Where the tough champion who, with
    Calvin's sword,
In wordy conflicts battled for the Lord ?
Where the grave scholar, lonely, calm,
    austere,
Whose voice like music charmed the
    listening ear,
Whose light rekindled, like the morn.
    ing star
Still shines upon us through the gates
    ajar ?
Where the still, solemn, weary, sad-eyed
    man,
Whose care-worn face my wandering
    eyes would scan, —
His features wasted in the lingering
    strife
With the pale foe that drains the stu-
    dent's life ?
Where my old friend, the scholar, teach-
    er, saint,
Whose creed, some hinted, showed a
    speck of taint ;
He broached his own opinion, which is
    not
Lightly to be forgiven or forgot ;
Some riddle's point, — I scarce remem-
    ber now, —
Homo*i*, perhaps, where they said homo
    —ou.
(If the unlettered greatly wish to know
Where lies the difference betwixt *oi*
    and *o*,
Those of the curious who have time may
    search
Among the stale conundrums of their
    church.)
Beneath his roof his peaceful life I
    shared,
And for his modes of faith I little cared,-
I, taught to judge men's dogmas by
    their deeds,
Long ere the days of india - rubber
    creeds.

Why should we look one common
    faith to find,
Where one in every score is color-blind?
If here on earth they know not red
    from green,
Will they see better into things unseen!
    Once more to time's old graveyard I
        return
And scrape the moss from memory's
    pictured urn.
Who, in these days when all things go
    by steam
Recalls the stage-coach with its four-
    horse team?
Its sturdy driver, — who remembers
    him?
Or the old landlord, saturnine and grim,
Who left our hill-top for a new abode
And reared his sign-post farther down
    the road?
Still in the waters of the dark Shaw-
    shine
Do the young bathers splash and think
    they 're clean?
Do pilgrims find their way to Indian
    Ridge,
Or journey onward to the far-off bridge,
And bring to younger ears the story
    back
Of the broad stream, the mighty Merri-
    mac?
Are there still truant feet that stray
    beyond
These circling bounds to Pomp's or
    Haggett's Pond,
Or where the legendary name recalls
The forest's earlier tenant, — " Deer-
    jump Falls " ?
    Yes, every nook these youthful feet
        explore,
Just as our sires and grandsires did of
    yore ;
So all life's opening paths, where na-
    ture led
Their father's feet, the children's chil-
    dren tread.

Roll the round century's five score years
    away,
Call from our storied past that earliest
    day
When great Eliphalet (I can see him
    now, —
Big name, big frame, big voice, and
    beetling brow),
Then *young* Eliphalet, — ruled the rows
    of boys
In homespun gray or old-world cordu-
    roys, —
And save for fashion's whims, the
    benches show
The self-same youths, the very boys we
    know.
Time works strange marvels : since I
    trod the green
And swung the gates, what wonders I
    have seen !
But come what will, — the sky itself
    may fall —
As things of course the boy accepts them
    all.
The prophet's chariot, drawn by steeds
    of flame,
For daily use our travelling millions
    claim ;
The face we love a sunbeam makes our
    own ;
No more the surgeon hears the suffer-
    er's groan ;
What unwrit histories wrapped in dark-
    ness lay
Till shovelling Schliemann bared them
    to the day !
Your Richelieu says, and says it well,
    my lord,
The pen is (sometimes) mightier than
    the sword ;
Great is the goosequill, say we all ;
    Amen !
Sometimes the spade is mightier than
    the pen ;
It shows where Babel's terraced walls
    were raised,

THE SCHOOL BOY. Page 349.

The slabs that cracked when Nimrod's
palace blazed,
Unearths Mycenæ, rediscovers Troy, —
Calmly he listens, that immortal boy.
A new Prometheus tips our wands with
fire,
A mightier Orpheus strains the whis-
pering wire,
Whose lightning thrills the lazy winds
outrun
And hold the hours as Joshua stayed
the sun, —
So swift, in truth, we hardly find a
place
For those dim fictions known as time
and space.
Still a new miracle each year sup-
plies, —
See at his work the chemist of the
skies,
Who questions Sirius in his tortured
rays
And steals the secret of the solar
blaze ;
Hush ! while the window-rattling bugles
play
The nation's airs a hundred miles away !
That wicked phonograph ! hark ! how
it swears !
Turn it again and make it say its pray-
ers !
And was it true, then, what the story
said
Of Oxford's friar and his brazen head ?
While wondering Science stands, herself
perplexed
At each day's miracle, and asks " What
next ? "
The immortal boy, the coming heir of
all,
Springs from his desk to " urge the fly-
ing ball,"
Cleaves with his bending oar the glassy
waves,
With sinewy arm the dashing current
braves,

The same bright creature in these haunts
of ours
That Eton shadowed with her " antique
towers."

Boy ! Where is he ? the long-limbed
youth inquires,
Whom his rough chin with manly pride
inspires ;
Ah, when the ruddy cheek no longer
glows,
When the bright hair is white as winter
snows,
When the dim eye has lost its lambent
flame,
Sweet to his ear will be his school-boy
name !
Nor think the difference mighty as it
seems
Between life's morning and its evening
dreams ;
Fourscore, like twenty, has its tasks
and toys ;
In earth's wide school-house all are girls
and boys.

Brothers, forgive my wayward fancy.
Who
Can guess beforehand what his pen will
do ?
Too light my strain for listeners such as
these,
Whom graver thoughts and soberer
speech shall please.
Is he not here whose breath of holy
song
Has raised the downcast eyes of Faith
so long ?
Are they not here, the strangers in your
gates,
For whom the wearied ear impatient
waits, —
The large-brained scholars whom their
toils release, —
The bannered heralds of the Prince of
Peace ?

Such was the gentle friend whose
    youth unblamed
In years long past our student-benches
    claimed ;
Whose name, illumined on the sacred
    page,
Lives in the labors of his riper age ;
Such he whose record time's destroying
    march
Leaves uneffaced on Zion's springing
    arch :
Not to the scanty phrase of measured
    song,
Cramped in its fetters, names like these
    belong ;
One ray they lend to gild my slender
    line —
Their praise I leave to sweeter lips than
    mine.

Homes of our sires, where Learning's
    temple rose,
While yet they struggled with their
    banded foes,
As in the West thy century's sun de-
    scends,
One parting gleam its dying radiance
    lends.
Darker and deeper though the shadows
    fall
From the gray towers on Doubting
    Castle's wall,
Though Pope and Pagan re-array their
    hosts,
And her new armor youthful Science
    boasts,
Truth, for whose altar rose this holy
    shrine,
Shall fly for refuge to these bowers of
    thine ;
No past shall chain her with its rusted
    vow,
No Jew's phylactery bind her Christian
    brow,
But Faith shall smile to find her sister
    free,

And nobler manhood draw its life from
    thee.

Long as the arching skies above thee
    spread,
As on thy groves the dews of heaven
    are shed,
With currents widening still from year
    to year,
And deepening channels, calm, un-
    troubled, clear,
Flow the twin streamlets from thy sa-
    cred hill —
Pieria's fount and Siloam's shaded
    rill !

THE SILENT MELODY.

"Bring me my broken harp," he said ;
    "We both are wrecks, — but as ye
        will, —
    Though all its ringing tones have
        fled,
        Their echoes linger round it still ;
    It had some golden strings, I know,
    But that was long, — how long ! —
        ago.

"I cannot see its tarnished gold,
        I cannot hear its vanished tone,
    Scarce can my trembling fingers hold
        The pillared frame so long their
            own ;
        We both are wrecks, — a while ago
        It had some silver strings, I know,

"But on them Time too long has played
        The solemn strain that knows no
            change,
        And where of old my fingers strayed
        The chords they find are new and
            strange, —
        Yes ! iron strings, — I know, — I
            know, —
    We both are wrecks of long ago.

" We both are wrecks, — a shattered
pair, —
Strange to ourselves in time's dis-
guise . . .
What say ye to the lovesick air
That brought the tears from Ma-
rian's eyes ?
Ay ! trust me, — under breasts of
snow
Hearts could be melted long ago !

" Or will ye hear the storm-song's crash
That from his dreams the soldier
woke,
And bade him face the lightning flash
When battle's cloud in thunder
broke ? . . .
Wrecks, — nought but wrecks ! — the
time was when
We two were worth a thousand men ! "

And so the broken harp they bring
With pitying smiles that none could
blame ;
Alas ! there 's not a single string
Of all that filled the tarnished
frame !
But see ! like children overjoyed,
His fingers rambling through the
void !

'I clasp thee ! Ay . . . mine ancient
lyre . . .
Nay, guide my wandering fingers.
. . . There !

They love to dally with the wire
As Isaac played with Esau's
hair. . . .
Hush ! ye shall hear the famous
tune
That Marian called the Breath of
June ! "

And so they softly gather round :
Rapt in his tuneful trance he
seems :
His fingers move : but not a sound !
A silence like the song of dreams. . . .
" There ! ye have heard the air," he
cries,
" That brought the tears from Marian's
eyes ! "

Ah, smile not at his fond conceit,
Nor deem his fancy wrought in
vain ;
To him the unreal sounds are sweet,—
No discord mars the silent strain
Scored on life's latest, starlit page —
The voiceless melody of age.

Sweet are the lips of all that sing,
When Nature's music breathes un-
sought,
But never yet could voice or string
So truly shape our tenderest
thought
As when by life's decaying fire
Our fingers sweep the stringless
lyre !

BEFORE THE CURFEW

AND OTHER POEMS.

AT MY FIRESIDE.

ALONE, beneath the darkened sky,
  With saddened heart and unstrung lyre,
I heap the spoils of years gone by,
And leave them with a long-drawn sigh,
Like drift-wood brands that glimmering
    lie,
  Before the ashes hide the fire.

Let not these slow declining days
  The rosy light of dawn outlast ;
Still round my lonely hearth it plays,
And gilds the east with borrowed rays,
While memory's mirrored sunset blaze
  Flames on the windows of the past.

March 1, 1888.

BEFORE THE CURFEW.

1829–1882.

NOTE. — The poems marked thus, 1829–1882,
etc., were written for and read at the annual meet-
ings of the class which graduated at Harvard University in 1829.

NOT bed-time yet !   The night-winds
    blow,
The stars are out, — full well we know
  The nurse is on the stair,
With hand of ice and cheek of snow,
And frozen lips that whisper low,
" Come, children, it is time to go
  My peaceful couch to share."

No years a wakeful heart can tire ;
Not bed-time yet !   Come, stir the fire
  And warm your dear old hands ;
Kind Mother Earth we love so well
Has pleasant stories yet to tell
Before we hear the curfew bell ;
  Still glow the burning brands.

Not bed-time yet !   We long to know
What wonders time has yet to show,
  What unborn years shall bring ;
What ship the Arctic pole shall reach,
What lessons Science waits to teach,
What sermons there are left to preach,
  What poems yet to sing.

What next ? we ask ; and is it true
The sunshine falls on nothing new,
  As Israel's king declared ?
Was ocean ploughed with harnessed fire ?
Were nations coupled with a wire ?
Did Tarshish telegraph to Tyre ?
  How Hiram would have stared !

And what if Sheba's curious queen,
Who came to see, — and to be seen, —
  Or something new to seek,
And swooned, as ladies sometimes do,
At sights that thrilled her through and
    through,
Had heard, as she was " coming to,"
  A locomotive's shriek,

And seen a rushing railway train
As she looked out along the plain

From David's lofty tower, —
A mile of smoke that blots the sky
And blinds the eagles as they fly
Behind the cars that thunder by
    A score of leagues an hour!

See to my *fiat lux* respond
This little slumbering fire-tipped wand, —
    One touch, — it bursts in flame!
Steal me a portrait from the sun, —
One look, — and lo! the picture done!
Are these old tricks, King Solomon,
    We lying moderns claim?

Could you have spectroscoped a star?
If both those mothers at your bar,
    The cruel and the mild,
The young and tender, old and tough,
Had said, "Divide, — you 're right, though
        rough," —
Did old Judea know enough
    To etherize the child?

These births of time our eyes have seen,
With but a few brief years between;
    What wonder if the text,
For other ages doubtless true,
For coming years will never do, —
Whereof we all should like a few
    If but to see what next.

If such things have been, such may
        be;
Who would not like to live and see —
    If Heaven may so ordain —
What waifs undreamed of, yet in store,
The waves that roll forevermore
On life's long beach may cast ashore
    From out the mist-clad main?

Will Earth to pagan dreams return
To find from misery's painted urn
    That all save hope has flown, —
Of Book and Church and Priest bereft,
The Rock of Ages vainly cleft,
Life's compass gone, its anchor left,
    Left, — lost, — in depths unknown?

Shall Faith the trodden path pursue
The *crux ansata* wearers knew
    Who sleep with folded hands,
Where, like a naked, lidless eye,
The staring Nile rolls wandering by
Those mountain slopes that climb the sky
    Above the drifting sands?

Or shall a nobler Faith return,
Its fanes a purer gospel learn,
    With holier anthems ring,
And teach us that our transient creeds
Were but the perishable seeds
Of harvests sown for larger needs,
    That ripening years shall bring?

Well, let the present do its best,
We trust our Maker for the rest,
    As on our way we plod;
Our souls, full dressed in fleshly suits,
Love air and sunshine, flowers and fruits,
The daisies better than their roots
    Beneath the grassy sod.

Not bed-time yet! The full-blown flower
Of all the year — this evening hour —
    With friendship's flame is bright;
Life still is sweet, the heavens are fair,
Though fields are brown and woods are
        bare,
And many a joy is left to share
    Before we say Good-night!

And when, our cheerful evening past,
The nurse, long waiting, comes at last,
    Ere on her lap we lie
In wearied nature's sweet repose,
At peace with all her waking foes,
Our lips shall murmur, ere they close,
    Good-night! and not Good-by!

A LOVING-CUP SONG.

1829–1883.

COME, heap the fagots! Ere we go
Again the cheerful hearth shall glow;

We'll have another blaze, my boys!
When clouds are black and snows are
     white,
Then Christmas logs lend ruddy light
    They stole from summer days, my boys,
       They stole from summer days.

And let the Loving-Cup go round,
The Cup with blessed memories crowned,
    That flows whene'er we meet, my boys;
No draught will hold a drop of sin
If love is only well stirred in
    To keep it sound and sweet, my boys,
       To keep it sound and sweet.

Give me, to pin upon my breast,
The blossoms twain I love the best,
    A rosebud and a pink, my boys;
Their leaves shall nestle next my heart,
Their perfumed breath shall own its part
    In every health we drink, my boys,
       In every health we drink.

The breathing blossoms stir my blood,
Methinks I see the lilacs bud
    And hear the bluebirds sing, my boys;
Why not?   Yon lusty oak has seen
Full tenscore years, yet leaflets green
    Peep out with every spring, my boys,
       Peep out with every spring.

Old Time his rusty scythe may whet,
The unmowed grass is glowing yet
    Beneath the sheltering snow, my boys;
And if the crazy dotard ask,
Is love worn out?   Is life a task?
    We'll bravely answer No! my boys,
       We'll bravely answer No!

For life's bright taper is the same
Love tipped of old with rosy flame
    That heaven's own altar lent, my boys,
To glow in every cup we fill
Till lips are mute and hearts are still,
    Till life and love are spent, my boys,
       Till life and love are spent.

THE GIRDLE OF FRIENDSHIP.

1829–1884.

She gathered at her slender waist
    The beauteous robe she wore;
Its folds a golden belt embraced,
    One rose-hued gem it bore.

The girdle shrank; its lessening round
    Still kept the shining gem,
But now her flowing locks it bound,
    A lustrous diadem.

And narrower still the circlet grew
    Behold! a glittering band,
Its roseate diamond set anew,
    Her neck's white column spanned.

Suns rise and set; the straining clasp
    The shortened links resist,
Yet flashes in a bracelet's grasp
    The diamond, on her wrist.

At length, the round of changes past
    The thieving years could bring,
The jewel, glittering to the last,
    Still sparkles in a ring.

So, link by link, our friendships part,
    So loosen, break, and fall,
A narrowing zone; the loving heart
    Lives changeless through them all.

THE LYRE OF ANACREON.

1829–1885.

The minstrel of the classic lay
    Of love and wine who sings
Still found the fingers run astray
    That touched the rebel strings.

Of Cadmus he would fain have sung,
    Of Atreus and his line;
But all the jocund echoes rung
    With songs of love and wine.

Ah, brothers! I would fain have caught
　　Some fresher fancy's gleam;
My truant accents find, unsought,
　　The old familiar theme.

Love, Love! but not the sportive child
　　With shaft and twanging bow,
Whose random arrows drove us wild
　　Some threescore years ago;

Not Eros, with his joyous laugh,
　　The urchin blind and bare,
But Love, with spectacles and staff,
　　And scanty, silvered hair.

Our heads with frosted locks are white,
　　Our roofs are thatched with snow,
But red, in chilling winter's spite,
　　Our hearts and hearthstones glow.

Our old acquaintance, Time, drops in,
　　And while the running sands
Their golden thread unheeded spin,
　　He warms his frozen hands.

Stay, wingèd hours, too swift, too sweet,
　　And waft this message o'er
To all we miss, from all we meet
　　On life's fast-crumbling shore:

Say that, to old affection true,
　　We hug the narrowing chain
That binds our hearts, — alas, how few
　　The links that yet remain!

The fatal touch awaits them all
　　That turns the rocks to dust;
From year to year they break and
　　　fall, —
They break, but never rust.

Say if one note of happier strain
　　This worn-out harp afford, —
One throb that trembles, not in vain, —
　　Their memory lent its chord.

Say that when Fancy closed her wings
　　And Passion quenched his fire,
Love, Love, still echoed from the strings
　　As from Anacreon's lyre!

THE OLD TUNE.

THIRTY–SIXTH VARIATION.

1829–1886.

This shred of song you bid me bring
　　Is snatched from fancy's embers;
Ah, when the lips forget to sing,
　　The faithful heart remembers!

Too swift the wings of envious Time
　　To wait for dallying phrases,
Or woven strands of labored rhyme
　　To thread their cunning mazes.

A word, a sigh, and lo, how plain
　　Its magic breath discloses
Our life's long vista through a lane
　　Of threescore summers' roses!

One language years alone can teach:
　　Its roots are young affections
That feel their way to simplest speech
　　Through silent recollections.

That tongue is ours. How few the words
　　We need to know a brother!
As simple are the notes of birds,
　　Yet well they know each other.

This freezing month of ice and snow
　　That brings our lives together
Lends to our year a living glow
　　That warms its wintry weather.

So let us meet as eve draws nigh,
　　And life matures and mellows,
Till Nature whispers with a sigh,
　　"Good-night, my dear old fellows!"

THE BROKEN CIRCLE.

1829–1887.

I STOOD on Sarum's treeless plain,
  The waste that careless Nature owns ;
Lone tenants of her bleak domain,
  Loomed huge and gray the Druid
    stones.

Upheaved in many a billowy mound
  The sea-like, naked turf arose,
Where wandering flocks went nibbling
  round
  The mingled graves of friends and
    foes.

The Briton, Roman, Saxon, Dane,
  This windy desert roamed in turn ;
Unmoved these mighty blocks remain
  Whose story none that lives may learn.

Erect, half buried, slant or prone,
  These awful listeners, blind and dumb,
Hear the strange tongues of tribes un-
  known,
  As wave on wave they go and come.

"Who are you, giants, whence and
  why ?"
  I stand and ask in blank amaze ;
My soul accepts their mute reply :
  "A mystery, as are you that gaze.

"A silent Orpheus wrought the charm
  From riven rocks their spoils to bring ;
A nameless Titan lent his arm
  To range us in our magic ring.

"But Ti__ __ith still and stealthy stride,
  Tha__ __d treads and levels all,
Tha__ __ing keystone slide,
  __ the crumbling

  __ied past,
  __ss the

They slant, they stoop, they fall at last,
  And strew the turf their priests have
    trod.

"No more our altar's wreath of smoke
  Floats up with morning's fragrant dew ;
The fires are dead, the ring is broke,
  Where stood the many stand the few."

— My thoughts had wandered far away,
  Borne off on Memory's outspread wing,
To where in deepening twilight lay
  The wrecks of friendship's broken ring.

Ah me ! of all our goodly train
  How few will find our banquet hall !
Yet why with coward lips complain
  That this must lean, and that must
    fall ?

Cold is the Druid's altar-stone,
  Its vanished flame no more returns ;
But ours no chilling damp has known, —
  Unchanged, unchanging, still it burns.

So let our broken circle stand
  A wreck, a remnant, yet the same,
While one last, loving, faithful hand
  Still lives to feed its altar-flame !

THE ANGEL-THIEF.

1829–1888.

TIME is a thief who leaves his tools be-
  hind him ;
  He comes by night, he vanishes at
    dawn ;
We track his footsteps, but we never find
  him :
  Strong locks are broken, massive bolts
    are drawn,

And all around are left the bars and
  borers,
  The splitting wedges and the prying
    keys,

Such aids as serve the soft-shod vault-
explorers
    To crack, wrench open, rifle as they
please.

Ah, these are tools which Heaven in
mercy lends us!
    When gathering rust has clenched our
shackles fast,
Time is the angel-thief that Nature sends
us
    To break the cramping fetters of our
past.

Mourn as we may for treasures he has
taken,
    Poor as we feel of hoarded wealth
bereft,
More precious are those implements forsaken,
    Found in the wreck his ruthless hands
have left.

Some lever that a casket's hinge has
broken
    Pries off a bolt, and lo! our souls are
free;
Each year some Open Sesame is spoken,
    And every decade drops its master-
key.

So as from year to year we count our
treasures,
    Our loss seems less, and larger look
our gains;
Time's wrongs repaid in more than even
measure, —
    We lose our jewels, but we break our
chains.

AT THE SATURDAY CLUB.

THIS is our place of meeting; opposite
That towered and pillared building: look
at it;
King's Chapel in the Second George's
day,

Rebellion stole its regal name away, —
Stone Chapel sounded better; but at last
The poisoned name of our provincial past
Had lost its ancient venom; then once
more
Stone Chapel was King's Chapel as
before.
(So let rechristened North Street, when it
can,
Bring back the days of Marlborough and
Queen Anne!)
    Next the old church your wandering
eye will meet
A granite pile that stares upon the
street, —
Our civic temple; slanderous tongues
have said
Its shape was modelled from St. Botolph's
head,
Lofty, but narrow; jealous passers-by
Say Boston always held her head too
high.
    Turn half-way round, and let your look
survey
The white façade that gleams across the
way, —
The many-windowed building, tall and
wide,
The palace-inn that shows its northern
side
In grateful shadow when the sunbeams
beat
The granite wall in summer's scorching
heat.
This is the place; whether its name you
spell
Tavern, or caravansera, or hotel.
Would I could steal its echoes! you
should find
Such store of vanished pleasures brought
to mind:
Such feasts! the laughs of many a
jocund hour
That shook the mortar from King
George's tower;
Such guests! What famous names its
record boasts,

Whose owners wander in the mob of
  ghosts!
Such stories! every beam and plank is
  filled
With juicy wit the joyous talkers spilled,
Ready to ooze, as once the mountain pine
The floors are laid with oozed its turpen-
  tine!

  A month had flitted since The Club
    had met;
The day came round; I found the table
    set,
The waiters lounging round the marble
    stairs,
Empty as yet the double row of chairs.
I was a full half hour before the rest,
Alone, the banquet-chamber's single
  guest.
So from the table's side a chair I took,
And having neither company nor book
To keep me waking, by degrees there
  crept
A torpor over me, — in short, I slept.
  Loosed from its chain, along the wreck-
    strown track
Of the dead years my soul goes travelling
  back;
My ghosts take on their robes of flesh; it
  seems
Dreaming is life; nay, life less life than
  dreams,
So real are the shapes that meet my
  eyes. —
They bring no sense of wonder, no sur-
  prise,
No hint of other than an earth-born
  source;
All seems plain daylight, everything of
  course.
  How dim the colors are, how poor and
    faint
This palette of weak words with which I
  paint!
Here sit my friends; if I could fix them so
As to my eyes they seem, my page would
  glow

Like a queen's missal, warm as if the
  brush
Of Titian or Velasquez brought the
  flush
Of life into their features.   Ay de mi!
If syllables were pigments, you should
  see
Such breathing portraitures as never
  man
Found in the Pitti or the Vatican.

  Here sits our POET, Laureate, if you
    will.
Long has he worn the wreath, and wears
  it still.
Dead? Nay, not so; and yet they say
  his bust
Looks down on marbles covering royal
  dust,
Kings by the Grace of God, or Nature's
  grace;
Dead! No! Alive! I see him in his
  place,
Full-featured, with the bloom that heaven
  denies
Her children, pinched by cold New Eng-
  land skies,
Too often, while the nursery's happier
  few
Win from a summer cloud its roseate
  hue.
Kind, soft-voiced, gentle, in his eye there
  shines
The ray serene that filled Evangeline's.
  Modest he seems, not shy; content to
    wait
Amid the noisy clamor of debate
The looked-for moment when a peaceful
  word
Smooths the rough ripples louder tongues
  have stirred.
In every tone I mark his tender grace
And all his poems hinted in his face;
What tranquil joy his friendly presence
  gives!
How could I think him dead? He lives!
  He lives!

There, at the table's further end I see
In his old place our Poet's *vis-à-vis*,
The great PROFESSOR, strong, broad-
    shouldered, square,
In life's rich noontide, joyous, debonair.
His social hour no leaden care alloys,
His laugh rings loud and mirthful as a
    boy's, —
That lusty laugh the Puritan forgot, —
What ear has heard it and remembers
    not ?

How often, halting at some wide crevasse
Amid the windings of his Alpine pass,
High up the cliffs, the climbing moun-
    taineer,
Listening the far-off avalanche to hear,
Silent, and leaning on his steel-shod staff,
Has heard that cheery voice, that ringing
    laugh,
From the rude cabin whose nomadic walls
Creep with the moving glacier as it
    crawls !

How does vast Nature lead her living
    train
In ordered sequence through that spacious
    brain,
As in the primal hour when Adam named
The new-born tribes that young creation
    claimed ! —
How will her realm be darkened, losing
    thee,
Her darling, whom we call *our* AGASSIZ !

But who is he whose massive frame
    belies
The maiden shyness of his downcast
    eyes ?
Who broods in silence till, by questions
    pressed,
Some answer struggles from his laboring
    breast ?
An artist Nature meant to dwell apart,
Locked in his studio with a human heart,
Tracking its caverned passions to their
    lair,
And all its throbbing mysteries laying
    bare.

Count it no marvel that he broods
    alone
Over the heart he studies, — 't is his own ;
So in his page whatever shape it wear,
The Essex wizard's shadowed self is
    there, —
The great ROMANCER, hid beneath his
    veil
Like the stern preacher of his sombre
    tale ;
Virile in strength, yet bashful as a girl,
Prouder than Hester, sensitive as Pearl.

From his mild throng of worshippers
    released,
Our Concord Delphi sends its chosen
    priest,
Prophet or poet, mystic, sage, or seer,
By every title always welcome here.
Why that ethereal spirit's frame describe ?
You know the race-marks of the Brahmin
    tribe, —
The spare, slight form, the sloping
    shoulders' droop,
The calm, scholastic mien, the clerkly
    stoop,
The lines of thought the sharpened fea-
    tures wear,
Carved by the edge of keen New England
    air.

List ! for he speaks ! As when a king
    would choose
The jewels for his bride, he might refuse
This diamond for its flaw, — find that
    less bright
Than those, its fellows, and a pearl less
    white
Than fits her snowy neck, and yet at last,
The fairest gems are chosen, and made
    fast
In golden fetters ; so, with light delays
He seeks the fittest word to fill his phrase ;
Nor vain nor idle his fastidious quest,
His chosen word is sure to prove the best.
Where in the realm of thought, whose
    air is song,
Does he, the Buddha of the West, belong ?

He seems a wingéd Franklin, sweetly
    wise,
Born to unlock the secrets of the skies ;
And which the nobler calling, — if 't is
    fair
Terrestrial with celestial to compare, —
To guide the storm-cloud's elemental
    flame,
Or walk the chambers whence the light-
    ning came,
Amidst the sources of its subtile fire,
And steal their effluence for his lips and
    lyre ?
  If lost at times in vague aerial flights,
None treads with firmer footstep when
    he lights ;
A soaring nature, ballasted with sense,
Wisdom without her wrinkles or pretence,
In every Bible he has faith to read,
And every altar helps to shape his creed.
Ask you what name this prisoned spirit
    bears
While with ourselves this fleeting breath
    it shares ?
Till angels greet him with a sweeter one
In heaven, on earth we call him EMERSON.

  I start ; I wake ; the vision is with-
    drawn ;
Its figures fading like the stars at dawn ;
Crossed from the roll of life their cher-
    ished names,
And memory's pictures fading in their
    frames ;
Yet life is lovelier for these transient
    gleams
Of buried friendships ; blest is he who
    dreams !

BENJAMIN PEIRCE :

ASTRONOMER, MATHEMATICIAN.

1809-1880.

FOR him the Architect of all
Unroofed our planet's starlit hall ;
Through voids unknown to worlds unseen
His clearer vision rose serene.

With us on earth he walked by day,
His midnight path how far away !
We knew him not so well who knew
The patient eyes his soul looked through ;

For who his untrod realm could share
Of us that breathe this mortal air,
Or camp in that celestial tent
Whose fringes gild our firmament ?

How vast the workroom where he brought
The viewless implements of thought !
The wit how subtle, how profound,
That Nature's tangled webs unwound ;

That through the clouded matrix saw
The crystal planes of shaping law,
Through these the sovereign skill that
    planned, —
The Father's care, the Master's hand !

To him the wandering stars revealed
The secrets in their cradle sealed :
The far-off, frozen sphere that swings
Through ether, zoned with lucid rings ;

The orb that rolls in dim eclipse
Wide wheeling round its long ellipse, —
His name Urania writes with these
And stamps it on her Pleiades.

We knew him not ? Ah, well we knew
The manly soul, so brave, so true,
The cheerful heart that conquered age,
The childlike silver-bearded sage.

No more his tireless thought explores
The azure sea with golden shores ;
Rest, wearied frame ! the stars shall
    keep
A loving watch where thou shalt sleep.

Farewell ! the spirit needs must rise,
So long a tenant of the skies, —
Rise to that home all worlds above
Whose sun is God, whose light is love.

OUR DEAD SINGER.

H. W. L.

Pride of the sister realm so long our
    own,
  We claim with her that spotless fame of
    thine,
  White as her snow and fragrant as her
    pine!
Ours was thy birthplace, but in every
    zone
Some wreath of song thy liberal hand has
    thrown
  Breathes perfume from its blossoms,
    that entwine
  Where'er the dewdrops fall, the sun-
    beams shine,
On life's long path with tangled cares
    o'ergrown.
Can Art thy truthful counterfeit com-
    mand, —
  The silver-haloed features, tranquil,
    mild, —
  Soften the lips of bronze as when they
    smiled,
Give warmth and pressure to the marble
    hand?
Seek the lost rainbow in the sky it
    spanned!
  Farewell, sweet Singer! Heaven re-
    claims its child.

Carved from the block or cast in clinging
    mould,
  Will grateful Memory fondly try her
    best
  The mortal vesture from decay to
    wrest;
His look shall greet us, calm, but ah, how
    cold!
No breath can stir the brazen drapery's
    fold,
  No throb can heave the statue's stony
    breast;
  "He is not here, but risen," will stand
    confest
In all we miss, in all our eyes behold.

How Nature loved him! On his placid
    brow,
  Thought's ample dome, she set the
    sacred sign
  That marks the priesthood of her
    holiest shrine,
Nor asked a leaflet from the laurel's
    bough
That envious Time might clutch or dis-
    allow,
  To prove her chosen minstrel's song
    divine.

On many a saddened hearth the evening
    fire
  Burns paler as the children's hour
    draws near, —
  That joyous hour his song made doubly
    dear, —
And tender memories touch the faltering
    choir.
He sings no more on earth; our vain
    desire
  Aches for the voice we loved so long
    to hear
  In Dorian flute-notes breathing soft and
    clear, —
The sweet contralto that could never tire.
Deafened with listening to a harsher
    strain,
  The Mænad's scream, the stark bar-
    barian's cry,
  Still for those soothing, loving tones
    we sigh;
Oh, for our vanished Orpheus once again!
The shadowy silence hears us call in vain!
  His lips are hushed; his song shall
    never die.

TO JAMES FREEMAN CLARKE.

APRIL 4, 1880.

I bring the simplest pledge of love,
  Friend of my earlier days;
Mine is the hand without the glove,
  The heart-beat, not the phrase.

How few still breathe this mortal air
  We called by schoolboy names!
You still, whatever robe you wear,
  To me are always James:

That name the kind apostle bore
  Who shames the sullen creeds,
Not trusting less, but loving more,
  And showing faith by deeds.

What blending thoughts our memories
    share!
  What visions yours and mine
Of May-days in whose morning air
  The dews were golden wine;

Of vistas bright with opening day,
  Whose all-awakening sun
Showed in life's landscape, far away,
  The summits to be won!

The heights are gained. — Ah, say
    not so
  For him who smiles at time,
Leaves his tired comrades down below,
  And only lives to climb!

His labors, — will they ever cease,
  With hand, and tongue, and pen?
Shall wearied Nature ask release
  At threescore years and ten?

Our strength the clustered seasons tax, —
  For him new life they mean;
Like rods around the lictor's axe
  They keep him bright and keen.

The wise, the brave, the strong, we
    know, —
  We mark them here or there;
But he, — we roll our eyes, and lo!
  We find him everywhere!

With truth's bold cohorts, or alone,
  He strides through error's field;
His lance is ever manhood's own,
  His breast is woman's shield.

Count not his years while earth has need
  Of souls that Heaven inflames
With sacred zeal to save, to lead, —
  Long live our dear Saint James!

TWO POEMS TO HARRIET BEECHER STOWE.

ON HER SEVENTIETH BIRTHDAY, JUNE 14, 1882.

I. AT THE SUMMIT.

SISTER, we bid you welcome, — we who
    stand
    On the high table-land;
We who have climbed life's slippery Al-
    pine slope,
And rest, still leaning on the staff of hope,
Looking along the silent Mer de Glace,
Leading our footsteps where the dark
    crevasse
Yawns in the frozen sea we all must
    pass, —
    Sister, we clasp your hand!

Rest with us in the hour that Heaven has
    lent
    Before the swift descent.
Look! the warm sunbeams kiss the glit-
    tering ice;
See! next the snow-drift blooms the edel-
    weiss;
The mated eagles fan the frosty air;
Life, beauty, love, around us everywhere,
And, in their time, the darkening hours
    that bear
    Sweet memories, peace, content.

Thrice welcome! shining names our mis-
    sals show
    Amid their rubrics' glow,
But search the blazoned record's starry
    line,
What halo's radiance fills the page like
    thine?
Thou who by some celestial clew couldst
    find

The way to all the hearts of all mankind,
On thee, already canonized, enshrined,
          What more can Heaven bestow.

II. THE WORLD'S HOMAGE.

IF every tongue that speaks her praise
For whom I shape my tinkling phrase
     Were summoned to the table,
The vocal chorus that would meet
Of mingling accents harsh or sweet,
From every land and tribe, would beat
     The polyglots at Babel.

Briton and Frenchman, Swede and Dane,
Turk, Spaniard, Tartar of Ukraine,
     Hidalgo, Cossack, Cadi,
High Dutchman and Low Dutchman,
     too,
The Russian serf, the Polish Jew,
Arab, Armenian, and Mantchoo,
     Would shout, "We know the lady!"

Know her! Who knows not Uncle
     Tom
And her he learned his gospel from
     Has never heard of Moses;
Full well the brave black hand we know
That gave to freedom's grasp the hoe
That killed the weed that used to grow
     Among the Southern roses.

When Archimedes, long ago,
Spoke out so grandly, " dos pou sto —
     Give me a place to stand on,
I 'll move your planet for you, now," —
He little dreamed or fancied how
The sto at last should find its pou
     For woman's faith to land on.

Her lever was the wand of art,
Her fulcrum was the human heart,
     Whence all unfailing aid is;
She moved the earth! Its thunders
     pealed,
Its mountains shook, its temples reeled,
The blood-red fountains were unsealed,
     And Moloch sunk to Hades.

All through the conflict, up and down
Marched Uncle Tom and Old John Brown,
     One ghost, one form ideal;
And which was false and which was true,
And which was mightier of the two,
The wisest sibyl never knew,
     For both alike were real.

Sister, the holy maid does well
Who counts her beads in convent cell,
     Where pale devotion lingers;
But she who serves the sufferer's needs,
Whose prayers are spelt in loving deeds,
May trust the Lord will count her beads
     As well as human fingers.

When Truth herself was Slavery's slave,
Thy hand the prisoned suppliant gave
     The rainbow wings of fiction.
And Truth who soared descends to-day
Bearing an angel's wreath away,
Its lilies at thy feet to lay
     With Heaven's own benediction.

A WELCOME TO DR. BENJAMIN APTHORP GOULD.

ON HIS RETURN FROM SOUTH AMERICA.

AFTER FIFTEEN YEARS DEVOTED TO CATALOGUING
THE STARS OF THE SOUTHERN HEMISPHERE.[1]

ONCE more Orion and the sister Seven
     Look on thee from the skies that hailed
          thy birth, —
How shall we welcome thee, whose home
          was heaven,
     From thy celestial wanderings back to
          earth?

Science has kept her midnight taper burn-
          ing
     To greet thy coming with its vestal
          flame;
Friendship has murmured, "When art
          thou returning?"

[1] Read at the Dinner given at the Hotel Vendome, May 6, 1885.

"Not yet! Not yet!" the answering
    message came.

Thine was unstinted zeal, unchilled de-
    votion,
    While the blue realm had kingdoms to
        explore, —
Patience, like his who ploughed the un-
    furrowed ocean,
    Till o'er its margin loomed San Salva-
        dor.

Through the long nights I see thee ever
    waking,
    Thy footstool earth, thy roof the hemi-
        sphere,
While with thy griefs our weaker hearts
    are aching,
    Firm as thine equatorial's rock-based
        pier.

The souls that voyaged the azure depths
    before thee
    Watch with thy tireless vigils, all un-
        seen, —
Tycho and Kepler bend benignant o'er
    thee,
    And with his toy-like tube the Floren-
        tine, —

He at whose word the orb that bore him
    shivered
    To find her central sovereignty dis-
        owned,
While the wan lips of priest and pontiff
    quivered,
    Their jargon stilled, their Baal disen-
        throned.

Flamsteed and Newton look with brows
    unclouded,
    Their strife forgotten with its faded
        scars, —
(Titans, who found the world of space
    too crowded
    To walk in peace among its myriad
        stars.)

All cluster round thee, — seers of earliest
    ages,
    Persians, Ionians, Mizraim's learned
        kings,
From the dim days of Shinar's hoary
    sages
    To his who weighed the planet's fluid
        rings.

And we, for whom the northern heavens
    are lighted,
    For whom the storm has passed, the
        sun has smiled,
Our clouds all scattered, all our stars
    united,
    We claim thee, clasp thee, like a long-
        lost child.

Fresh from the spangled vault's o'erarch-
    ing splendor,
    Thy lonely pillar, thy revolving dome,
In heartfelt accents, proud, rejoicing,
    tender,
    We bid thee welcome to thine earthly
        home!

TO FREDERICK HENRY HEDGE.

AT A DINNER GIVEN HIM ON HIS
    EIGHTIETH BIRTHDAY, DECEMBER,
    12, 1885.

*With a bronze statuette of John of Bologna's
    Mercury, presented by a few friends.*

FIT emblem for the altar's side,
    And him who serves its daily need,
The stay, the solace, and the guide
    Of mortal men, whate'er his creed!

Flamen or Auspex, Priest or Bonze,
    He feeds the upward-climbing fire,
Still teaching, like the deathless bronze,
    Man's noblest lesson, — to aspire.

Hermes lies prone by fallen Jove,
    Crushed are the wheels of Krishna's
        çar,

And o'er Dodona's silent grove
  Streams the white ray from Bethle-
      hem's star.

Yet snatched from Time's relentless
      clutch,
  A godlike shape, that human hands
Have fired with Art's electric touch,
  The herald of Olympus stands.

Ask not what ore the furnace knew;
  Love mingled with the flowing mass,
And lends its own unchanging hue,
  Like gold in Corinth's molten brass.

Take then our gift; this airy form
  Whose bronze our benedictions gild,
The hearts of all its givers warm
  With love by freezing years unchilled.

With eye undimmed, with strength un-
      worn,
  Still toiling in your Master's field,
Before you wave the growths unshorn,
  Their ripened harvest yet to yield.

True servant of the Heavenly Sire,
  To you our tried affection clings,
Bids you still labor, still aspire,
  But clasps your feet and steals their
      wings.

TO JAMES RUSSELL LOWELL.

THIS is your month, the month of "per-
      fect days,"
Birds in full song and blossoms all ablaze.
Nature herself your earliest welcome
      breathes,
Spreads every leaflet, every bower in-
      wreathes;
Carpets her paths for your returning
      feet,
Puts forth her best your coming steps to
      greet;
And Heaven must surely find the earth in
      tune

When Home, sweet Home, exhales the
      breath of June.
  These blessed days are waning all too
      fast,
And June's bright visions mingling with
      the past;
Lilacs have bloomed and faded, and the
      rose
Has dropped its petals, but the clover
      blows,
And fills its slender tubes with honeyed
      sweets;
The fields are pearled with milk-white
      margarites;
The dandelion, which you sang of old,
Has lost its pride of place, its crown of
      gold,
But still displays its feathery-mantled
      globe,
Which children's breath, or wandering
      winds unrobe.
These were your humble friends; your
      opened eyes
Nature had trained her common gifts to
      prize;
Not Cam nor Isis taught you to de-
      spise
Charles, with his muddy margin and the
      harsh,
Plebeian grasses of the reeking marsh.
New England's home-bred scholar, well
      you knew
Her soil, her speech, her people, through
      and through,
And loved them ever with the love that
      holds
All sweet, fond memories in its fragrant
      folds.
Though far and wide your wingèd words
      have flown,
Your daily presence kept you all our
      own,
Till, with a sorrowing sigh, a thrill of
      pride,
We heard your summons, and you left our
      side
For larger duties and for tasks untried.

How pleased the Spaniards for a while
    to claim
This frank Hidalgo with the liquid name,
Who stored their classics on his crowded
    shelves
And loved their Calderon as they did
    themselves!
Before his eyes what changing pageants
    pass!
The bridal feast how near the funeral
    mass!
The death-stroke falls, — Misereres wail;
The joy - bells ring, — the tear - stained
    cheeks unveil,
While, as the playwright shifts his pictured
    scene,
The royal mourner crowns his second
    queen.

From Spain to Britain is a goodly
    stride, —
Madrid and London long-stretched leagues
    divide.
What if I send him, " Uncle S., says he,"
To my good cousin whom he calls " J.B." ?
A nation's servants go where they are
    sent, —
He heard his Uncle's orders, and he went.
  By what enchantments, what alluring
    arts,
Our truthful James led captive British
    hearts, —
Whether his shrewdness made their states-
    men halt,
Or if his learning found their Dons at
    fault,
Or if his virtue was a strange surprise,
Or if his wit flung star-dust in their
    eyes, —
Like honest Yankees we can simply guess;
But that he did it all must needs confess.
England herself without a blush may
    claim
Her only conqueror since the Norman
    came.
  Eight years an exile! What a weary
    while

Since first our herald sought the mother
    isle !
His snow-white flag no churlish wrong
    has soiled, —
He left unchallenged, he returns un-
    spoiled.

Here let us keep him, here he saw the
    light, —
His genius, wisdom, wit, are ours by right;
And if we lose him our lament will be
We have " five hundred " — *not* " as good
    as he."

TO JOHN GREENLEAF WHITTIER.

ON HIS EIGHTIETH BIRTHDAY.

1887

FRIEND, whom thy fourscore winters
    leave more dear
Than when life's roseate summer on thy
    cheek
Burned in the flush of manhood's man-
    liest year,
Lonely, how lonely ! is the snowy peak
Thy feet have reached, and mine have
    climbed so near !
Close on thy footsteps 'mid the landscape
    drear
I stretch my hand thine answering grasp
    to seek,
Warm with the love no rippling rhymes
    can speak !
Look backwards ! From thy lofty height
    survey
Thy years of toil, of peaceful victories
    won,
Of dreams made real, largest hopes out-
    run !
Look forward ! Brighter than earth's
    morning ray
Streams the pure light of Heaven's un-
    setting sun,
The unclouded dawn of life's immortal
    day !

PRELUDE TO A VOLUME PRINTED IN RAISED LETTERS FOR THE BLIND.

DEAR friends, left darkling in the long
 eclipse
That veils the noonday, — you whose
 finger-tips
A meaning in these ridgy leaves can find
Where ours go stumbling, senseless, help-
 less, blind,
This wreath of verse how dare I offer you
To whom the garden's choicest gifts are
 due ?
The hues of all its glowing beds are ours,
Shall you not claim its sweetest-smelling
 flowers ?

Nay, those I have I bring you, — at their
 birth
Life's cheerful sunshine warmed the
 grateful earth ;
If my rash boyhood dropped some idle
 seeds,
And here and there you light on saucy
 weeds
Among the fairer growths, remember still
Song comes of grace, and not of human
 will :
We get a jarring note when most we try,
Then strike the chord we know not how
 or why ;
Our stately verse with too aspiring art
Oft overshoots and fails to reach the heart,
While the rude rhyme one human throb
 endears
Turns grief to smiles, and softens mirth
 to tears.
Kindest of critics, ye whose fingers read,
From Nature's lesson learn the poet's
 creed ;
The queenly tulip flaunts in robes of
 flame,
The wayside seedling scarce a tint may
 claim,
Yet may the lowliest leaflets that unfold
A dewdrop fresh from heaven's own chal-
 ice hold.

BOSTON TO FLORENCE.

SENT TO "THE PHILOLOGICAL CIRCLE" OF FLORENCE FOR ITS MEETING IN COMMEMORATION OF DANTE, JANU-ARY 27, 1881, ANNIVERSARY OF HIS FIRST CONDEMNATION.

PROUD of her clustering spires, her new-
 built towers,
 Our Venice, stolen from the slumbering
  sea,
 A sister's kindliest greeting wafts to
  thee,
Rose of Val d' Arno, Queen of all its
 flowers !
Thine exile's shrine thy sorrowing love
 embowers,
 Yet none with truer homage bends the
  knee,
 Or stronger pledge of fealty brings, than
  we,
Whose poets make thy dead Immortal
 ours.
Lonely the height, but ah, to heaven how
 near !
 Dante, whence flowed that solemn verse
  of thine
 Like the stern river from its Apennine
Whose name the far-off Scythian thrilled
 with fear :
Now to all lands thy deep-toned voice is
 dear,
 And every language knows the Song
  Divine !

AT THE UNITARIAN FESTIVAL.
MARCH 8, 1882.

THE waves unbuild the wasting shore ;
 Where mountains towered the billows
  sweep,
Yet still their borrowed spoils restore,
 And build new empires from the deep.
So while the floods of thought lay waste
 The proud domain of priestly creeds,
Its heaven-appointed tides will haste
 To plant new homes for human needs.

Be ours to mark with hearts unchilled
　　The change an outworn church de-
　　　plores ;
The legend sinks, but Faith shall build
　　A fairer throne on new-found shores.

POEM

FOR THE TWO HUNDRED AND FIFTIETH
ANNIVERSARY OF THE FOUNDING OF
HARVARD COLLEGE.

TWICE had the mellowing sun of autumn
　　crowned
The hundredth circle of his yearly round,
When, as we meet to-day, our fathers
　　met:
That joyous gathering who can e'er
　　forget,
When Harvard's nurslings, scattered far
　　and wide,
Through mart and village, lake's and
　　ocean's side,
Came, with one impulse, one fraternal
　　throng,
And crowned the hours with banquet,
　　speech, and song ?

Once more revived in fancy's magic glass,
I see in state the long procession pass :
Tall, courtly, leader as by right divine,
Winthrop, our Winthrop, rules the mar-
　　shalled line,
Still seen in front, as on that far-off day
His ribboned baton showed the column's
　　way.
Not all are gone who marched in manly
　　pride
And waved their truncheons at their
　　leader's side ;
Gray, Lowell, Dixwell, who his empire
　　shared,
These to be with us envious Time has
　　spared.

Few are the faces, so familiar then,
Our eyes still meet amid the haunts of
　　men ;
Scarce one of all the living gathered
　　there,
Whose unthinned locks betrayed a silver
　　hair,
Greets us to-day, and yet we seem the
　　same
As our own sires and grandsires, save in
　　name.

There are the patriarchs, looking vaguely
　　round
For classmates' faces, hardly known if
　　found ;
See the cold brow that rules the busy
　　mart ;
Close at its side the pallid son of art,
Whose purchased skill with borrowed
　　meaning clothes,
And stolen hues, the smirking face he
　　loathes.
Here is the patient scholar ; in his looks
You read the titles of his learned books ;
What classic lore those spidery crow's-
　　feet speak !
What problems figure on that wrinkled
　　cheek !
For never thought but left its stiffened
　　trace,
Its fossil footprint, on the plastic face,
As the swift record of a raindrop stands,
Fixed on the tablet of the hardening
　　sands.
On every face as on the written page
Each year renews the autograph of age ;
One trait alone may wasting years
　　defy, —
The fire still lingering in the poet's
　　eye,
While Hope, the siren, sings her sweetest
　　strain, —
Non omnis moriar is its proud refrain.

Sadly we gaze upon the vacant chair ;
He who should claim its honors is not
　　there, —
Otis, whose lips the listening crowd en-
　　thrall

That press and pack the floor of Boston's
hall.
But Kirkland smiles, released from toil
and care
Since the silk mantle younger shoulders
wear, —
Quincy's, whose spirit breathes the self-
same fire
That filled the bosom of his youthful
sire,
Who for the altar bore the kindled torch
To freedom's temple, dying in its porch.
  Three grave professions in their sons
appear,
Whose words well studied all well
pleased will hear:
Palfrey, ordained in varied walks to
shine,
Statesman, historian, critic, and divine ;
Solid and square behold majestic Shaw,
A mass of wisdom and a mine of law;
Warren, whose arm the doughtiest war-
riors fear,
Asks of the startled crowd to lend its
ear, —
Proud of his calling, him the world loves
best,
Not as the coming, but the parting guest.

Look on that form, — with eye dilating
scan
The stately mould of nature's kingliest
man !
Tower-like he stands in life's unfaded
prime ;
Ask you his name ? None asks a second
time !
He from the land his outward semblance
takes,
Where storm-swept mountains watch o'er
slumbering lakes.
See in the impress which the body wears
How its imperial might the soul declares :
The forehead's large expansion, lofty,
wide,
That locks unsilvered vainly strive to
hide ;

The lines of thought that plough the
sober cheek ;
Lips that betray their wisdom ere they
speak
In tones like answers from Dodona's
grove ;
An eye like Juno's when she frowns on
Jove.
I look and wonder ; will he be content —
This man, this monarch, for the purple
meant —
The meaner duties of his tribe to share,
Clad in the garb that common mortals
wear ?
Ah, wild Ambition, spread thy restless
wings,
Beneath whose plumes the hidden œstrum
stings ;
Thou whose bold flight would leave
earth's vulgar crowds,
And like the eagle soar above the clouds,
Must feel the pang that fallen angels
know
When the red lightning strikes thee from
below !

Less bronze, more silver, mingles in the
mould
Of him whom next my roving eyes be-
hold ;
His, more the scholar's than the states-
man's face,
Proclaims him born of academic race.
Weary his look, as if an aching brain
Left on his brow the frozen prints of
pain ;
His voice far-reaching, grave, sonorous,
owns
A shade of sadness in its plaintive tones,
Yet when its breath some loftier thought
inspires
Glows with a heat that every bosom
fires.
Such Everett seems ; no chance-sown
wild flower knows
The full-blown charms of culture's double
rose, —

Alas, how soon, by death's unsparing frost,
Its bloom is faded and its fragrance lost !

Two voices, only two, to earth belong,
Of all whose accents met the listening throng :
Winthrop, alike for speech and guidance framed,
On that proud day a twofold duty claimed ;
One other yet, — remembered or forgot, —
Forgive my silence if I name him not.
Can I believe it ? I, whose youthful voice
Claimed a brief gamut, — notes not over choice, —
Stood undismayed before the solemn throng,
And *propria voce* sung that saucy song
Which even in memory turns my soul aghast, —
Felix audacia was the verdict cast.

What were the glory of these festal days
Shorn of their grand illumination's blaze ?
Night comes at last with all her starry train
To find a light in every glittering pane.
From "Harvard's" windows see the sudden flash, —
Old "Massachusetts" glares through every sash ;
From wall to wall the kindling splendors run
Till all is glorious as the noonday sun.

How to the scholar's mind each object brings
What some historian tells, some poet sings !
The good gray teacher whom we all revered —
Loved, honored, laughed at, and by freshmen feared,
As from old "Harvard," where its light began,

From hall to hall the clustering splendors ran —
Took down his well-worn Æschylus and read,
Lit by the rays a thousand tapers shed,
How the swift herald crossed the leagues between
Mycenæ's monarch and his faithless queen ;
And thus he read, — my verse but ill displays
The Attic picture, clad in modern phrase :

On Ida's summit flames the kindling pile,
And Lemnos answers from his rocky isle ;
From Athos next it climbs the reddening skies,
Thence where the watch-towers of Macistus rise.
The sentries of Mesapius in their turn
Bid the dry heath in high-piled masses burn,
Cithæron's crag the crimson billows stain,
Far Ægiplanctus joins the fiery train.
Thus the swift courier through the pathless night
Has gained at length the Arachnæan height,
Whence the glad tidings, borne on wings of flame,
"Ilium has fallen !" reach the royal dame.

So ends the day ; before the midnight stroke
The lights expiring cloud the air with smoke ;
While these the toil of younger hands employ,
The slumbering **Grecian** dreams of smouldering **Troy**.

As to that hour with backward steps I turn,
Midway I pause ; behold a funeral urn !
Ah, sad memorial ! known but all too well
The tale which thus its golden letters tell :

This dust, once breathing, changed its joy-
ous life
For toil and hunger, wounds and mortal
strife;
Love, friendship, learning's all-prevailing
charms,
For the cold bivouac and the clash of
arms.
The cause of freedom won, a race enslaved
Called back to manhood, and a nation
saved,
These sons of Harvard, falling ere their
prime,
Leave their proud memory to the coming
time.

While in their still retreats our scholars
turn
The mildewed pages of the past, to learn
With endless labor of the sleepless brain
What once has been and ne'er shall be
again,
We reap the harvest of their ceaseless
toil
And find a fragrance in their midnight
oil.
But let a purblind mortal dare the task
The embryo future of itself to ask,
The world reminds him, with a scornful
laugh,
That times have changed since Prospero
broke his staff.
Could all the wisdom of the schools fore-
tell
The dismal hour when Lisbon shook and
fell,
Or name the shuddering night that top-
pled down
Our sister's pride, beneath whose mural
crown
Scarce had the scowl forgot its angry
lines,
When earth's blind prisoners fired their
fatal mines?
New realms, new worlds, exulting Sci-
ence claims,
Still the dim future unexplored remains;

Her trembling scales the far-off planet
weigh,
Her torturing prisms its elements be-
tray, —
We know what ores the fires of Sirius
melt,
What vaporous metals gild Orion's belt;
Angels, archangels, may have yet to learn
Those hidden truths our heaven-taught
eyes discern;
Yet vain is Knowledge, with her mystic
wand,
To pierce the cloudy screen and read
beyond;
Once to the silent stars the fates were
known,
To us they tell no secrets but their own.

At Israel's altar still we humbly bow,
But where, oh where, are Israel's prophets
now?
Where is the sibyl with her hoarded
leaves?
Where is the charm the weird enchantress
weaves?
No croaking raven turns the auspex pale,
No reeking altars tell the morrow's tale;
The measured footsteps of the Fates are
dumb,
Unseen, unheard, unheralded, they come,
Prophet and priest and all their following
fail.
Who then is left to rend the future's
veil?
Who but the poet, he whose nicer sense
No film can baffle with its slight defence,
Whose finer vision marks the waves that
stray,
Felt, but unseen, beyond the violet
ray? —
Who, while the storm-wind waits its
darkening shroud,
Foretells the tempest ere he sees the
cloud, —
Stays not for time his secrets to reveal,
But reads his message ere he breaks the
seal.

So Mantua's bard foretold the coming
    day
Ere Bethlehem's infant in the manger
    lay;
The promise trusted to a mortal tongue
Found listening ears before the angels
    sung.
So while his load the creeping pack-horse
    galled,
While inch by inch the dull canal-boat
    crawled,
Darwin beheld a Titan from " afar
Drag the slow barge or drive the rapid
    car,"
That panting giant fed by air and flame,
The mightiest forges task their strength
    to tame.

Happy the poet! him no tyrant fact
Holds in its clutches to be chained and
    racked;
Him shall no mouldy document convict,
No stern statistics gravely contradict;
No rival sceptre threats his airy throne;
He rules o'er shadows, but he reigns
    alone.
Shall I the poet's broad dominion claim
Because you bid me wear his sacred name
For these few moments? Shall I boldly
    clash
My flint and steel, and by the sudden
    flash
Read the fair vision which my soul de-
    scries
Through the wide pupils of its wondering
    eyes?
List then awhile; the fifty years have
    sped;
The third full century's opened scroll is
    spread,
Blank to all eyes save his who dimly
    sees
The shadowy future told in words like
    these:

How strange the prospect to my sight ap-
    pears,

Changed by the busy hands of fifty years!
Full well I know our ocean-salted Charles,
Filling and emptying through the sands
    and marls
That wall his restless stream on either
    bank,
Not all unlovely when the sedges rank
Lend their coarse veil the sable ooze to
    hide
That bares its blackness with the ebbing
    tide.
In other shapes to my illumined eyes
Those ragged margins of our stream
    arise:
Through walls of stone the sparkling
    waters flow,
In clearer depths the golden sunsets glow,
On purer waves the lamps of midnight
    gleam,
That silver o'er the unpolluted stream.
Along his shores what stately temples
    rise,
What spires, what turrets, print the
    shadowed skies!
Our smiling Mother sees her broad do-
    main
Spread its tall roofs along the western
    plain;
Those blazoned windows' blushing glories
    tell
Of grateful hearts that loved her long
    and well;
Yon gilded dome that glitters in the sun
Was Dives' gift, — alas, his only one!
These buttressed walls enshrine a banker's
    name,
That hallowed chapel hides a miser's
    shame;
Their wealth they left, — their memory
    cannot fade
Though age shall crumble every stone
    they laid.
    Great lord of millions, — let me call
        thee great,
Since countless servants at thy bidding
    wait, —
Richesse oblige : no mortal must be blind

To all but self, or look at human kind
Laboring and suffering, — all its want
    and woe, —
Through sheets of crystal, as a pleasing
    show
That makes life happier for the chosen
    few
Duty for whom is something not to do.
    When thy last page of life at length is
      filled,
What shall thine heirs to keep thy
    memory build ?
Will piles of stone in Auburn's mourn-
    ful shade
Save from neglect the spot where thou
    art laid ?
Nay, deem not thus; the sauntering
    stranger's eye
Will pass unmoved thy columned tomb-
    stone by,
No memory wakened, not a teardrop
    shed,
Thy name uncared for and thy date un-
    read.
    But if thy record thou indeed dost
      prize,
Bid from the soil some stately temple
    rise, —
Some hall of learning, some memorial
    shrine,
With names long honored to associate
    thine :
So shalt thy fame outlive thy shattered
    bust
When all around thee slumber in the
    dust.
Thus England's Henry lives in Eton's
    towers,
Saved from the spoil oblivion's gulf de-
    vours ;
Our later records with as fair a fame
Have wreathed each uncrowned bene-
    factor's name;
The walls they reared the memories still
    retain
That churchyard marbles try to keep in
    vain.

In vain the delving antiquary tries
To find the tomb where generous Harvard
    lies :
Here, here, his lasting monument is
    found,
Where every spot is consecrated ground !
O'er Stoughton's dust the crumbling
    stone decays, —
Fast fade its lines of lapidary praise ;
There the wild bramble weaves its ragged
    nets,
There the dry lichen spreads its gray
    rosettes ;
Still in yon walls his memory lives un-
    spent,
Nor asks a braver, nobler monument.
Thus Hollis lives, and Holden, honored,
    praised,
And good Sir Matthew, in the halls they
    raised ;
Thus live the worthies of these later
    times,
Who shine in deeds, less brilliant,
    grouped in rhymes.
Say, shall the Muse with faltering steps
    retreat,
Or dare these names in rhythmic form
    repeat ?
Why not as boldly as from Homer's
    lips
The long array of Argive battle-ships ?
When o'er our graves a thousand years
    have past
(If to such date our threatened globe
    shall last)
These classic precincts, myriad feet have
    pressed,
Will show on high, in beauteous garlands
    dressed,
Those honored names that grace our later
    day, —
Weld, Matthews, Sever, Thayer, Austin,
    Gray,
Sears, Phillips, Lawrence, Hemenway, —
    to the list
Add Sanders, Sibley, — all the Muse has
    missed.

Once more I turn to read the pictured
page
Bright with the promise of the coming
age.
Ye unborn sons of children yet unborn,
Whose youthful eyes shall greet that far-
off morn,
Blest are those eyes that all undimmed
behold
The sights so longed for by the wise of
old.

From high-arched alcoves, through re-
sounding halls,
Clad in full robes majestic Science calls,
Tireless, unsleeping, still at Nature's feet,
Whate'er she utters fearless to repeat,
Her lips at last from every cramp released
That Israel's prophet caught from Egypt's
priest.

I see the statesman, firm, sagacious,
bold,
For life's long conflict cast in amplest
mould:
Not his to clamor with the senseless
throng
That shouts unshamed, "Our party, right
or wrong,"
But in the patriot's never-ending fight
To side with Truth, who changes wrong
to right.

I see the scholar; in that wondrous
time
Men, women, children, all can write in
rhyme.
These four brief lines addressed to youth
inclined
To idle rhyming in his notes I find:

*Who writes in verse that should have writ
in prose*
Is like a traveller walking on his toes;
Happy the rhymester who in time has found
*The heels he lifts were made to touch the
ground.*

I see gray teachers, — on their work
intent,

Their lavished lives, in endless labor
spent,
Had closed at last in age and penury
wrecked,
Martyrs, not burned, but frozen in
neglect,
Save for the generous hands that stretched
in aid
Of worn-out servants left to die half paid.
Ah, many a year will pass, I thought, ere
we
Such kindly forethought shall rejoice to
see, —
Monarchs are mindful of the sacred debt
That cold republics hasten to forget.

I see the priest, — if such a name he
bears
Who without pride his sacred vestment
wears;
And while the symbols of his tribe I seek
Thus my first impulse bids me think and
speak:

Let not the mitre England's prelate
wears
Next to the crown whose regal pomp it
shares,
Though low before it courtly Christians
bow,
Leave its red mark on Younger England's
brow.
We love, we honor, the maternal dame,
But let her priesthood wear a modest
name,
While through the waters of the Pil-
grim's bay
A new-born Mayflower shows her keels
the way.
Too old grew Britain for her mother's
beads, —
Must we be necklaced with her children's
creeds?
Welcome alike in surplice or in gown
The loyal lieges of the Heavenly Crown!
We greet with cheerful, not submissive,
mien
A sister church, but not a mitred Queen!

A few brief flutters, and the unwilling
    Muse,
Who feared the flight she hated to refuse,
Shall fold the wings whose gayer plumes
    are shed,
Here where at first her half-fledged
    pinions spread.
  Well I remember in the long ago
How in the forest shades of Fontaine-
    bleau,
Strained through a fissure in a rocky cell,
One crystal drop with measured cadence
    fell.
Still, as of old, forever bright and clear,
The fissured cavern drops its wonted tear,
And wondrous virtue, simple folk aver,
Lies in that teardrop of *la roche qui pleure*.
  Of old I wandered by the river's side
Between whose banks the mighty waters
    glide,
Where vast Niagara, hurrying to its fall,
Builds and unbuilds its ever-tumbling
    wall;
Oft in my dreams I hear the rush and roar
Of battling floods, and feel the trembling
    shore,
As the huge torrent, girded for its leap,
With bellowing thunders plunges down
    the steep.
  Not less distinct, from memory's pic-
    tured urn,
The gray old rock, the leafy woods, re-
    turn;
Robed in their pride the lofty oaks ap-
    pear,
And once again with quickened sense I
    hear,
Through the low murmur of the leaves
    that stir,
The tinkling teardrop of *la roche qui
    pleure*.

So when the third ripe century stands
    complete,
As once again the sons of Harvard meet,
Rejoicing, numerous as the seashore
    sands,

Drawn from all quarters, — farthest dis-
    tant lands,
Where through the reeds the scaly sau-
    rian steals,
Where cold Alaska feeds her floundering
    seals,
Where Plymouth, glorying, wears her
    iron crown,
Where Sacramento sees the suns go
    down;
Nay, from the cloisters whence the reflu-
    ent tide
Wafts their pale students to our Mother's
    side, —
Mid all the tumult that the day shall bring,
While all the echoes shout, and roar, and
    ring,
These tinkling lines, oblivion's easy prey,
Once more emerging to the light of day,
Not all unpleasing to the listening ear
Shall wake the memories of this bygone
    year,
Heard as I hear the measured drops that
    flow
From the gray rock of wooded Fontaine-
    bleau.

Yet, ere I leave, one loving word for all
Those fresh young lives that wait our
    Mother's call:
  One gift is yours, kind Nature's richest
    dower, —
Youth, the fair bud that holds life's
    opening flower,
Full of high hopes no coward doubts en-
    chain,
With all the future throbbing in its brain,
And mightiest instincts which the beating
    heart
Fills with the fire its burning waves im-
    part.
  O joyous youth, whose glory is to
    dare, —
Thy foot firm planted on the lowest stair,
Thine eye uplifted to the loftiest height
Where Fame stands beckoning in the
    rosy light,

Thanks for thy flattering tales, thy fond
  deceits,
Thy loving lies, thy cheerful smiling
  cheats!
Nature's rash promise every day is
  broke, —
A thousand acorns breed a single oak,
The myriad blooms that make the orchard
  gay
In barren beauty throw their lives away;
Yet shall we quarrel with the sap that
  yields
The painted blossoms which adorn the
  fields,
When the fair orchard wears its May-day
  suit
Of pink-white petals, for its scanty fruit?
Thrice happy hours, in hope's illusion
  dressed,
In fancy's cradle nurtured and caressed,
Though rich the spoils that ripening
  years may bring,
To thee the dewdrops of the Orient
  cling, —
Not all the dye-stuffs from the vats of
  truth
Can match the rainbow on the robes of
  youth!

Dear unborn children, to our Mother's
  trust
We leave you, fearless, when we lie in
  dust:
While o'er these walls the Christian ban-
  ner waves
From hallowed lips shall flow the truth
  that saves;
While o'er those portals *Veritas* you read
No church shall bind you with its human
  creed.
Take from the past the best its toil has
  won,
But learn betimes its slavish ruts to shun.
Pass the old tree whose withered leaves
  are shed,
Quit the old paths that error loved to
  tread,

And a new wreath of living blossoms
  seek,
A narrower pathway up a loftier peak;
Lose not your reverence, but unmanly fear
Leave far behind you, all who enter here!

As once of old from Ida's lofty height
The flaming signal flashed across the
  night,
So Harvard's beacon sheds its unspent rays
Till every watch-tower shows its kindling
  blaze.
Caught from a spark and fanned by every
  gale,
A brighter radiance gilds the roofs of
  Yale;
Amherst and Williams bid their flambeaus
  shine,
And Bowdoin answers through her groves
  of pine;
O'er Princeton's sands the far reflections
  steal,
Where mighty Edwards stamped his iron
  heel;
Nay, on the hill where old beliefs were
  bound
Fast as if Styx had girt them nine times
  round,
Bursts such a light that trembling souls
  inquire
If the whole church of Calvin is on
  fire!
Well may they ask, for what so brightly
  burns
As a dry creed that nothing ever learns?
Thus link by link is knit the flaming
  chain
Lit by the torch of Harvard's hallowed
  plain.

Thy son, thy servant, dearest Mother
  mine,
Lays this poor offering on thy holy shrine,
An autumn leaflet to the wild winds
  tost,
Touched by the finger of November's
  frost,

With sweet, sad memories of that earlier
  day,
And all that listened to my first-born lay.
With grateful heart this glorious morn I
  see, —
Would that my tribute worthier were of
  thee !

POST-PRANDIAL.

PHI BETA KAPPA.

WENDELL PHILLIPS, ORATOR ; CHARLES GODFREY
LELAND, POET.

1881.

"THE Dutch have taken Holland," — so
  the schoolboys used to say ;
The Dutch have taken Harvard, — no
  doubt of that to-day !
For the Wendells were low Dutchmen,
  and all their vrows were Vans ;
And the Breitmanns are high Dutchmen,
  and here is honest Hans.

Mynheers, you both are welcome ! Fair
  cousin Wendell P.,
Our ancestors were dwellers beside the
  Zuyder Zee ;
Both Grotius and Erasmus were country-
  men of we,
And Vondel was our namesake, though
  he spelt it with a V.

It is well old Evert Jansen sought a
  dwelling over sea
On the margin of the Hudson, where he
  sampled you and me
Through our grandsires and great-grand-
  sires, for you would n't quite agree
With the steady-going burghers along the
  Zuyder Zee.

Like our Motley's John of Barnveld, you
  have always been inclined
To speak, — well, — somewhat frankly, —
  to let us know your mind,

And the Mynheers would have told you
  to be cautious what you said,
Or else that silver tongue of yours might
  cost your precious head.

But we 're very glad you 've kept it ; it
  was always Freedom's own,
And whenever Reason chose it she found
  a royal throne ;
You have whacked us with your sceptre ;
  our backs were little harmed,
And while we rubbed our bruises we
  owned we had been charmed.

And you, our *quasi* Dutchman, what welcome should be yours
For all the wise prescriptions that work
  your laughter-cures ?
" Shake before taking " ? — not a bit, —
  the bottle-cure 's a sham ;
Take before shaking, and you 'll find it
  shakes your diaphragm.

" Hans Breitmann gif a barty, — vhere is
  dot barty now ? "
On every shelf where wit is stored to
  smooth the careworn brow !
A health to stout Hans Breitmann ! How
  long before we see
Another Hans as handsome, — as bright
  a man as he !

THE FLANEUR.

BOSTON COMMON, DECEMBER 6, 1882.

DURING THE TRANSIT OF VENUS.

I LOVE all sights of earth and skies,
From flowers that glow to stars that
  shine ;
The comet and the penny show,
All curious things, above, below,
Hold each in turn my wandering eyes :
I claim the Christian Pagan's line,
Humani nihil, — even so, —
And is not human life divine ?

When soft the western breezes blow,
And strolling youths meet sauntering
          maids,
I love to watch the stirring trades
Beneath the Vallombrosa shades
Our much-enduring elms bestow;
The vender and his rhetoric's flow,
That lambent stream of liquid lies;
The bait he dangles from his line,
The gudgeon and his gold-washed prize.
I halt before the blazoned sign
That bids me linger to admire
The drama time can never tire,
The little hero of the hunch,
With iron arm and soul of fire,
And will that works his fierce desire, —
Untamed, unscared, unconquered Punch!
My ear a pleasing torture finds
In tones the withered sibyl grinds, —
The *dame sans merci's* broken strain,
Whom I erewhile, perchance, have known,
When Orleans filled the Bourbon throne,
A siren singing by the Seine.

But most I love the tube that spies
The orbs celestial in their march;
That shows the comet as it whisks
Its tail across the planets' disks,
As if to blind their blood-shot eyes;
Or wheels so close against the sun
We tremble at the thought of risks
Our little spinning ball may run,
To pop like corn that children parch,
From summer something overdone,
And roll, a cinder, through the skies.

Grudge not to-day the scanty fee
To him who farms the firmament,
To whom the milky way is free;
Who holds the wondrous crystal key,
The silent Open Sesame
That Science to her sons has lent;
Who takes his toll, and lifts the bar
That shuts the road to sun and star.
If Venus only comes to time,
(And prophets say she must and shall,)
To-day will hear the tinkling chime

Of many a ringing silver dime,
For him whose optic glass supplies
The crowd with astronomic eyes, —
The Galileo of the Mall.

Dimly the transit morning broke;
The sun seemed doubting what to do,
As one who questions how to dress,
And takes his doublets from the press,
And halts between the old and new.
Please Heaven he wear his suit of blue,
Or don, at least, his ragged cloak,
With rents that show the azure through!

I go the patient crowd to join
That round the tube my eyes discern,
The last new-comer of the file,
And wait, and wait, a weary while,
And gape, and stretch, and shrug, and
          smile,
(For each his place must fairly earn,
Hindmost and foremost, in his turn,)
Till hitching onward, pace by pace,
I gain at last the envied place,
And pay the white exiguous coin:
The sun and I are face to face;
He glares at me, I stare at him;
And lo! my straining eye has found
A little spot that, black and round,
Lies near the crimsoned fire-orb's rim.
O blessed, beauteous evening star,
Well named for her whom earth adores, —
The Lady of the dove-drawn car, —
I know thee in thy white simar;
But veiled in black, a rayless spot,
Blank as a careless scribbler's blot,
Stripped of thy robe of silvery flame, —
The stolen robe that Night restores
When Day has shut his golden doors, —
I see thee, yet I know thee not;
And canst thou call thyself the same?

A black, round spot, — and that is all;
And such a speck our earth would be
If he who looks upon the stars
Through the red atmosphere of Mars
Could see our little creeping ball

Across the disk of crimson crawl
As I our sister planet see.

And art thou, then, a world like ours,
Flung from the orb that whirled our own
A molten pebble from its zone?
How must thy burning sands absorb
The fire-waves of the blazing orb,
Thy chain so short, thy path so near,
Thy flame-defying creatures hear
The maelstroms of the photosphere!
And is thy bosom decked with flowers
That steal their bloom from scalding
   showers?
And hast thou cities, domes, and towers,
And life, and love that makes it dear,
And death that fills thy tribes with fear?

Lost in my dream, my spirit soars
Through paths the wandering angels
   know;
My all-pervading thought explores
The azure ocean's lucent shores;
I leave my mortal self below,
As up the star-lit stairs I climb,
And still the widening view reveals
In endless rounds the circling wheels
That build the horologe of time.
New spheres, new suns, new systems
   gleam;
The voice no earth-born echo hears
Steals softly on my ravished ears:
I hear them "singing as they shine"—
—A mortal's voice dissolves my dream:
My patient neighbor, next in line,
Hints gently there are those who wait.
O guardian of the starry gate,
What coin shall pay this debt of mine?
Too slight thy claim, too small the fee
That bids thee turn the potent key
The Tuscan's hand has placed in thine.
Forgive my own the small affront,
The insult of the proffered dime;
Take it, O friend, since this thy wont,
But still shall faithful memory be
A bankrupt debtor unto thee,
And pay thee with a grateful rhyme.

AVE.

PRELUDE TO "ILLUSTRATED POEMS."

FULL well I know the frozen hand has
   come
That smites the songs of grove and
   garden dumb,
And chills sad autumn's last chrysanthemum;

Yet would I find one blossom, if I might,
Ere the dark loom that weaves the robe of
   white
Hides all the wrecks of summer out of
   sight.

Sometimes in dim November's narrowing
   day,
When all the season's pride has passed
   away,
As mid the blackened stems and leaves
   we stray,

We spy in sheltered nook or rocky cleft
A starry disk the hurrying winds have
   left,
Of all its blooming sisterhood bereft:

Some pansy, with its wondering baby
   eyes—
Poor wayside nursling!—fixed in blank
   surprise
At the rough welcome of unfriendly
   skies;

Or golden daisy,—will it dare disclaim
The lion's tooth, to wear this gentler
   name?
Or blood-red salvia, with its lips aflame:

The storms have stripped the lily and the
   rose,
Still on its cheek the flush of summer
   glows,
And all its heart-leaves kindle as it blows.

So had I looked some bud of song to find

The careless winds of autumn left behind,
With these of earlier seasons' growth to
    bind.

Ah me! my skies are dark with sudden
    grief,
A flower lies faded on my garnered
    sheaf;
Yet let the sunshine gild this virgin
    leaf, —

The joyous, blessed sunshine of the past,
Still with me, though the heavens are
    overcast, —
The light that shines while life and
    memory last.

Go, pictured rhymes, for loving readers
    meant;
Bring back the smiles your jocund morn-
    ing lent,
And warm their hearts with sunbeams
    yet unspent!

BEVERLY FARMS, *July* 24, 1884.

KING'S CHAPEL.

READ AT THE TWO HUNDREDTH ANNI-
VERSARY.

Is it a weanling's weakness for the past
  That in the stormy, rebel-breeding town,
Swept clean of relics by the levelling
    blast,
Still keeps our gray old chapel's name of
    "King's," —
Still to its outworn symbols fondly clings,
  Its unchurched mitres and its empty
    crown?

Poor harmless emblems! All has shrunk
    away
  That made them gorgons in the pa-
    triot's eyes;
The priestly plaything harms us not
    to-day;
The gilded crown is but a pleasing show,

An old-world heirloom, left from long
    ago,
  Wreck of the past that memory bids
    us prize.

Lightly we glance the fresh-cut marbles
    o'er;
  Those two of earlier date our eyes en-
    thrall:
The proud old Briton's by the western
    door,
And hers, the Lady of Colonial days,
Whose virtues live in long-drawn classic
    phrase, —
  The fair Francesca of the southern
    wall.

Ay! those were goodly men that Reynolds
    drew,
  And stately dames our Copley's canvas
    holds,
To their old Church, their Royal Master,
    true,
Proud of the claim their valiant sires had
    earned,
That "gentle blood," not lightly to be
    spurned,
Save by the churl ungenerous Nature
    moulds.

All vanished! It were idle to complain
  That ere the fruits shall come the
    flowers must fall;
Yet somewhat we have lost amidst our
    gain,
Some rare ideals time may not restore, —
The charm of courtly breeding, seen no
    more,
  And reverence, dearest ornament of all.

— Thus musing, to the western wall I
    came,
  Departing: lo! a tablet fresh and fair,
Where glistened many a youth's remem-
    bered name
In golden letters on the snow-white
    stone, —

Young lives these aisles and arches once
    have known,
    Their country's bleeding altar might
        not spare.

These died that we might claim a soil
        unstained,
    Save by the blood of heroes; their be-
        quests
A realm unsevered and a race unchained.
Has purer blood through Norman veins
    come down
From the rough knights that clutched
    the Saxon's crown
    Than warmed the pulses in these faith-
        ful breasts ?

These, too, shall live in history's deathless
        page,
    High on the slow-wrought pedestals of
        fame,
Ranged with the heroes of remoter age;
They could not die who left their nation
    free,
Firm as the rock, unfettered as the sea,
    Its heaven unshadowed by the cloud of
        shame.

While on the storied past our memory
    dwells,
    Our grateful tribute shall not be de-
        nied, —
The wreath, the cross of rustling immor-
    telles;
And willing hands shall clear each dark-
    ening bust,
As year by year sifts down the clinging
    dust
    On Shirley's beauty and on Vassall's
        pride.

But for our own, our loved and lost, we
    bring
    With throbbing hearts and tears that
        still must flow,
In full-heaped hands, the opening flowers
    of spring,

Lilies half-blown, and budding roses, red
As their young cheeks, before the blood
    was shed
    That lent their morning bloom its gen-
        erous glow.

Ah, who shall count a rescued nation's
    debt,
    Or sum in words our martyrs' silent
        claims ?
Who shall our heroes' dread exchange
    forget, —
All life, youth, hope, could promise to
    allure
For all that soul could brave or flesh en-
    dure ?
    They shaped our future; we but carve
        their names.

HYMN

FOR THE SAME OCCASION.

SUNG BY THE CONGREGATION TO THE TUNE OF TAL-
LIS'S EVENING HYMN.

O'ERSHADOWED by the walls that climb,
    Piled up in air by living hands,
A rock amid the waves of time,
    Our gray old house of worship stands.

High o'er the pillared aisles we love
    The symbols of the past look down;
Unharmed, unharming, throned above,
    Behold the mitre and the crown!

Let not our younger faith forget
    The loyal souls that held them dear;
The prayers we read their tears have wet,
    The hymns we sing they loved to hear.

The memory of their earthly throne
    Still to our holy temple clings,
But here the kneeling suppliants own
    One only Lord, the King of kings.

Hark! while our hymn of grateful praise
    The solemn echoing vaults prolong,

The far-off voice of earlier days
  Blends with our own in hallowed song:

To Him who ever lives and reigns,
  Whom all the hosts of heaven adore,
Who lent the life His breath sustains,
  Be glory now and evermore!

HYMN. — THE WORD OF PROMISE.

(by supposition)

An Hymn set forth to be sung by the Great
  Assembly at Newtown, [Mass.] Mo. 12. 1.
  1636.

[Written by OLIVER WENDELL HOLMES, eldest son
  of Rev. ABIEL HOLMES, eighth Pastor of the
  First Church in Cambridge, Massachusetts.]

LORD, Thou hast led us as of old
  Thine Arm led forth the chosen Race
Through Foes that raged, through Floods
    that roll'd,
  To Canaan's far-off Dwelling-Place.

Here is Thy bounteous Table spread,
  Thy Manna falls on every Field,
Thy Grace our hungering Souls hath fed,
  Thy Might hath been our Spear and
    Shield.

Lift high Thy Buckler, Lord of Hosts!
  Guard Thou Thy Servants, Sons and
    Sires,
While on the Godless heathen Coasts
  They light Thine Israel's Altar-fires!

The salvage Wilderness remote
  Shall hear Thy Works and Wonders
    sung;
So from the Rock that Moses smote
  The Fountain of the Desart sprung.

Soon shall the slumbering Morn awake,
  From wandering Stars of Errour freed,
When Christ the Bread of Heaven shall
    break
  For Saints that own a common Creed.

The Walls that fence His Flocks apart
  Shall crack and crumble in Decay,
And every Tongue and every Heart
  Shall welcome in the new-born Day.

Then shall His glorious Church rejoice
  His Word of Promise to recall, —
ONE SHELTERING FOLD, ONE SHEP-
    HERD'S VOICE,
  ONE GOD AND FATHER OVER ALL!

HYMN.

READ AT THE DEDICATION OF THE
OLIVER WENDELL HOLMES HOSPITAL
AT HUDSON, WISCONSIN, JUNE 7, 1887.

ANGEL of love, for every grief
  Its soothing balm thy mercy brings,
For every pang its healing leaf,
  For homeless want, thine outspread
    wings.

Enough for thee the pleading eye,
  The knitted brow of silent pain;
The portals open to a sigh
  Without the clank of bolt or chain.

Who is our brother? He that lies
  Left at the wayside, bruised and sore:
His need our open hand supplies,
  His welcome waits him at our door.

Not ours to ask in freezing tones
  His race, his calling, or his creed;
Each heart the tie of kinship owns,
  When those are human veins that
    bleed.

Here stand the champions to defend
  From every wound that flesh can feel;
Here science, patience, skill, shall blend
  To save, to calm, to help, to heal.

Father of Mercies! Weak and frail,
  Thy guiding hand Thy children ask;
Let not the Great Physician fail
  To aid us in our holy task.

Source of all truth, and love, and light,
  That warm and cheer our earthly days,
Be ours to serve Thy will aright,
  Be Thine the glory and the praise!

ON THE DEATH OF PRESIDENT GARFIELD.

I.

FALLEN with autumn's falling leaf
  Ere yet his summer's noon was past,
Our friend, our guide, our trusted chief, —
  What words can match a woe so vast!

And whose the chartered claim to speak
  The sacred grief where all have part,
Where sorrow saddens every cheek
  And broods in every aching heart?

Yet Nature prompts the burning phrase
  That thrills the hushed and shrouded hall,
The loud lament, the sorrowing praise,
  The silent tear that love lets fall.

In loftiest verse, in lowliest rhyme,
  Shall strive unblamed the minstrel choir, —
The singers of the new-born time,
  And trembling age with outworn lyre.

No room for pride, no place for blame, —
  We fling our blossoms on the grave,
Pale, — scentless, — faded, — all we claim,
  This only, — what we had we gave.

Ah, could the grief of all who mourn
  Blend in one voice its bitter cry,
The wail to heaven's high arches borne
  Would echo through the caverned sky.

II.

O happiest land, whose peaceful choice
  Fills with a breath its empty throne!
God, speaking through thy people's voice,
  Has made that voice for once His own.

No angry passion shakes the state
  Whose weary servant seeks for rest;
And who could fear that scowling hate
  Would strike at that unguarded breast?

He stands, unconscious of his doom,
  In manly strength, erect, serene;
Around him Summer spreads her bloom;
  He falls, — what horror clothes the scene!

How swift the sudden flash of woe
  Where all was bright as childhood's dream!
As if from heaven's ethereal bow
  Had leaped the lightning's arrowy gleam.

Blot the foul deed from history's page;
  Let not the all-betraying sun
Blush for the day that stains an age
  When murder's blackest wreath was won.

III.

Pale on his couch the sufferer lies,
  The weary battle-ground of pain:
Love tends his pillow; Science tries
  Her every art, alas! in vain.

The strife endures how long! how long!
  Life, death, seem balanced in the scale,
While round his bed a viewless throng
  Await each morrow's changing tale.

In realms the desert ocean parts
  What myriads watch with tear-filled eyes,
His pulse-beats echoing in their hearts,
  His breathings counted with their sighs!

Slowly the stores of life are spent,
  Yet hope still battles with despair;
Will Heaven not yield when knees are bent?
  Answer, O Thou that hearest prayer!

But silent is the brazen sky;
  On sweeps the meteor's threatening
    train,
Unswerving Nature's mute reply,
  Bound in her adamantine chain.

Not ours the verdict to decide
  Whom death shall claim or skill shall
    save;
The hero's life though Heaven denied,
  It gave our land a martyr's grave.

Nor count the teaching vainly sent
  How human hearts their griefs may
    share, —
The lesson woman's love has lent,
  What hope may do, what faith can
    bear!

Farewell! the leaf-strown earth enfolds
  Our stay, our pride, our hopes, our
    fears,
And autumn's golden sun beholds
  A nation bowed, a world in tears.

THE GOLDEN FLOWER.

WHEN Advent dawns with lessening days,
  While earth awaits the angels' hymn;
When bare as branching coral sways
  In whistling winds each leafless limb;
When spring is but a spendthrift's dream,
  And summer's wealth a wasted dower,
Nor dews nor sunshine may redeem, —
  Then autumn coins his Golden Flower.

Soft was the violet's vernal hue,
  Fresh was the rose's morning red,
Full-orbed the stately dahlia grew, —
  All gone! their short-lived splendors
    shed.
The shadows, lengthening, stretch at
    noon;
  The fields are stripped, the groves are
    dumb;
The frost-flowers greet the icy moon, —

Then blooms the bright chrysanthe-
    mum.

The stiffening turf is white with snow,
  Yet still its radiant disks are seen
Where soon the hallowed morn will show
    The wreath and cross of Christmas
      green;
As if in autumn's dying days
  It heard the heavenly song afar,
And opened all its glowing rays,
    The herald lamp of Bethlehem's star.

Orphan of summer, kindly sent
  To cheer the fading year's decline,
In all that pitying Heaven has lent
  No fairer pledge of hope than thine.
Yes! June lies hid beneath the snow,
  And winter's unborn heir shall claim
For every seed that sleeps below
  A spark that kindles into flame.

Thy smile the scowl of winter braves
  Last of the bright-robed, flowery train,
Soft sighing o'er the garden graves,
  "Farewell! farewell! we meet again!"
So may life's chill November bring
  Hope's golden flower, the last of all,
Before we hear the angels sing
  Where blossoms never fade and fall!

NO TIME LIKE THE OLD TIME.

THERE is no time like the old time, when
    you and I were young,
When the buds of April blossomed, and
    the birds of spring-time sung!
The garden's brightest glories by summer
    suns are nursed,
But oh, the sweet, sweet violets, the
    flowers that opened first!

There is no place like the old place, where
    you and I were born,
Where we lifted first our eyelids on the
    splendors of the morn

From the milk-white breast that warmed
  us, from the clinging arms that
  bore,
Where the dear eyes glistened o'er us that
  will look on us no more !

There is no friend like the old friend, who
  has shared our morning days,
No greeting like his welcome, no homage
  like his praise :
Fame is the scentless sunflower, with
  gaudy crown of gold ;
But friendship is the breathing rose, with
  sweets in every fold.

There is no love like the old love, that we
  courted in our pride ;
Though our leaves are falling, falling,
  and we 're fading side by side,
There are blossoms all around us with the
  colors of our dawn,
And we live in borrowed sunshine when
  the day-star is withdrawn.

There are no times like the old times, —
  they shall never be forgot !
There is no place like the old place, —
  keep green the dear old spot !
There are no friends like our old friends,
  — may Heaven prolong their lives !
There are no loves like our old loves, —
  God bless our loving wives !
1865.

THE MORNING VISIT.

A SICK man's chamber, though it often
  boast
The grateful presence of a literal toast,
Can hardly claim, amidst its various
  wealth,
The right unchallenged to propose a
  health ;
Yet though its tenant is denied the feast,
Friendship must launch his sentiment at
  least,
As prisoned damsels, locked from lovers'
  lips,

Toss them a kiss from off their fingers'
  tips.

The morning visit, — not till sickness
  falls
In the charmed circles of your own safe
  walls ;
Till fever's throb and pain's relentless
  rack
Stretch you all helpless on your aching
  back ;
Not till you play the patient in your
  turn,
The morning visit's mystery shall you
  learn.

'T is a small matter, in your neighbor's
  case,
To charge your fee for showing him your
  face ;
You skip up-stairs, inquire, inspect, and
  touch,
Prescribe, take leave, and off to twenty
  such.

But when at length by fate's transferred
  decree
The visitor becomes the visitee :
Oh, then, indeed, it pulls another string ;
Your ox is gored, and that 's a different
  thing !
Your friend is sick : phlegmatic as a
  Turk,
You write your recipe and let it work ;
Not yours to stand the shiver and the
  frown,
And sometimes worse, with which your
  draught goes down.
Calm as a clock your knowing hand
  directs,
Rhei, jalapæ ana grana sex,
Or traces on some tender missive's back,
Scrupulos duos pulveris ipecac:
And leaves your patient to his qualms
  and gripes,
Cool as a sportsman banging at his
  snipes.

But change the time, the person, and the place,
And be yourself " the interesting case,"
You 'll gain some knowledge which it 's well to learn ;
In future practice it may serve your turn.
Leeches, for instance, — pleasing creatures quite,
Try them, — and bless you, — don't you find they bite ?
You raise a blister for the smallest cause,
But be yourself the sitter whom it draws,
And trust my statement, you will not deny
The worst of draughtsmen is your Spanish fly !
It 's mighty easy ordering when you please
Infusi sennæ capiat uncias tres ;
It 's mighty different when you quackle down
Your own three ounces of the liquid brown.
Pilula, pulvis, — pleasant words enough,
When other throats receive the shocking stuff ;
But oh, what flattery can disguise the groan
That meets the gulp which sends it through your own !
Be gentle, then, though Art's unsparing rules
Give you the handling of her sharpest tools ;
Use them not rashly, — sickness is enough ;
Be always " ready," but be never "rough."

Of all the ills that suffering man endures,
The largest fraction liberal Nature cures ;
Of those remaining, 't is the smallest part
Yields to the efforts of judicious Art ;
But simple *Kindness*, kneeling by the bed

To shift the pillow for the sick man's head,
Give the fresh draught to cool the lips that burn,
Fan the hot brow, the weary frame to turn, —
Kindness, untutored by our grave M. D.'s,
But Nature's graduate, when she schools to please,
Wins back more sufferers with her voice and smile
Than all the trumpery in the druggist's pile.

Once more, be *quiet:* coming up the stair,
Don't be a plantigrade, a human bear,
But, stealing softly on the silent toe,
Reach the sick chamber ere you 're heard below.
Whatever changes there may greet your eyes,
Let not your looks proclaim the least surprise ;
It 's not your business by your face to show
All that your patient does not want to know ;
Nay, use your optics with considerate care,
And don't abuse your privilege to stare.
But if your eyes may probe him over-much,
Beware still further how you rudely touch ;
Don't clutch his carpus in your icy fist,
But warm your fingers ere you take the wrist.
If the poor victim needs must be percussed,
Don't make an anvil of his aching bust ;
(Doctors exist within a hundred miles
Who thump a thorax as they 'd hammer piles ;)
If you must listen to his doubtful chest,
Catch the essentials, and ignore the rest.
Spare him ; the sufferer wants of you and art

A track to steer by, not a finished chart.
So of your questions : don't in mercy try
To pump your patient absolutely dry ;
He 's not a mollusk squirming in a dish,
You 're not Agassiz, and he 's not a fish.

And last, not least, in each perplexing
    case,
Learn the sweet magic of a *cheerful face ;*
Not always smiling, but at least serene,
When grief and anguish cloud the
    anxious scene.
Each look, each movement, every word
    and tone,
Should tell your patient you are all his
    own ;
Not the mere artist purchased to attend,
But the warm, ready, self-forgetting
    friend,
Whose genial visit in itself combines
The best of cordials, tonics, anodynes.

Such is the *visit* that from day to day
Sheds o'er my chamber its benignant ray·
I give his health, who never cared to
    claim
Her babbling homage from the tongue of
    Fame ;
Unmoved by praise, he stands by all con-
    fest,
The truest, noblest, wisest, kindest, best.
1849.

HAIL, COLUMBIA!

1798.

THE FIRST VERSE OF THE SONG, BY
JOSEPH HOPKINSON.

" HAIL, Columbia ! Happy land !
  Hail, ye heroes, heaven-born band,
    Who fought and bled in Freedom's cause
    Who fought and bled in Freedom's cause,
  And when the storm of war was gone
  Enjoy'd the peace your valor won.
    Let independence be our boast,
    Ever mindful what it cost ;
    Ever grateful for the prize,
    Let its altar reach the skies.

" Firm — united — let us be,
  Rallying round our Liberty ;
  As a band of brothers join'd,
  Peace and safety we shall find."

. . . .

ADDITIONAL VERSES

WRITTEN AT THE REQUEST OF THE COMMITTEE FOR
THE CONSTITUTIONAL CENTENNIAL CELEBRATION AT
PHILADELPHIA, 1887.

LOOK our ransomed shores around,
Peace and safety we have found !
  Welcome, friends who once were foes !
  Welcome, friends who once were foes,
To all the conquering years have
    gained, —
A nation's rights, a race unchained !
  Children of the day new-born,
  Mindful of its glorious morn,
  Let the pledge our fathers signed
  Heart to heart forever bind !

    While the stars of heaven shall burn,
    While the ocean tides return,
    Ever may the circling sun
    Find the Many still are One !

Graven deep with edge of steel,
Crowned with Victory's crimson seal,
  All the world their names shall read !
  All the world their names shall read,
Enrolled with his, the Chief that led
The hosts whose blood for us was shed.
  Pay our sires their children's debt,
  Love and honor, nor forget
  Only Union's golden key
  Guards the Ark of Liberty !

    While the stars of heaven shall burn,
    While the ocean tides return.
    Ever may the circling sun
    Find the Many still are One !

Hail, Columbia ! strong and free,
Throned in hearts from sea to sea !
  Thy march triumphant still pursue !
  Thy march triumphant still pursue

With peaceful stride from zone to zone,
Till Freedom finds the world her own!
  Blest in Union's holy ties,
  Let our grateful song arise,
  Every voice its tribute lend,
  All in loving chorus blend!

  While the stars in heaven shall burn,
  While the ocean tides return,
  Ever shall the circling sun
  Find the Many still are One!

POEM

FOR THE DEDICATION OF THE FOUN-
TAIN AT STRATFORD-ON-AVON, PRE-
SENTED BY GEORGE W. CHILDS, OF
PHILADELPHIA.

WELCOME, thrice welcome is thy silvery
    gleam,
  Thou long-imprisoned stream!
Welcome the tinkle of thy crystal beads
As plashing raindrops to the flowery
    meads,
As summer's breath to Avon's whispering
    reeds!
From rock-walled channels, drowned in
    rayless night,
  Leap forth to life and light;
Wake from the darkness of thy troubled
    dream,
And greet with answering smile the
    morning's beam!

No purer lymph the white-limbed Naiad
    knows
  Than from thy chalice flows;
Not the bright spring of Afric's sunny
    shores,
Starry with spangles washed from golden
    ores,
Nor glassy stream Bandusia's fountain
    pours,
Nor wave translucent where Sabrina fair
    Braids her loose-flowing hair,
Nor the swift current, stainless as it rose

Where chill Arveiron steals from Alpine
    snows.

Here shall the traveller stay his weary
    feet
  To seek thy calm retreat;
Here at high noon the brown-armed
    reaper rest;
Here, when the shadows, lengthening
    from the west,
Call the mute song-bird to his leafy nest,
Matron and maid shall chat the cares
    away
  That brooded o'er the day,
While flocking round them troops of
    children meet,
And all the arches ring with laughter
    sweet.

Here shall the steed, his patient life who
    spends
  In toil that never ends,
Hot from his thirsty tramp o'er hill and
    plain,
Plunge his red nostrils, while the torturing
    rein
Drops in loose loops beside his floating
    mane;
Nor the poor brute that shares his master's
    lot
  Find his small needs forgot, —
Truest of humble, long-enduring friends,
Whose presence cheers, whose guardian
    care defends!

Here lark and thrush and nightingale
    shall sip,
  And skimming swallows dip,
And strange shy wanderers fold their
    lustrous plumes
Fragrant from bowers that lent their
    sweet perfumes
Where Pæstum's rose or Persia's lilac
    blooms;
Here from his cloud the eagle stoop to
    drink
  At the full basin's brink,

And whet his beak against its rounded lip,
His glossy feathers glistening as they
drip.

Here shall the dreaming poet linger long,
　Far from his listening throng, —
Nor lute nor lyre his trembling hand shall
　bring ;
Here no frail Muse shall imp her crippled
　wing,
No faltering minstrel strain his throat to
　sing !
These hallowed echoes who shall dare to
　claim
　Whose tuneless voice would shame,
Whose jangling chords with jarring notes
　would wrong
The nymphs that heard the Swan of
　Avon's song ?

What visions greet the pilgrim's raptured
　eyes !
　What ghosts made real rise !
The dead return, — they breathe, — they
　live again,
Joined by the host of Fancy's airy train,
Fresh from the springs of Shakespeare's
　quickening brain !
The stream that slakes the soul's diviner
　thirst
　Here found the sunbeams first ;
Rich with his fame, not less shall memory
　prize
The gracious gift that humbler wants
　supplies.

O'er the wide waters reached the hand
　that gave
　To all this bounteous wave,
With health and strength and joyous
　beauty fraught ;
Blest be the generous pledge of friend-
　ship, brought
From the far home of brothers' love, un-
　bought !
Long may fair Avon's fountain flow, en-
　rolled

With storied shrines of old,
Castalia's spring, Egeria's dewy cave,
And Horeb's rock the God of Israel
　clave !

Land of our fathers, ocean makes us two,
　But heart to heart is true !
Proud is your towering daughter in the
　West,
Yet in her burning life-blood reign confest
Her mother's pulses beating in her breast.
This holy fount, whose rills from heaven
　descend,
　Its gracious drops shall lend, —
Both foreheads bathed in that baptismal
　dew,
And love make one the old home and the
　new !
August 29, 1887.

TO THE POETS WHO ONLY READ AND LISTEN.

WHEN evening's shadowy fingers fold
　The flowers of every hue,
Some shy, half-opened bud will hold
　Its drop of morning's dew.

Sweeter with every sunlit hour
　The trembling sphere has grown,
Till all the fragrance of the flower
　Becomes at last its own.

We that have sung perchance may find
　Our little meed of praise,
And round our pallid temples bind
　The wreath of fading bays :

Ah, Poet, who hast never spent
　Thy breath in idle strains,
For thee the dewdrop morning lent
　Still in thy heart remains ;

Unwasted, in its perfumed cell
　It waits the evening gale ;
Then to the azure whence it fell
　Its lingering sweets exhale.

NOTES.

Page 1.
"OLD IRONSIDES."

This was the popular name by which the frigate "Constitution" was known. The poem was first printed in the Boston Daily Advertiser, at the time when it was proposed to break up the old ship as unfit for service.

Page 3.
"THE CAMBRIDGE CHURCHYARD."

"The Goblet and the Sun" (Vas-Sol), sculptured on a freestone slab supported by five pillars, are the only designation of the family tomb of the Vassalls.

Page 25.
"Thou calm, chaste scholar."

Charles Chauncy Emerson; died May 9, 1836.

Page 26.
"And thou, dear friend."

James Jackson, Jr., M. D.; died March 28, 1834.

Page 53.
"Hark! The sweet bells renew their welcome sound."

The churches referred to in the lines which follow are, —

1. "King's Chapel," the foundation of which was laid by Governor Shirley in 1749.

2. Brattle Street Church, consecrated in 1773. The completion of this edifice, the design of which included a spire, was prevented by the troubles of the Revolution, and its plain, square tower presents nothing more attractive than a massive simplicity. In the front of this tower is still seen, half imbedded in the brick-work, a cannon-ball, which was thrown from the American fortifications at Cambridge, during the bombardment of the city, then occupied by the British troops.

3. The "Old South," first occupied for public worship in 1730.

4. Park Street Church, built in 1809, the tall white steeple of which is the most conspicuous of all the Boston spires.

5. Christ Church, opened for public worship in 1723, and containing a set of eight bells, until of late years the only chime in Boston.

Page 89.
AGNES.

The story of Sir Harry Frankland and Agnes Surraige is told in the ballad with a very strict adhesion to the facts. These were obtained from information afforded me by the Rev. Mr. Webster of Hopkinton, in company with whom I visited the Frankland Mansion in that town, then standing; from a very interesting Memoir, by the Rev. Elias Nason of Medford, not yet published; and from the manuscript diary of Sir Harry, or more properly Sir Charles Henry Frankland, now in the library of the Massachusetts Historical Society.

At the time of the visit referred to, old

Julia was living, and on our return we called at the house where she resided.[1] Her account is little more than paraphrased in the poem. If the incidents are treated with a certain liberality at the close of the fifth part, the essential fact that Agnes rescued Sir Harry from the ruins after the earthquake, and their subsequent marriage as related, may be accepted as literal truth. So with regard to most of the trifling details which are given; they are taken from the record.

It is to be hoped that the Rev. Mr. Nason's Memoir will be published, that this extraordinary romance of our sober New England life may become familiar to that class of readers who prefer a rigorous statement to an embellished narrative. It will be found to contain many historical facts and allusions which add much to its romantic interest.

It is greatly to be regretted that the Frankland Mansion no longer exists. It was accidentally burned on the 23d of January, 1858, a year or two after the first sketch of this ballad was written. A visit to it was like stepping out of the century into the years before the Revolution. A new house, similar in plan and arrange-

[1] She was living June 10, 1861, when this ballad was published.

ments to the old one, has been built upon its site, and the terraces, the clump of box, and the lilacs, doubtless remain to bear witness to the truth of this story.

———

Since the above note was written the Rev. Mr. Nason's interesting Memoir of Sir Harry Frankland has been published.

Page 300.

GRANDMOTHER'S STORY OF BUNKER-HILL BATTLE.

" They 're as safe as Dan'l Malcolm."

The following epitaph is still to be read on a tall gravestone standing as yet undisturbed among the transplanted monuments of the dead in Copp's Hill Burial-ground, one of the three city cemeteries which have been desecrated and ruined within my own remembrance : —

" Here lies buried in a
Stone Grave 10 feet deep,
Capt DANIEL MALCOLM Mercht
Who departed this Life
October 23d, 1769,
Aged 44 years,
a true son of Liberty,
a Friend to the Publick,
an Enemy to oppression,
and one of the foremost
in opposing the Revenue Acts
on America."

INDEX OF FIRST LINES.

INDEX OF TITLES.